Yamada-kun and the Seven Witches

2

Miki Yoshikawa

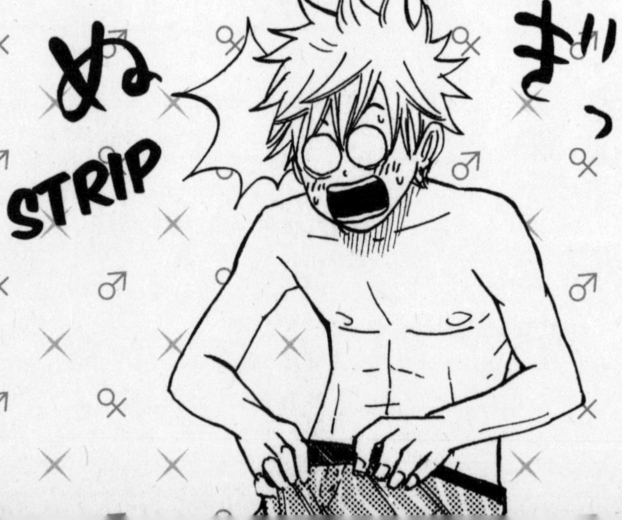
ぬぎっ
STRIP

CONTENTS

CHAPTER 8: My Shiraishi-san...

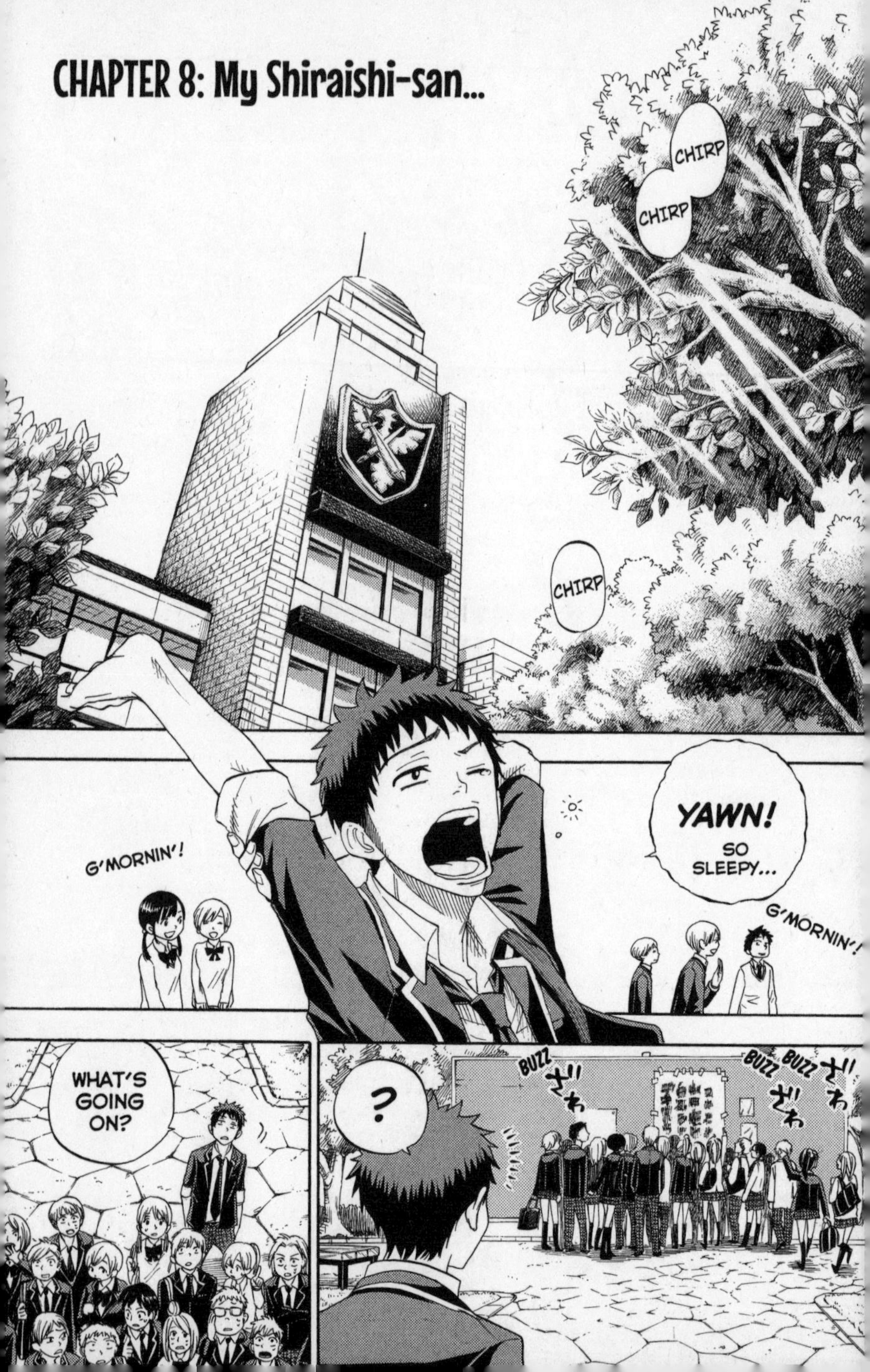
CHIRP
CHIRP
CHIRP
YAWN! SO SLEEPY...
G'MORNIN'!
G'MORNIN'!
BUZZ BUZZ BUZZ
ざわ ざわ ざわ
?
WHAT'S GOING ON?

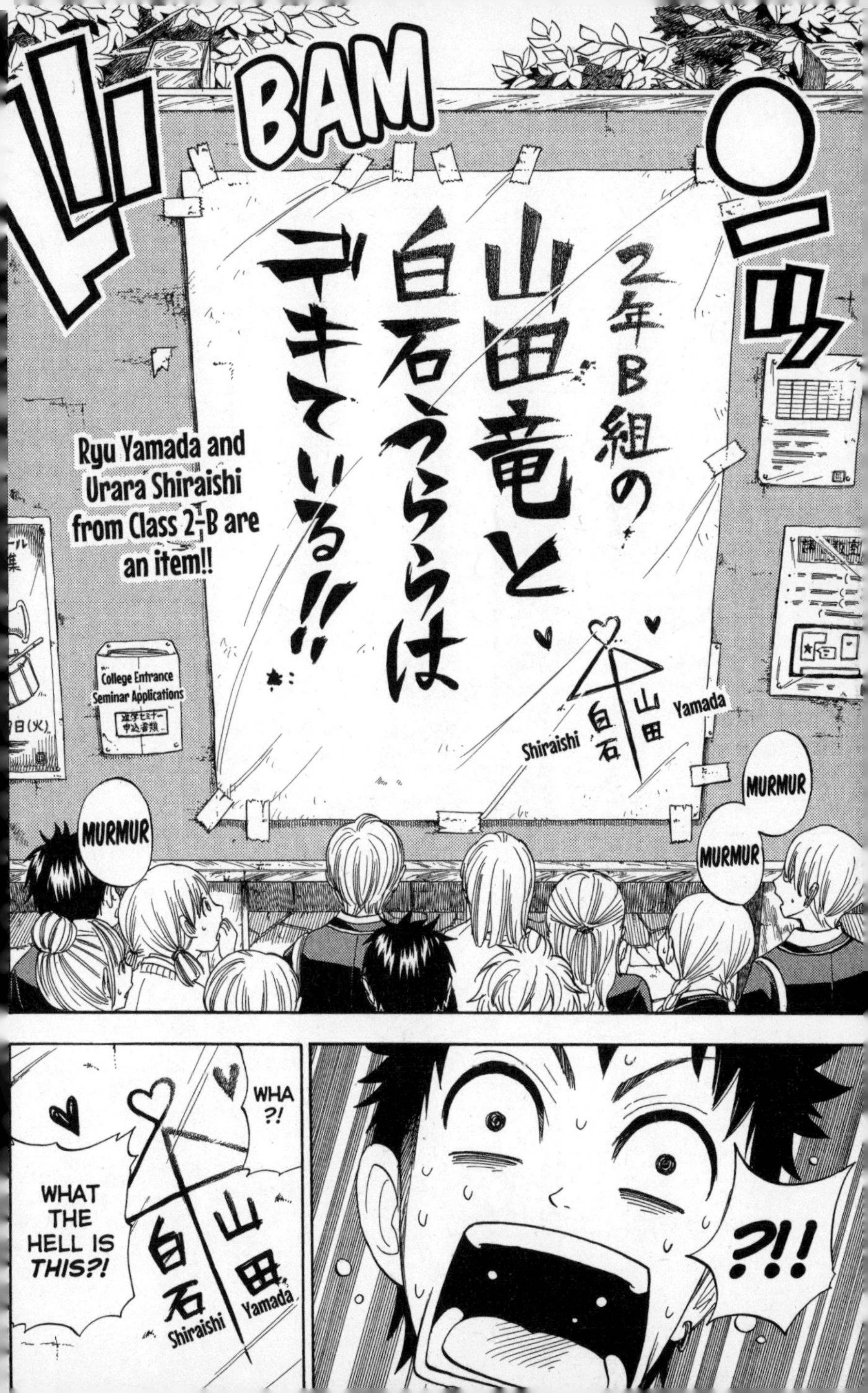
BAM
2年B組の山田竜と白石うららはデキている!!
Ryu Yamada and Urara Shiraishi from Class 2-B are an item!!
山田
Yamada
白石
Shiraishi
College Entrance Seminar Applications
進学セミナー申込書類
MURMUR
MURMUR
MURMUR
?!!
WHA?!
WHAT THE HELL IS THIS?!
山田
Yamada
白石
Shiraishi

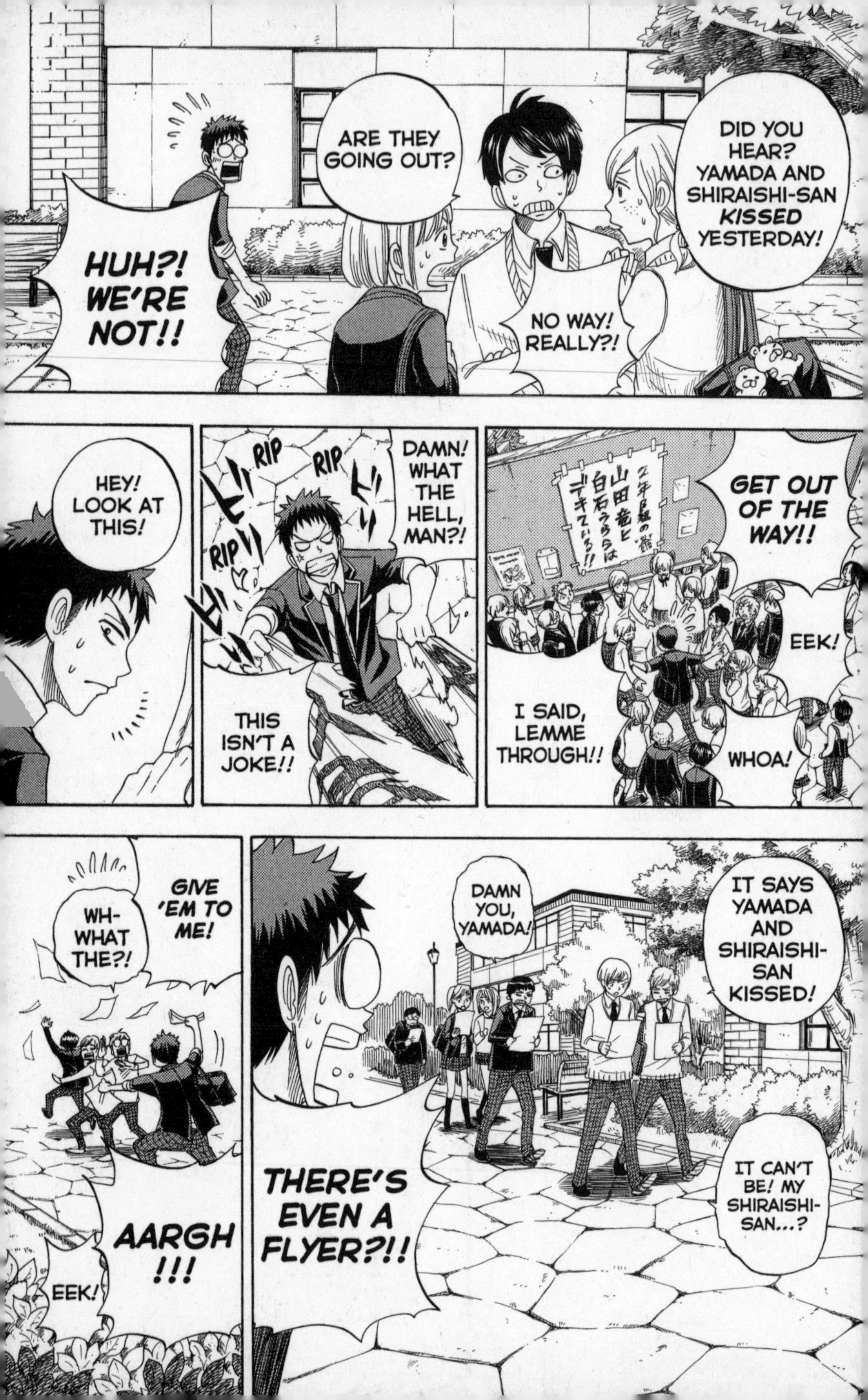
DID YOU HEAR? YAMADA AND SHIRAISHI-SAN *KISSED* YESTERDAY!
NO WAY! REALLY?!
ARE THEY GOING OUT?
HUH?! WE'RE NOT!!
GET OUT OF THE WAY!!
2年B組の山田竜と白石うららはデキている!!
EEK!
I SAID, LEMME THROUGH!!
WHOA!
DAMN! WHAT THE HELL, MAN?!
RIP
RIP
RIP
THIS ISN'T A JOKE!!
HEY! LOOK AT THIS!
IT SAYS YAMADA AND SHIRAISHI-SAN KISSED!
DAMN YOU, YAMADA!
IT CAN'T BE! MY SHIRAISHI-SAN...?
THERE'S EVEN A FLYER?!!
GIVE 'EM TO ME!
WH-WHAT THE?!
AARGH!!!
EEK!

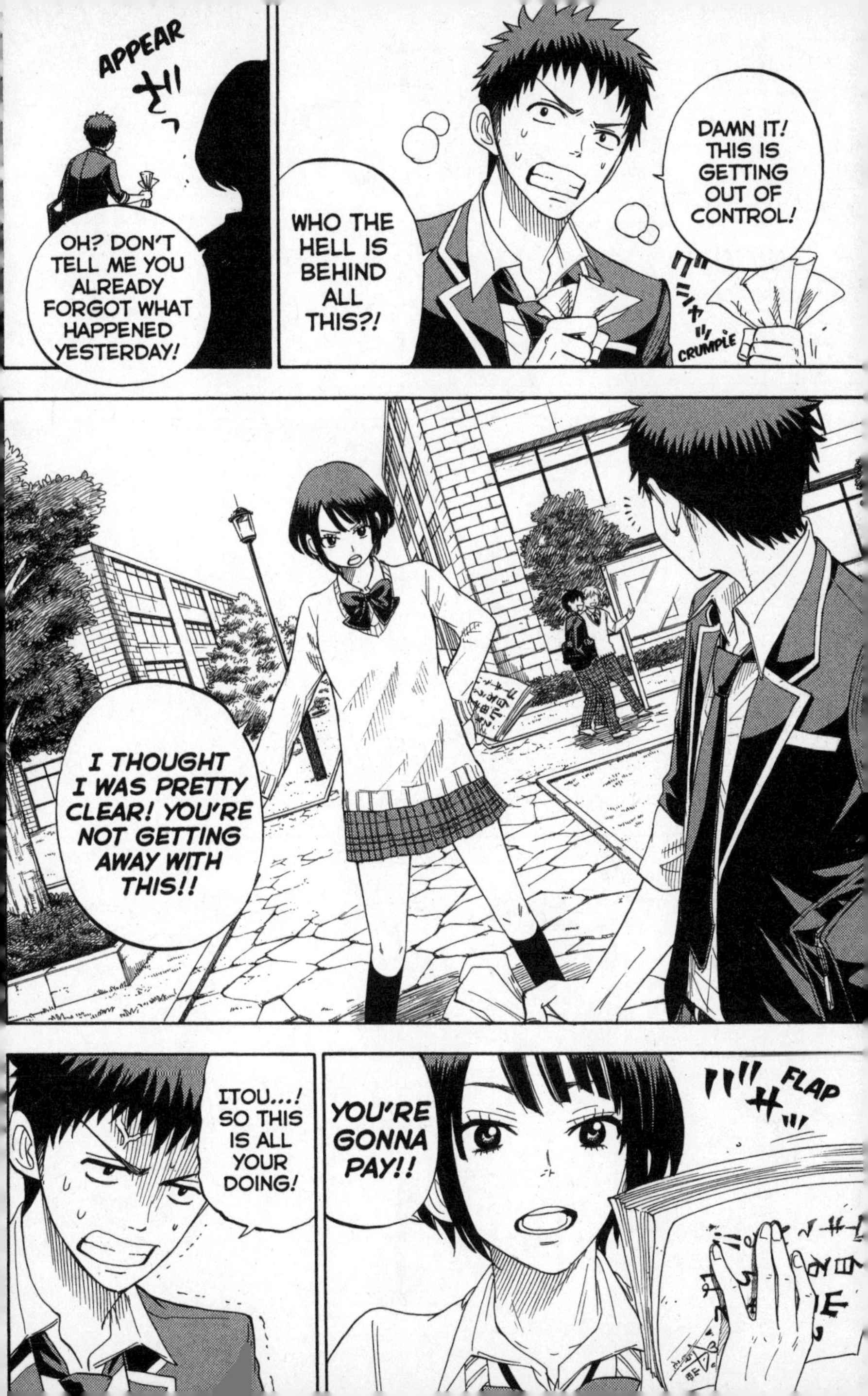
DAMN IT! THIS IS GETTING OUT OF CONTROL!
WHO THE HELL IS BEHIND ALL THIS?!
CRUMPLE
APPEAR
OH? DON'T TELL ME YOU ALREADY FORGOT WHAT HAPPENED YESTERDAY!
I THOUGHT I WAS PRETTY CLEAR! YOU'RE NOT GETTING AWAY WITH THIS!!
FLAP
YOU'RE GONNA PAY!!
ITOU...! SO THIS IS ALL YOUR DOING!

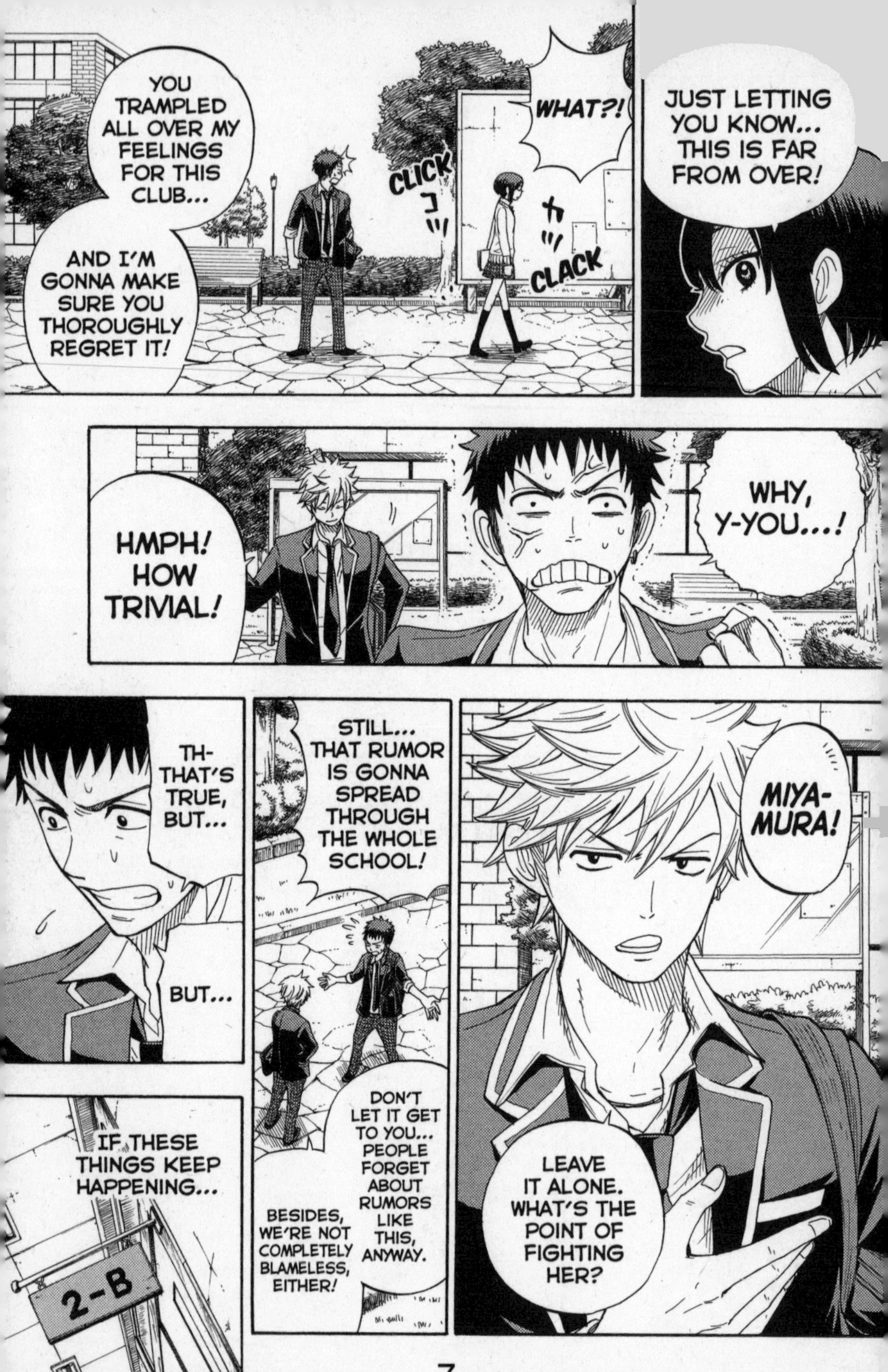
JUST LETTING YOU KNOW... THIS IS FAR FROM OVER!
WHAT?!
カッ
CLACK
CLICK
コッ
YOU TRAMPLED ALL OVER MY FEELINGS FOR THIS CLUB...
AND I'M GONNA MAKE SURE YOU THOROUGHLY REGRET IT!
WHY, Y-YOU...!
HMPH! HOW TRIVIAL!
MIYA-MURA!
LEAVE IT ALONE. WHAT'S THE POINT OF FIGHTING HER?
STILL... THAT RUMOR IS GONNA SPREAD THROUGH THE WHOLE SCHOOL!
DON'T LET IT GET TO YOU... PEOPLE FORGET ABOUT RUMORS LIKE THIS, ANYWAY.
BESIDES, WE'RE NOT COMPLETELY BLAMELESS, EITHER!
TH-THAT'S TRUE, BUT...
BUT...
IF THESE THINGS KEEP HAPPENING...
2-B

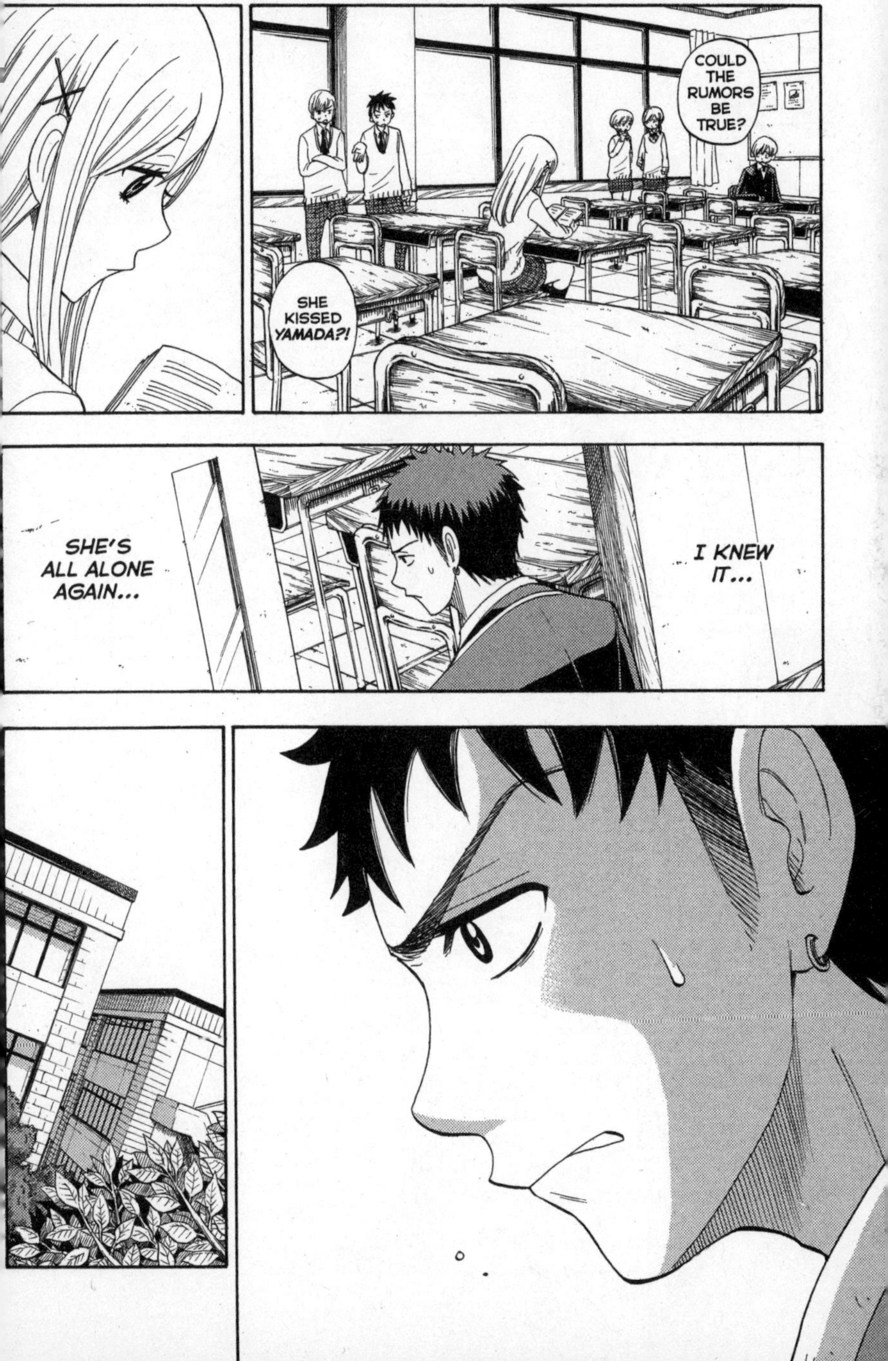
COULD THE RUMORS BE TRUE?
SHE KISSED YAMADA?!
I KNEW IT...
SHE'S ALL ALONE AGAIN...

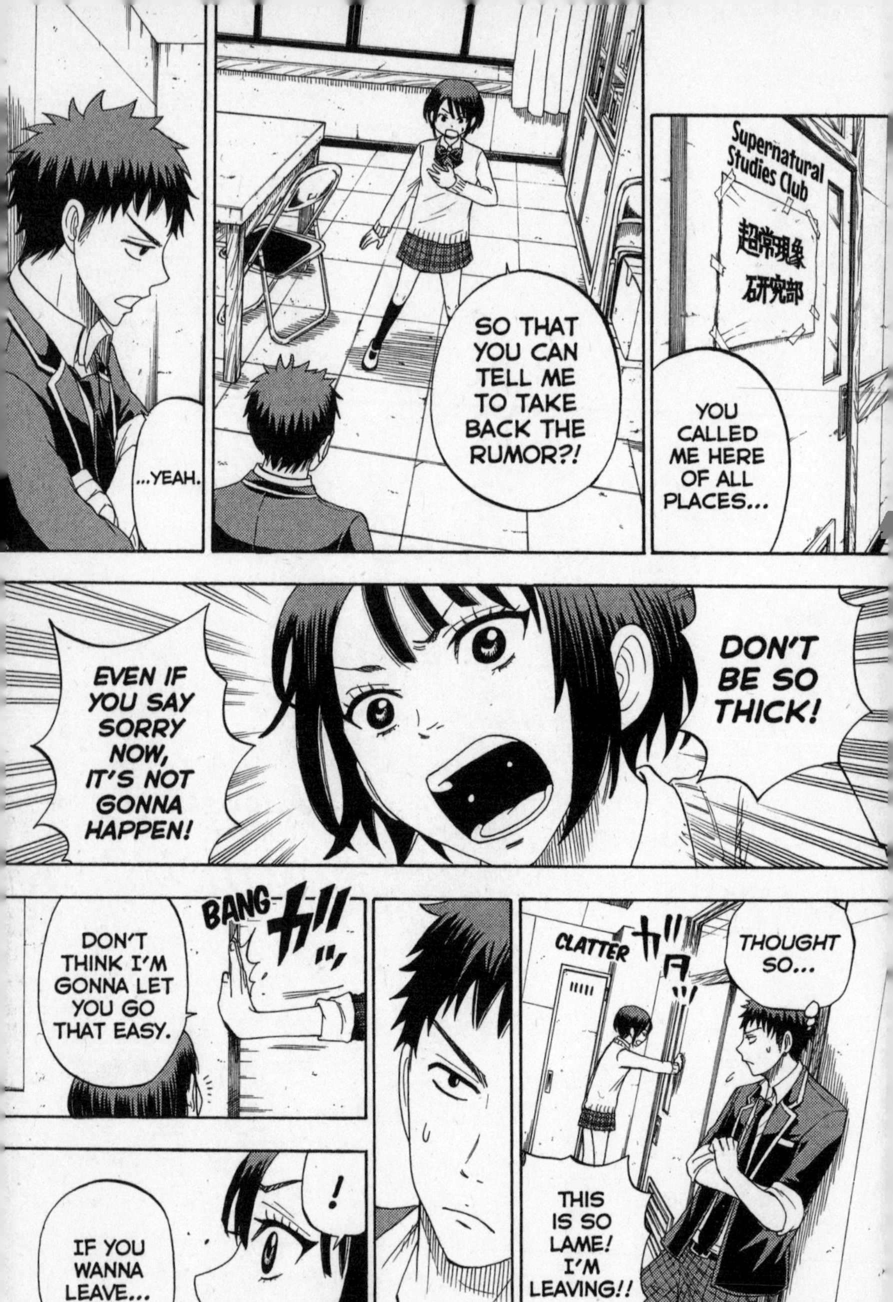

Supernatural Studies Club
超常現象
研究部
YOU CALLED ME HERE OF ALL PLACES...
SO THAT YOU CAN TELL ME TO TAKE BACK THE RUMOR?!
...YEAH.
DON'T BE SO THICK!
EVEN IF YOU SAY SORRY NOW, IT'S NOT GONNA HAPPEN!
THOUGHT SO...
CLATTER
THIS IS SO LAME! I'M LEAVING!!
BANG
DON'T THINK I'M GONNA LET YOU GO THAT EASY.
!
IF YOU WANNA LEAVE...

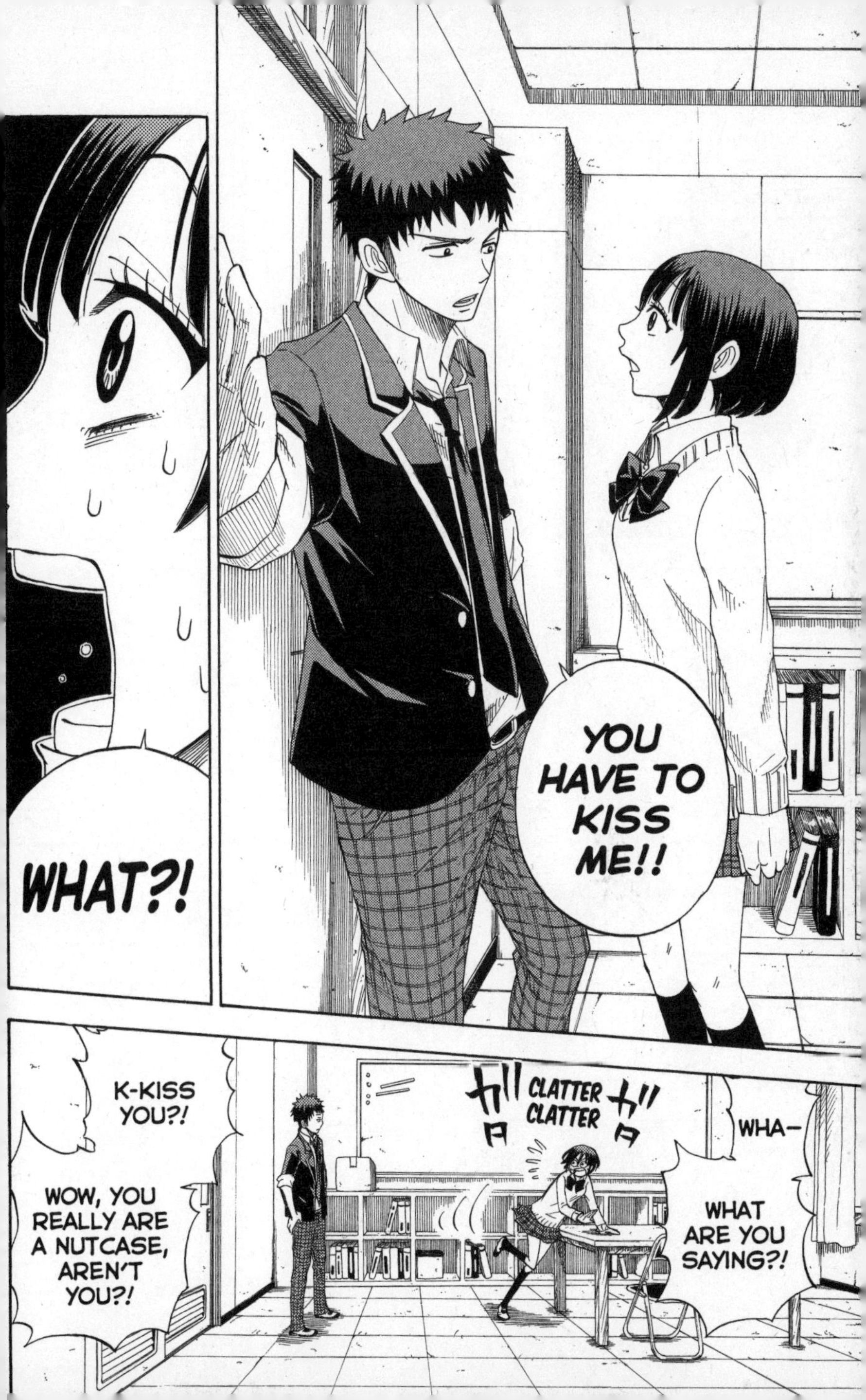
YOU HAVE TO KISS ME!!
WHAT?!
WHA-
WHAT ARE YOU SAYING?!
ガタ ガタ
CLATTER CLATTER
K-KISS YOU?!
WOW, YOU REALLY ARE A NUTCASE, AREN'T YOU?!

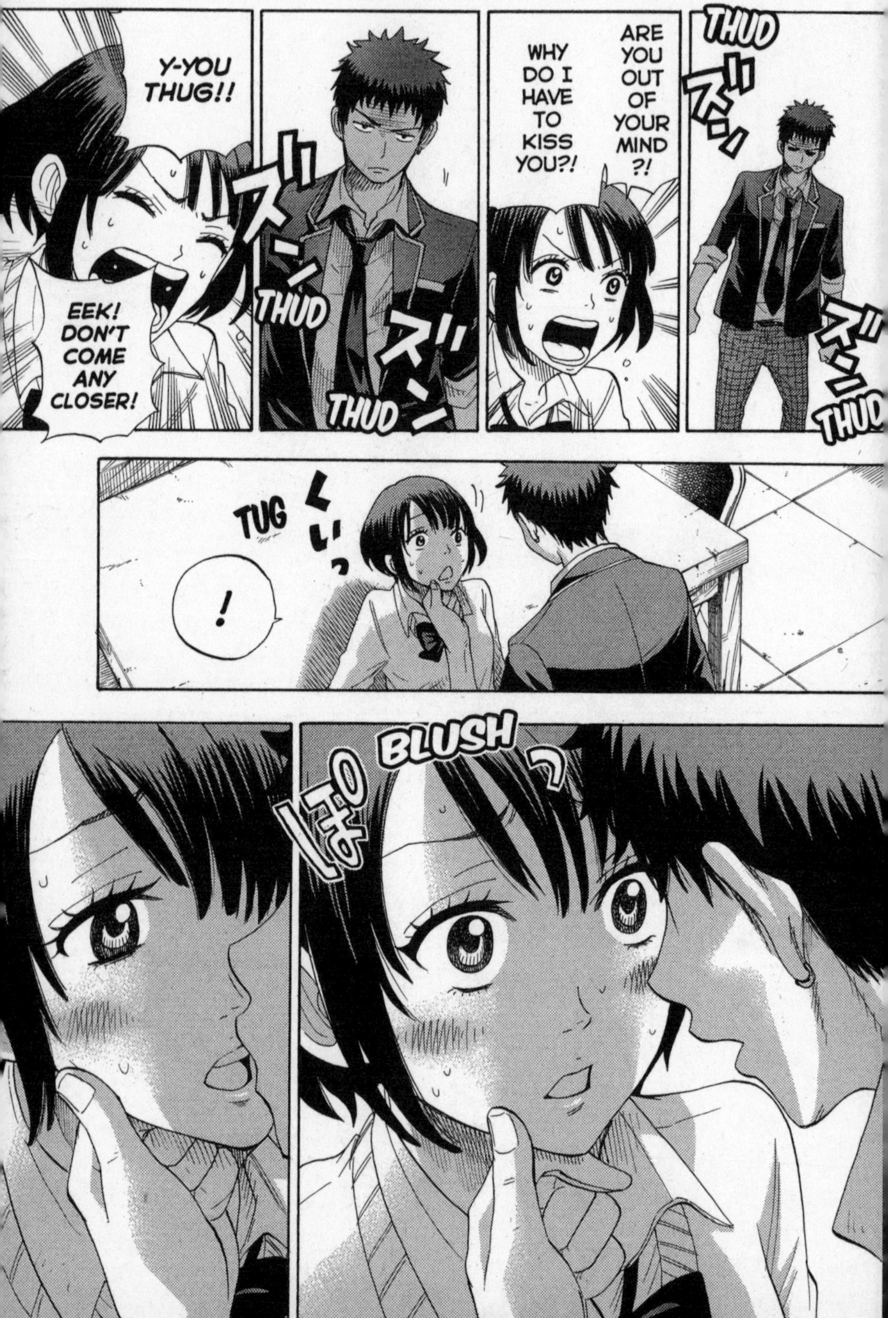
THUD
THUD
ARE YOU OUT OF YOUR MIND?!
WHY DO I HAVE TO KISS YOU?!
THUD
THUD
Y-YOU THUG!!
EEK! DON'T COME ANY CLOSER!
TUG
!
BLUSH

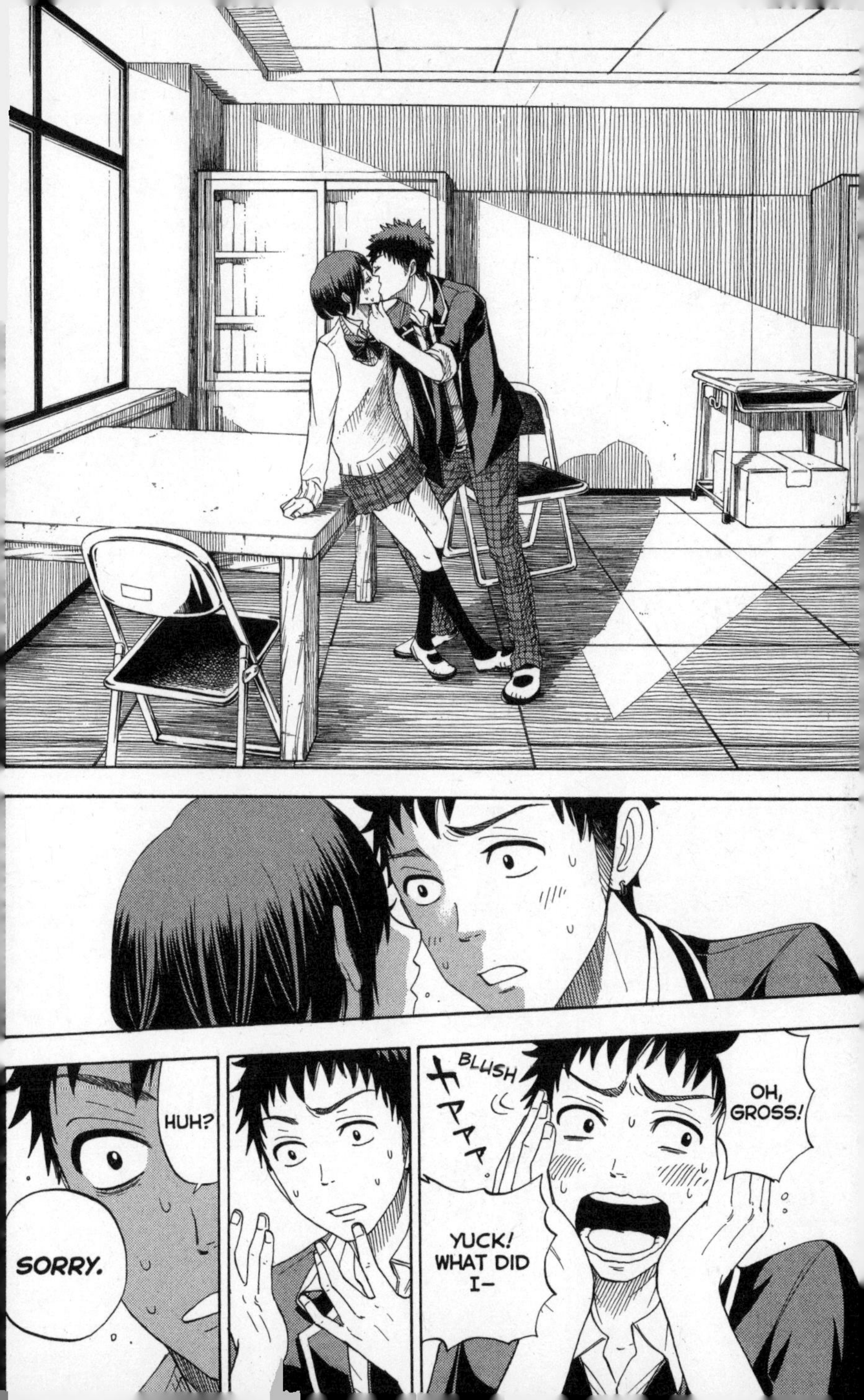
OH, GROSS!
BLUSH
YUCK! WHAT DID I–
HUH?
SORRY.

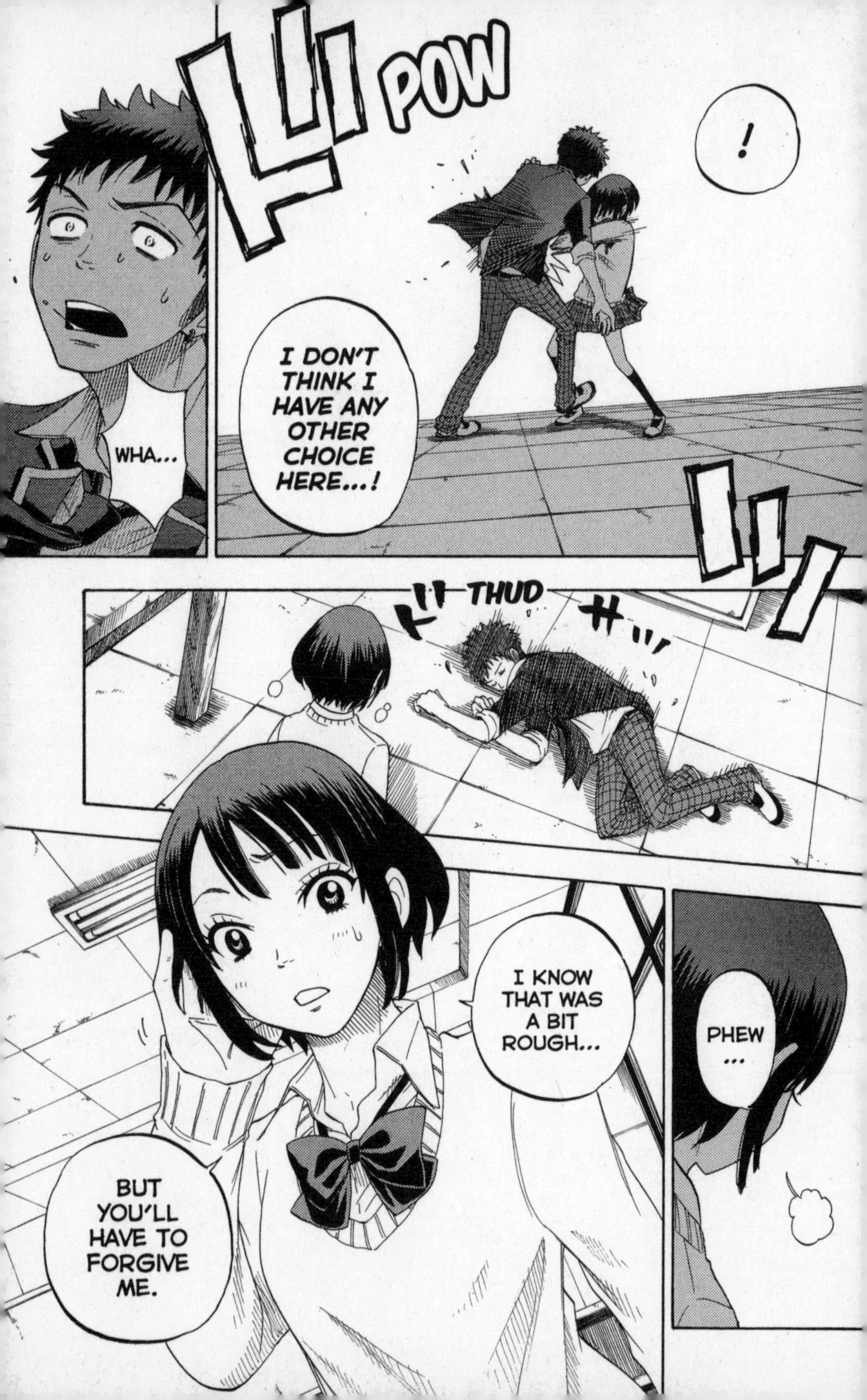
!
POW
I DON'T THINK I HAVE ANY OTHER CHOICE HERE...!
WHA...
THUD
PHEW ...
I KNOW THAT WAS A BIT ROUGH...
BUT YOU'LL HAVE TO FORGIVE ME.

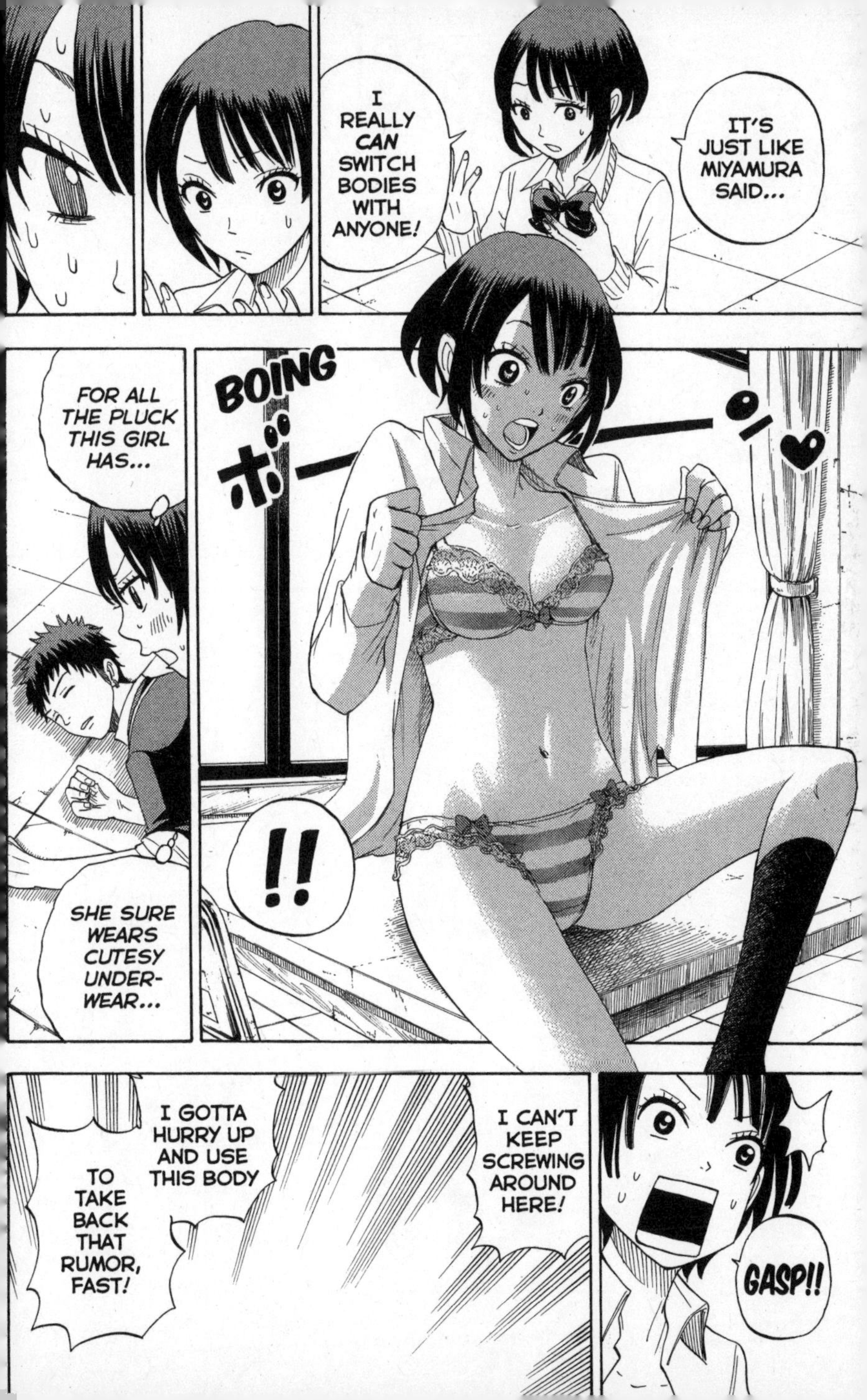
IT'S JUST LIKE MIYAMURA SAID...
I REALLY CAN SWITCH BODIES WITH ANYONE!
BOING
!!
FOR ALL THE PLUCK THIS GIRL HAS...
SHE SURE WEARS CUTESY UNDER-WEAR...
GASP!!
I CAN'T KEEP SCREWING AROUND HERE!
I GOTTA HURRY UP AND USE THIS BODY
TO TAKE BACK THAT RUMOR, FAST!

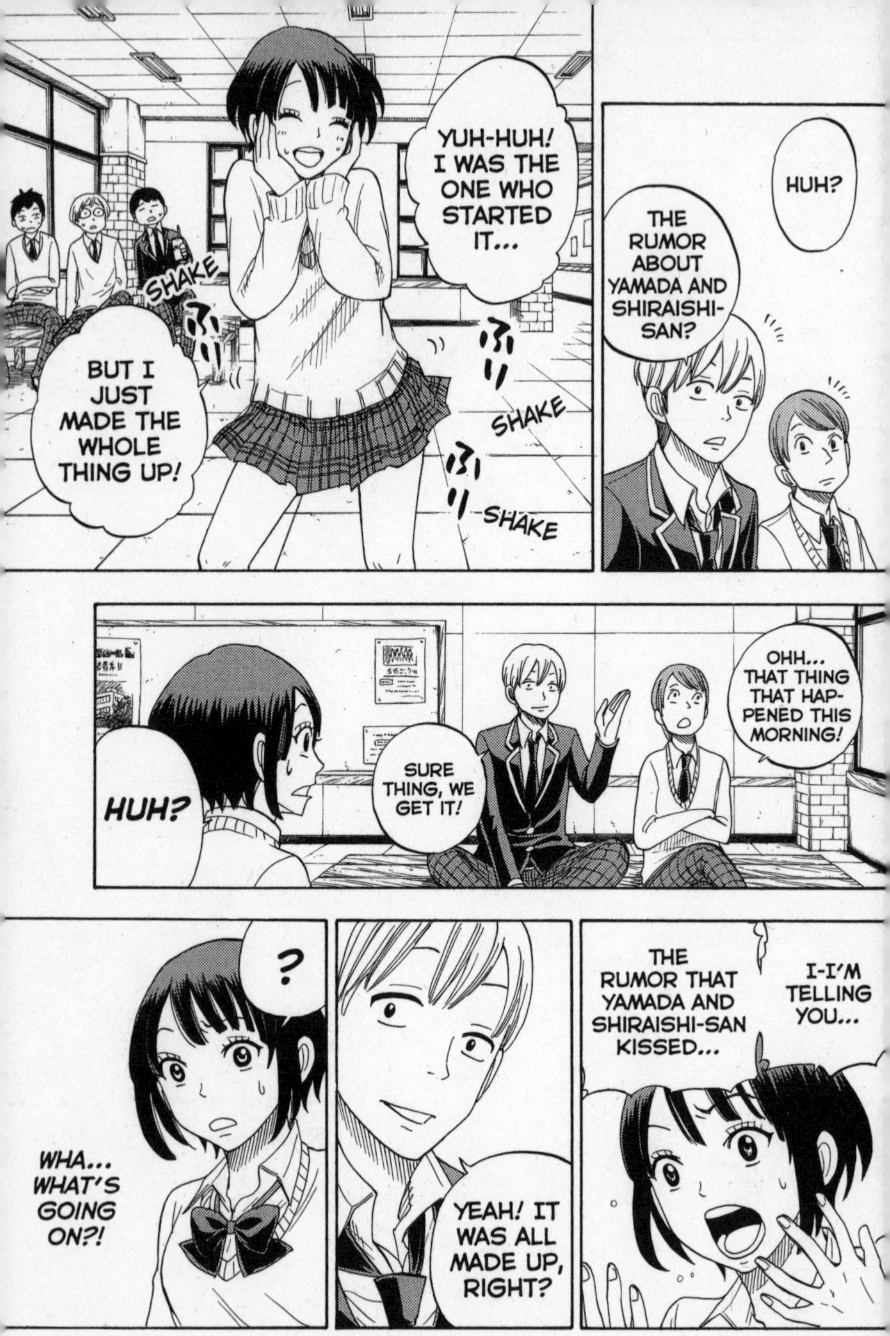
HUH?
THE RUMOR ABOUT YAMADA AND SHIRAISHI-SAN?
YUH-HUH! I WAS THE ONE WHO STARTED IT...
ふり
SHAKE
ふり
SHAKE
ふり
SHAKE
BUT I JUST MADE THE WHOLE THING UP!
OHH... THAT THING THAT HAPPENED THIS MORNING!
SURE THING, WE GET IT!
HUH?
I-I'M TELLING YOU...
THE RUMOR THAT YAMADA AND SHIRAISHI-SAN KISSED...
YEAH! IT WAS ALL MADE UP, RIGHT?
?
WHA... WHAT'S GOING ON?!

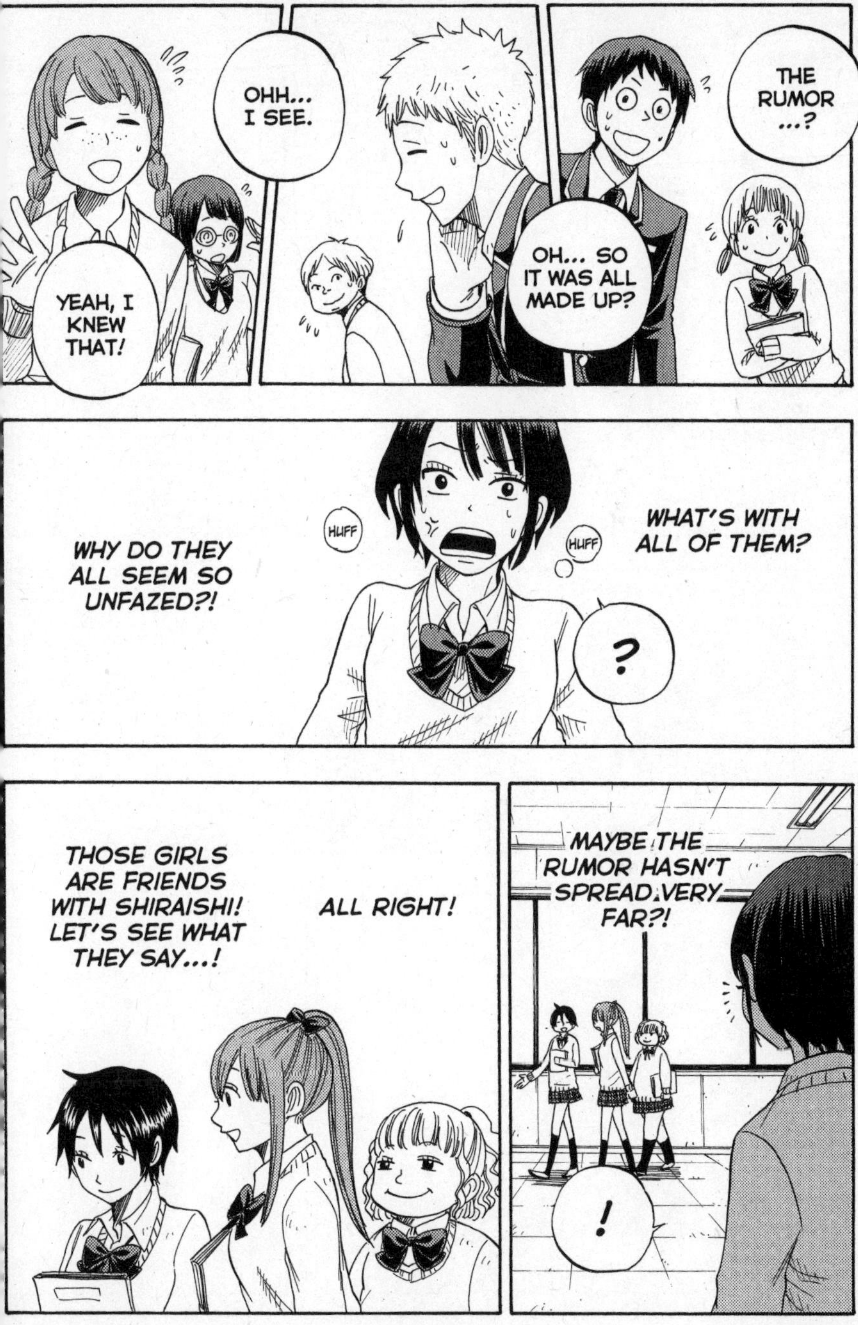
THE RUMOR ...?
OH... SO IT WAS ALL MADE UP?
OHH... I SEE.
YEAH, I KNEW THAT!
WHAT'S WITH ALL OF THEM?
HUFF
?
HUFF
WHY DO THEY ALL SEEM SO UNFAZED?!
MAYBE THE RUMOR HASN'T SPREAD VERY FAR?!
!
ALL RIGHT!
THOSE GIRLS ARE FRIENDS WITH SHIRAISHI! LET'S SEE WHAT THEY SAY...!

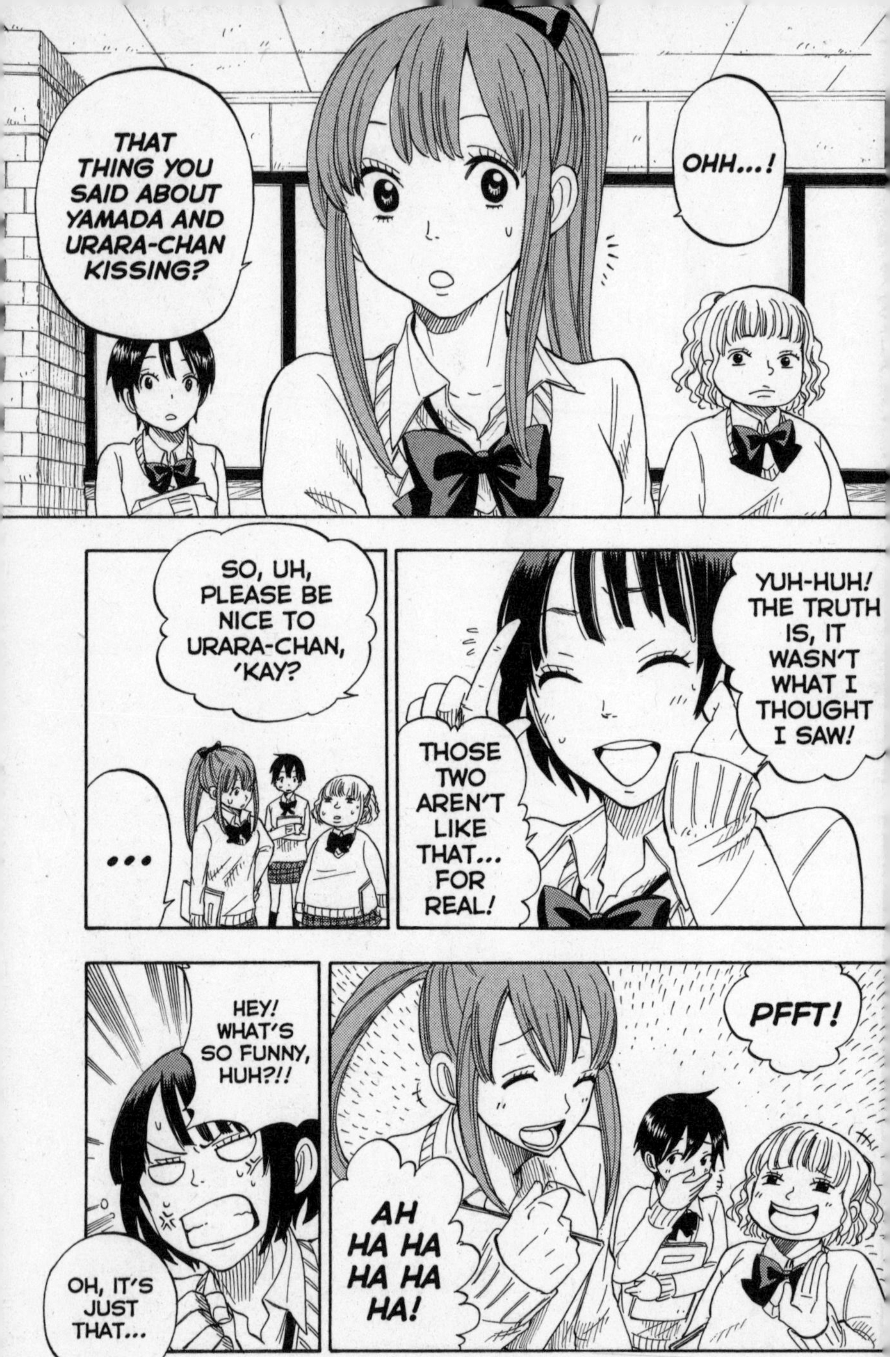
OHH...!
THAT THING YOU SAID ABOUT YAMADA AND URARA-CHAN KISSING?
YUH-HUH! THE TRUTH IS, IT WASN'T WHAT I THOUGHT I SAW!
THOSE TWO AREN'T LIKE THAT... FOR REAL!
SO, UH, PLEASE BE NICE TO URARA-CHAN, 'KAY?
...
PFFT!
AH HA HA HA HA HA!
HEY! WHAT'S SO FUNNY, HUH?!!
OH, IT'S JUST THAT...

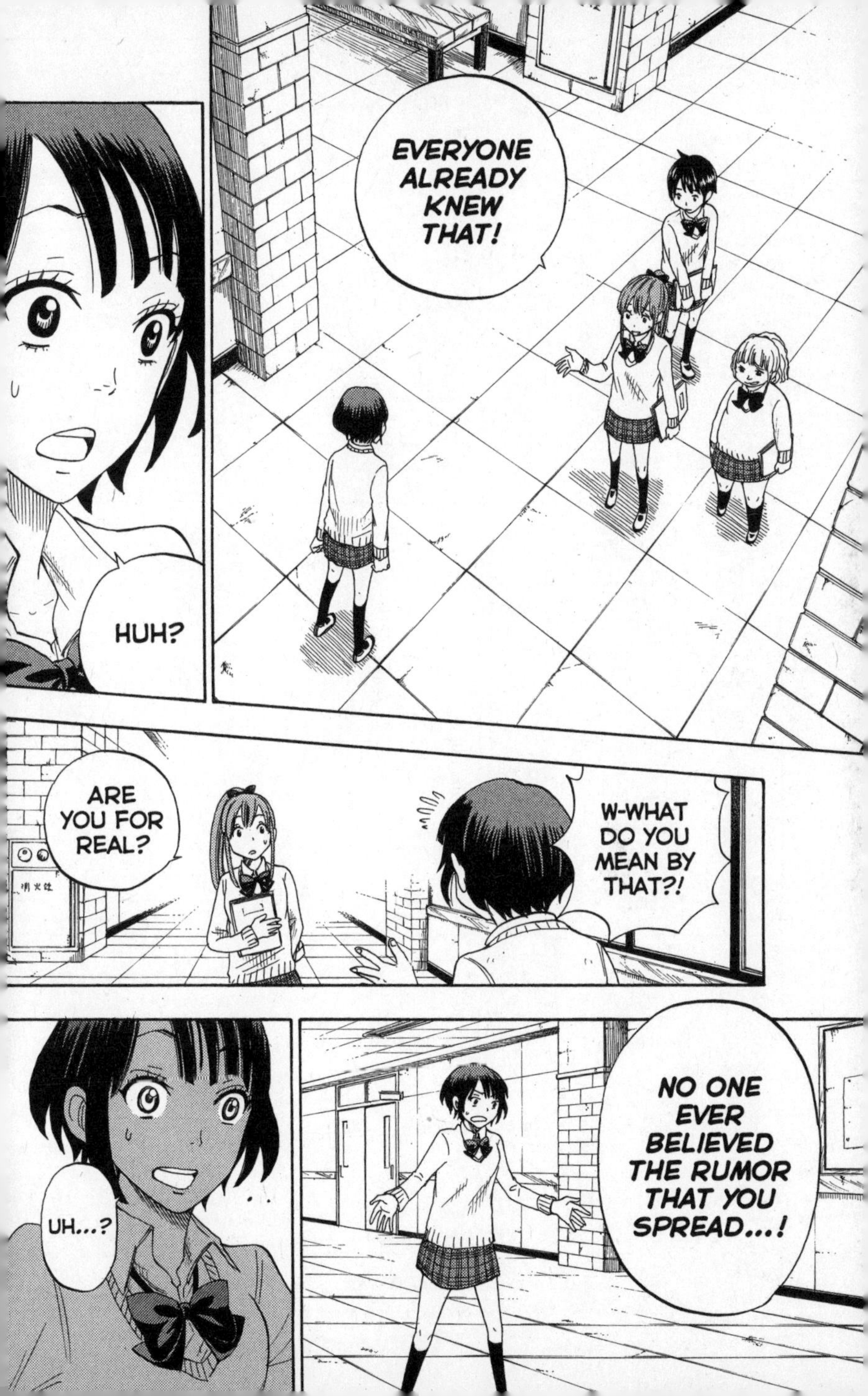
EVERYONE ALREADY KNEW THAT!
HUH?
W-WHAT DO YOU MEAN BY THAT?!
ARE YOU FOR REAL?
NO ONE EVER BELIEVED THE RUMOR THAT YOU SPREAD...!
UH...?

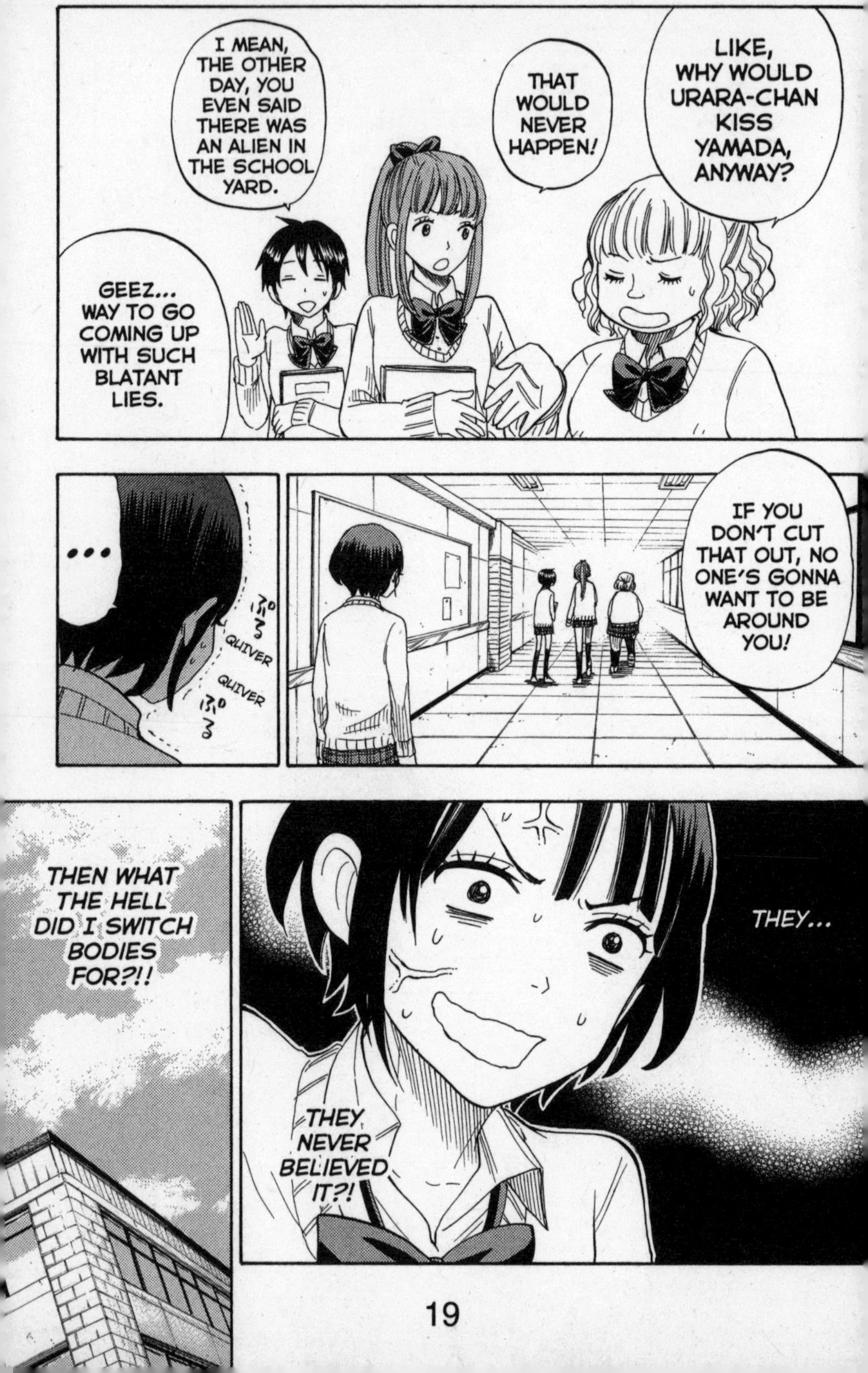
LIKE, WHY WOULD URARA-CHAN KISS YAMADA, ANYWAY?
THAT WOULD NEVER HAPPEN!
I MEAN, THE OTHER DAY, YOU EVEN SAID THERE WAS AN ALIEN IN THE SCHOOL YARD.
GEEZ... WAY TO GO COMING UP WITH SUCH BLATANT LIES.
IF YOU DON'T CUT THAT OUT, NO ONE'S GONNA WANT TO BE AROUND YOU!
...
ぷる
QUIVER
QUIVER
ぷる
THEY...
THEY NEVER BELIEVED IT?!
THEN WHAT THE HELL DID I SWITCH BODIES FOR?!!

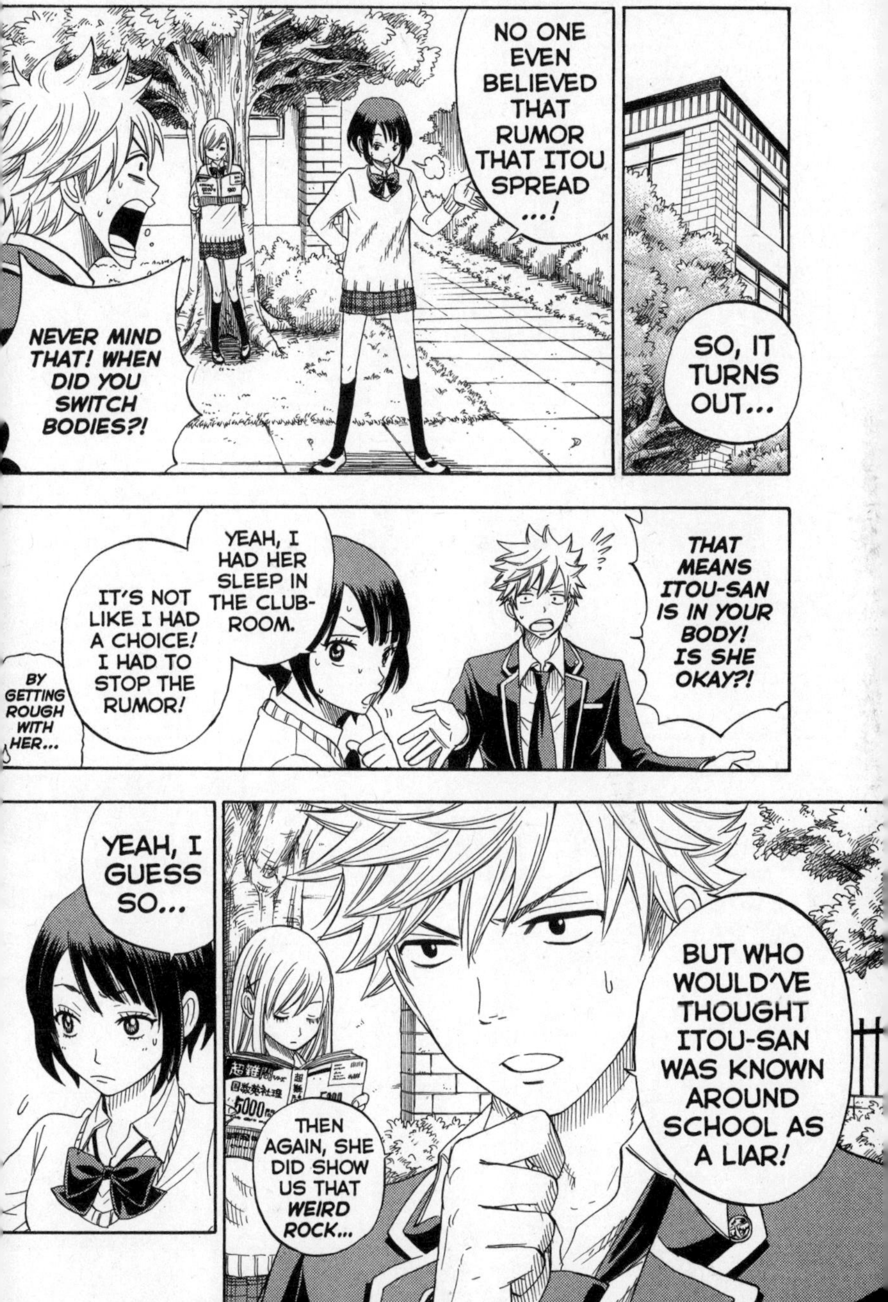
SO, IT TURNS OUT...
NO ONE EVEN BELIEVED THAT RUMOR THAT ITOU SPREAD ...!
NEVER MIND THAT! WHEN DID YOU SWITCH BODIES?!
THAT MEANS ITOU-SAN IS IN YOUR BODY! IS SHE OKAY?!
YEAH, I HAD HER SLEEP IN THE CLUB-ROOM.
IT'S NOT LIKE I HAD A CHOICE! I HAD TO STOP THE RUMOR!
BY GETTING ROUGH WITH HER...
BUT WHO WOULD'VE THOUGHT ITOU-SAN WAS KNOWN AROUND SCHOOL AS A LIAR!
THEN AGAIN, SHE DID SHOW US THAT WEIRD ROCK...
YEAH, I GUESS SO...

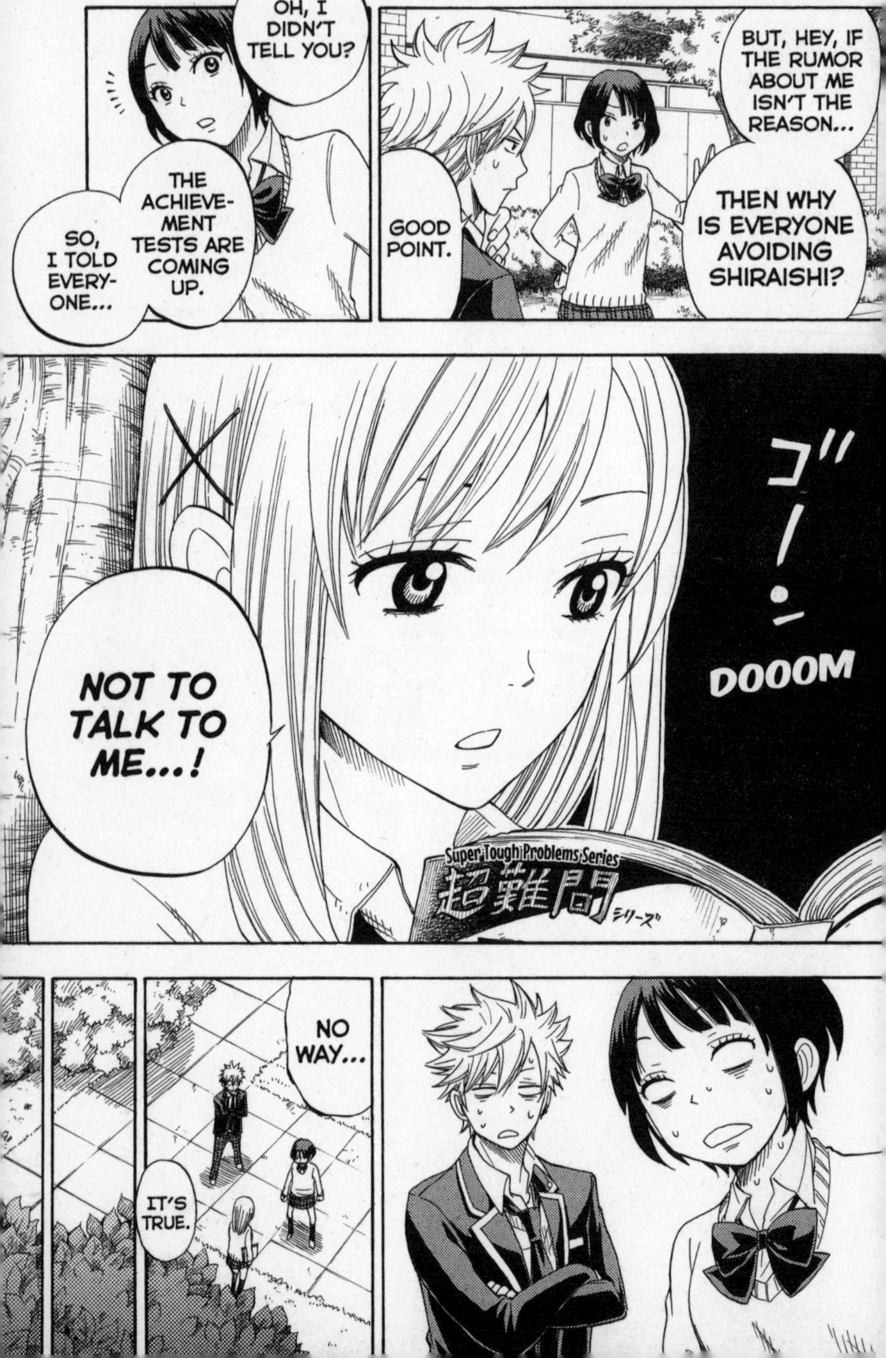
BUT, HEY, IF THE RUMOR ABOUT ME ISN'T THE REASON...
THEN WHY IS EVERYONE AVOIDING SHIRAISHI?
GOOD POINT.
OH, I DIDN'T TELL YOU?
THE ACHIEVEMENT TESTS ARE COMING UP.
SO, I TOLD EVERYONE...
NOT TO TALK TO ME...!
ゴーン
DOOOM
Super Tough Problems Series
超難問シリーズ
NO WAY...
IT'S TRUE.

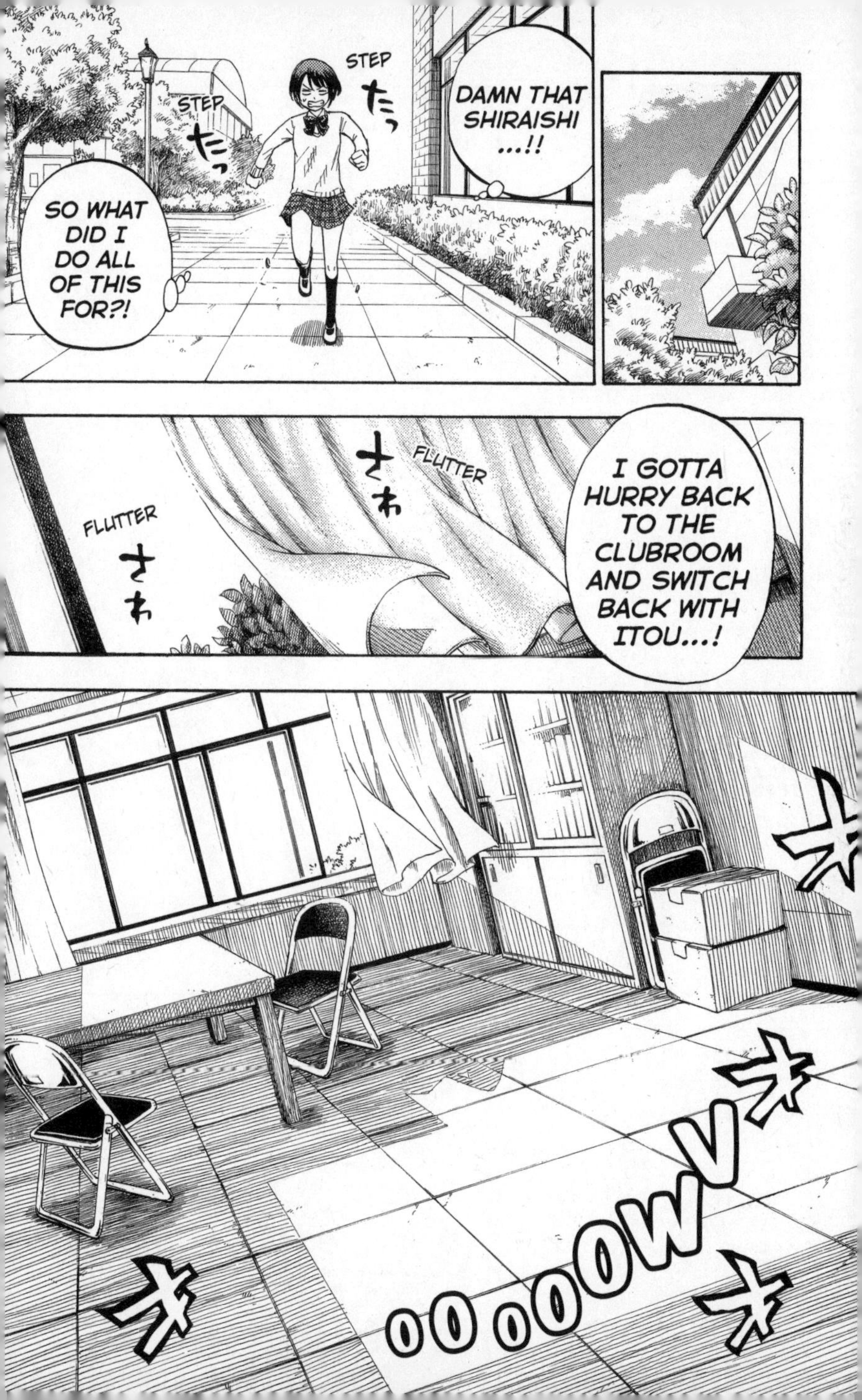
DAMN THAT SHIRAISHI...!!
STEP
たっ
STEP
たっ
SO WHAT DID I DO ALL OF THIS FOR?!
I GOTTA HURRY BACK TO THE CLUBROOM AND SWITCH BACK WITH ITOU...!
FLUTTER
さわ
FLUTTER
さわ
オ
オ
オ
オ
OO OOOOWV

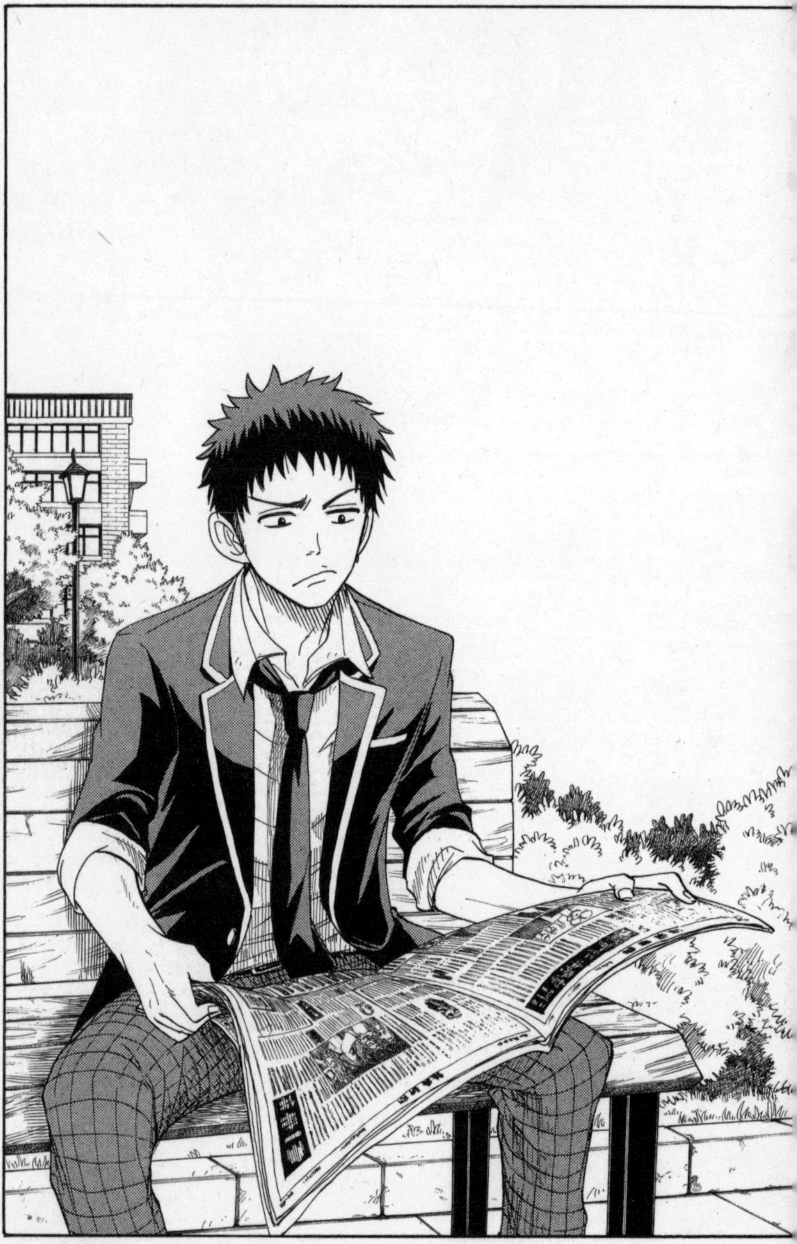

CHAPTER 9: Crushing Tornado Kick!

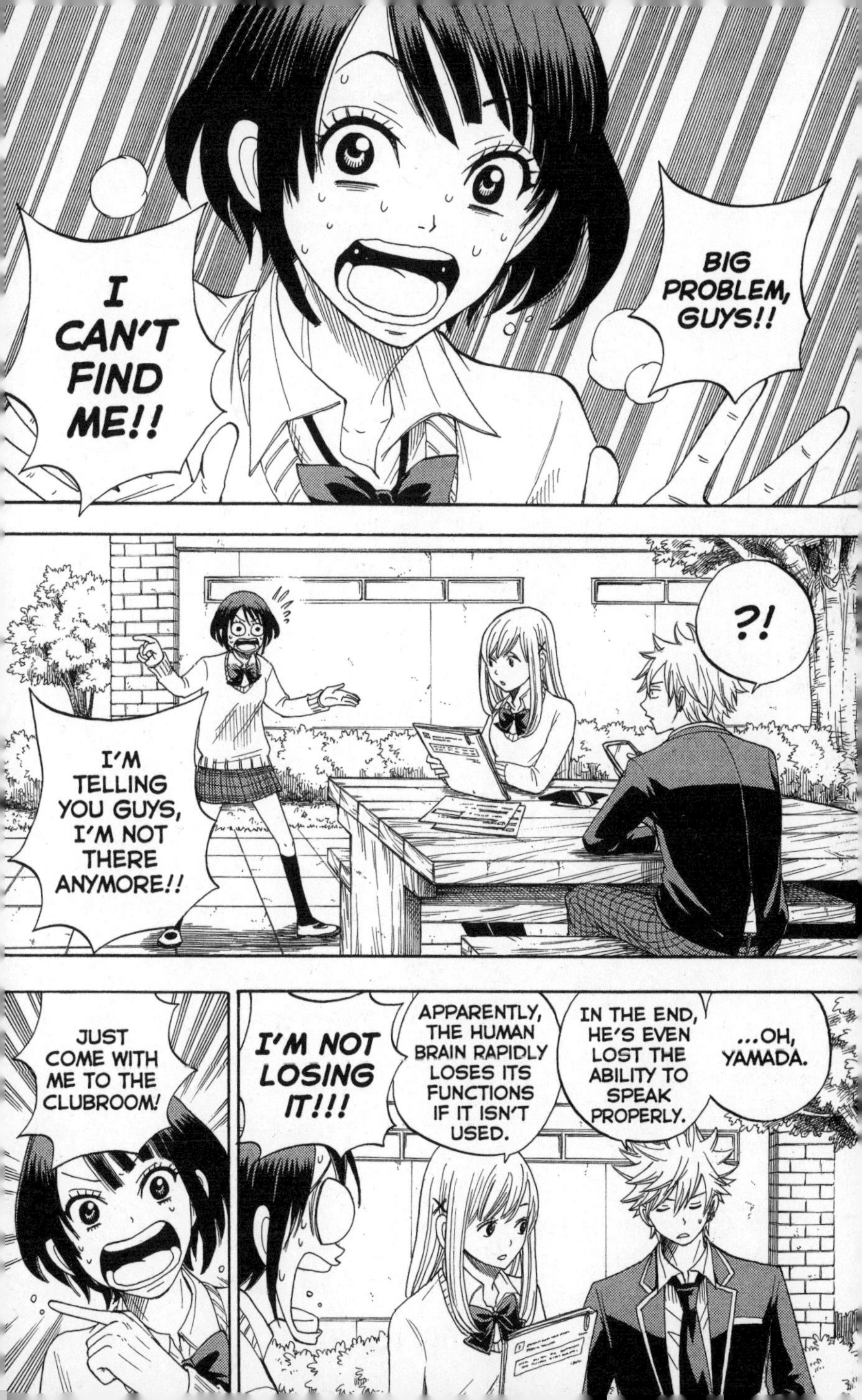
BIG PROBLEM, GUYS!!
I CAN'T FIND ME!!
?!
I'M TELLING YOU GUYS, I'M NOT THERE ANYMORE!!
...OH, YAMADA.
IN THE END, HE'S EVEN LOST THE ABILITY TO SPEAK PROPERLY.
APPARENTLY, THE HUMAN BRAIN RAPIDLY LOSES ITS FUNCTIONS IF IT ISN'T USED.
I'M NOT LOSING IT!!!
JUST COME WITH ME TO THE CLUBROOM!

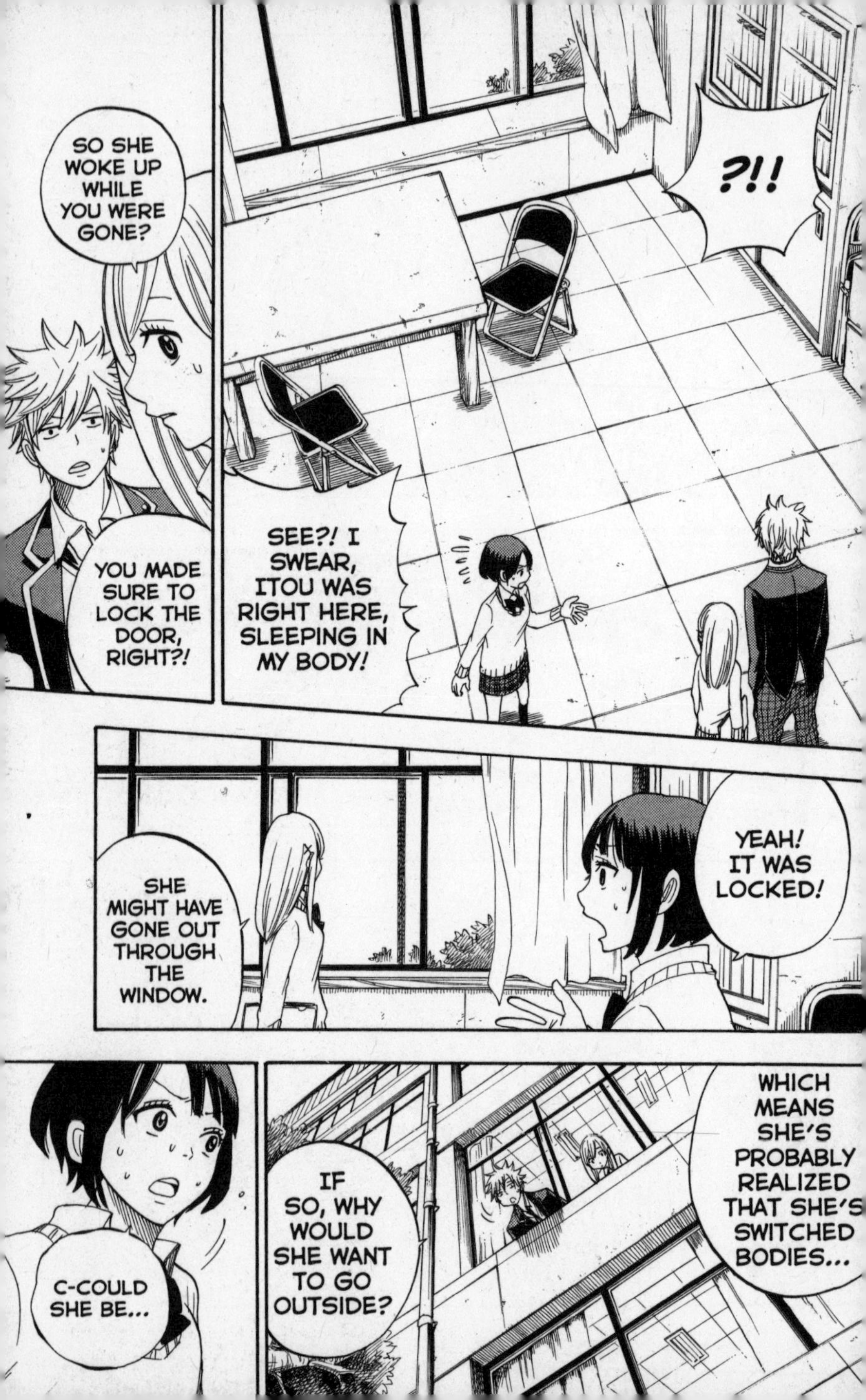

?!!
SEE?! I SWEAR, ITOU WAS RIGHT HERE, SLEEPING IN MY BODY!
SO SHE WOKE UP WHILE YOU WERE GONE?
YOU MADE SURE TO LOCK THE DOOR, RIGHT?!
YEAH! IT WAS LOCKED!
SHE MIGHT HAVE GONE OUT THROUGH THE WINDOW.
WHICH MEANS SHE'S PROBABLY REALIZED THAT SHE'S SWITCHED BODIES...
IF SO, WHY WOULD SHE WANT TO GO OUTSIDE?
C-COULD SHE BE...

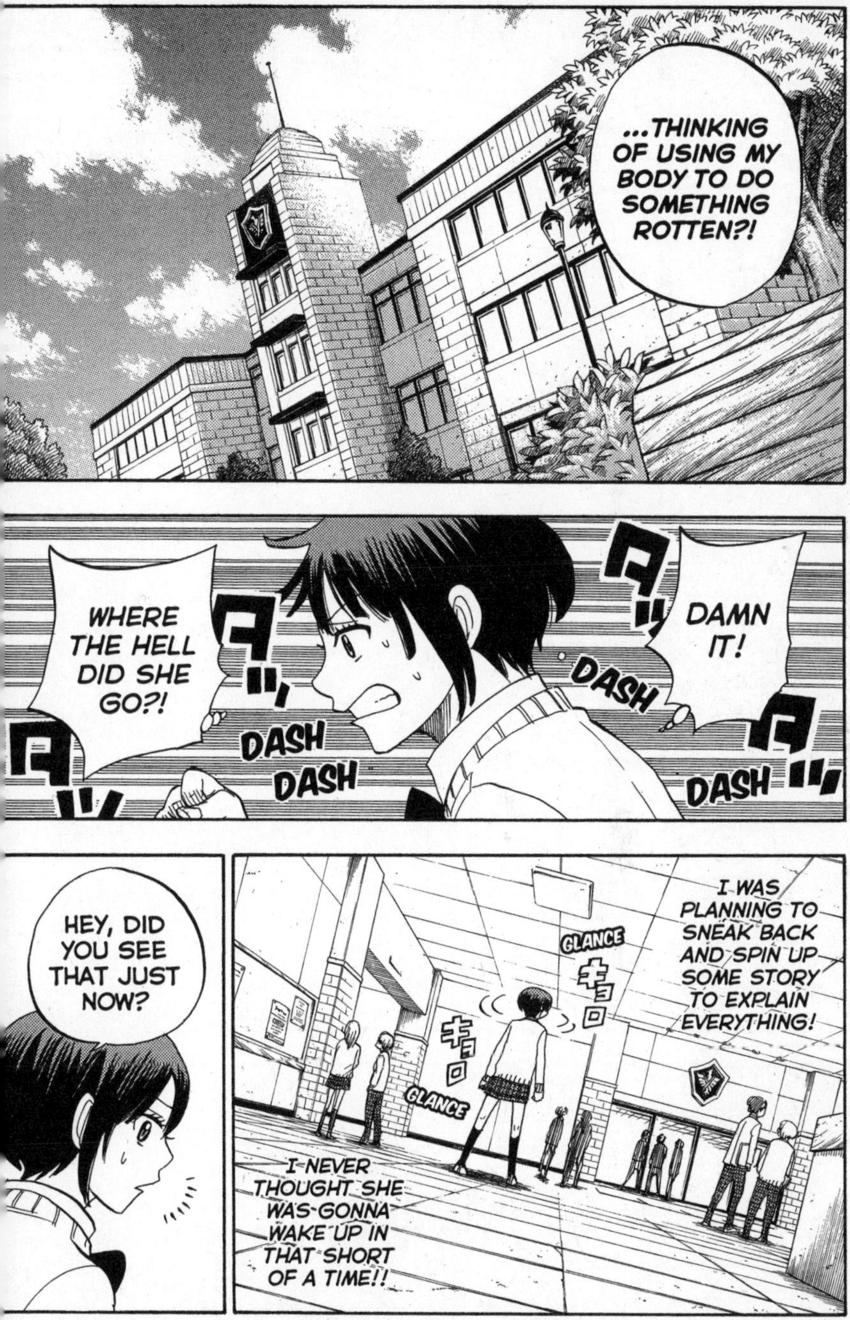
...THINKING OF USING MY BODY TO DO SOMETHING ROTTEN?!
DAMN IT!
DASH
DASH
WHERE THE HELL DID SHE GO?!
DASH
DASH
I WAS PLANNING TO SNEAK BACK AND SPIN UP SOME STORY TO EXPLAIN EVERYTHING!
GLANCE
GLANCE
I NEVER THOUGHT SHE WAS GONNA WAKE UP IN THAT SHORT OF A TIME!!
HEY, DID YOU SEE THAT JUST NOW?

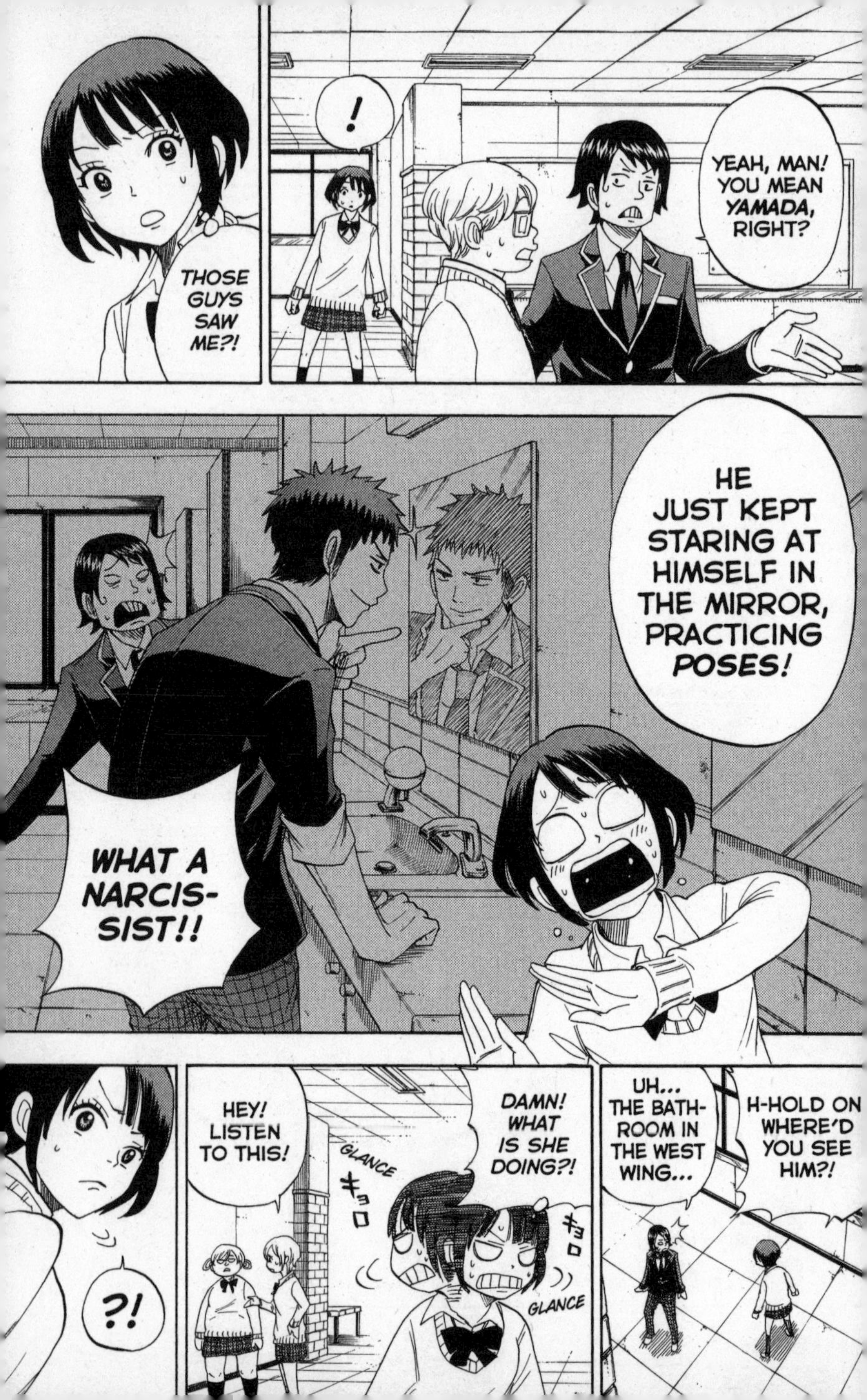
YEAH, MAN! YOU MEAN YAMADA, RIGHT?
!
THOSE GUYS SAW ME?!
HE JUST KEPT STARING AT HIMSELF IN THE MIRROR, PRACTICING POSES!
WHAT A NARCIS-SIST!!
H-HOLD ON WHERE'D YOU SEE HIM?!
UH... THE BATH-ROOM IN THE WEST WING...
DAMN! WHAT IS SHE DOING?!
キョロ
GLANCE
HEY! LISTEN TO THIS!
GLANCE
キョロ
?!

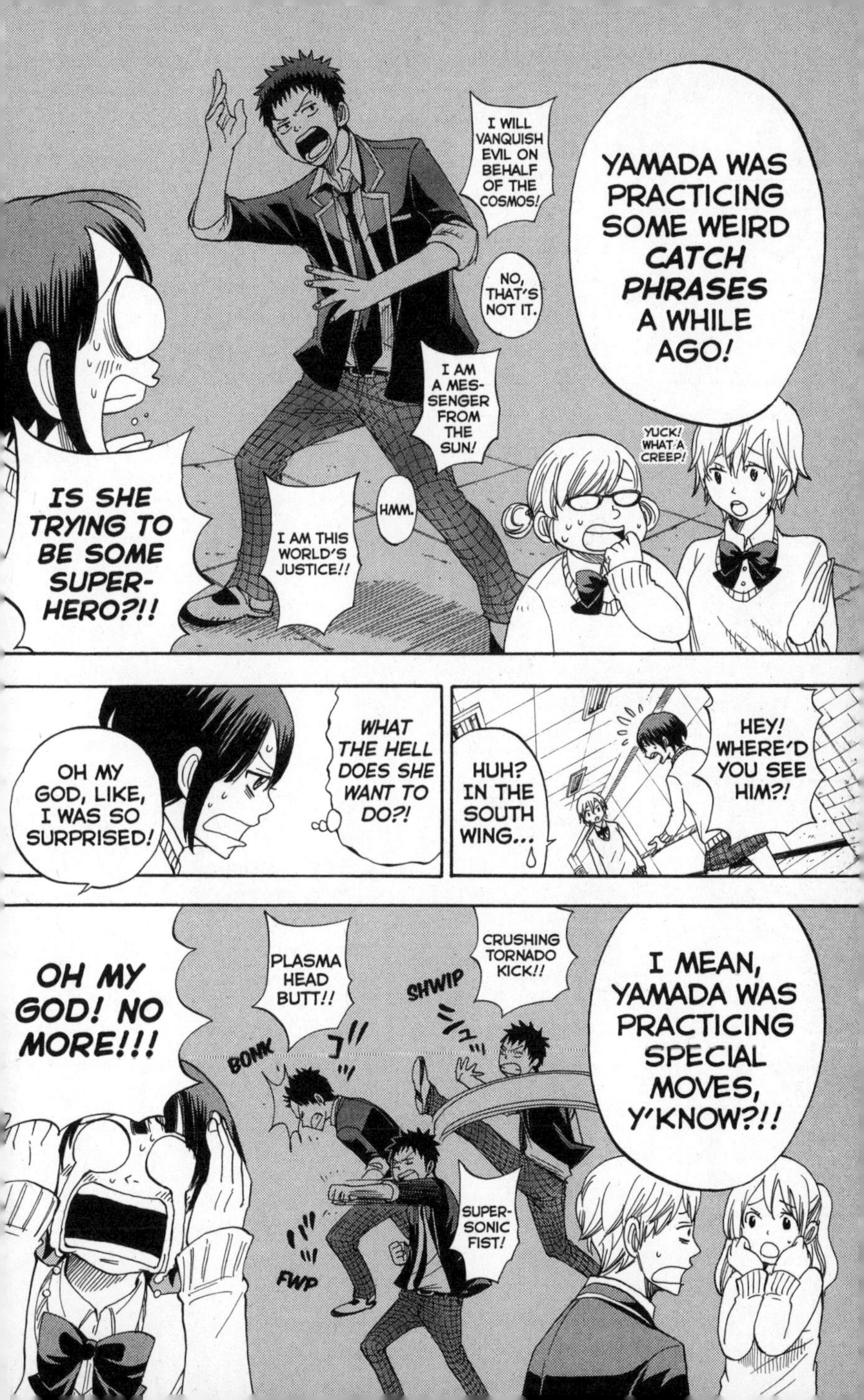
YAMADA WAS PRACTICING SOME WEIRD CATCH PHRASES A WHILE AGO!
YUCK! WHAT A CREEP!
I WILL VANQUISH EVIL ON BEHALF OF THE COSMOS!
NO, THAT'S NOT IT.
I AM A MESSENGER FROM THE SUN!
HMM.
I AM THIS WORLD'S JUSTICE!!
IS SHE TRYING TO BE SOME SUPERHERO?!!
HEY! WHERE'D YOU SEE HIM?!
HUH? IN THE SOUTH WING...
WHAT THE HELL DOES SHE WANT TO DO?!
OH MY GOD, LIKE, I WAS SO SURPRISED!
I MEAN, YAMADA WAS PRACTICING SPECIAL MOVES, Y'KNOW?!!
CRUSHING TORNADO KICK!!
SHWIP
PLASMA HEAD BUTT!!
BONK
SUPERSONIC FIST!
FWP
OH MY GOD! NO MORE!!!

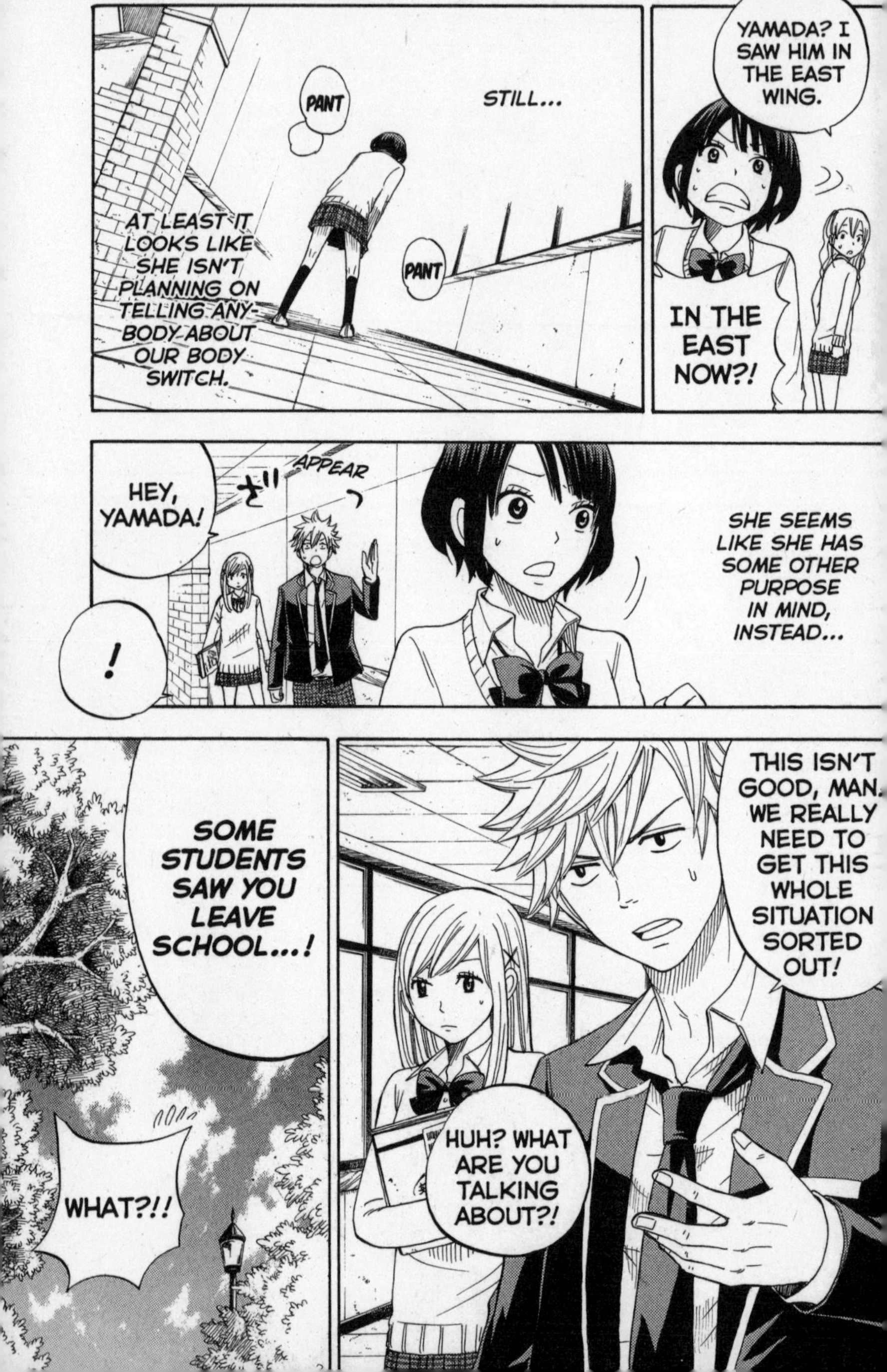
YAMADA? I SAW HIM IN THE EAST WING.
IN THE EAST NOW?!
STILL...
PANT
PANT
AT LEAST IT LOOKS LIKE SHE ISN'T PLANNING ON TELLING ANY-BODY ABOUT OUR BODY SWITCH.
SHE SEEMS LIKE SHE HAS SOME OTHER PURPOSE IN MIND, INSTEAD...
APPEAR
HEY, YAMADA!
!
THIS ISN'T GOOD, MAN. WE REALLY NEED TO GET THIS WHOLE SITUATION SORTED OUT!
HUH? WHAT ARE YOU TALKING ABOUT?!
SOME STUDENTS SAW YOU LEAVE SCHOOL...!
WHAT?!!

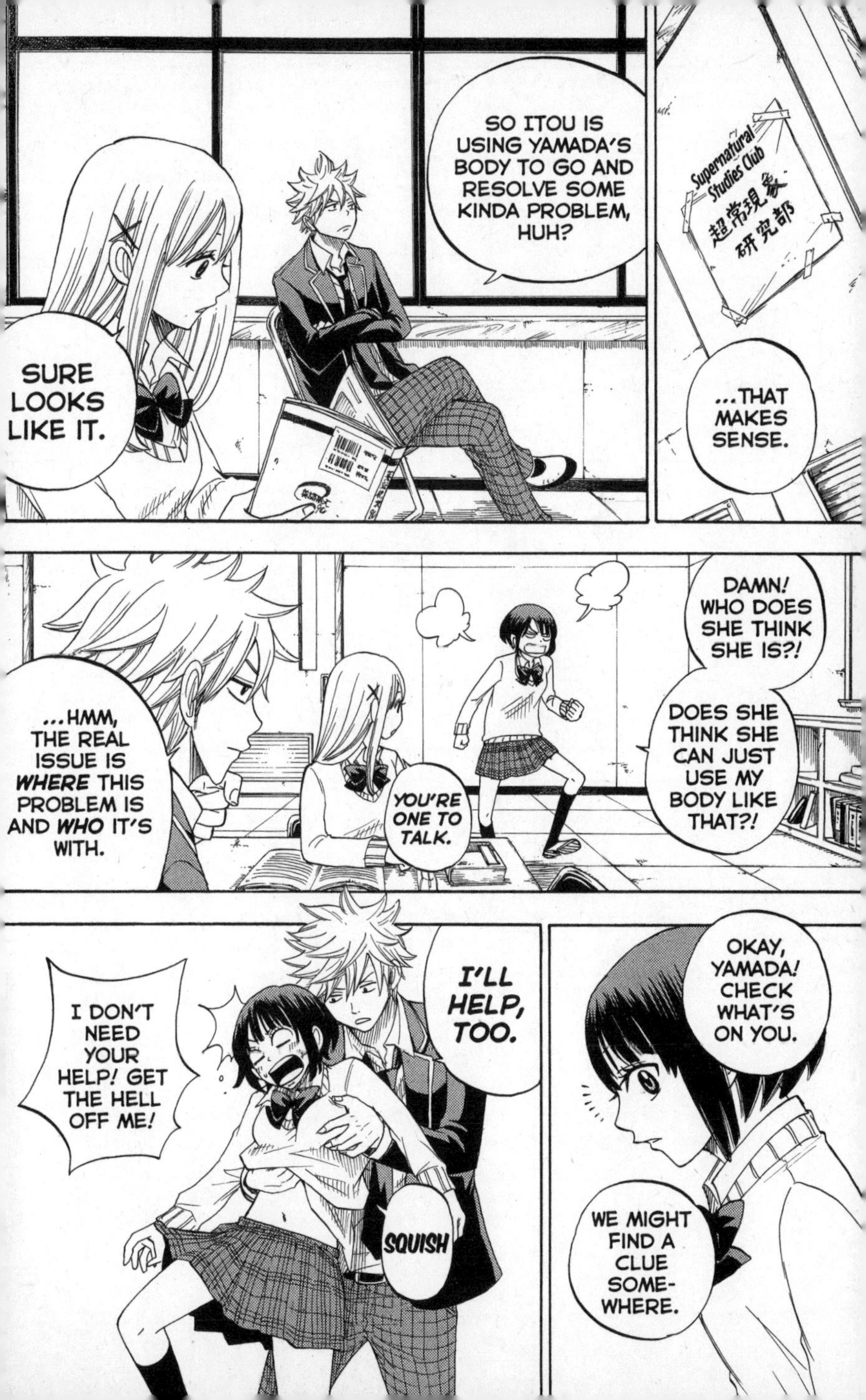
Supernatural Studies Club
超常現象研究部
...THAT MAKES SENSE.
SO ITOU IS USING YAMADA'S BODY TO GO AND RESOLVE SOME KINDA PROBLEM, HUH?
SURE LOOKS LIKE IT.
DAMN! WHO DOES SHE THINK SHE IS?!
DOES SHE THINK SHE CAN JUST USE MY BODY LIKE THAT?!
YOU'RE ONE TO TALK.
...HMM, THE REAL ISSUE IS *WHERE* THIS PROBLEM IS AND *WHO* IT'S WITH.
OKAY, YAMADA! CHECK WHAT'S ON YOU.
WE MIGHT FIND A CLUE SOME-WHERE.
I'LL HELP, TOO.
SQUISH
I DON'T NEED YOUR HELP! GET THE HELL OFF ME!

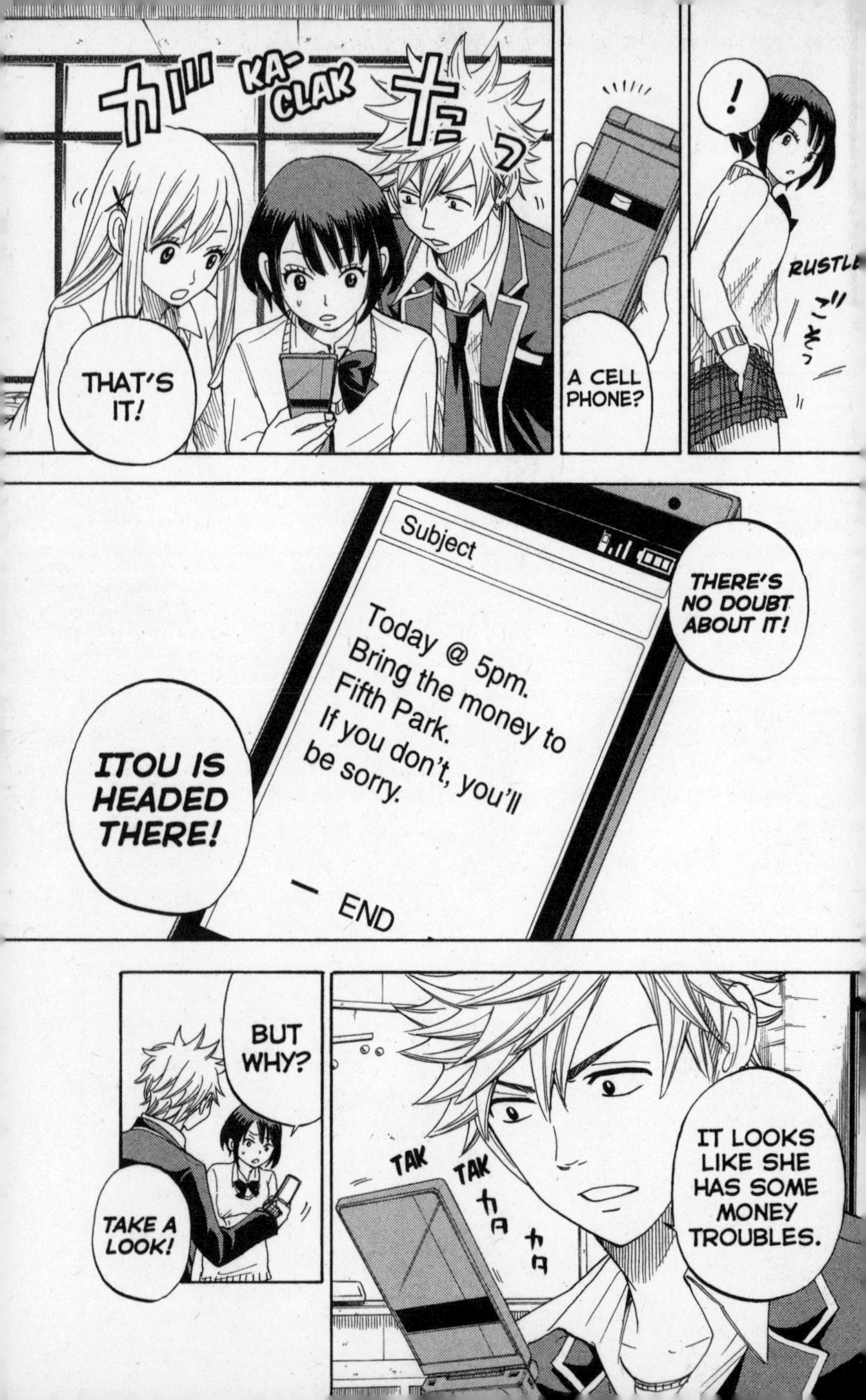
!
RUSTLE
A CELL PHONE?
KA-CLAK
THAT'S IT!
THERE'S NO DOUBT ABOUT IT!
Subject
Today @ 5pm.
Bring the money to Fifth Park.
If you don't, you'll be sorry.
— END
ITOU IS HEADED THERE!
TAK
TAK
カタ
カタ
IT LOOKS LIKE SHE HAS SOME MONEY TROUBLES.
BUT WHY?
TAKE A LOOK!

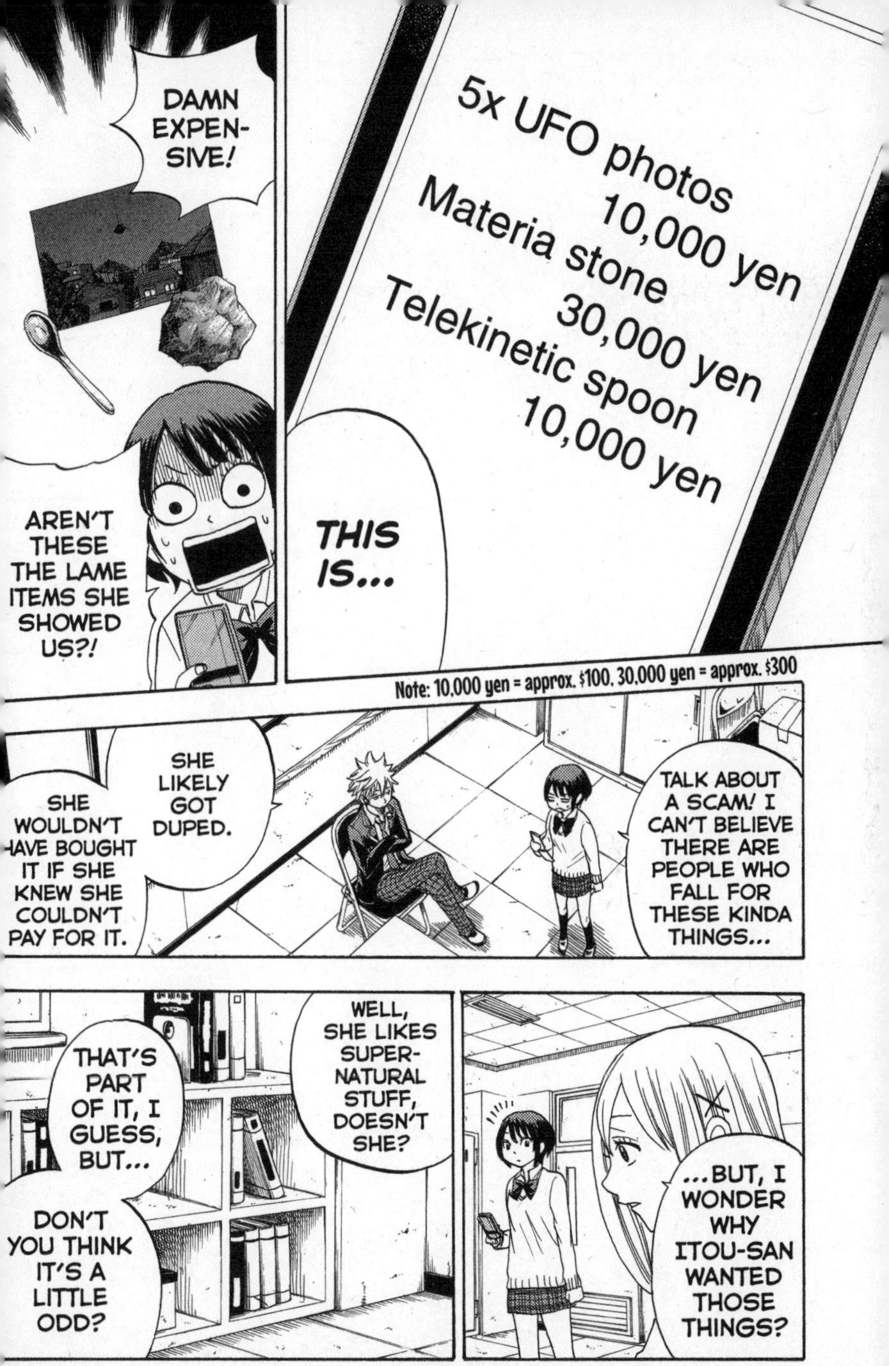
5x UFO photos 10,000 yen
Materia stone 30,000 yen
Telekinetic spoon 10,000 yen
THIS IS...
DAMN EXPENSIVE!
AREN'T THESE THE LAME ITEMS SHE SHOWED US?!
Note: 10,000 yen = approx. $100, 30,000 yen = approx. $300
TALK ABOUT A SCAM! I CAN'T BELIEVE THERE ARE PEOPLE WHO FALL FOR THESE KINDA THINGS...
SHE LIKELY GOT DUPED.
SHE WOULDN'T HAVE BOUGHT IT IF SHE KNEW SHE COULDN'T PAY FOR IT.
...BUT, I WONDER WHY ITOU-SAN WANTED THOSE THINGS?
WELL, SHE LIKES SUPER-NATURAL STUFF, DOESN'T SHE?
THAT'S PART OF IT, I GUESS, BUT...
DON'T YOU THINK IT'S A LITTLE ODD?

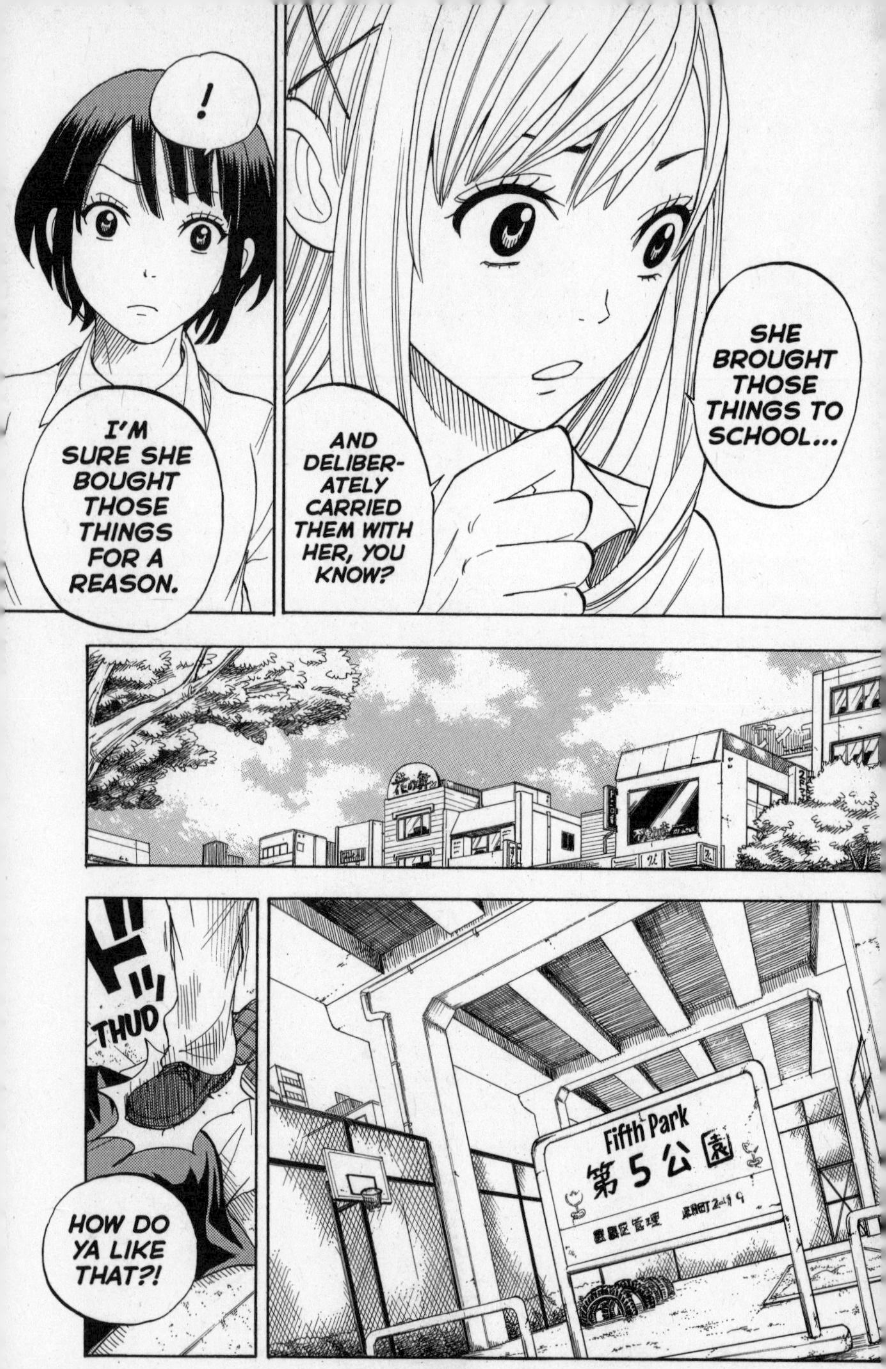
SHE BROUGHT THOSE THINGS TO SCHOOL...
AND DELIBER-ATELY CARRIED THEM WITH HER, YOU KNOW?
!
I'M SURE SHE BOUGHT THOSE THINGS FOR A REASON.
Fifth Park
第5公園
THUD
HOW DO YA LIKE THAT?!

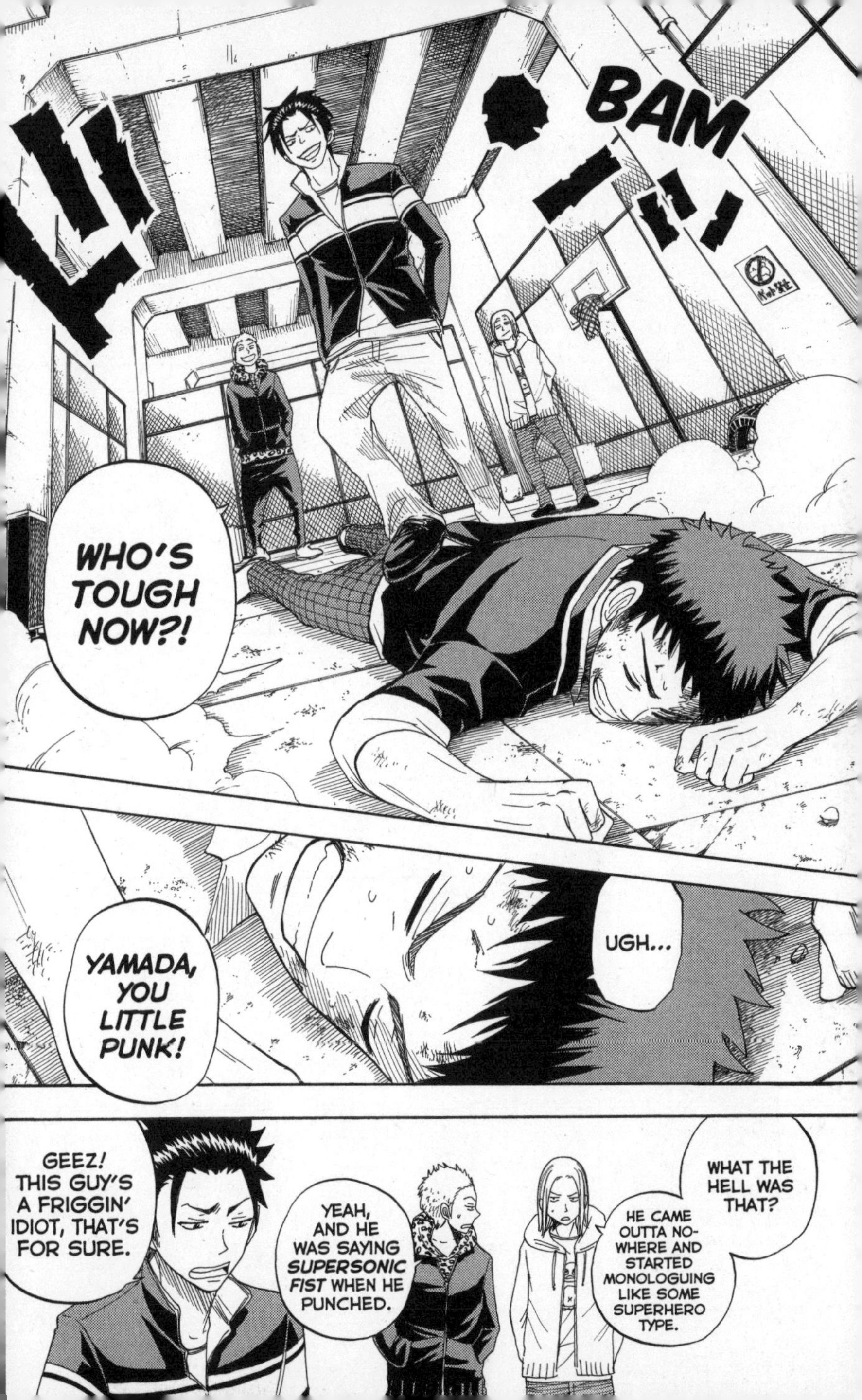
BAM
WHO'S TOUGH NOW?!
UGH...
YAMADA, YOU LITTLE PUNK!
WHAT THE HELL WAS THAT?
HE CAME OUTTA NO-WHERE AND STARTED MONOLOGUING LIKE SOME SUPERHERO TYPE.
YEAH, AND HE WAS SAYING *SUPERSONIC FIST* WHEN HE PUNCHED.
GEEZ! THIS GUY'S A FRIGGIN' IDIOT, THAT'S FOR SURE.

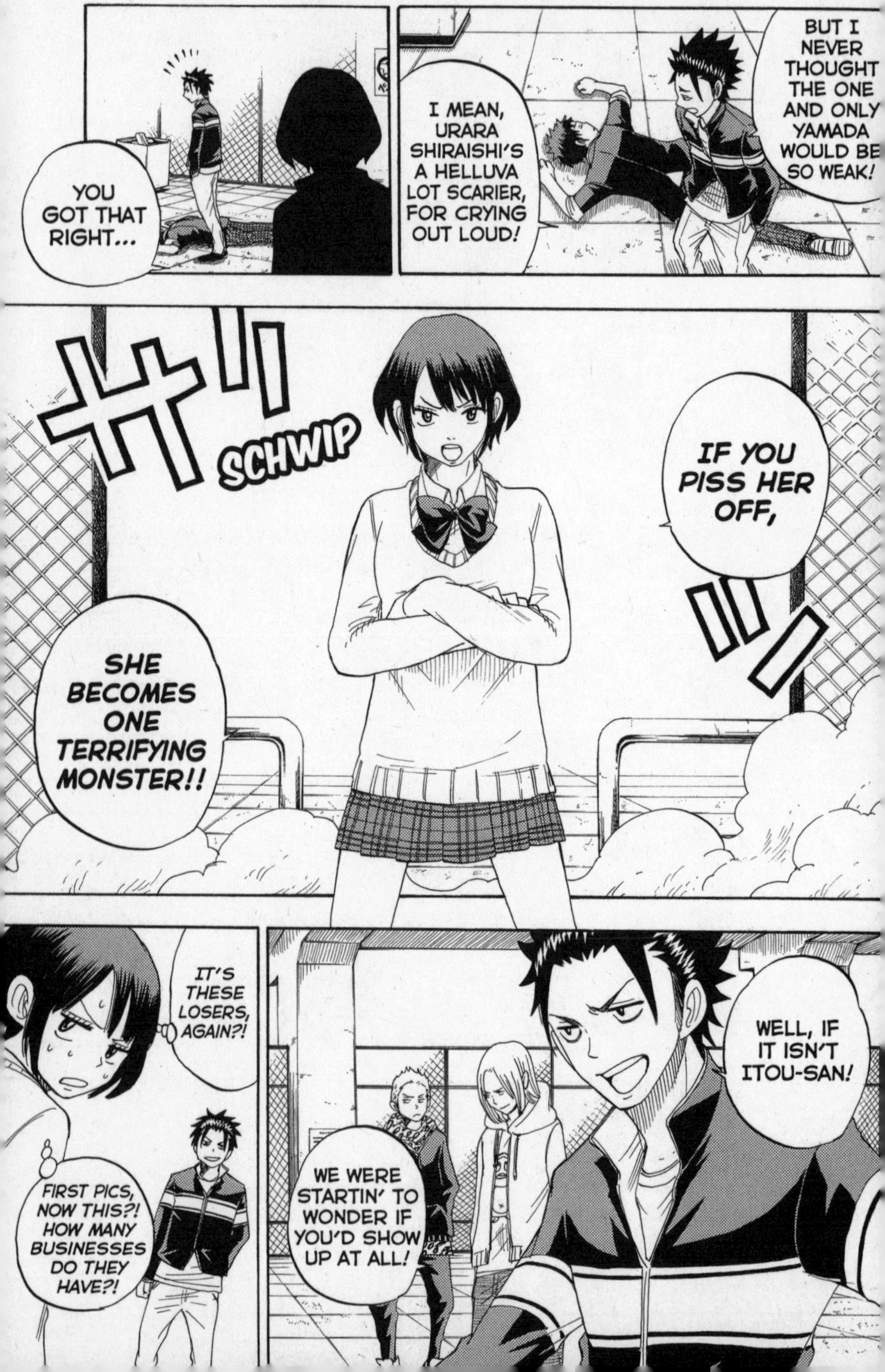
BUT I NEVER THOUGHT THE ONE AND ONLY YAMADA WOULD BE SO WEAK!
I MEAN, URARA SHIRAISHI'S A HELLUVA LOT SCARIER, FOR CRYING OUT LOUD!
YOU GOT THAT RIGHT...
IF YOU PISS HER OFF,
SCHWIP
SHE BECOMES ONE TERRIFYING MONSTER!!
WELL, IF IT ISN'T ITOU-SAN!
WE WERE STARTIN' TO WONDER IF YOU'D SHOW UP AT ALL!
IT'S THESE LOSERS, AGAIN?!
FIRST PICS, NOW THIS?! HOW MANY BUSINESSES DO THEY HAVE?!

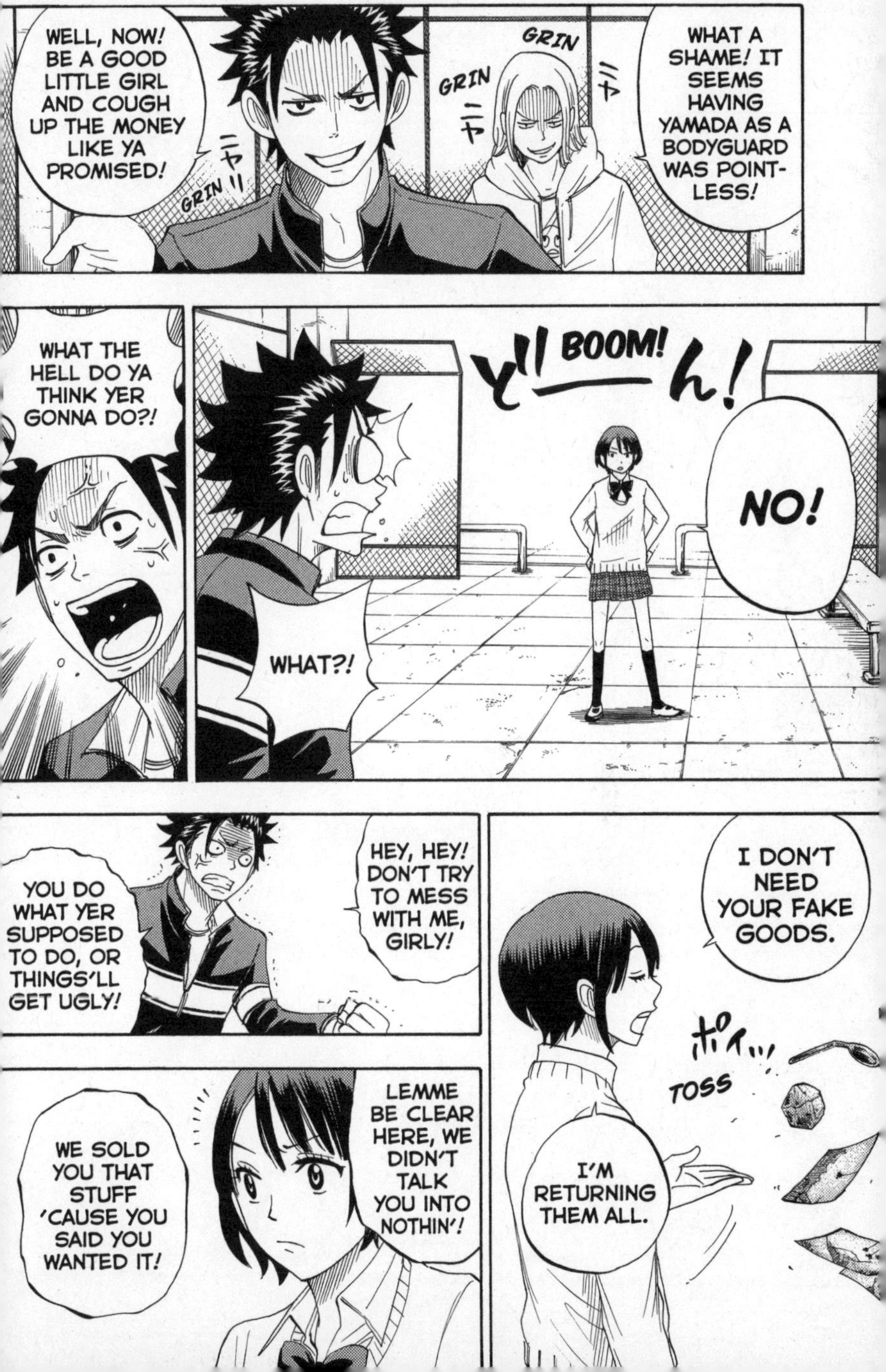
WHAT A SHAME! IT SEEMS HAVING YAMADA AS A BODYGUARD WAS POINTLESS!
ニヤ
GRIN
ニヤ
GRIN
WELL, NOW! BE A GOOD LITTLE GIRL AND COUGH UP THE MONEY LIKE YA PROMISED!
ニヤ
GRIN
NO!
どーん!
BOOM!
WHAT?!
WHAT THE HELL DO YA THINK YER GONNA DO?!
I DON'T NEED YOUR FAKE GOODS.
ポイ
TOSS
I'M RETURNING THEM ALL.
HEY, HEY! DON'T TRY TO MESS WITH ME, GIRLY!
YOU DO WHAT YER SUPPOSED TO DO, OR THINGS'LL GET UGLY!
LEMME BE CLEAR HERE, WE DIDN'T TALK YOU INTO NOTHIN'!
WE SOLD YOU THAT STUFF 'CAUSE YOU SAID YOU WANTED IT!

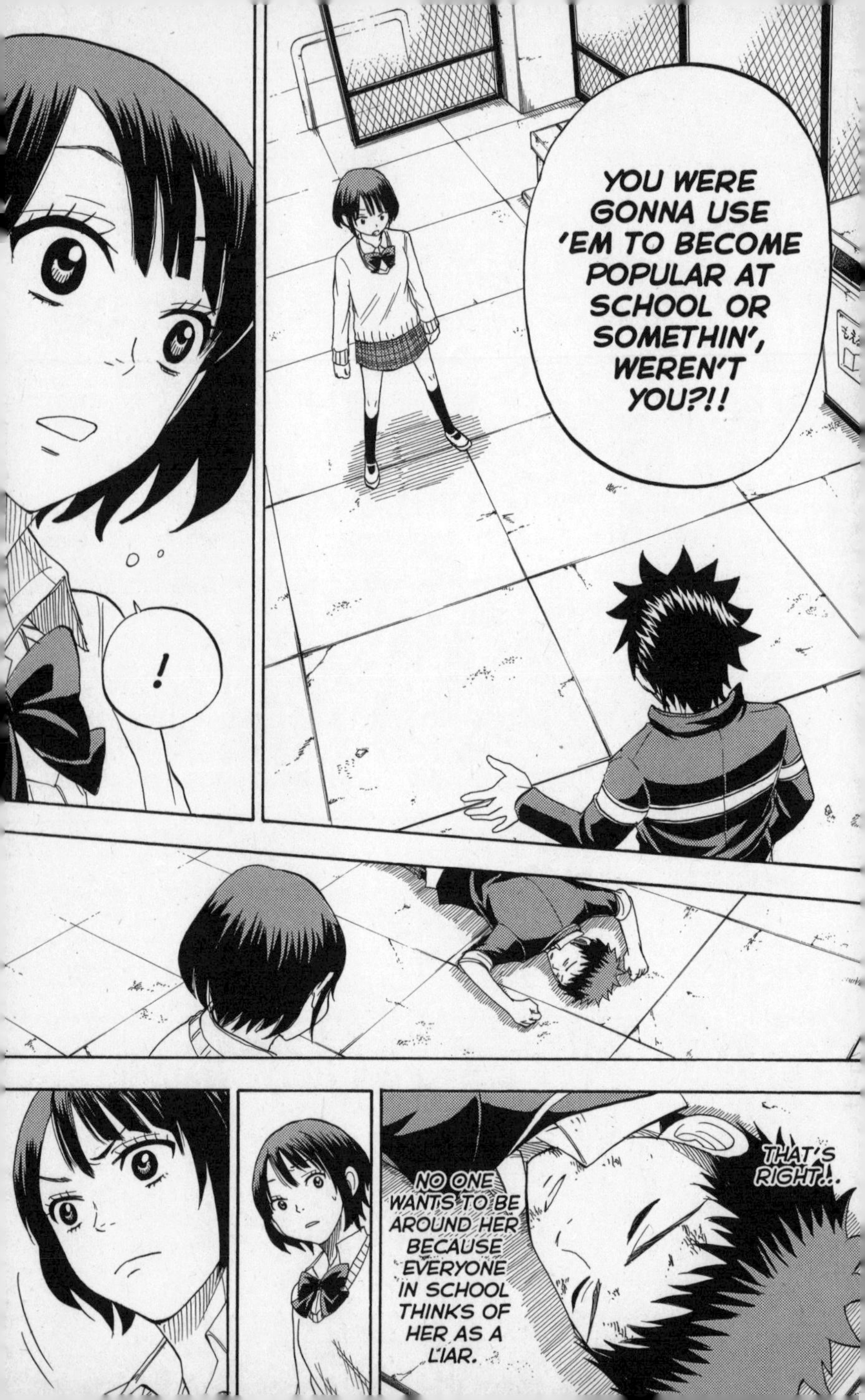
YOU WERE GONNA USE 'EM TO BECOME POPULAR AT SCHOOL OR SOMETHIN', WEREN'T YOU?!!
!
THAT'S RIGHT...
NO ONE WANTS TO BE AROUND HER BECAUSE EVERYONE IN SCHOOL THINKS OF HER AS A LIAR.

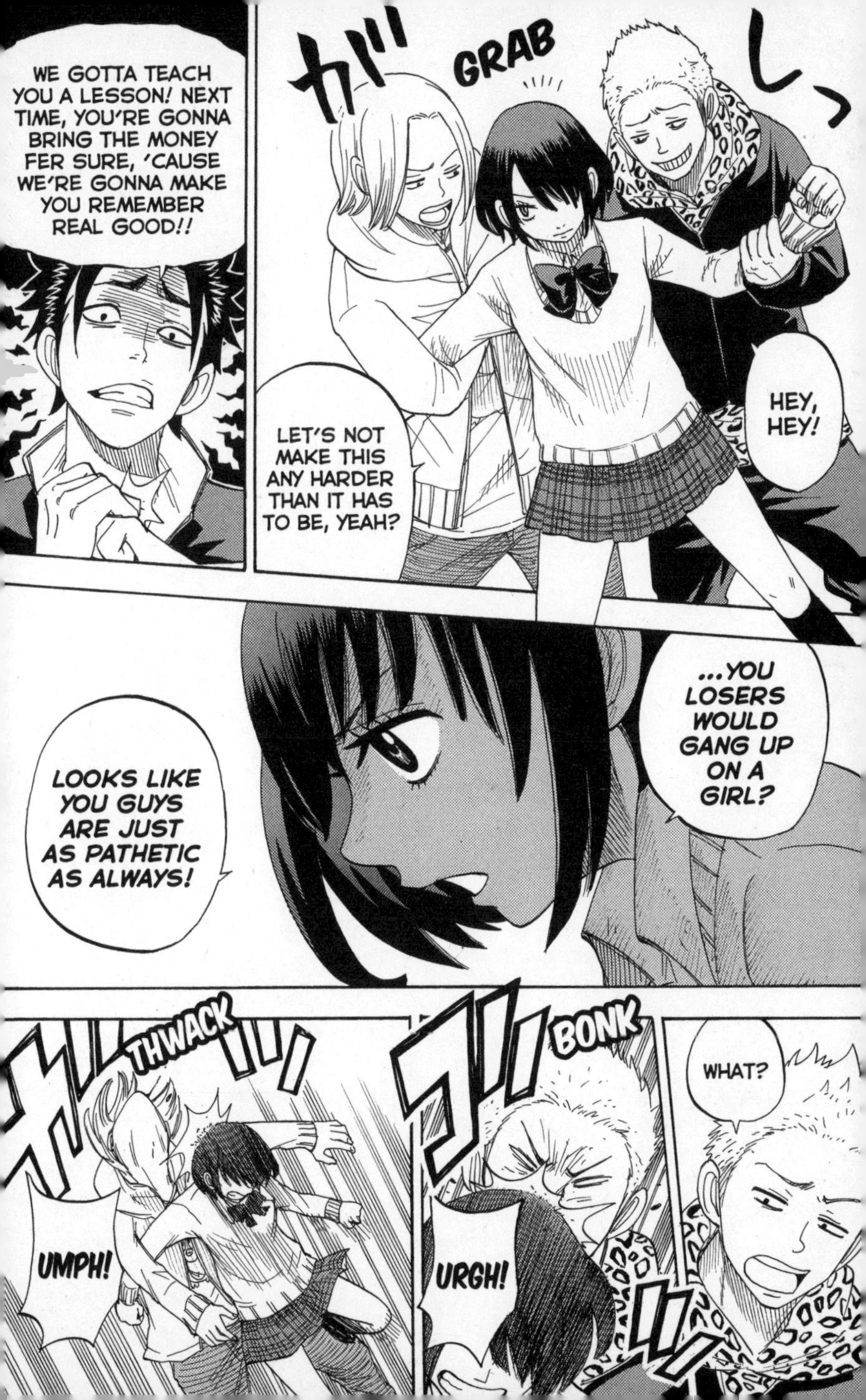
GRAB
HEY, HEY!
LET'S NOT MAKE THIS ANY HARDER THAN IT HAS TO BE, YEAH?
WE GOTTA TEACH YOU A LESSON! NEXT TIME, YOU'RE GONNA BRING THE MONEY FER SURE, 'CAUSE WE'RE GONNA MAKE YOU REMEMBER REAL GOOD!!
...YOU LOSERS WOULD GANG UP ON A GIRL?
LOOKS LIKE YOU GUYS ARE JUST AS PATHETIC AS ALWAYS!
WHAT?
BONK
URGH!
THWACK
UMPH!

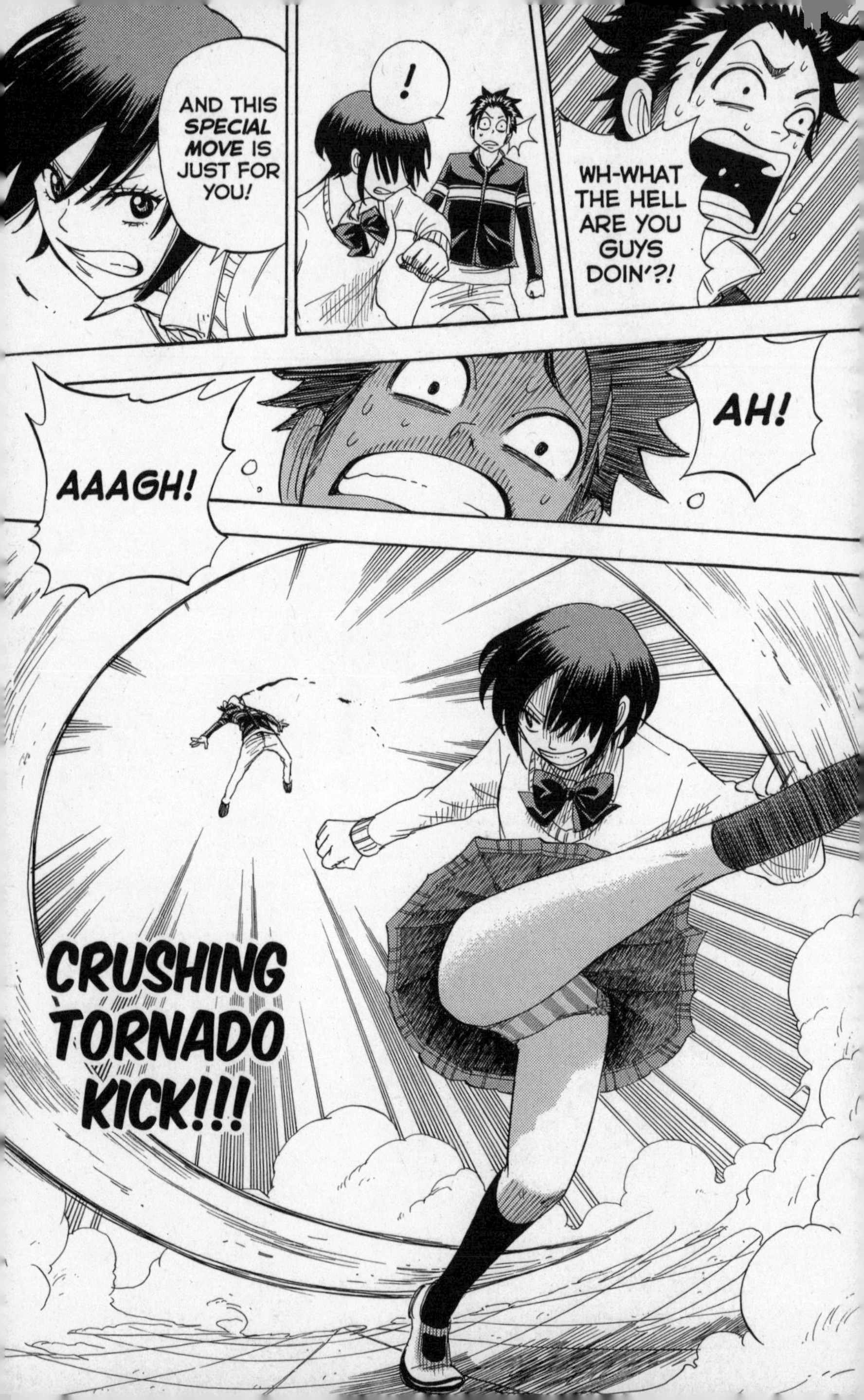
WH-WHAT THE HELL ARE YOU GUYS DOIN'?!
!
AND THIS SPECIAL MOVE IS JUST FOR YOU!
AH!
AAAGH!
CRUSHING TORNADO KICK!!!

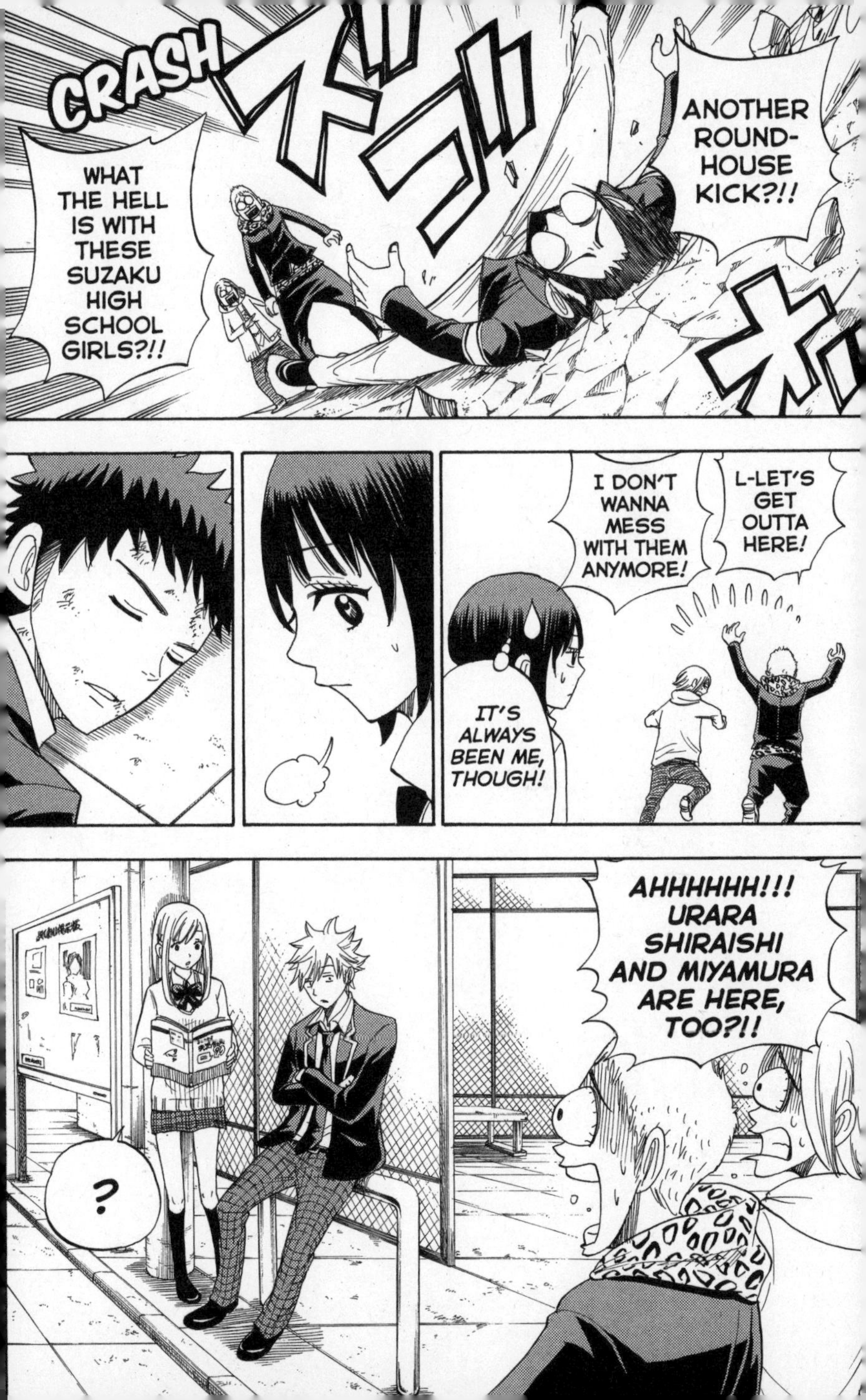
ANOTHER ROUND-HOUSE KICK?!!
CRASH
WHAT THE HELL IS WITH THESE SUZAKU HIGH SCHOOL GIRLS?!!
L-LET'S GET OUTTA HERE!
I DON'T WANNA MESS WITH THEM ANYMORE!
IT'S ALWAYS BEEN ME, THOUGH!
AHHHHHH!!! URARA SHIRAISHI AND MIYAMURA ARE HERE, TOO?!!
?

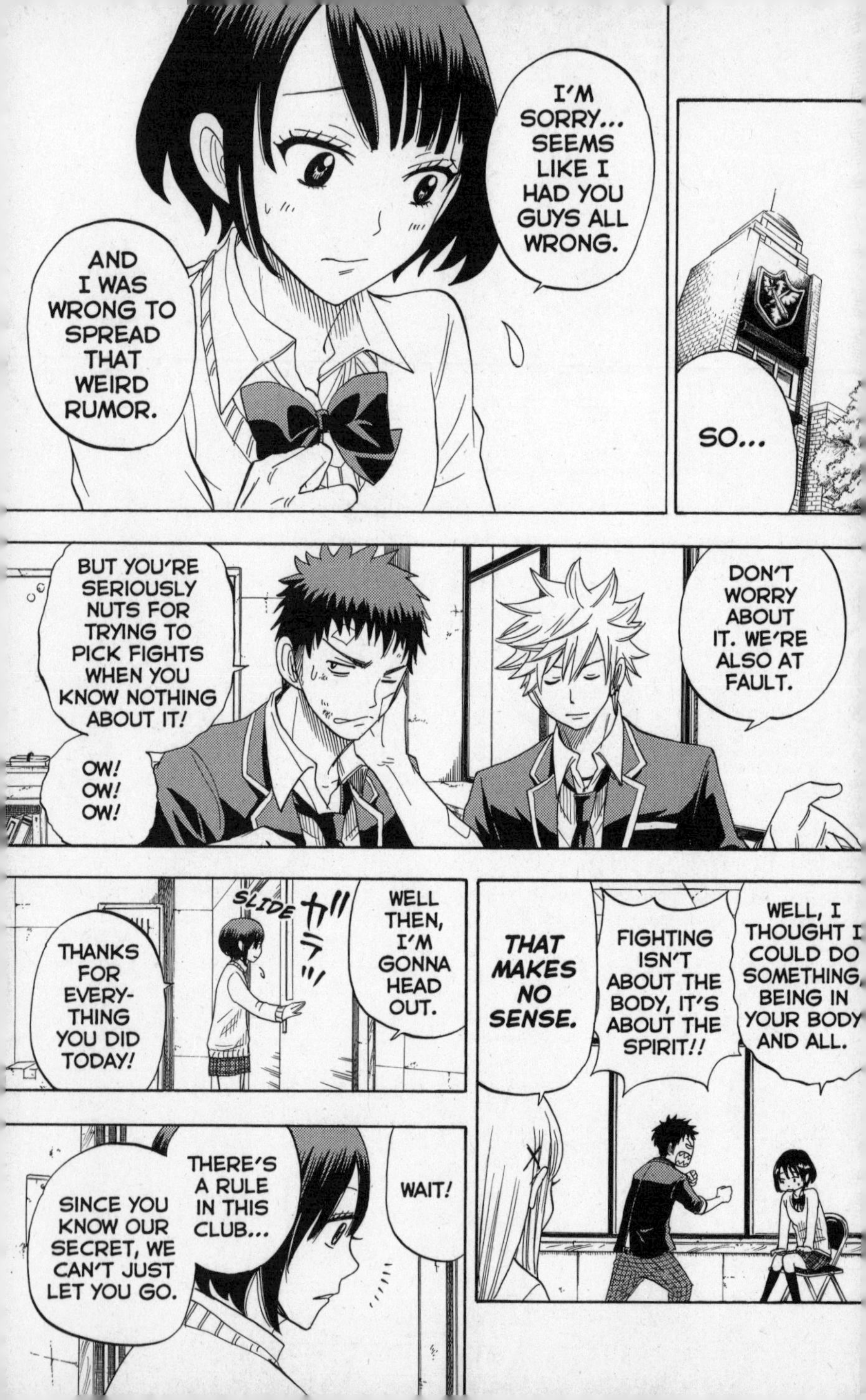
SO...
I'M SORRY... SEEMS LIKE I HAD YOU GUYS ALL WRONG.
AND I WAS WRONG TO SPREAD THAT WEIRD RUMOR.
DON'T WORRY ABOUT IT. WE'RE ALSO AT FAULT.
BUT YOU'RE SERIOUSLY NUTS FOR TRYING TO PICK FIGHTS WHEN YOU KNOW NOTHING ABOUT IT!
OW! OW! OW!
WELL, I THOUGHT I COULD DO SOMETHING, BEING IN YOUR BODY AND ALL.
FIGHTING ISN'T ABOUT THE BODY, IT'S ABOUT THE SPIRIT!!
THAT MAKES NO SENSE.
WELL THEN, I'M GONNA HEAD OUT.
SLIDE
THANKS FOR EVERYTHING YOU DID TODAY!
WAIT!
THERE'S A RULE IN THIS CLUB...
SINCE YOU KNOW OUR SECRET, WE CAN'T JUST LET YOU GO.

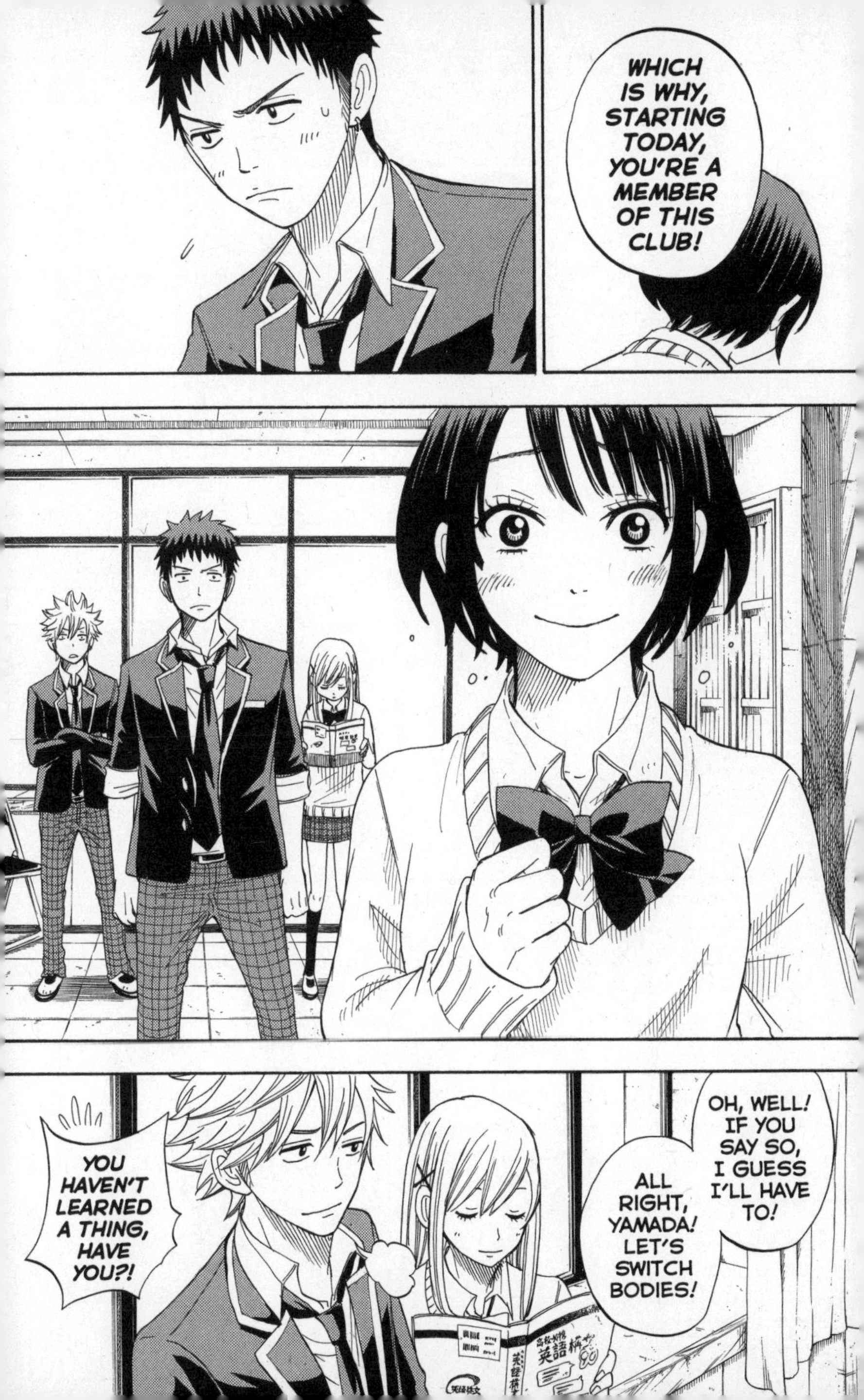
WHICH IS WHY, STARTING TODAY, YOU'RE A MEMBER OF THIS CLUB!
OH, WELL! IF YOU SAY SO, I GUESS I'LL HAVE TO!
ALL RIGHT, YAMADA! LET'S SWITCH BODIES!
YOU HAVEN'T LEARNED A THING, HAVE YOU?!

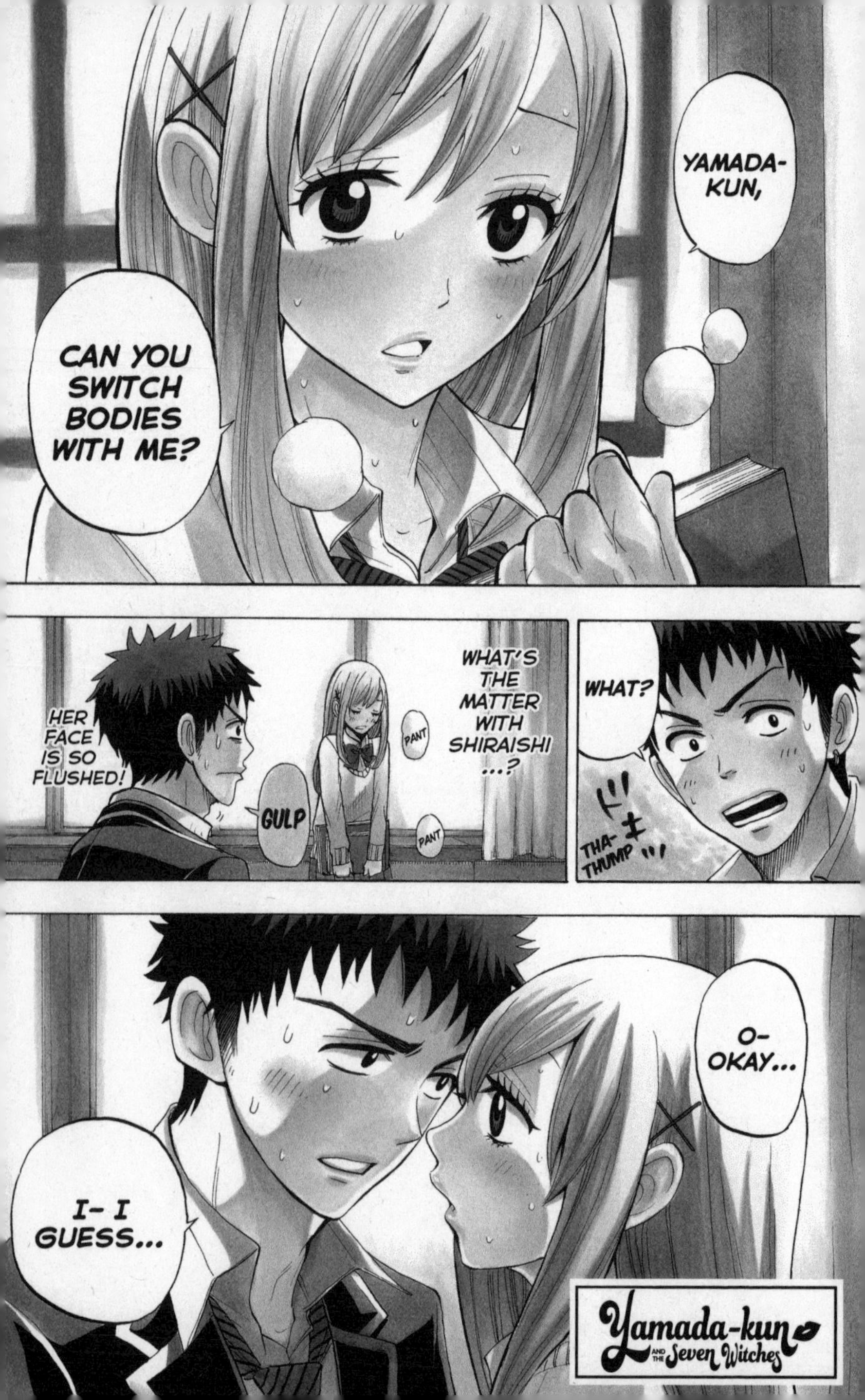
YAMADA-KUN,
CAN YOU SWITCH BODIES WITH ME?
WHAT?
ドキ
THA-THUMP
WHAT'S THE MATTER WITH SHIRAISHI ...?
PANT
PANT
HER FACE IS SO FLUSHED!
GULP
O-OKAY...
I- I GUESS...
Yamada-kun AND THE Seven Witches

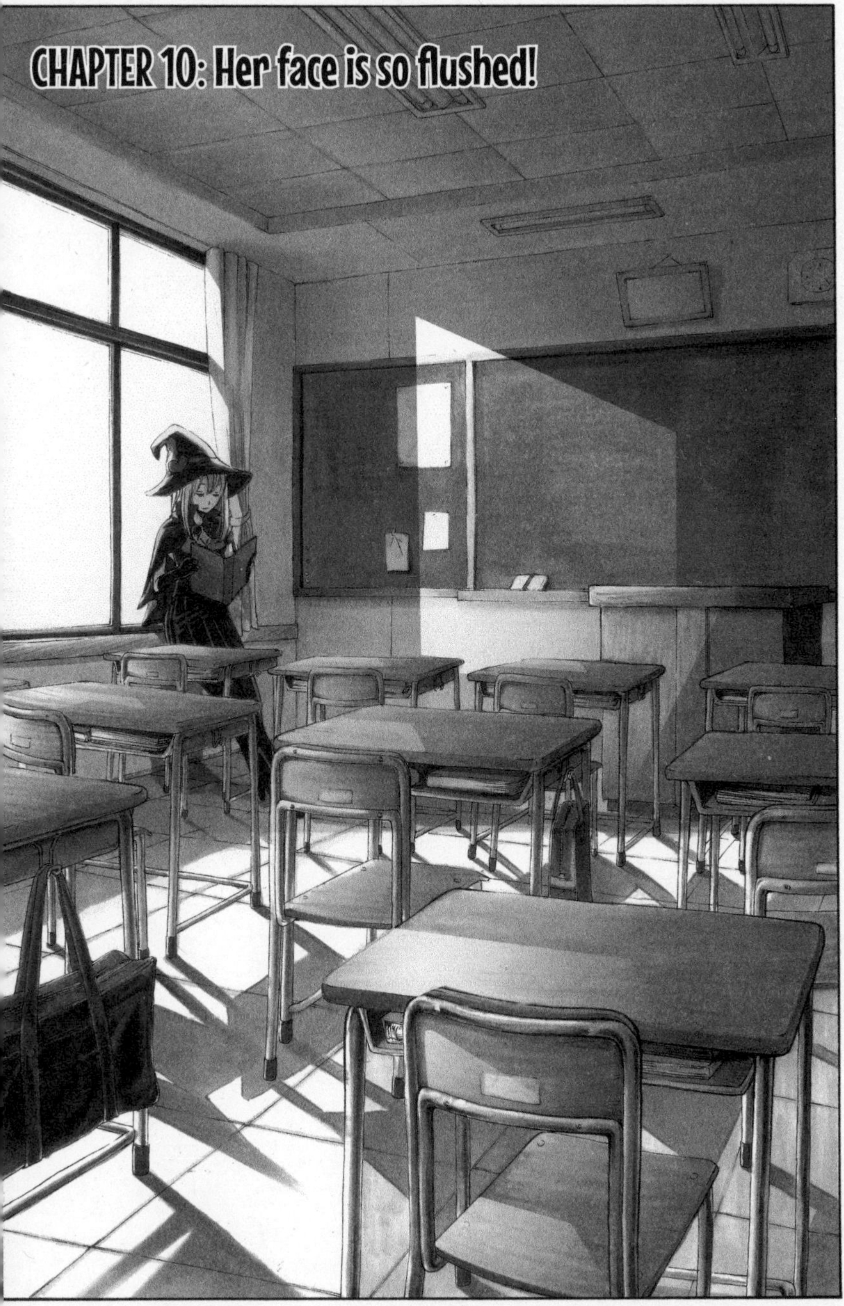
CHAPTER 10: Her face is so flushed!

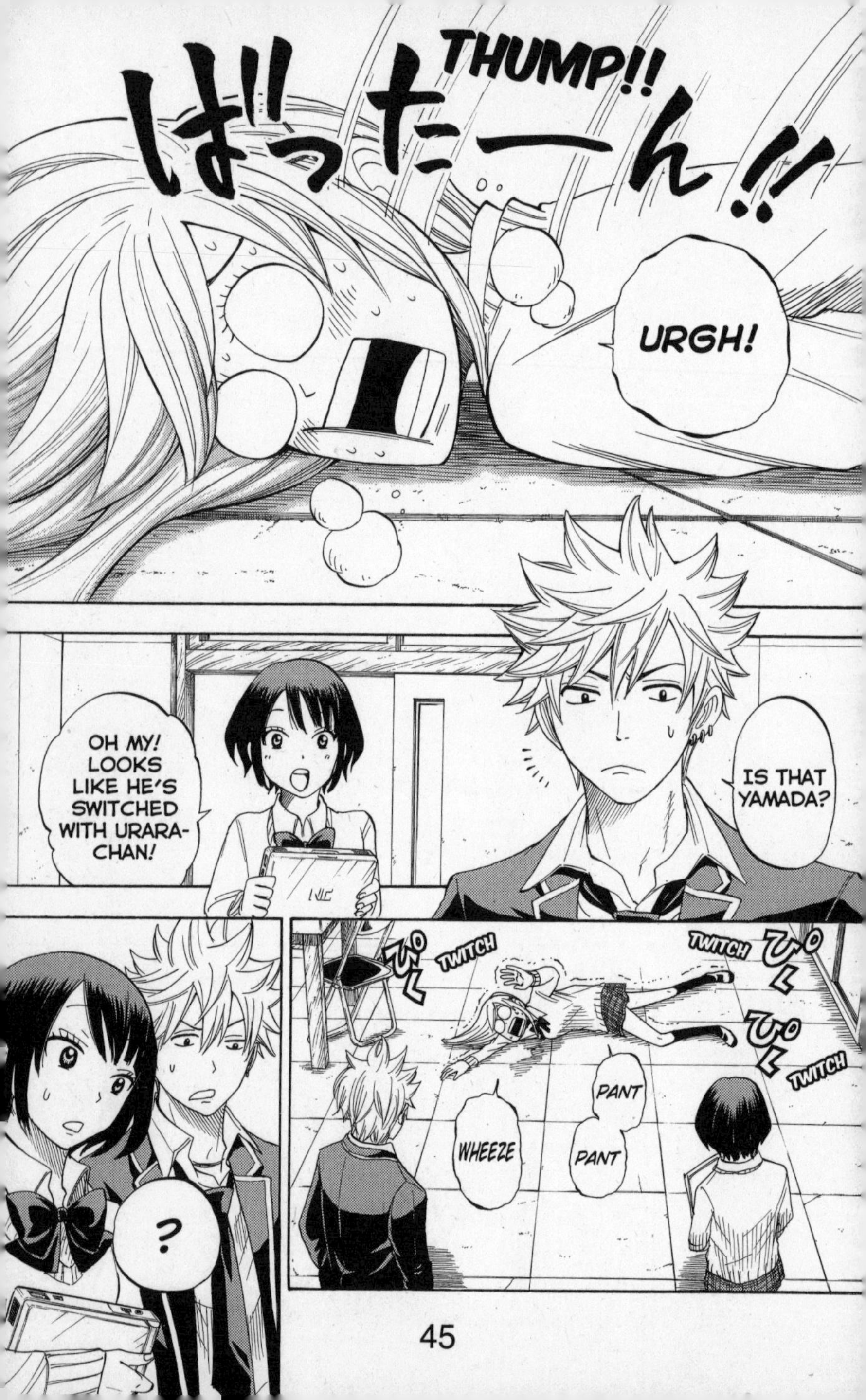
ばったーん!!
THUMP!!
URGH!
IS THAT YAMADA?
OH MY! LOOKS LIKE HE'S SWITCHED WITH URARA-CHAN!
ぴくぴく
TWITCH
ぴく
TWITCH
ぴく
TWITCH
PANT PANT
WHEEZE
?

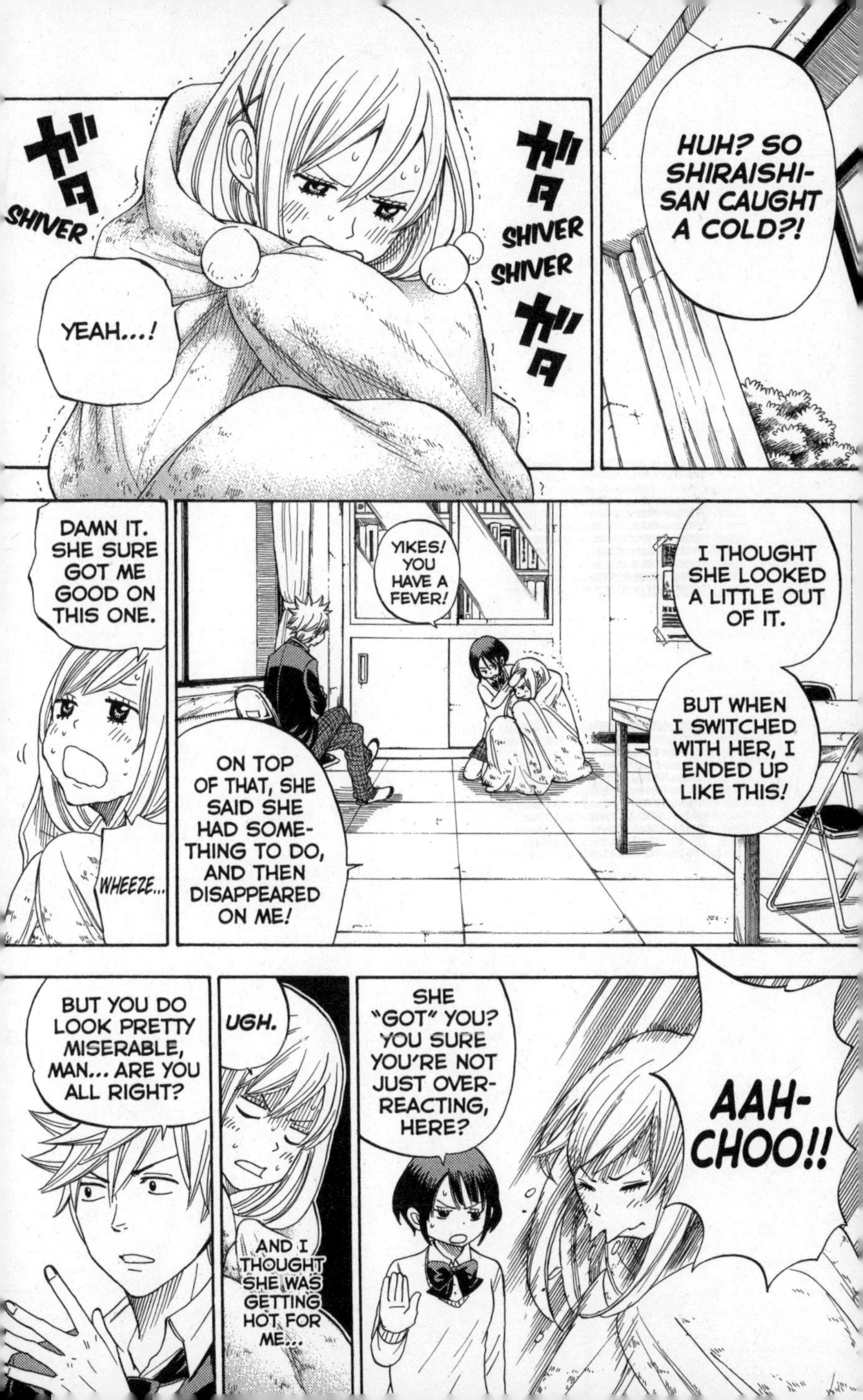
HUH? SO SHIRAISHI-SAN CAUGHT A COLD?!
ガタ
SHIVER SHIVER
ガタ
SHIVER
YEAH...!
I THOUGHT SHE LOOKED A LITTLE OUT OF IT.
BUT WHEN I SWITCHED WITH HER, I ENDED UP LIKE THIS!
YIKES! YOU HAVE A FEVER!
ON TOP OF THAT, SHE SAID SHE HAD SOME-THING TO DO, AND THEN DISAPPEARED ON ME!
DAMN IT. SHE SURE GOT ME GOOD ON THIS ONE.
WHEEZE...
AAH-CHOO!!
SHE "GOT" YOU? YOU SURE YOU'RE NOT JUST OVER-REACTING, HERE?
UGH.
AND I THOUGHT SHE WAS GETTING HOT FOR ME...
BUT YOU DO LOOK PRETTY MISERABLE, MAN... ARE YOU ALL RIGHT?

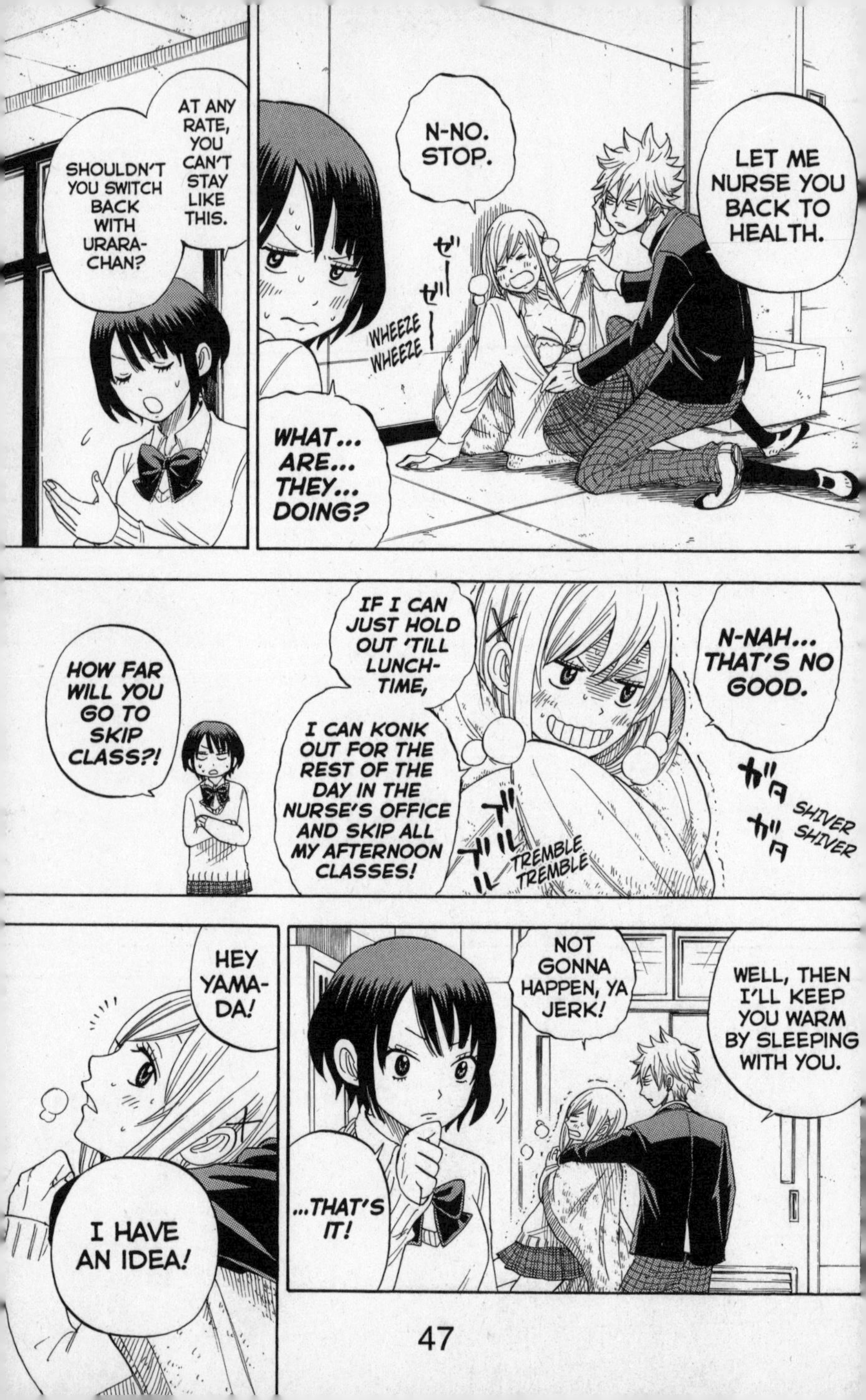
LET ME NURSE YOU BACK TO HEALTH.
N-NO. STOP.
ゼーゼー
WHEEZE WHEEZE
WHAT... ARE... THEY... DOING?
AT ANY RATE, YOU CAN'T STAY LIKE THIS.
SHOULDN'T YOU SWITCH BACK WITH URARA-CHAN?
N-NAH... THAT'S NO GOOD.
ガタガタ
SHIVER SHIVER
IF I CAN JUST HOLD OUT 'TILL LUNCH-TIME,
I CAN KONK OUT FOR THE REST OF THE DAY IN THE NURSE'S OFFICE AND SKIP ALL MY AFTERNOON CLASSES!
ブルブル
TREMBLE TREMBLE
HOW FAR WILL YOU GO TO SKIP CLASS?!
WELL, THEN I'LL KEEP YOU WARM BY SLEEPING WITH YOU.
NOT GONNA HAPPEN, YA JERK!
...THAT'S IT!
HEY YAMADA!
I HAVE AN IDEA!

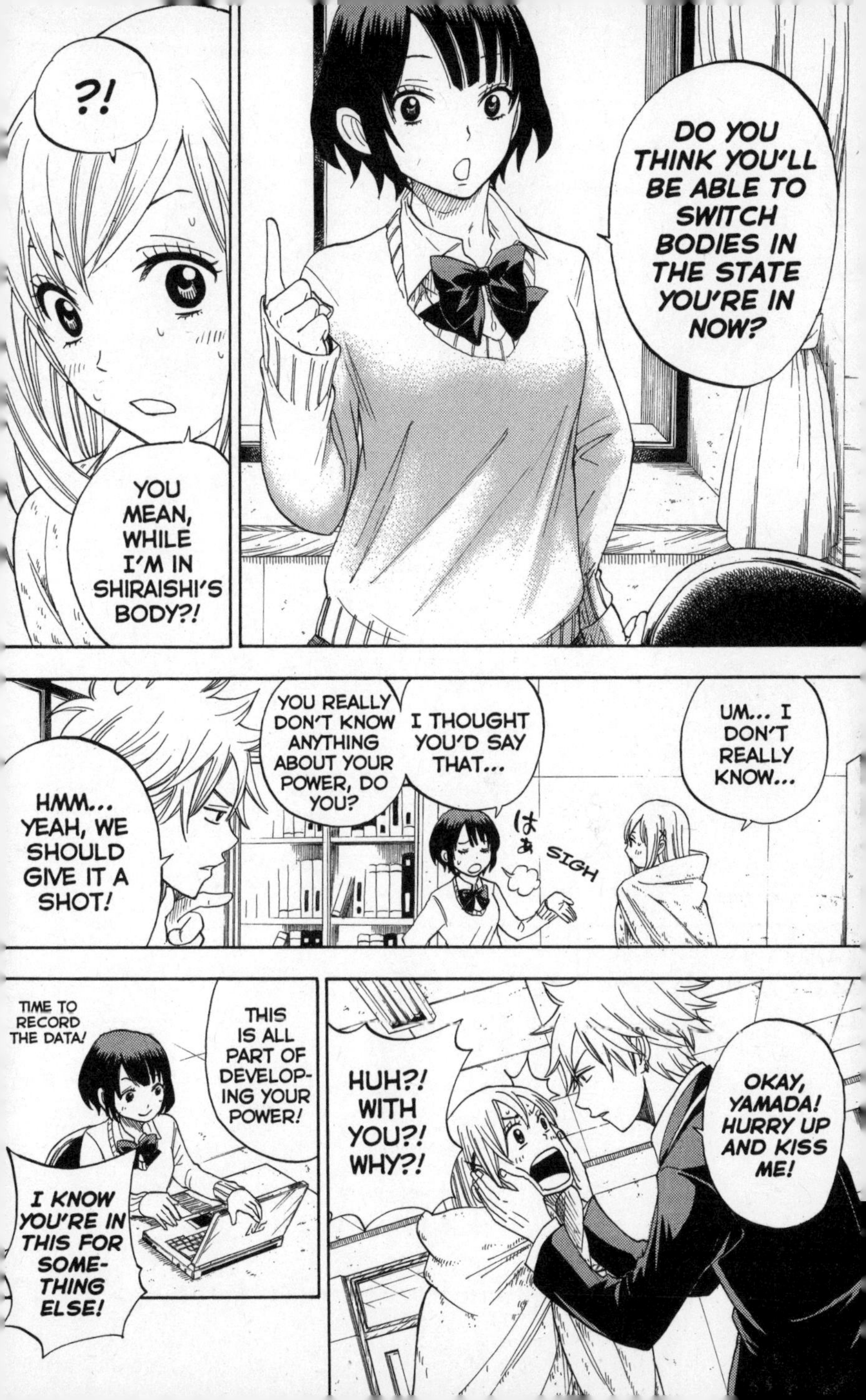
DO YOU THINK YOU'LL BE ABLE TO SWITCH BODIES IN THE STATE YOU'RE IN NOW?
?!
YOU MEAN, WHILE I'M IN SHIRAISHI'S BODY?!
UM... I DON'T REALLY KNOW...
I THOUGHT YOU'D SAY THAT...
はぁ SIGH
YOU REALLY DON'T KNOW ANYTHING ABOUT YOUR POWER, DO YOU?
HMM... YEAH, WE SHOULD GIVE IT A SHOT!
OKAY, YAMADA! HURRY UP AND KISS ME!
HUH?! WITH YOU?! WHY?!
THIS IS ALL PART OF DEVELOP-ING YOUR POWER!
TIME TO RECORD THE DATA!
I KNOW YOU'RE IN THIS FOR SOME-THING ELSE!

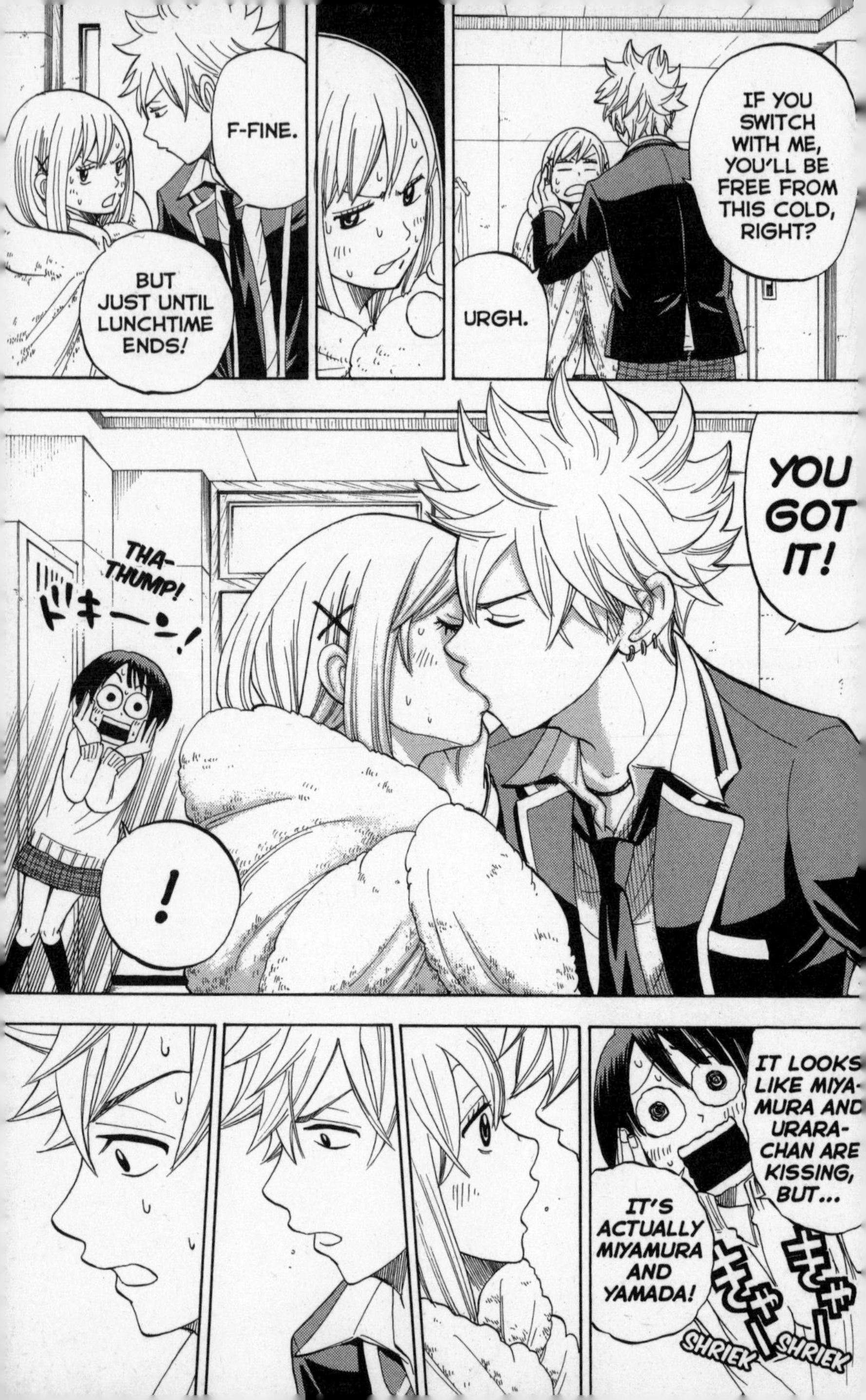
IF YOU SWITCH WITH ME, YOU'LL BE FREE FROM THIS COLD, RIGHT?
URGH.
F-FINE.
BUT JUST UNTIL LUNCHTIME ENDS!
YOU GOT IT!
!
THA-THUMP!
IT LOOKS LIKE MIYAMURA AND URARA-CHAN ARE KISSING, BUT...
IT'S ACTUALLY MIYAMURA AND YAMADA!
SHRIEK
SHRIEK

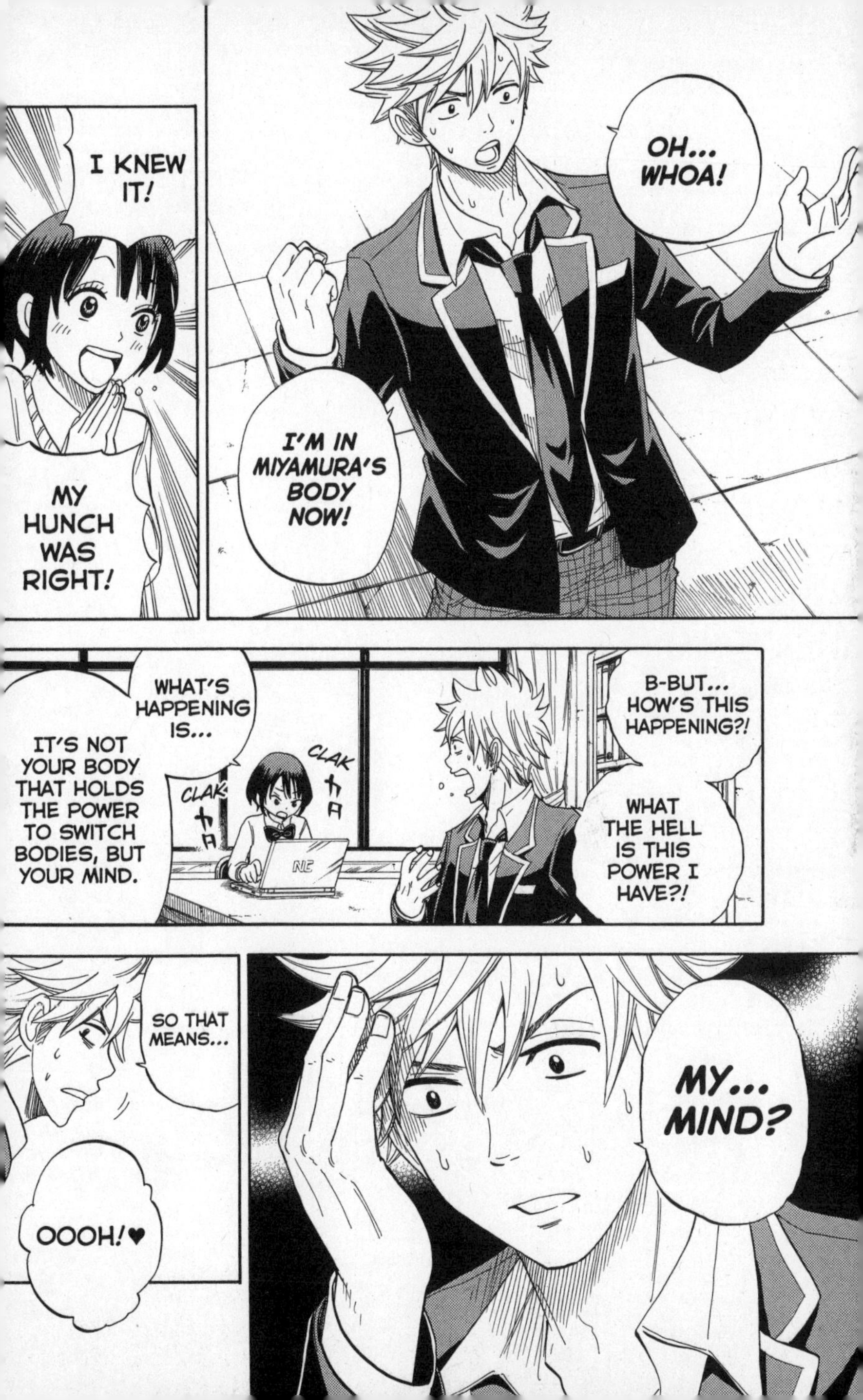
OH... WHOA!
I'M IN MIYAMURA'S BODY NOW!
I KNEW IT!
MY HUNCH WAS RIGHT!
B-BUT... HOW'S THIS HAPPENING?!
WHAT THE HELL IS THIS POWER I HAVE?!
CLAK カタ
CLAK カタ
WHAT'S HAPPENING IS...
IT'S NOT YOUR BODY THAT HOLDS THE POWER TO SWITCH BODIES, BUT YOUR MIND.
MY... MIND?
SO THAT MEANS...
OOOH!♥

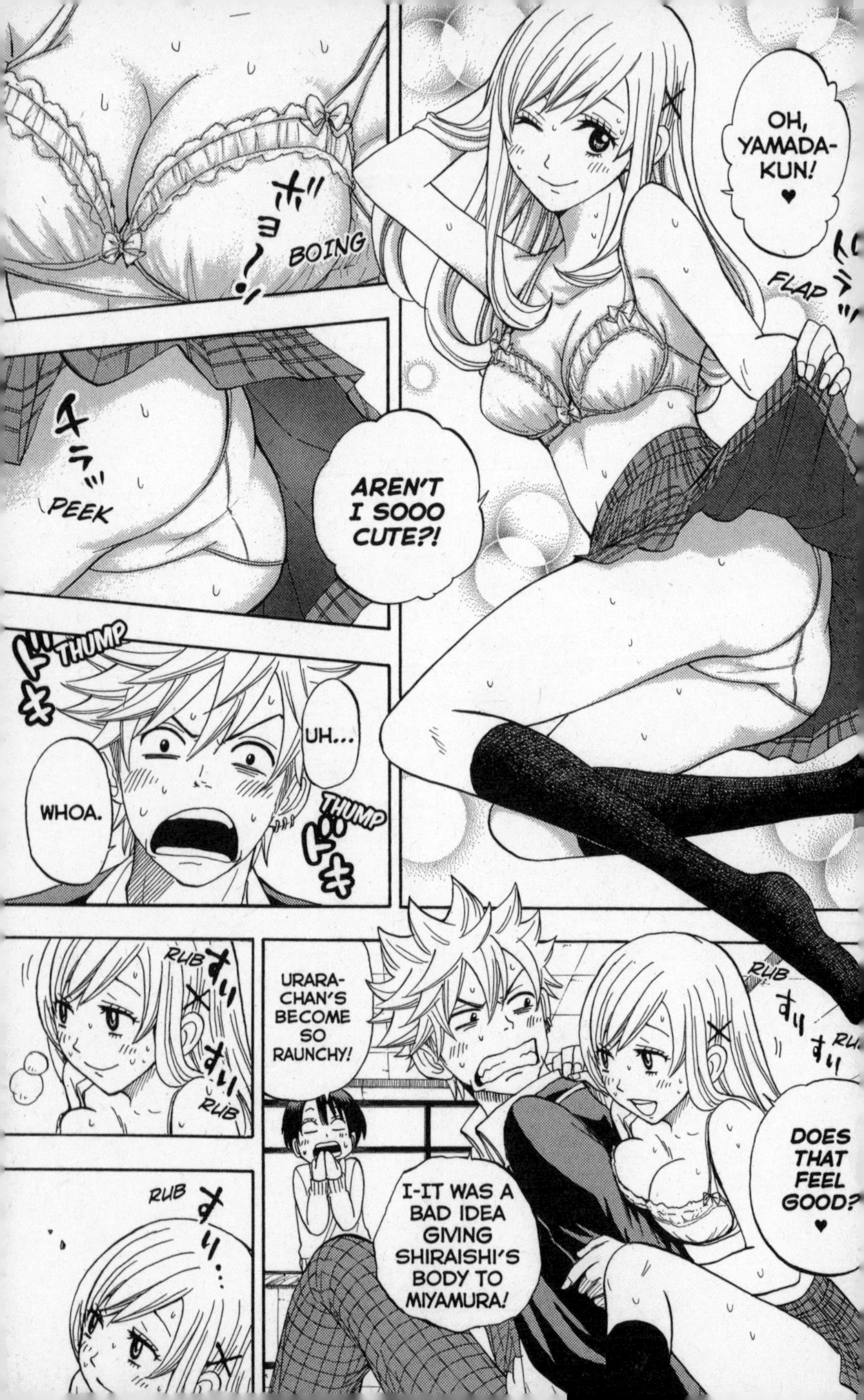
OH, YAMADA-KUN! ♥
FLAP
AREN'T I SOOO CUTE?!
BOING
PEEK
THUMP
UH...
WHOA.
THUMP
DOES THAT FEEL GOOD? ♥
RUB
RUB
URARA-CHAN'S BECOME SO RAUNCHY!
I-IT WAS A BAD IDEA GIVING SHIRAISHI'S BODY TO MIYAMURA!
RUB
RUB
RUB

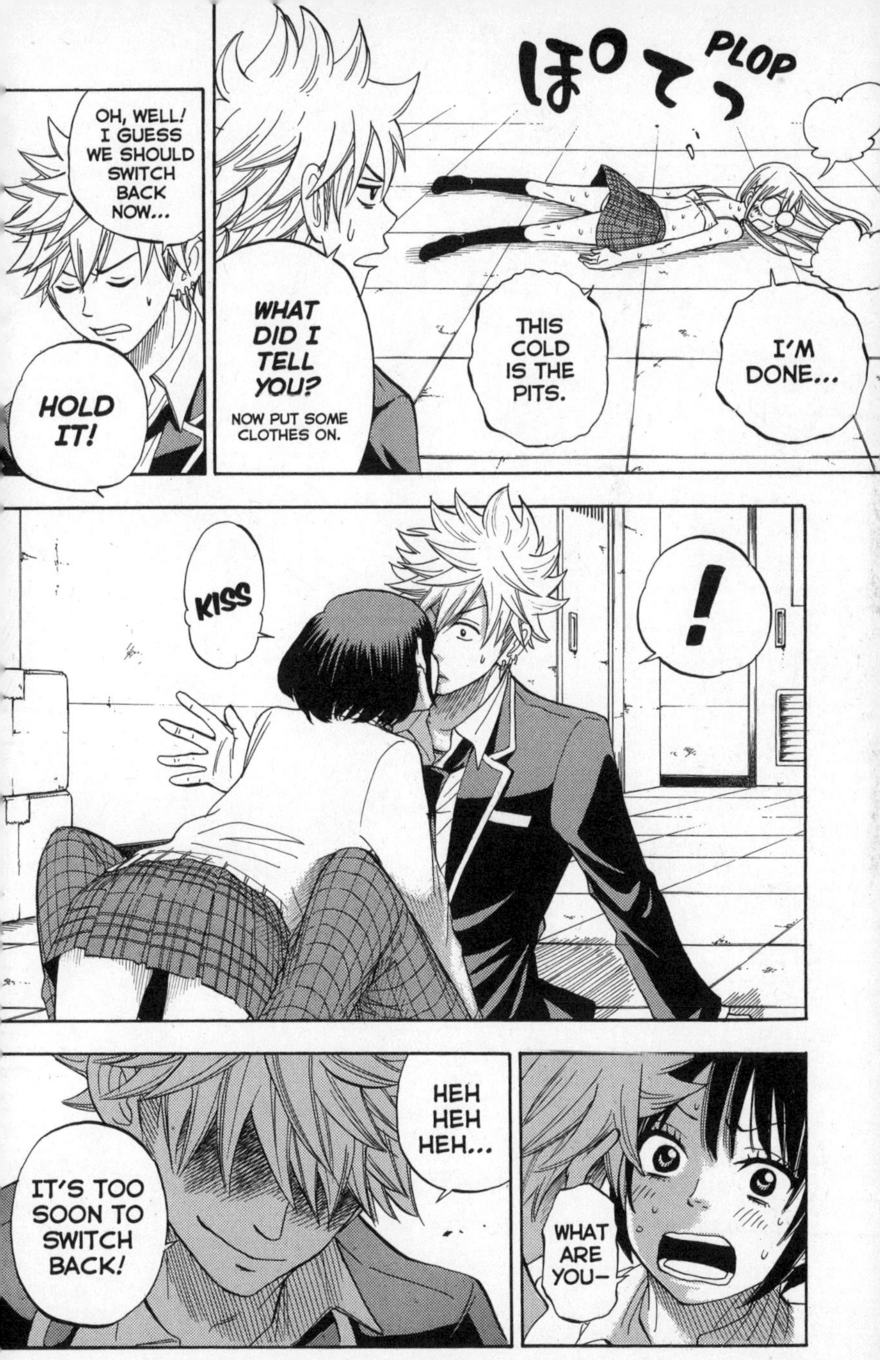
ぽてっ
PLOP
I'M DONE...
THIS COLD IS THE PITS.
WHAT DID I TELL YOU?
NOW PUT SOME CLOTHES ON.
OH, WELL! I GUESS WE SHOULD SWITCH BACK NOW...
HOLD IT!
!
KISS
WHAT ARE YOU—
HEH HEH HEH...
IT'S TOO SOON TO SWITCH BACK!

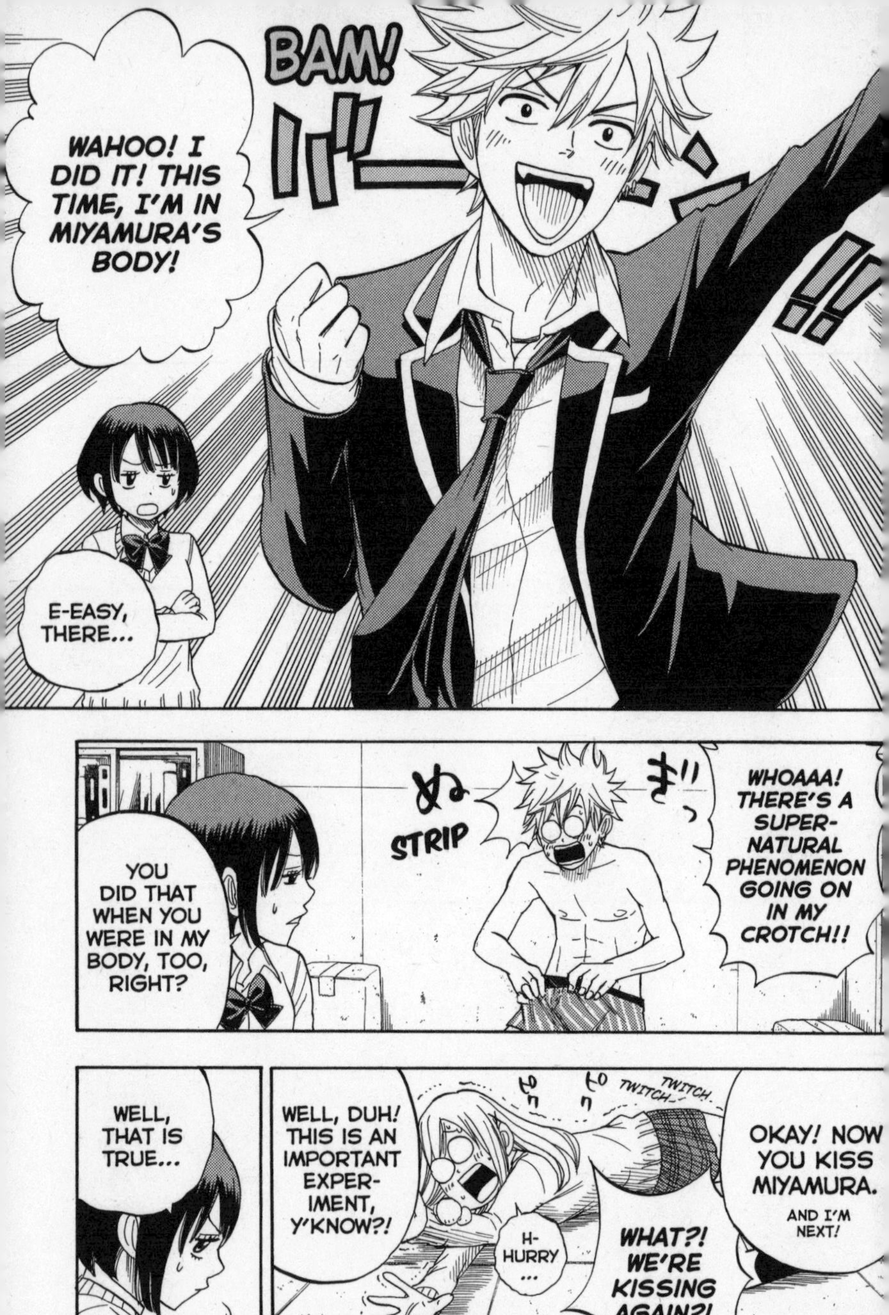
BAM!
WAHOO! I DID IT! THIS TIME, I'M IN MIYAMURA'S BODY!
E-EASY, THERE...
WHOAAA! THERE'S A SUPER-NATURAL PHENOMENON GOING ON IN MY CROTCH!!
STRIP
YOU DID THAT WHEN YOU WERE IN MY BODY, TOO, RIGHT?
OKAY! NOW YOU KISS MIYAMURA.
AND I'M NEXT!
TWITCH TWITCH
WHAT?! WE'RE KISSING AGAIN?!
H-HURRY...
WELL, DUH! THIS IS AN IMPORTANT EXPER-IMENT, Y'KNOW?!
WELL, THAT IS TRUE...

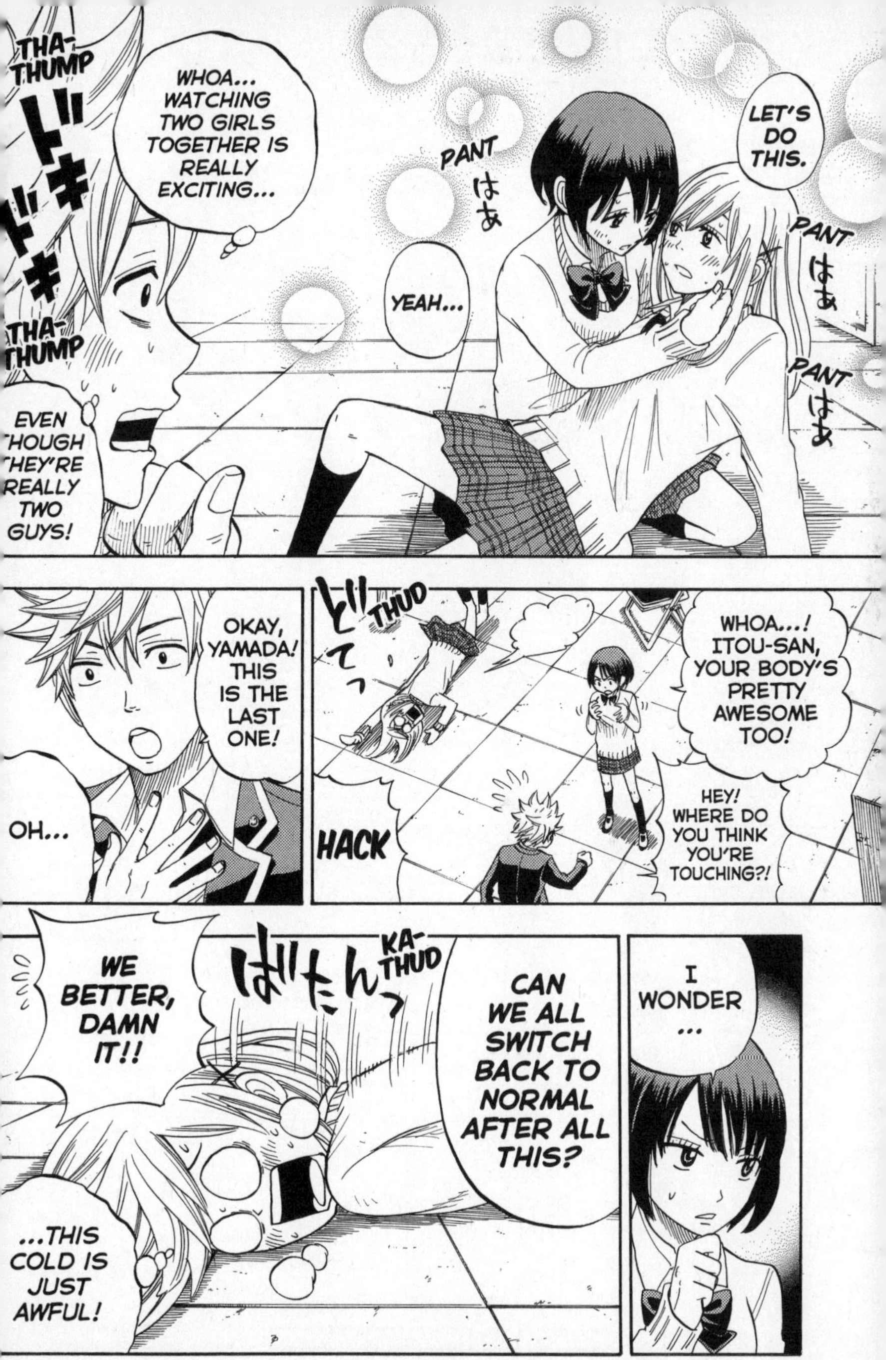
LET'S DO THIS.
PANT はあ
PANT はあ
YEAH...
PANT はあ
WHOA... WATCHING TWO GIRLS TOGETHER IS REALLY EXCITING...
THA-THUMP
ドキドキ
THA-THUMP
EVEN THOUGH THEY'RE REALLY TWO GUYS!
WHOA...! ITOU-SAN, YOUR BODY'S PRETTY AWESOME TOO!
HEY! WHERE DO YOU THINK YOU'RE TOUCHING?!
THUD
HACK
OKAY, YAMADA! THIS IS THE LAST ONE!
OH...
I WONDER...
CAN WE ALL SWITCH BACK TO NORMAL AFTER ALL THIS?
KA-THUD
WE BETTER, DAMN IT!!
...THIS COLD IS JUST AWFUL!

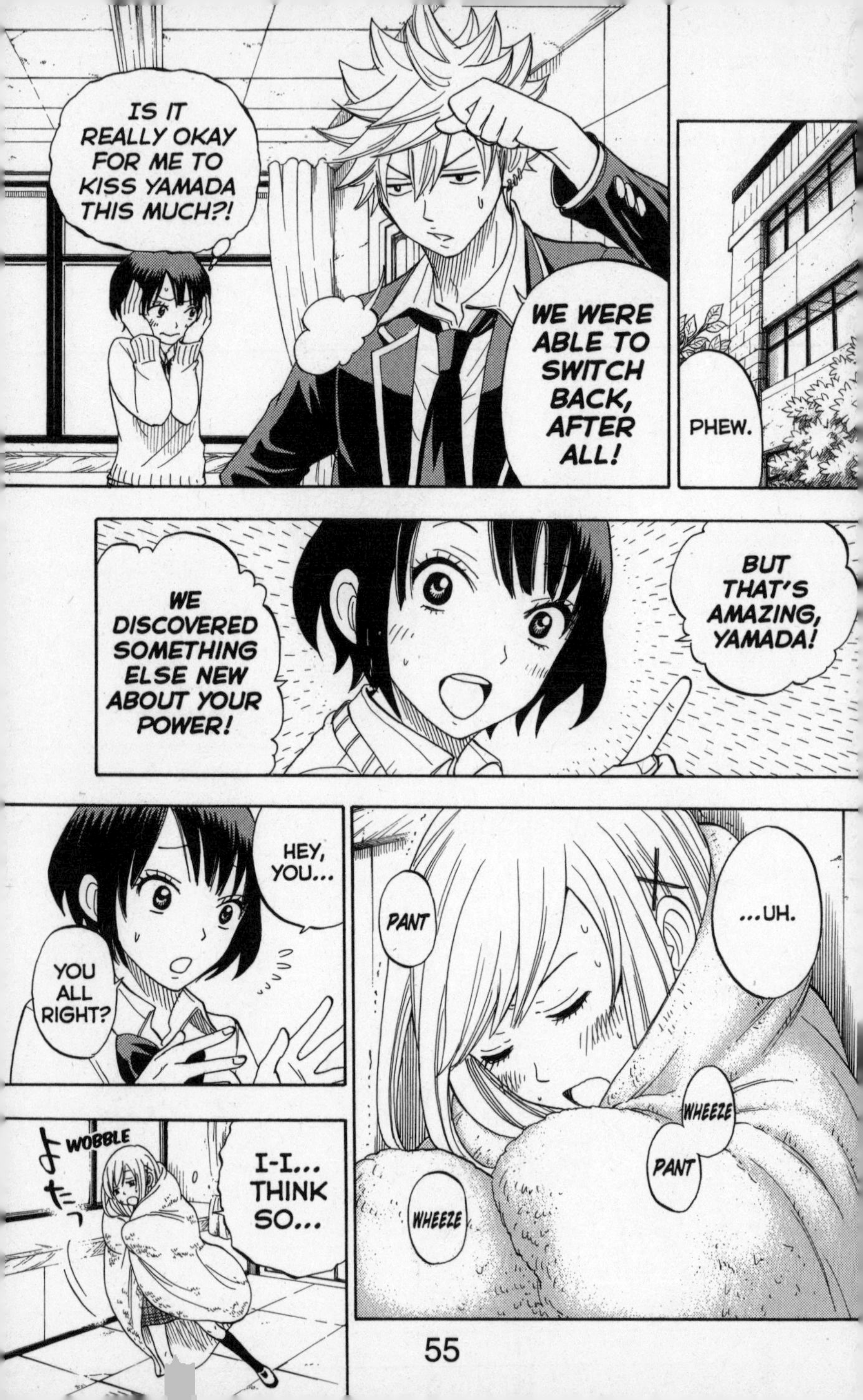
PHEW.
WE WERE ABLE TO SWITCH BACK, AFTER ALL!
IS IT REALLY OKAY FOR ME TO KISS YAMADA THIS MUCH?!
BUT THAT'S AMAZING, YAMADA!
WE DISCOVERED SOMETHING ELSE NEW ABOUT YOUR POWER!
...UH.
PANT
WHEEZE
PANT
WHEEZE
HEY, YOU...
YOU ALL RIGHT?
I-I... THINK SO...
WOBBLE
よたっ

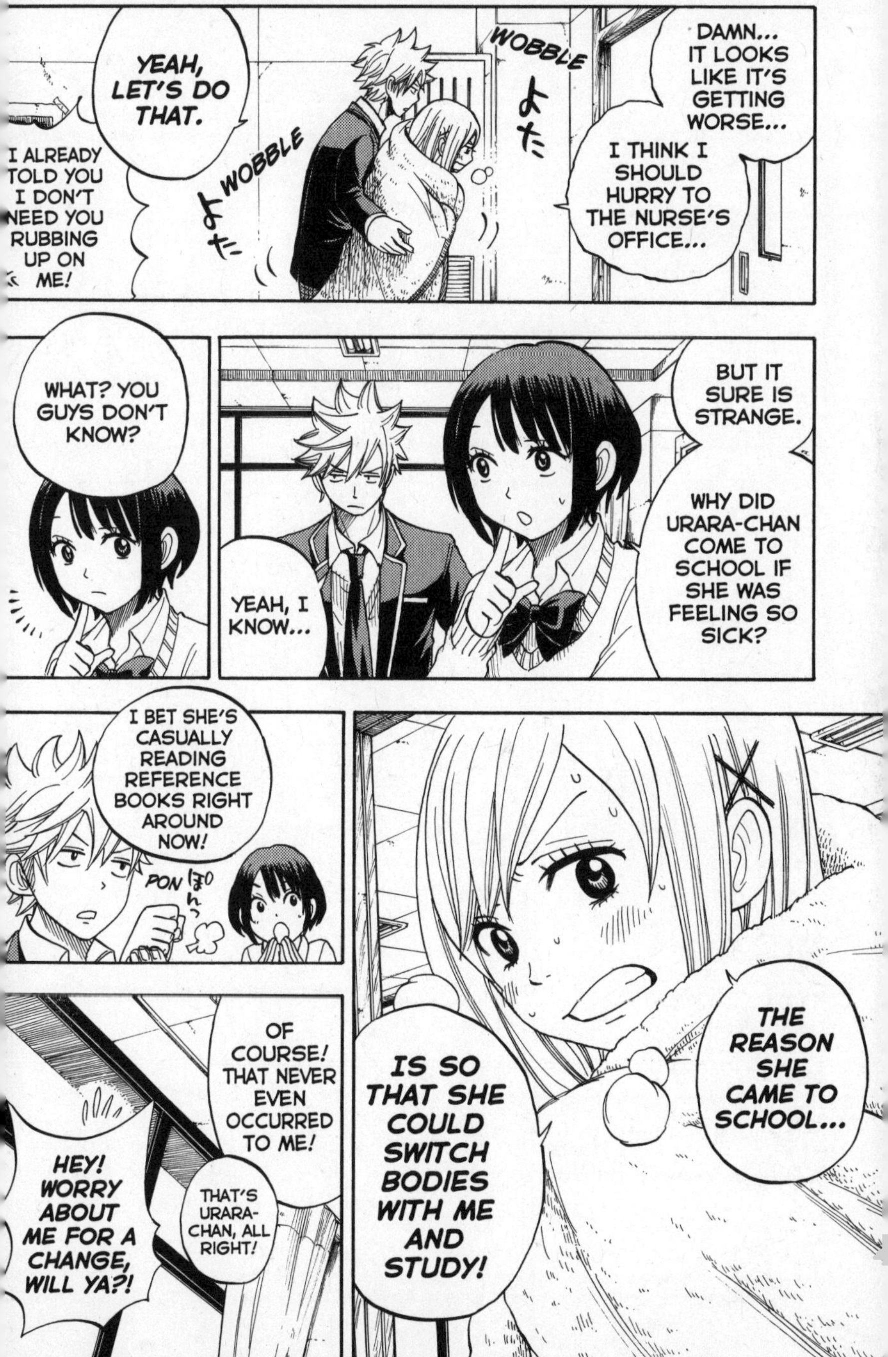
DAMN... IT LOOKS LIKE IT'S GETTING WORSE...
I THINK I SHOULD HURRY TO THE NURSE'S OFFICE...
WOBBLE よた
WOBBLE よた
YEAH, LET'S DO THAT.
I ALREADY TOLD YOU I DON'T NEED YOU RUBBING UP ON ME!
BUT IT SURE IS STRANGE.
WHY DID URARA-CHAN COME TO SCHOOL IF SHE WAS FEELING SO SICK?
YEAH, I KNOW...
WHAT? YOU GUYS DON'T KNOW?
THE REASON SHE CAME TO SCHOOL...
IS SO THAT SHE COULD SWITCH BODIES WITH ME AND STUDY!
I BET SHE'S CASUALLY READING REFERENCE BOOKS RIGHT AROUND NOW!
PON ぽん
OF COURSE! THAT NEVER EVEN OCCURRED TO ME!
THAT'S URARA-CHAN, ALL RIGHT!
HEY! WORRY ABOUT ME FOR A CHANGE, WILL YA?!

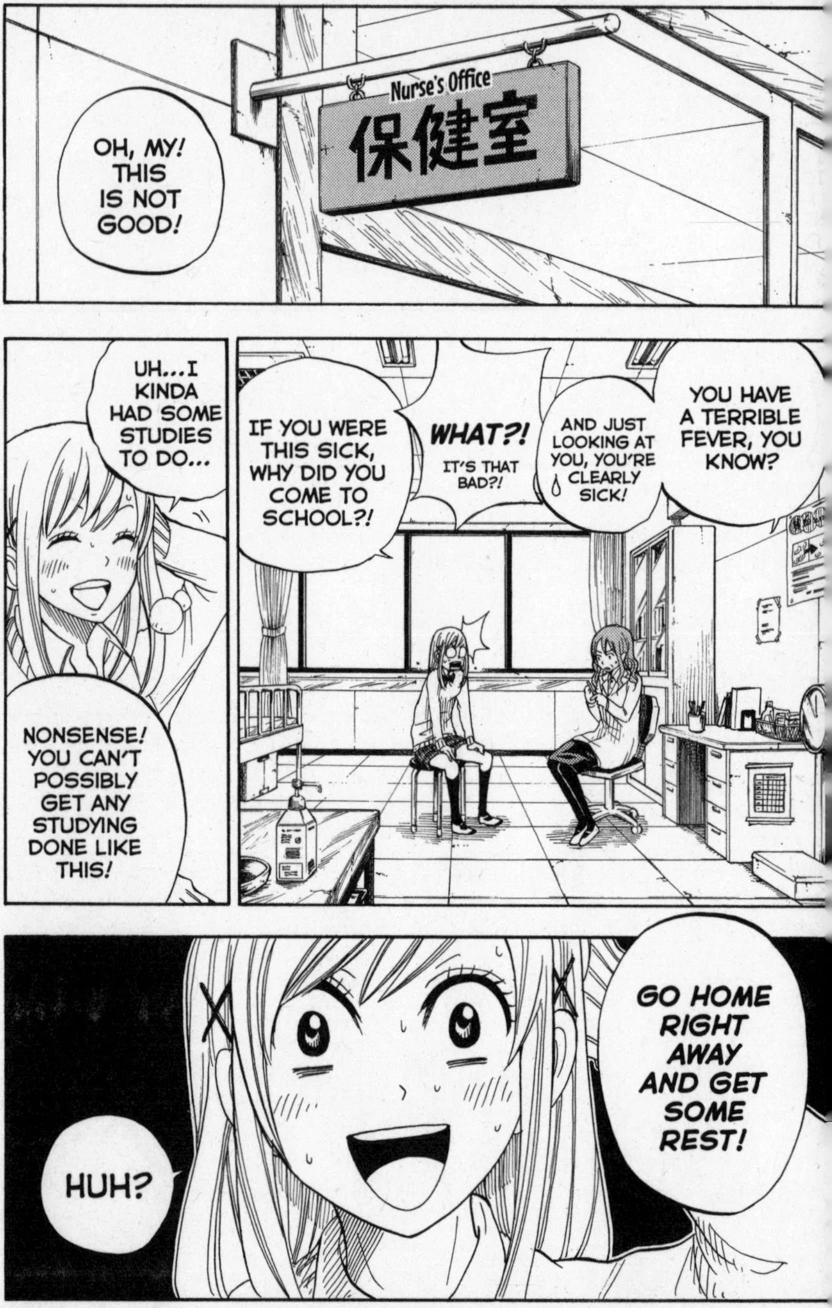
Nurse's Office
保健室
OH, MY! THIS IS NOT GOOD!
YOU HAVE A TERRIBLE FEVER, YOU KNOW?
AND JUST LOOKING AT YOU, YOU'RE CLEARLY SICK!
WHAT?!
IT'S THAT BAD?!
IF YOU WERE THIS SICK, WHY DID YOU COME TO SCHOOL?!
UH...I KINDA HAD SOME STUDIES TO DO...
NONSENSE! YOU CAN'T POSSIBLY GET ANY STUDYING DONE LIKE THIS!
GO HOME RIGHT AWAY AND GET SOME REST!
HUH?

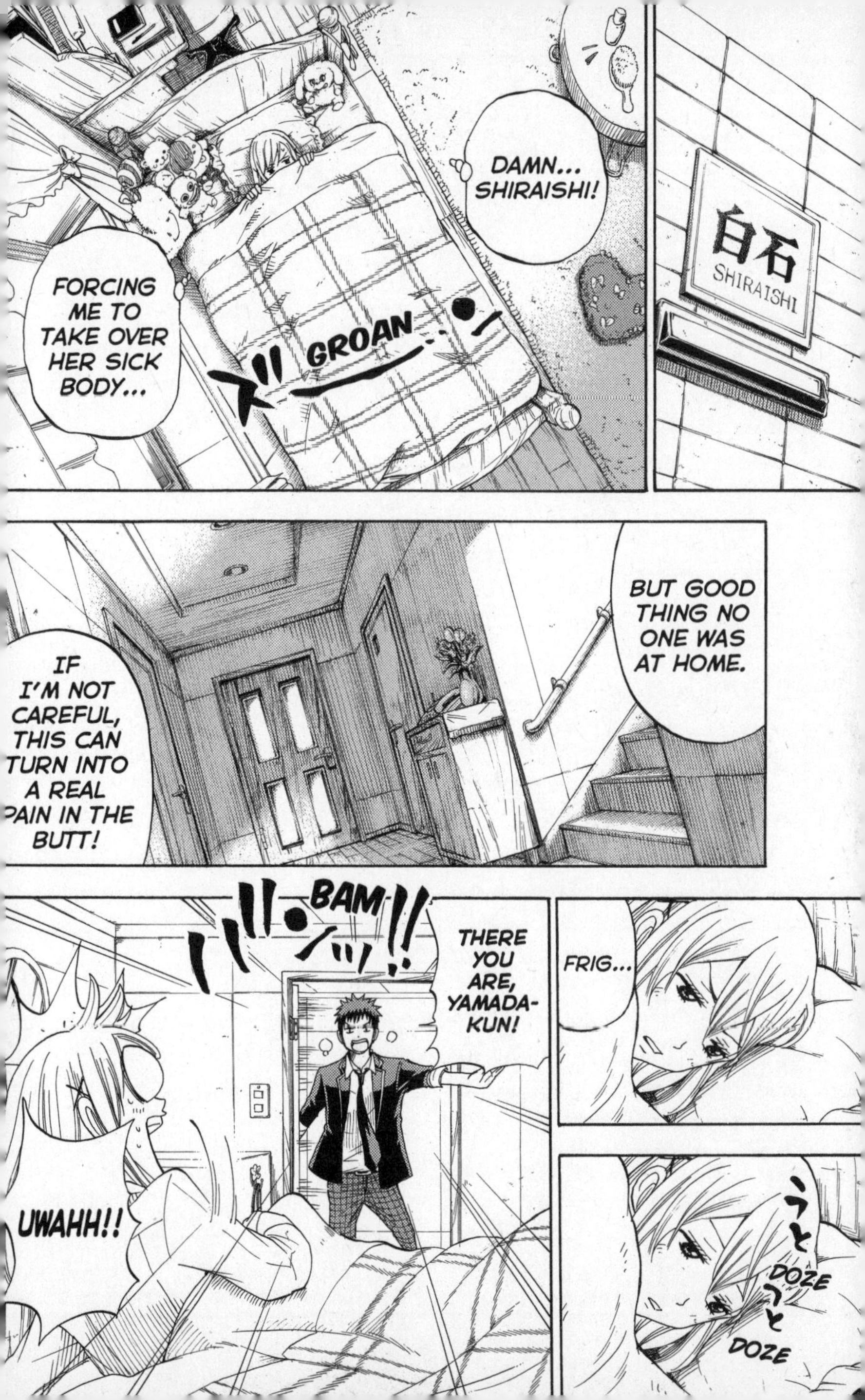
白石
SHIRAISHI
DAMN... SHIRAISHI!
FORCING ME TO TAKE OVER HER SICK BODY...
GROAN
BUT GOOD THING NO ONE WAS AT HOME.
IF I'M NOT CAREFUL, THIS CAN TURN INTO A REAL PAIN IN THE BUTT!
FRIG...
DOZE
DOZE
BAM
THERE YOU ARE, YAMADA-KUN!
UWAHH!!

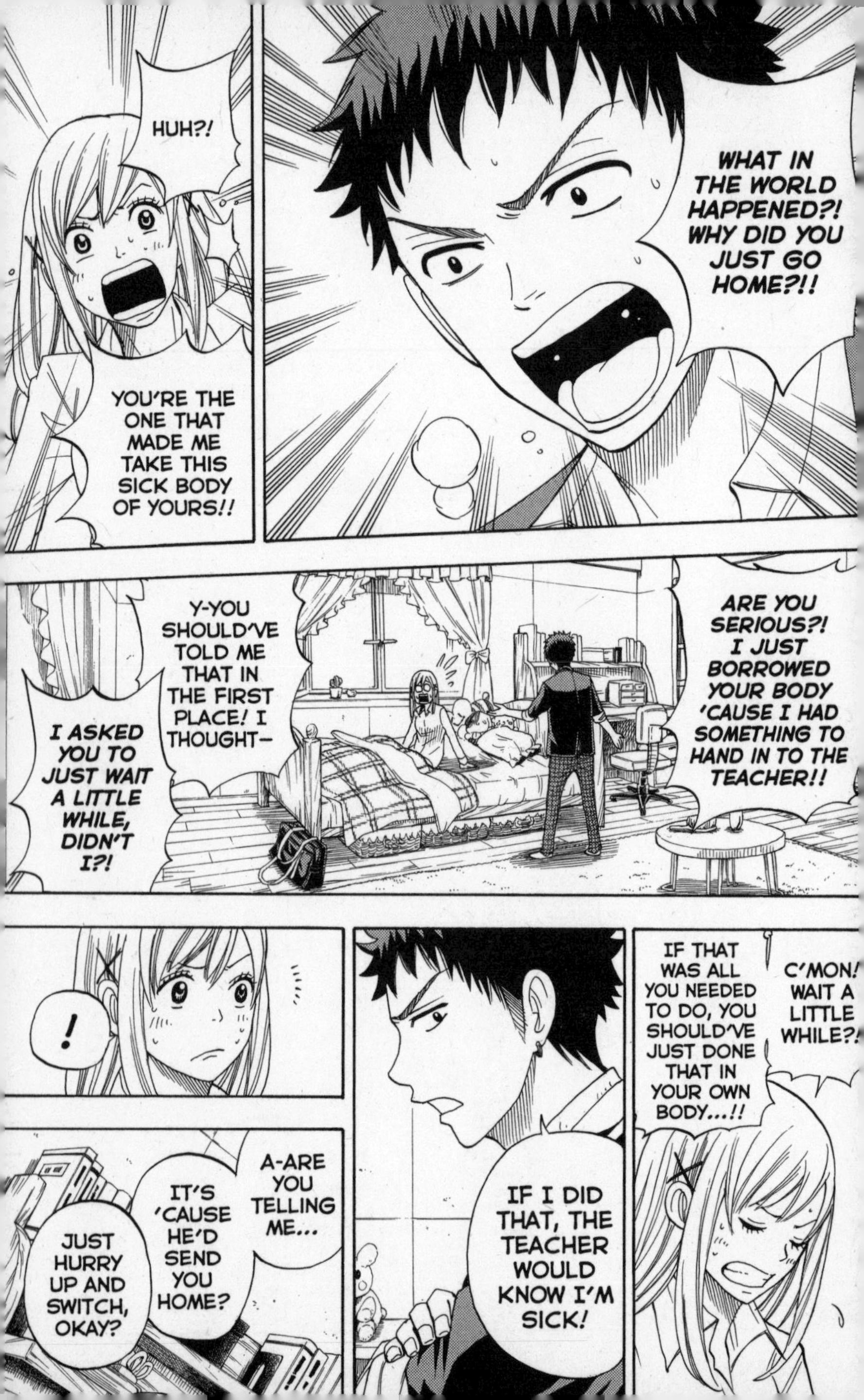
WHAT IN THE WORLD HAPPENED?! WHY DID YOU JUST GO HOME?!!
HUH?!
YOU'RE THE ONE THAT MADE ME TAKE THIS SICK BODY OF YOURS!!
ARE YOU SERIOUS?! I JUST BORROWED YOUR BODY 'CAUSE I HAD SOMETHING TO HAND IN TO THE TEACHER!!
Y-YOU SHOULD'VE TOLD ME THAT IN THE FIRST PLACE! I THOUGHT—
I ASKED YOU TO JUST WAIT A LITTLE WHILE, DIDN'T I?!
C'MON! WAIT A LITTLE WHILE?!
IF THAT WAS ALL YOU NEEDED TO DO, YOU SHOULD'VE JUST DONE THAT IN YOUR OWN BODY...!!
IF I DID THAT, THE TEACHER WOULD KNOW I'M SICK!
!
A-ARE YOU TELLING ME...
IT'S 'CAUSE HE'D SEND YOU HOME?
JUST HURRY UP AND SWITCH, OKAY?

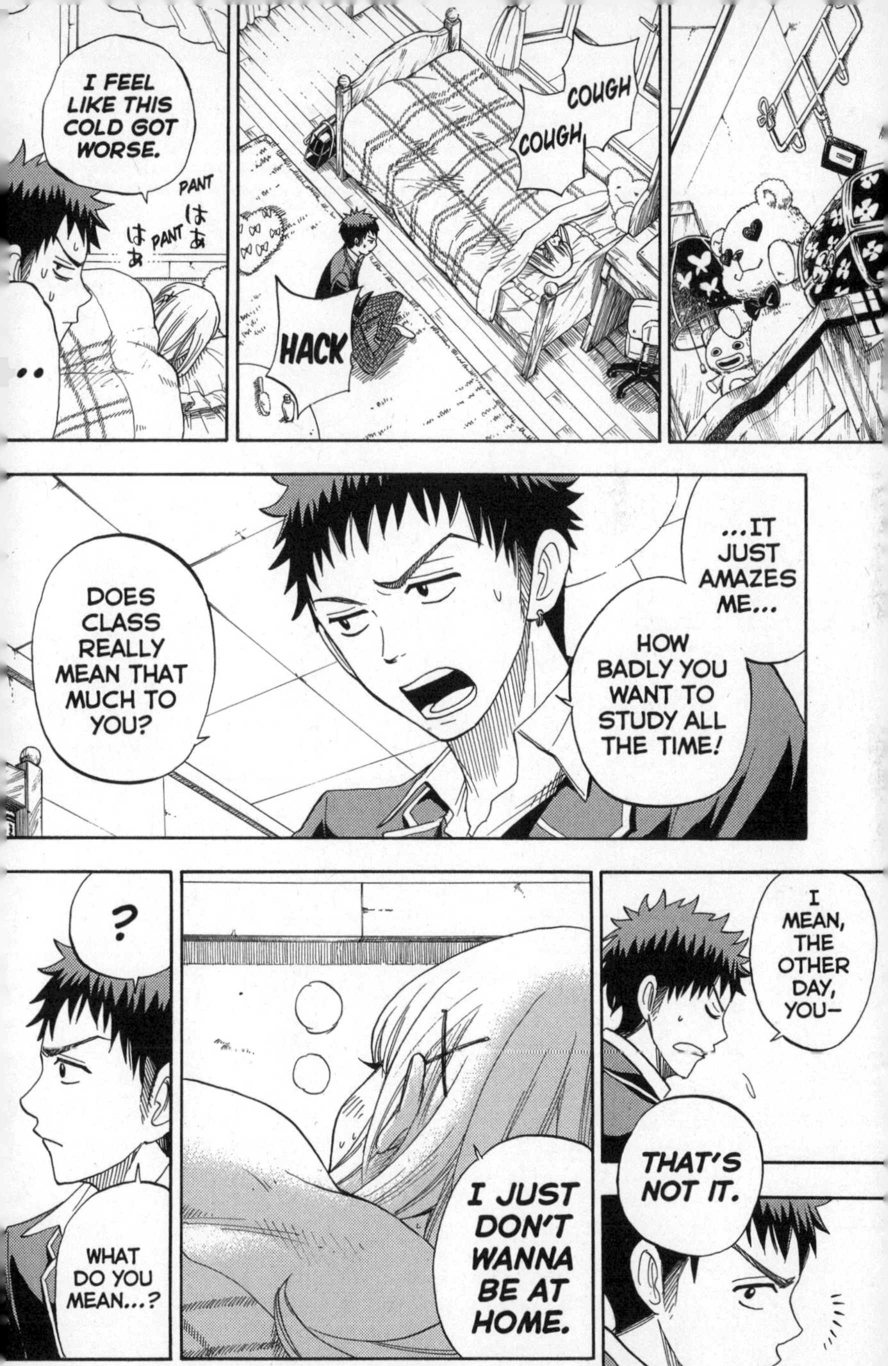
COUGH
COUGH
HACK
I FEEL LIKE THIS COLD GOT WORSE.
PANT はあ
PANT はあ
..
...IT JUST AMAZES ME...
HOW BADLY YOU WANT TO STUDY ALL THE TIME!
DOES CLASS REALLY MEAN THAT MUCH TO YOU?
I MEAN, THE OTHER DAY, YOU–
THAT'S NOT IT.
I JUST DON'T WANNA BE AT HOME.
?
WHAT DO YOU MEAN...?

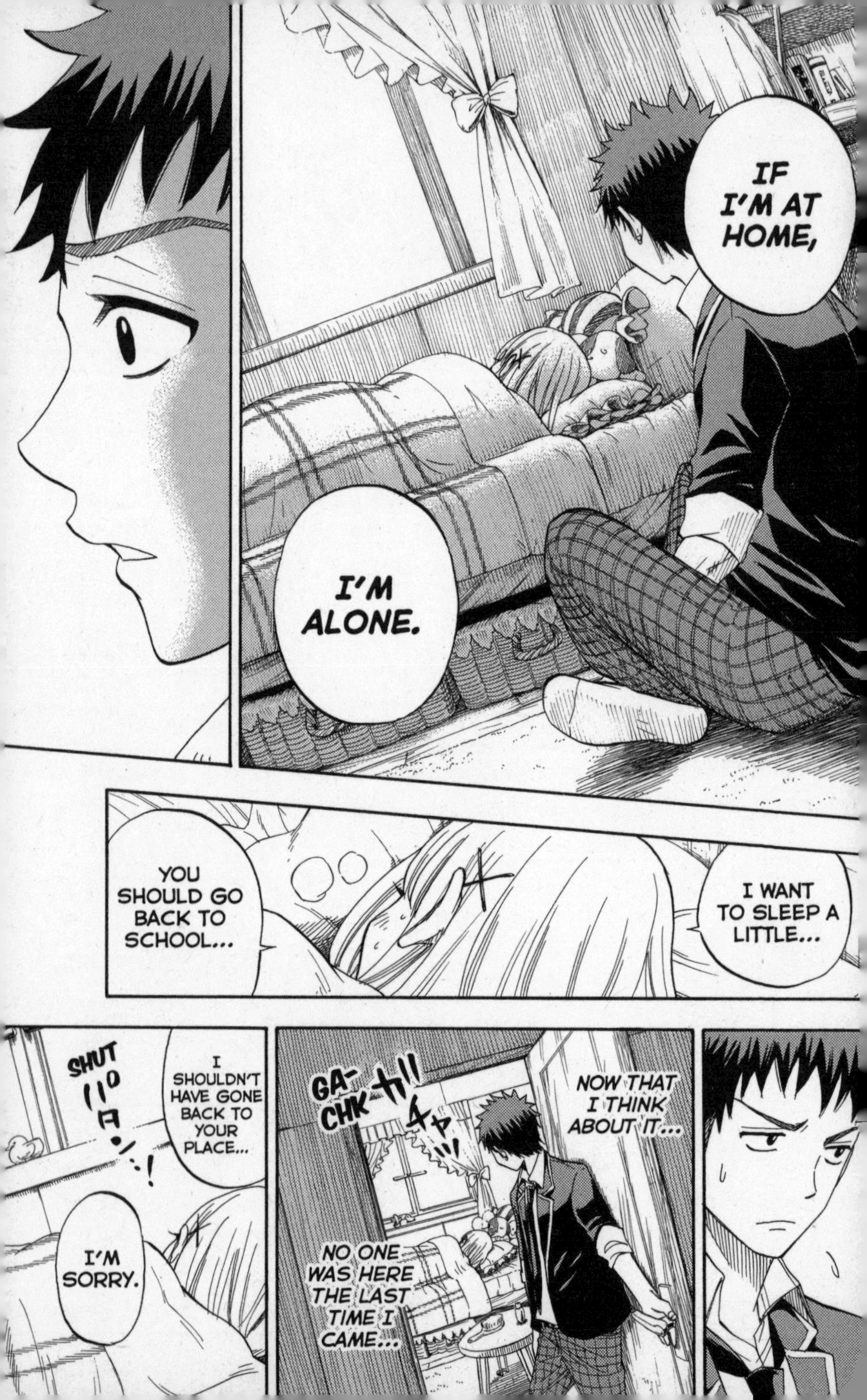
IF I'M AT HOME,
I'M ALONE.
I WANT TO SLEEP A LITTLE...
YOU SHOULD GO BACK TO SCHOOL...
NOW THAT I THINK ABOUT IT...
GA-CHK
NO ONE WAS HERE THE LAST TIME I CAME...
I SHOULDN'T HAVE GONE BACK TO YOUR PLACE...
SHUT
I'M SORRY.

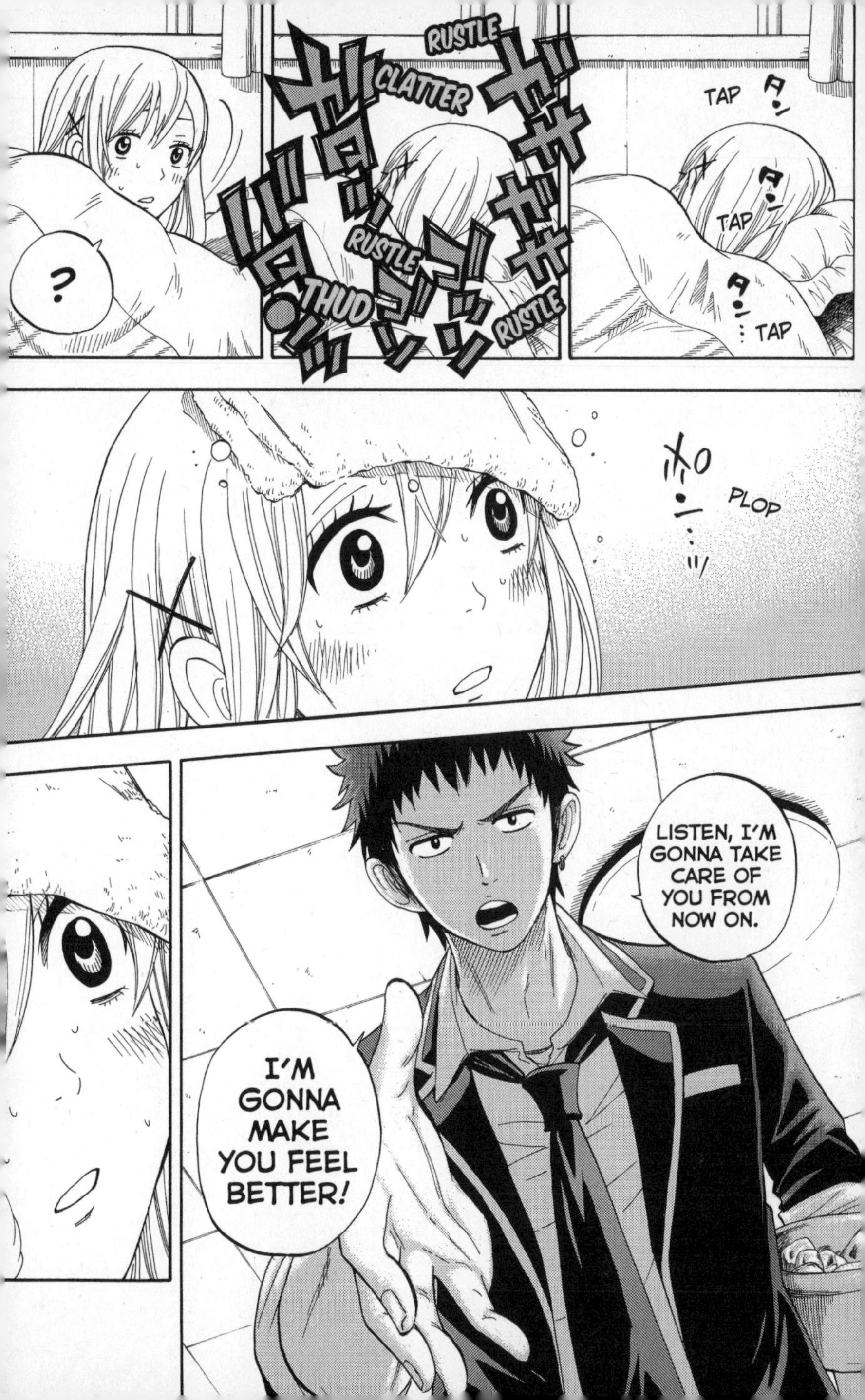
TAP
TAP
TAP
RUSTLE
CLATTER
RUSTLE
THUD
RUSTLE
?
PLOP
LISTEN, I'M GONNA TAKE CARE OF YOU FROM NOW ON.
I'M GONNA MAKE YOU FEEL BETTER!

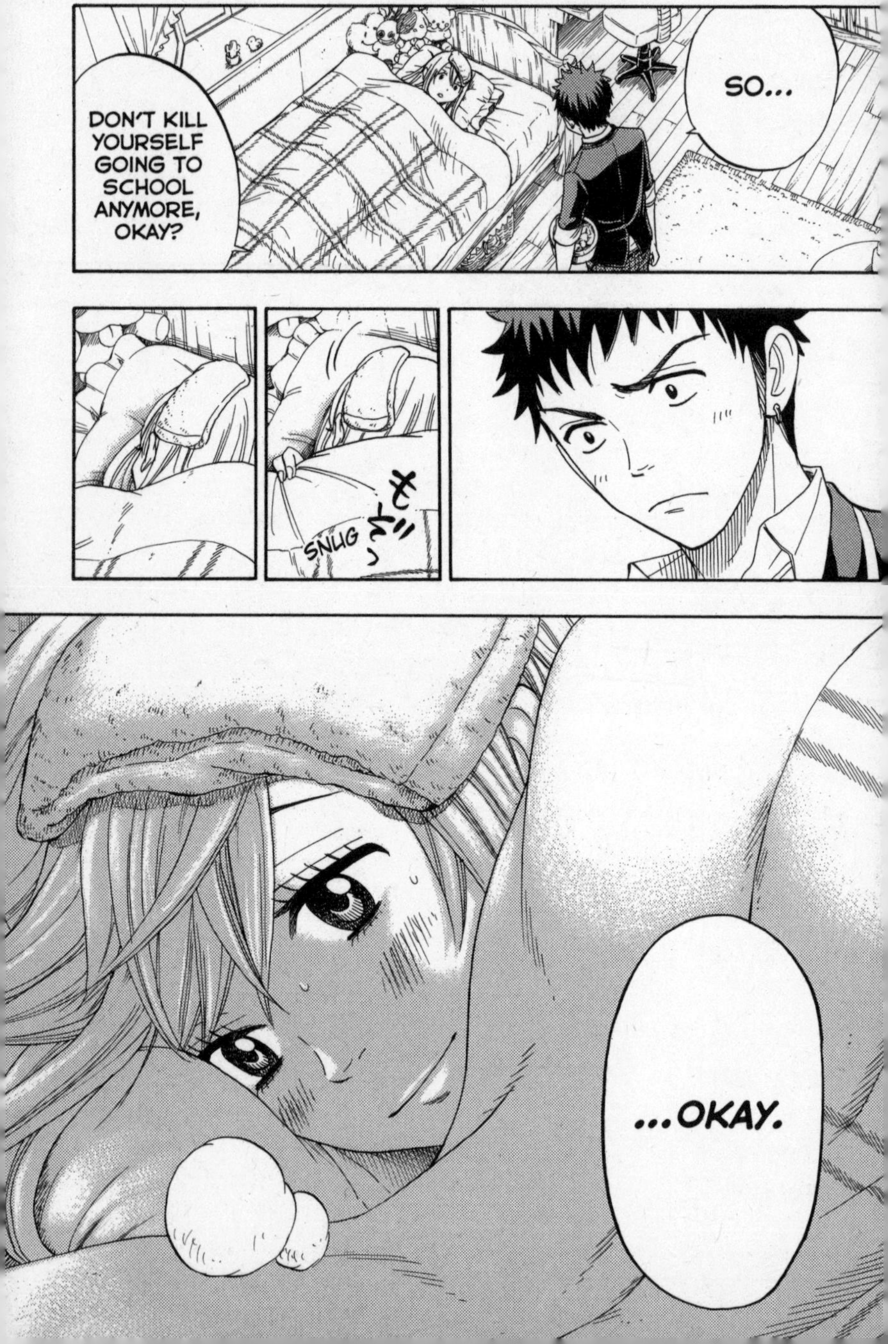
SO...
DON'T KILL YOURSELF GOING TO SCHOOL ANYMORE, OKAY?
SNUG
...OKAY.

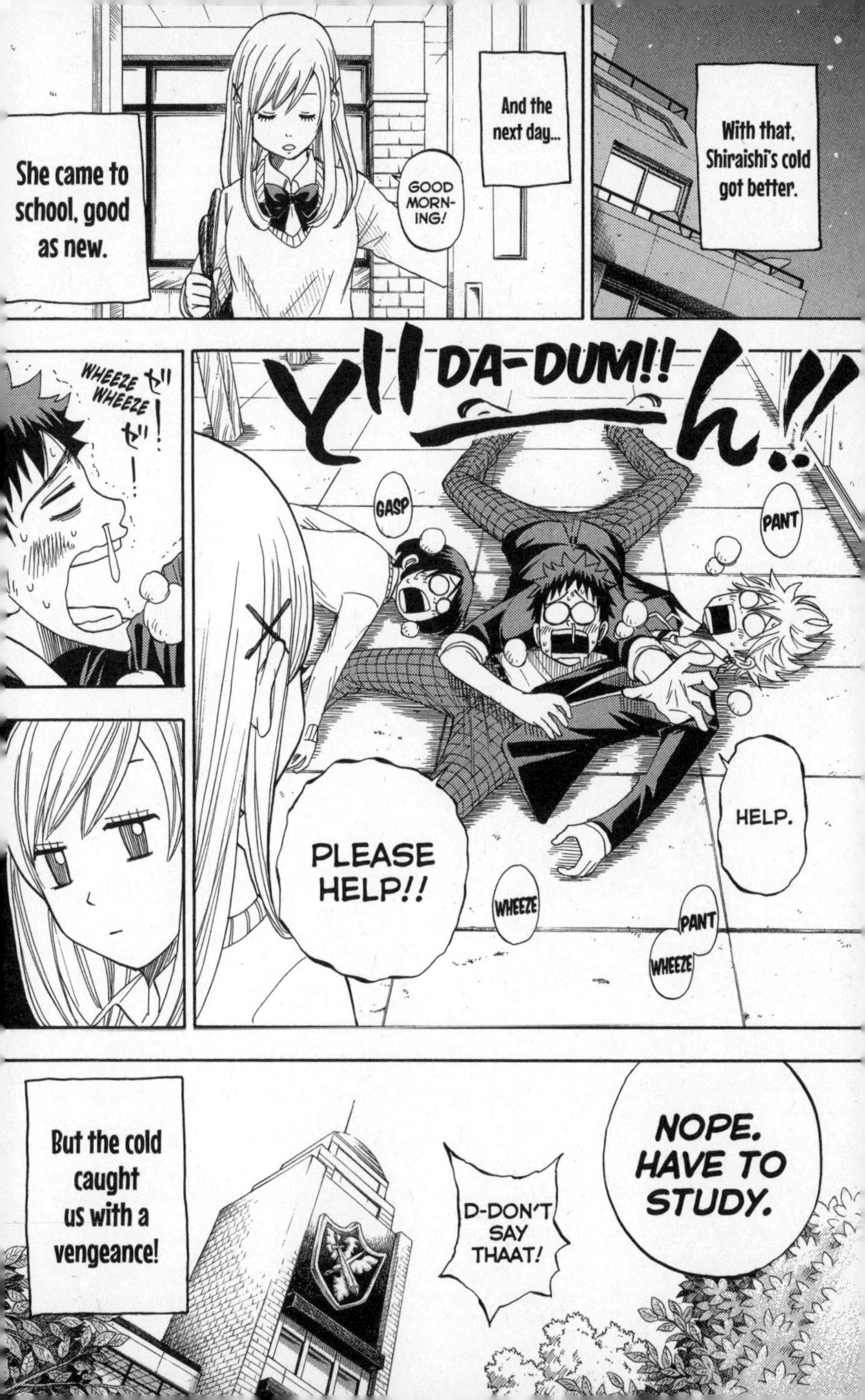
With that, Shiraishi's cold got better.
And the next day...
GOOD MORNING!
She came to school, good as new.
DA-DUM!!
PANT
GASP
HELP.
PANT
WHEEZE
WHEEZE
PLEASE HELP!!
WHEEZE WHEEZE
ぜ ぜ
NOPE. HAVE TO STUDY.
D-DON'T SAY THAAT!
But the cold caught us with a vengeance!

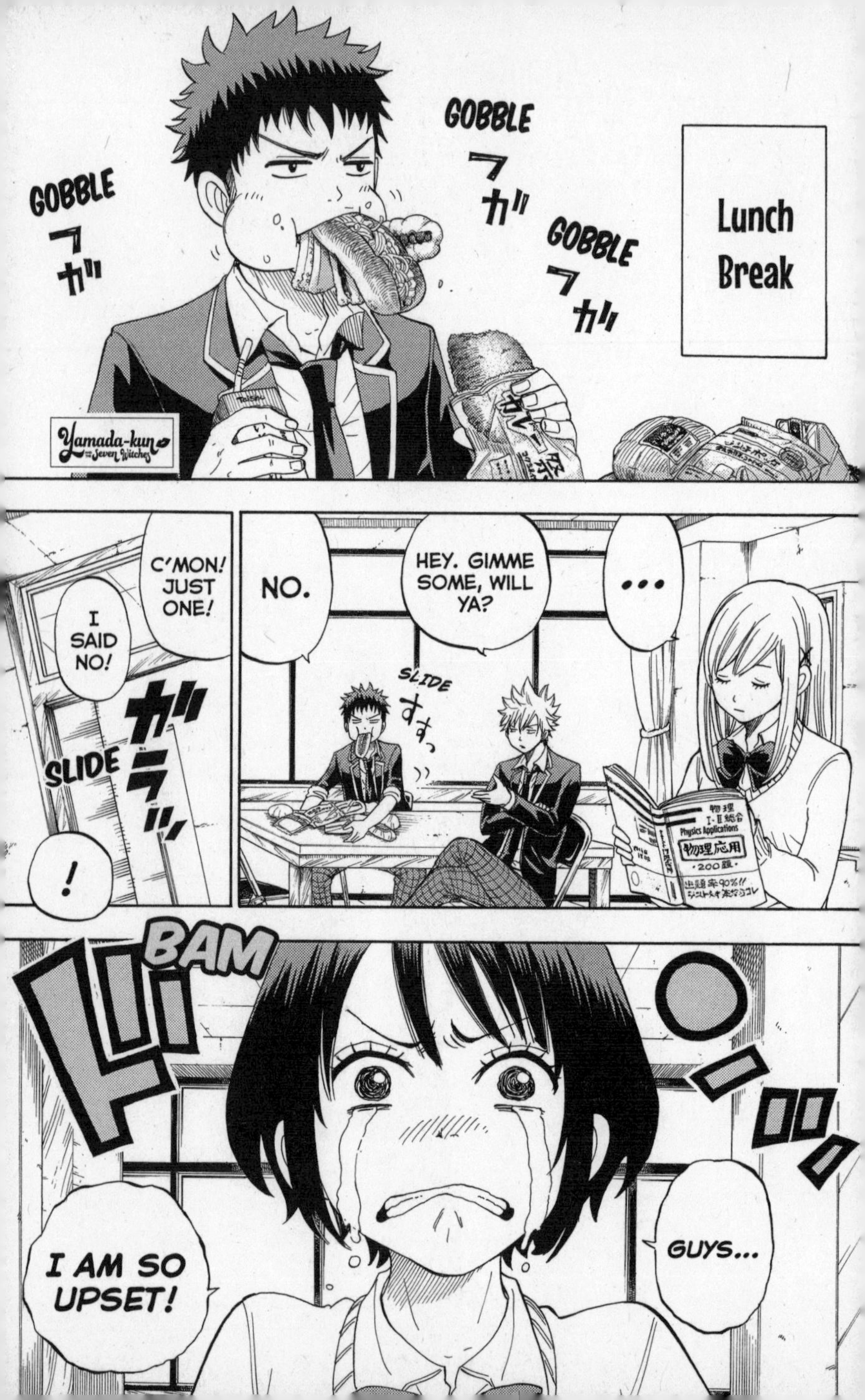
Lunch Break
GOBBLE
フガ
GOBBLE
フガ
GOBBLE
フガ
Yamada-kun and the Seven Witches
...
HEY. GIMME SOME, WILL YA?
NO.
SLIDE
すすっ
C'MON! JUST ONE!
I SAID NO!
SLIDE
ガラッ
!
BAM
GUYS...
I AM SO UPSET!

Chapter 11: Now then, Suzuki-kun!

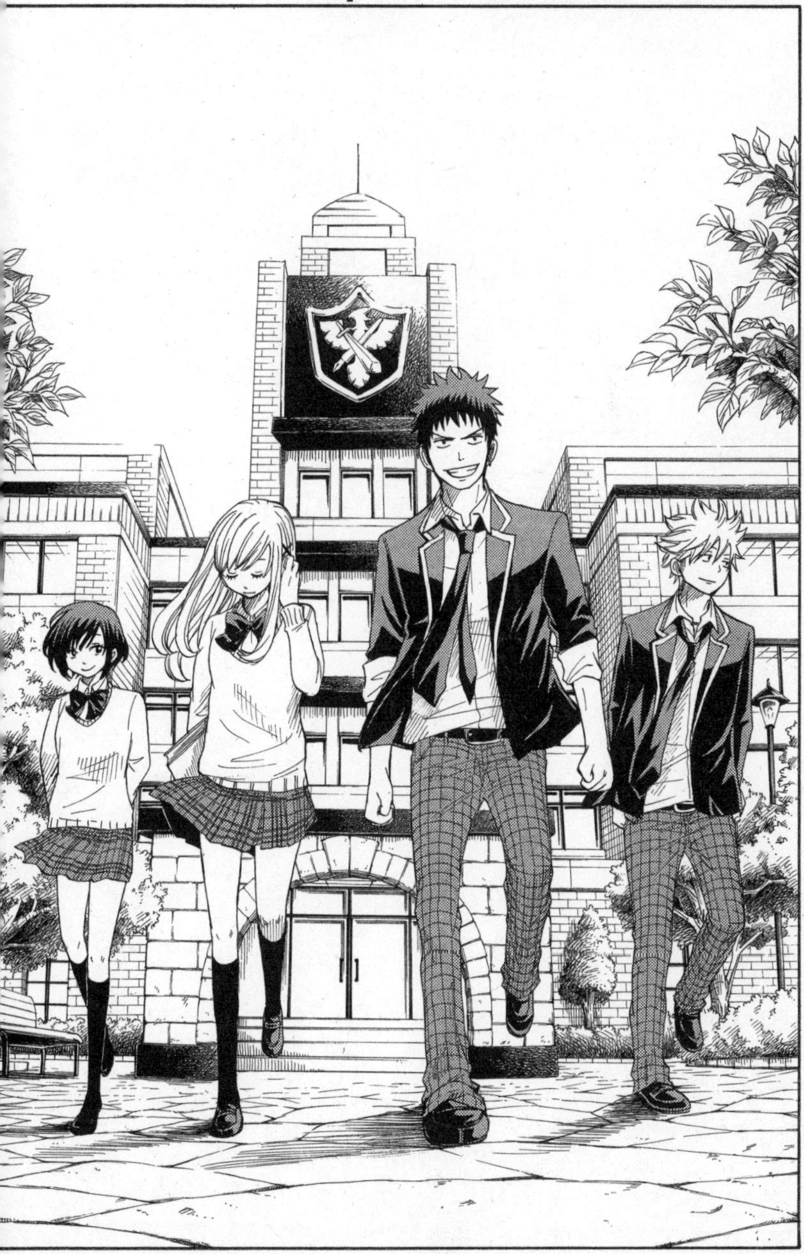

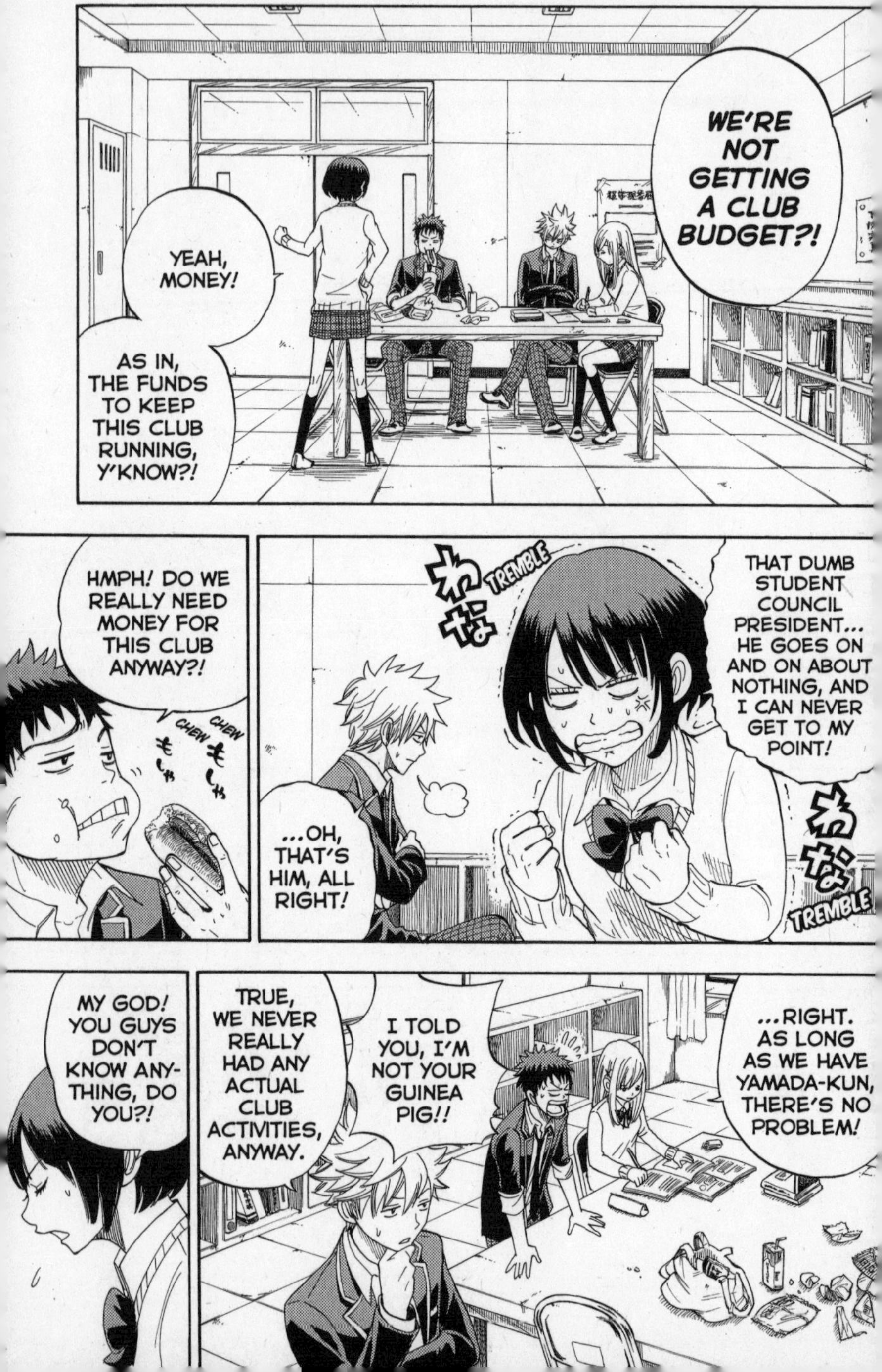
WE'RE NOT GETTING A CLUB BUDGET?!
YEAH, MONEY!
AS IN, THE FUNDS TO KEEP THIS CLUB RUNNING, Y'KNOW?!
THAT DUMB STUDENT COUNCIL PRESIDENT... HE GOES ON AND ON ABOUT NOTHING, AND I CAN NEVER GET TO MY POINT!
TREMBLE
TREMBLE
...OH, THAT'S HIM, ALL RIGHT!
HMPH! DO WE REALLY NEED MONEY FOR THIS CLUB ANYWAY?!
CHEW CHEW
...RIGHT. AS LONG AS WE HAVE YAMADA-KUN, THERE'S NO PROBLEM!
I TOLD YOU, I'M NOT YOUR GUINEA PIG!!
TRUE, WE NEVER REALLY HAD ANY ACTUAL CLUB ACTIVITIES, ANYWAY.
MY GOD! YOU GUYS DON'T KNOW ANY-THING, DO YOU?!

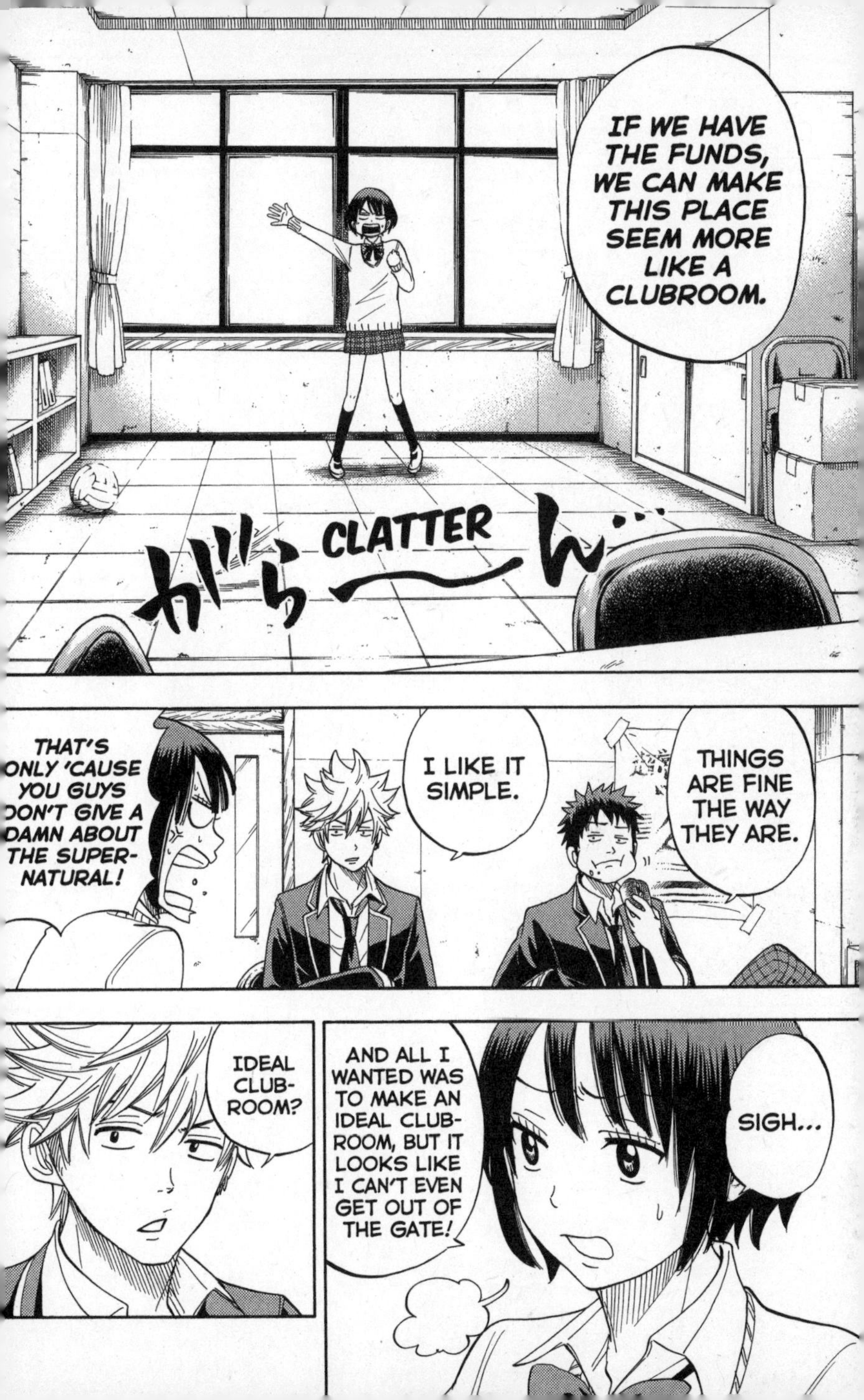
IF WE HAVE THE FUNDS, WE CAN MAKE THIS PLACE SEEM MORE LIKE A CLUBROOM.
がら〜ん…
CLATTER
THINGS ARE FINE THE WAY THEY ARE.
I LIKE IT SIMPLE.
THAT'S ONLY 'CAUSE YOU GUYS DON'T GIVE A DAMN ABOUT THE SUPER-NATURAL!
SIGH...
AND ALL I WANTED WAS TO MAKE AN IDEAL CLUB-ROOM, BUT IT LOOKS LIKE I CAN'T EVEN GET OUT OF THE GATE!
IDEAL CLUB-ROOM?

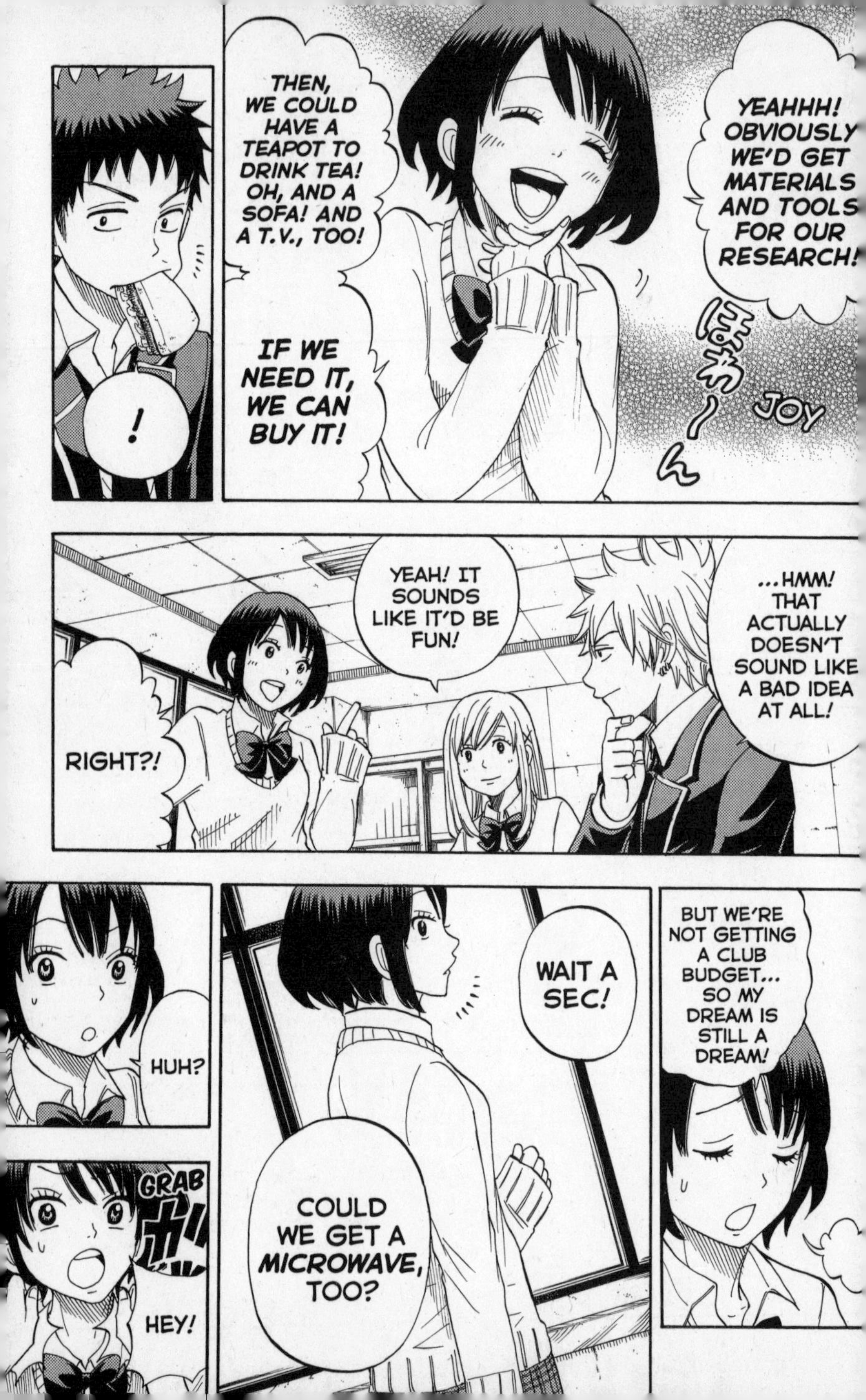
YEAHHH! OBVIOUSLY WE'D GET MATERIALS AND TOOLS FOR OUR RESEARCH!
ほわーん
JOY
THEN, WE COULD HAVE A TEAPOT TO DRINK TEA! OH, AND A SOFA! AND A T.V., TOO!
IF WE NEED IT, WE CAN BUY IT!
!
...HMM! THAT ACTUALLY DOESN'T SOUND LIKE A BAD IDEA AT ALL!
YEAH! IT SOUNDS LIKE IT'D BE FUN!
RIGHT?!
BUT WE'RE NOT GETTING A CLUB BUDGET... SO MY DREAM IS STILL A DREAM!
WAIT A SEC!
COULD WE GET A MICROWAVE, TOO?
HUH?
GRAB
HEY!

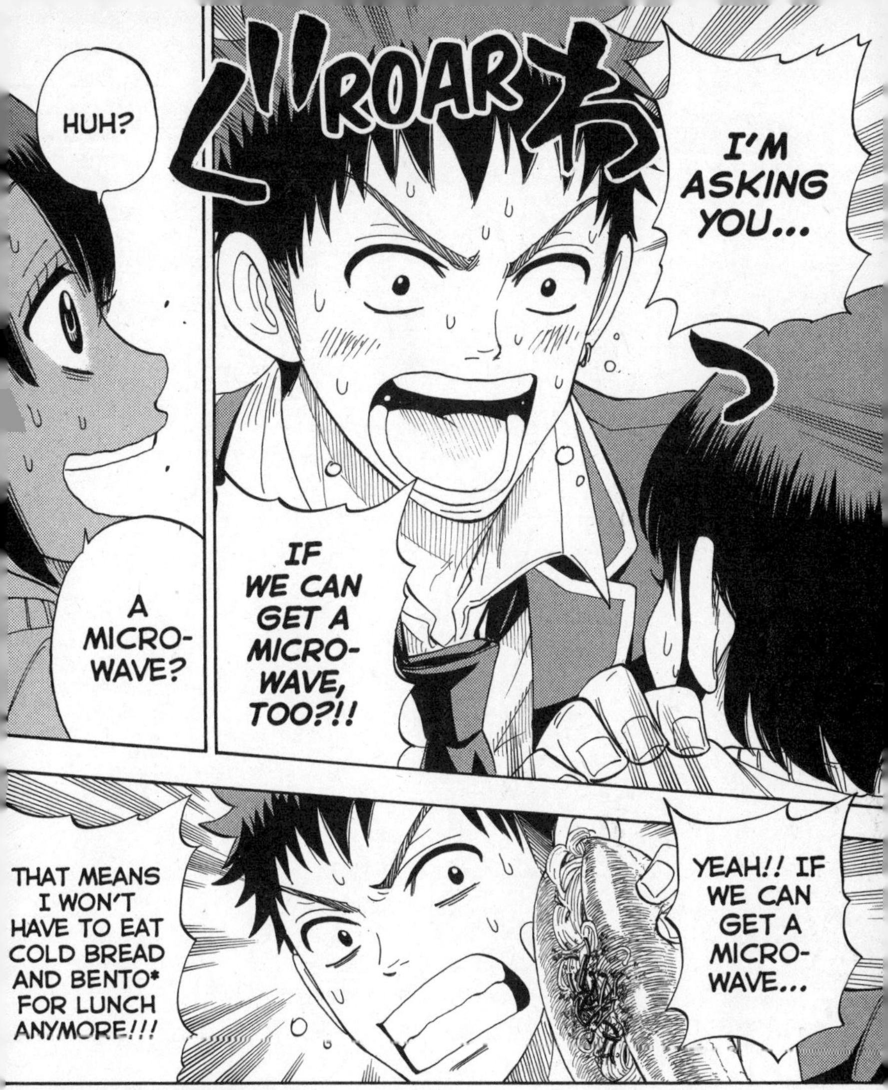
ROAR
I'M ASKING YOU...
IF WE CAN GET A MICROWAVE, TOO?!!
HUH?
A MICRO-WAVE?
YEAH!! IF WE CAN GET A MICRO-WAVE...
THAT MEANS I WON'T HAVE TO EAT COLD BREAD AND BENTO* FOR LUNCH ANYMORE!!!

*Bento: Japanese home-packed box lunches

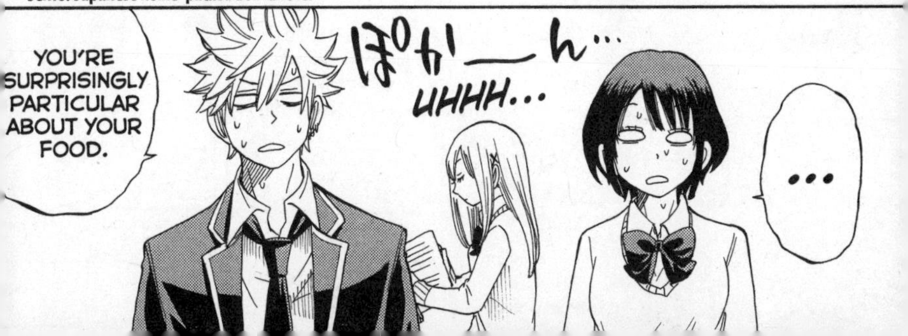
...
UHHH...
YOU'RE SURPRISINGLY PARTICULAR ABOUT YOUR FOOD.

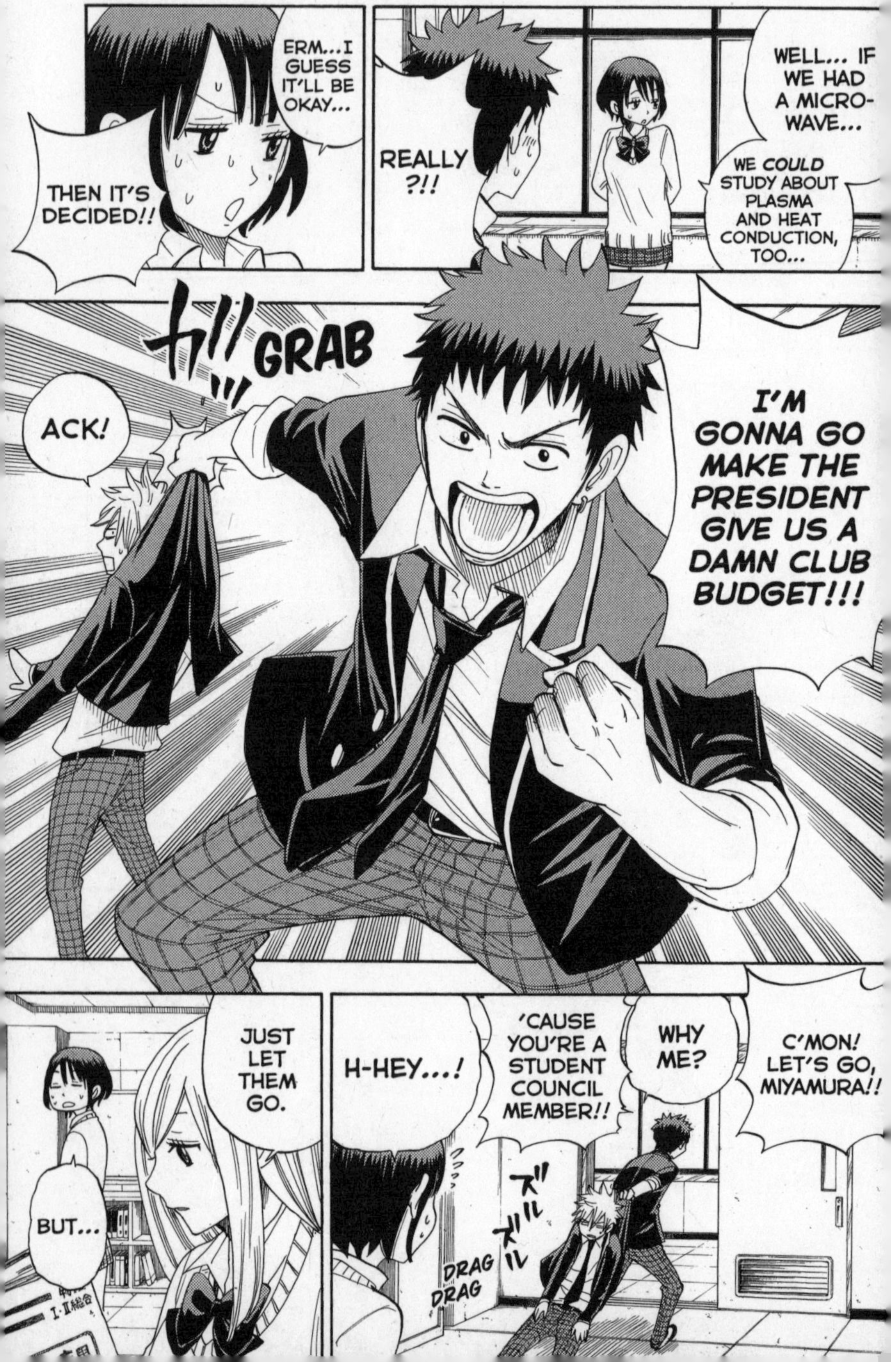
WELL... IF WE HAD A MICRO-WAVE...
WE COULD STUDY ABOUT PLASMA AND HEAT CONDUCTION, TOO...
REALLY ?!!
ERM...I GUESS IT'LL BE OKAY...
THEN IT'S DECIDED!!
I'M GONNA GO MAKE THE PRESIDENT GIVE US A DAMN CLUB BUDGET!!!
GRAB
ACK!
C'MON! LET'S GO, MIYAMURA!!
WHY ME?
'CAUSE YOU'RE A STUDENT COUNCIL MEMBER!!
DRAG DRAG
H-HEY...!
JUST LET THEM GO.
BUT...

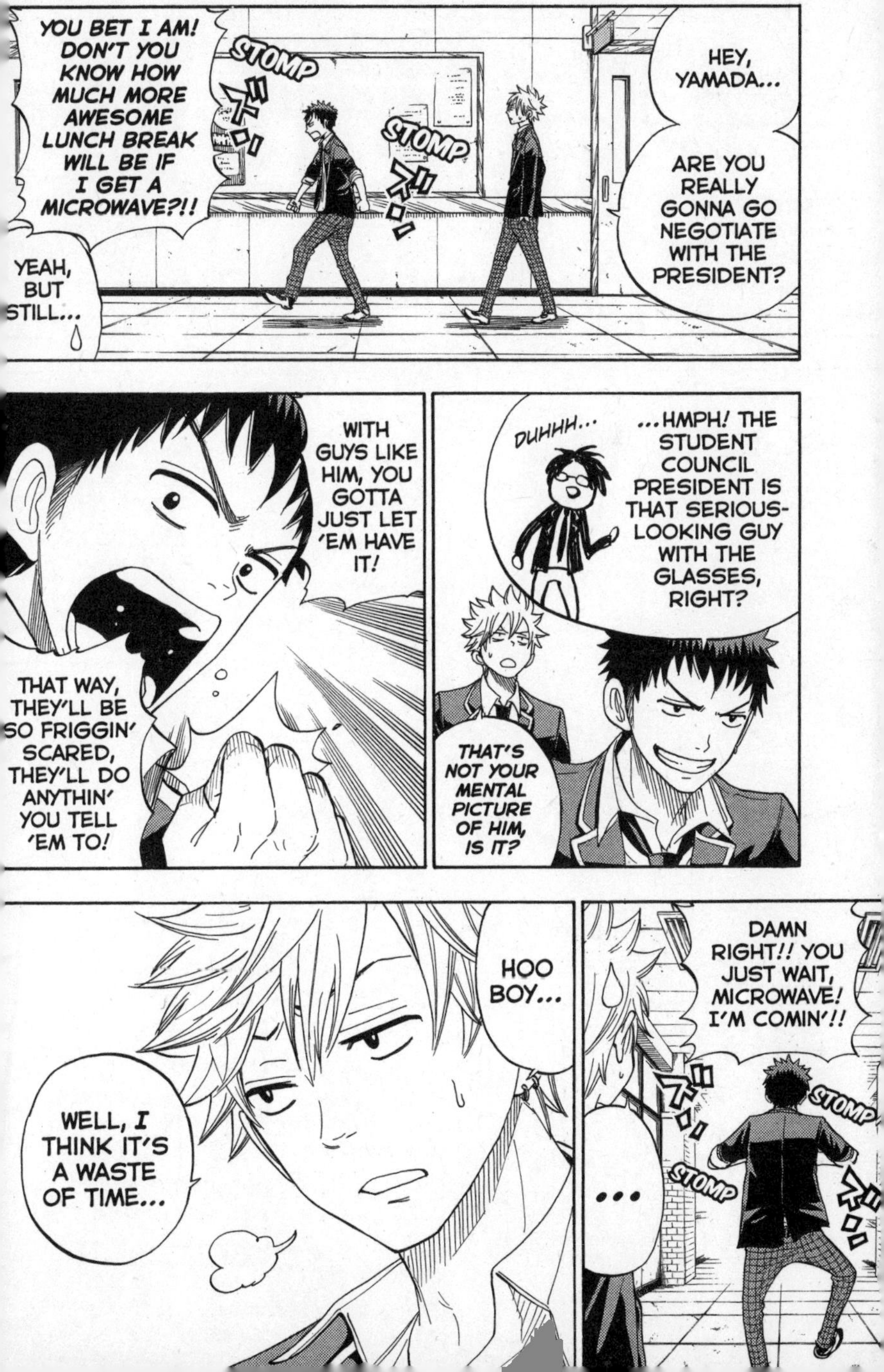
HEY, YAMADA...
ARE YOU REALLY GONNA GO NEGOTIATE WITH THE PRESIDENT?
STOMP
STOMP
YOU BET I AM! DON'T YOU KNOW HOW MUCH MORE AWESOME LUNCH BREAK WILL BE IF I GET A MICROWAVE?!!
YEAH, BUT STILL...
...HMPH! THE STUDENT COUNCIL PRESIDENT IS THAT SERIOUS-LOOKING GUY WITH THE GLASSES, RIGHT?
DUHHH...
THAT'S NOT YOUR MENTAL PICTURE OF HIM, IS IT?
WITH GUYS LIKE HIM, YOU GOTTA JUST LET 'EM HAVE IT!
THAT WAY, THEY'LL BE SO FRIGGIN' SCARED, THEY'LL DO ANYTHIN' YOU TELL 'EM TO!
DAMN RIGHT!! YOU JUST WAIT, MICROWAVE! I'M COMIN'!!
STOMP
STOMP
...
HOO BOY...
WELL, I THINK IT'S A WASTE OF TIME...

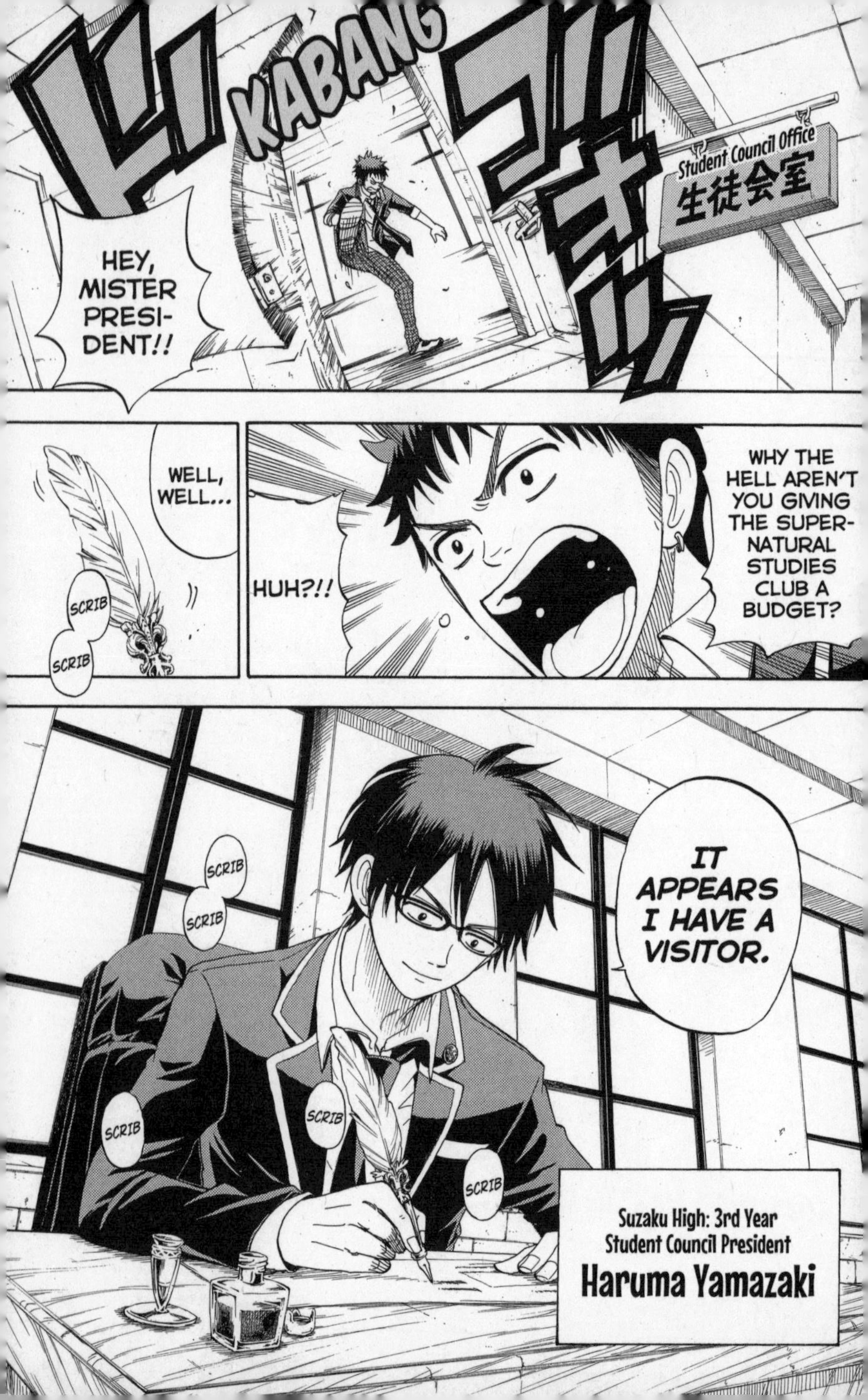
Student Council Office
生徒会室
KABANG
HEY, MISTER PRESI-DENT!!
WHY THE HELL AREN'T YOU GIVING THE SUPER-NATURAL STUDIES CLUB A BUDGET?
HUH?!!
WELL, WELL...
SCRIB
SCRIB
IT APPEARS I HAVE A VISITOR.
SCRIB
SCRIB
SCRIB
SCRIB
SCRIB
Suzaku High: 3rd Year
Student Council President
Haruma Yamazaki

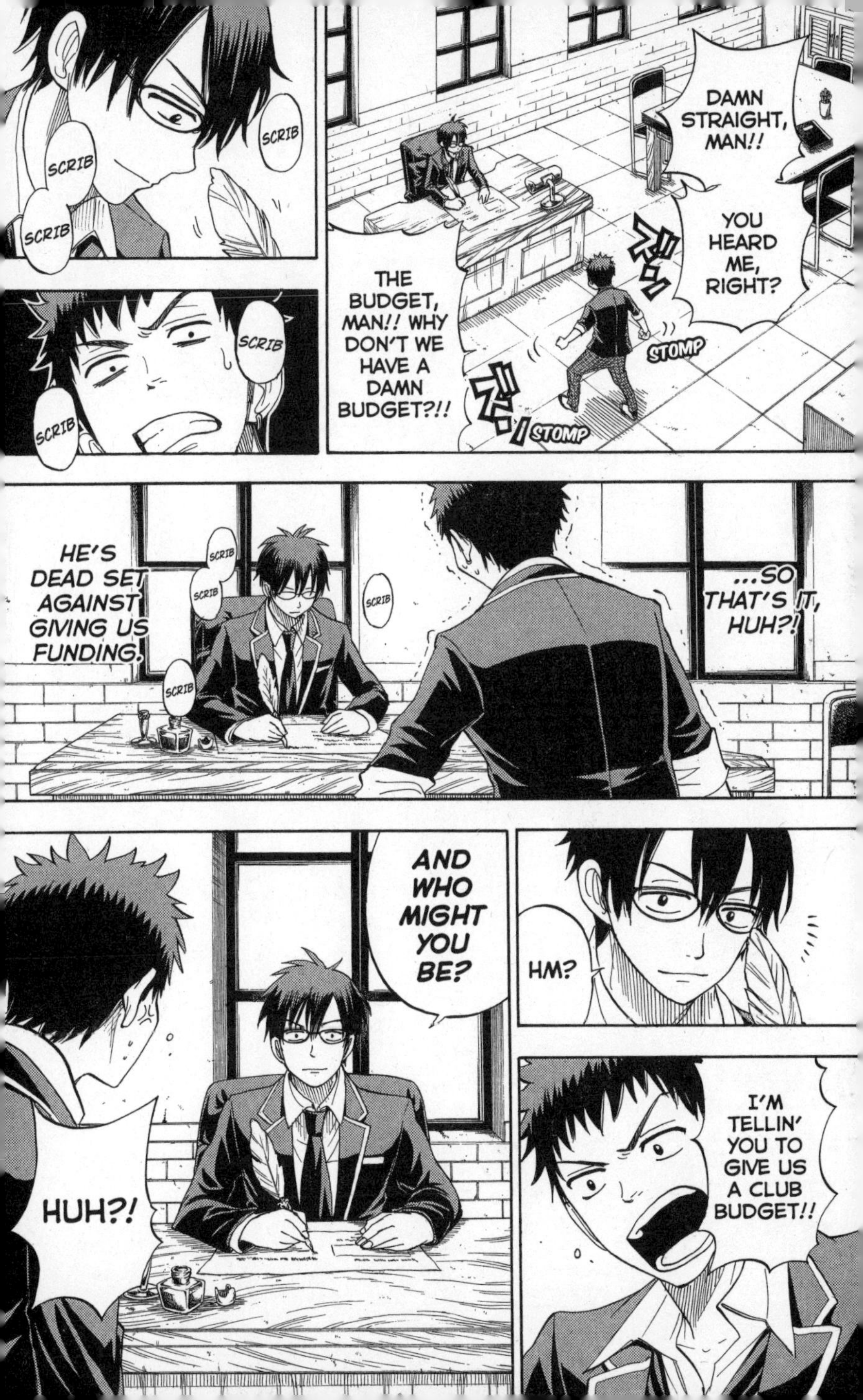
DAMN STRAIGHT, MAN!!
YOU HEARD ME, RIGHT?
THE BUDGET, MAN!! WHY DON'T WE HAVE A DAMN BUDGET?!!
STOMP
STOMP
SCRIB
SCRIB
SCRIB
SCRIB
SCRIB
...SO THAT'S IT, HUH?!
SCRIB
SCRIB
SCRIB
SCRIB
HE'S DEAD SET AGAINST GIVING US FUNDING.
HM?
I'M TELLIN' YOU TO GIVE US A CLUB BUDGET!!
AND WHO MIGHT YOU BE?
HUH?!

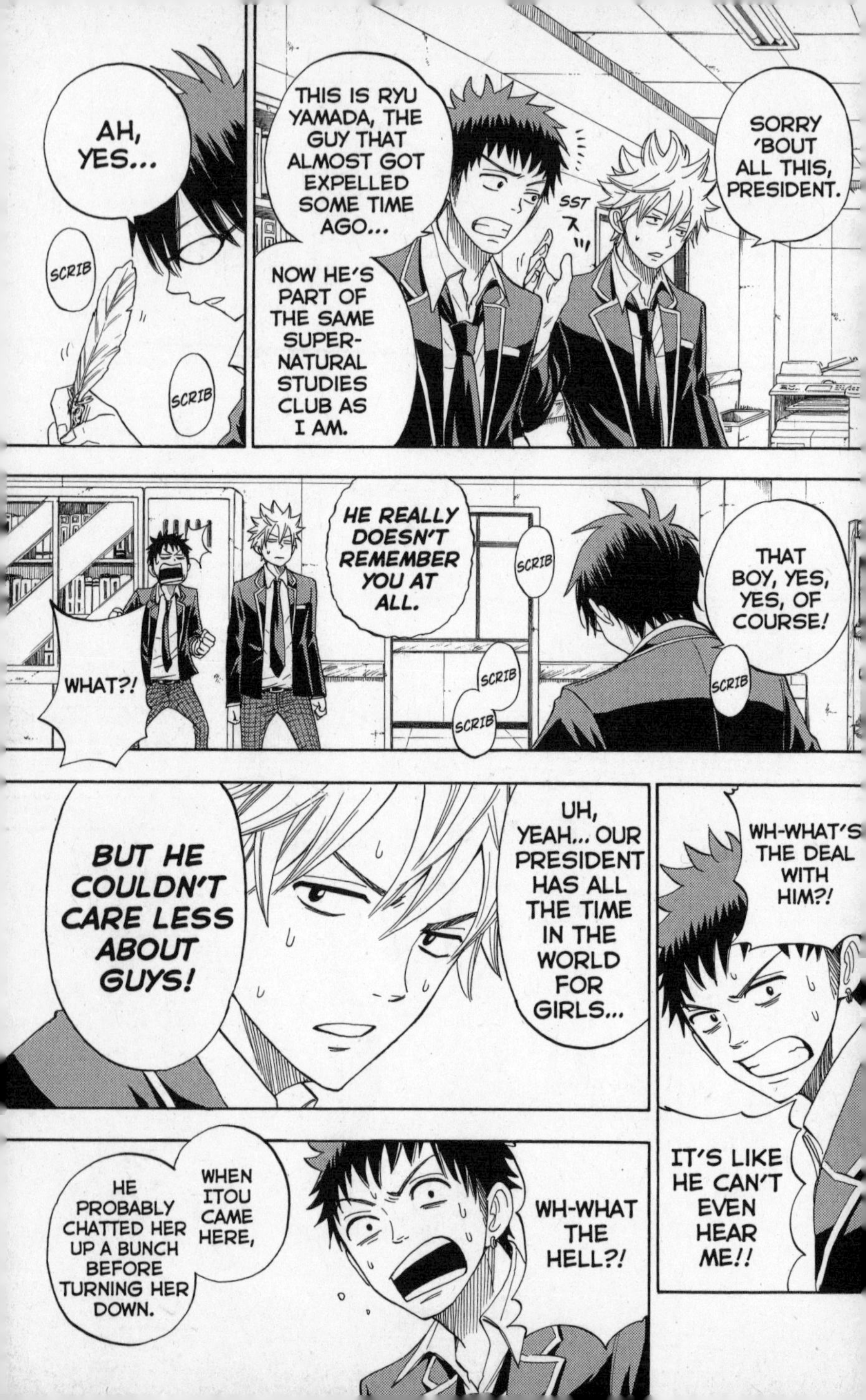

SORRY 'BOUT ALL THIS, PRESIDENT.
SST
THIS IS RYU YAMADA, THE GUY THAT ALMOST GOT EXPELLED SOME TIME AGO...
NOW HE'S PART OF THE SAME SUPER-NATURAL STUDIES CLUB AS I AM.
AH, YES...
SCRIB
SCRIB
THAT BOY, YES, YES, OF COURSE!
SCRIB
SCRIB
SCRIB
SCRIB
HE REALLY DOESN'T REMEMBER YOU AT ALL.
WHAT?!
WH-WHAT'S THE DEAL WITH HIM?!
IT'S LIKE HE CAN'T EVEN HEAR ME!!
UH, YEAH... OUR PRESIDENT HAS ALL THE TIME IN THE WORLD FOR GIRLS...
BUT HE COULDN'T CARE LESS ABOUT GUYS!
WH-WHAT THE HELL?!
WHEN ITOU CAME HERE,
HE PROBABLY CHATTED HER UP A BUNCH BEFORE TURNING HER DOWN.

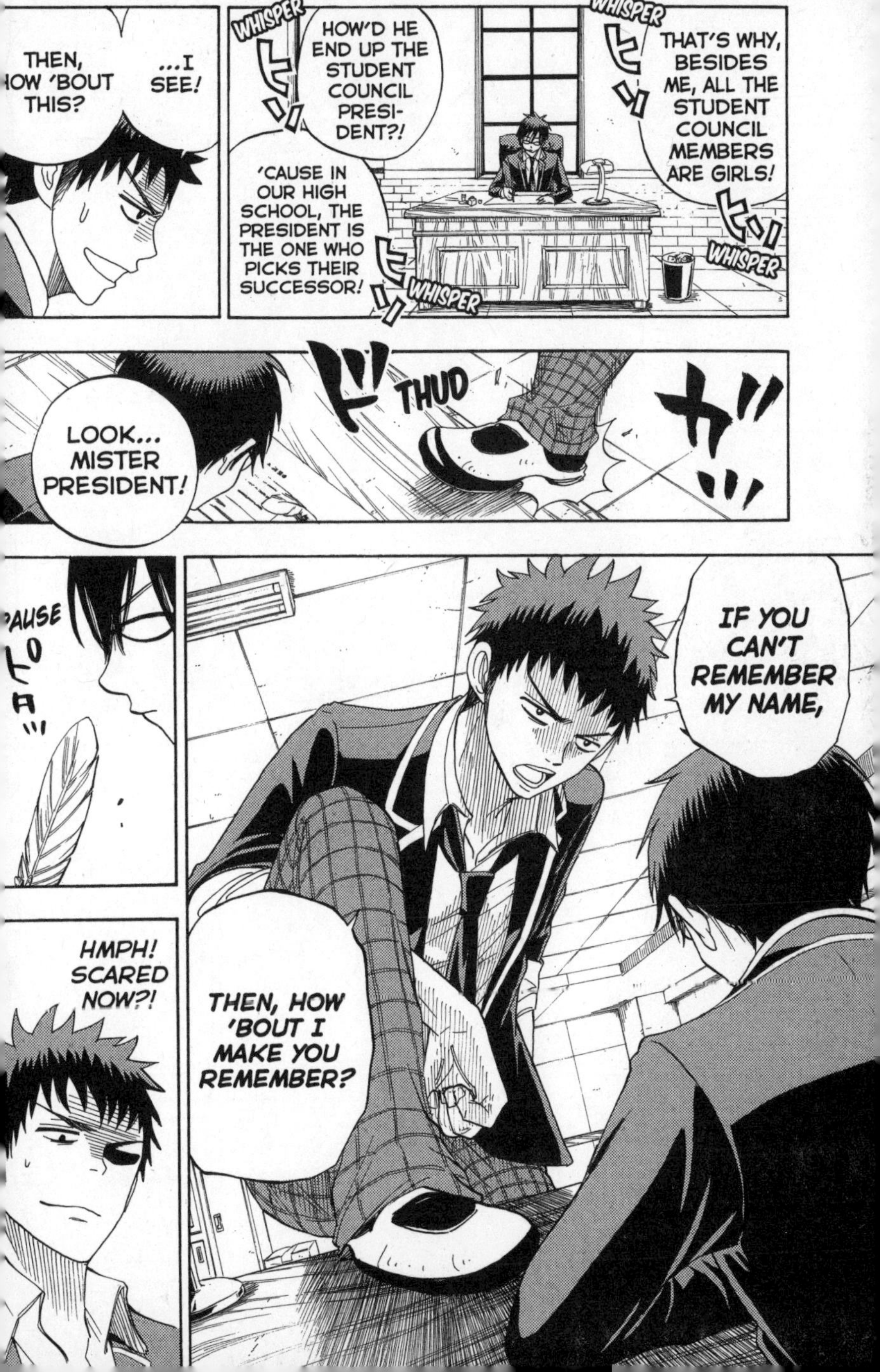
WHISPER
HOW'D HE END UP THE STUDENT COUNCIL PRESIDENT?!
'CAUSE IN OUR HIGH SCHOOL, THE PRESIDENT IS THE ONE WHO PICKS THEIR SUCCESSOR!
WHISPER
WHISPER
THAT'S WHY, BESIDES ME, ALL THE STUDENT COUNCIL MEMBERS ARE GIRLS!
WHISPER
...I SEE!
THEN, HOW 'BOUT THIS?
THUD
LOOK... MISTER PRESIDENT!
IF YOU CAN'T REMEMBER MY NAME,
THEN, HOW 'BOUT I MAKE YOU REMEMBER?
AUSE
HMPH! SCARED NOW?!

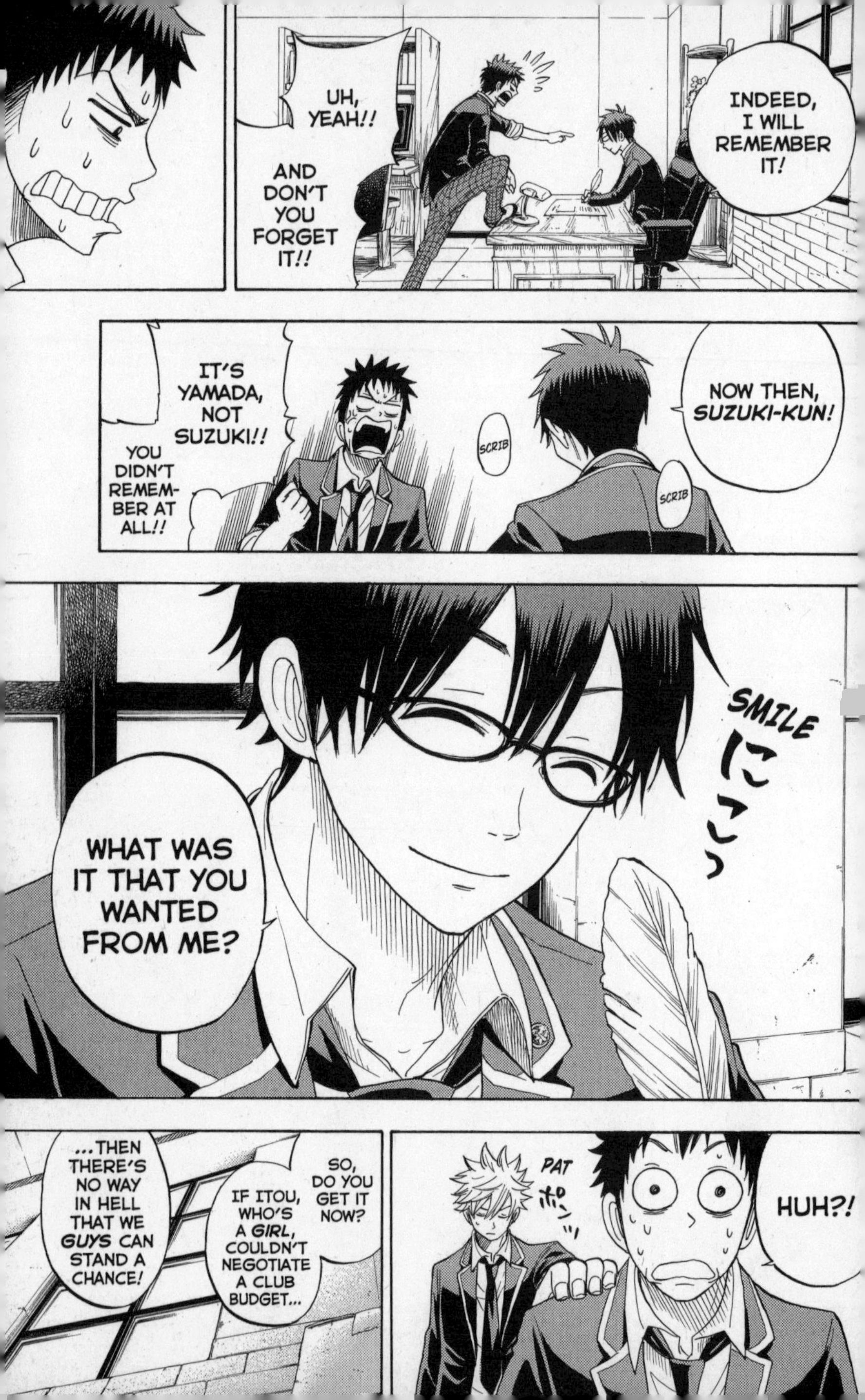
INDEED, I WILL REMEMBER IT!
UH, YEAH!!
AND DON'T YOU FORGET IT!!
NOW THEN, SUZUKI-KUN!
SCRIB
SCRIB
IT'S YAMADA, NOT SUZUKI!!
YOU DIDN'T REMEMBER AT ALL!!
SMILE
にこっ
WHAT WAS IT THAT YOU WANTED FROM ME?
HUH?!
PAT
ポンッ
SO, DO YOU GET IT NOW?
IF ITOU, WHO'S A GIRL, COULDN'T NEGOTIATE A CLUB BUDGET...
...THEN THERE'S NO WAY IN HELL THAT WE GUYS CAN STAND A CHANCE!

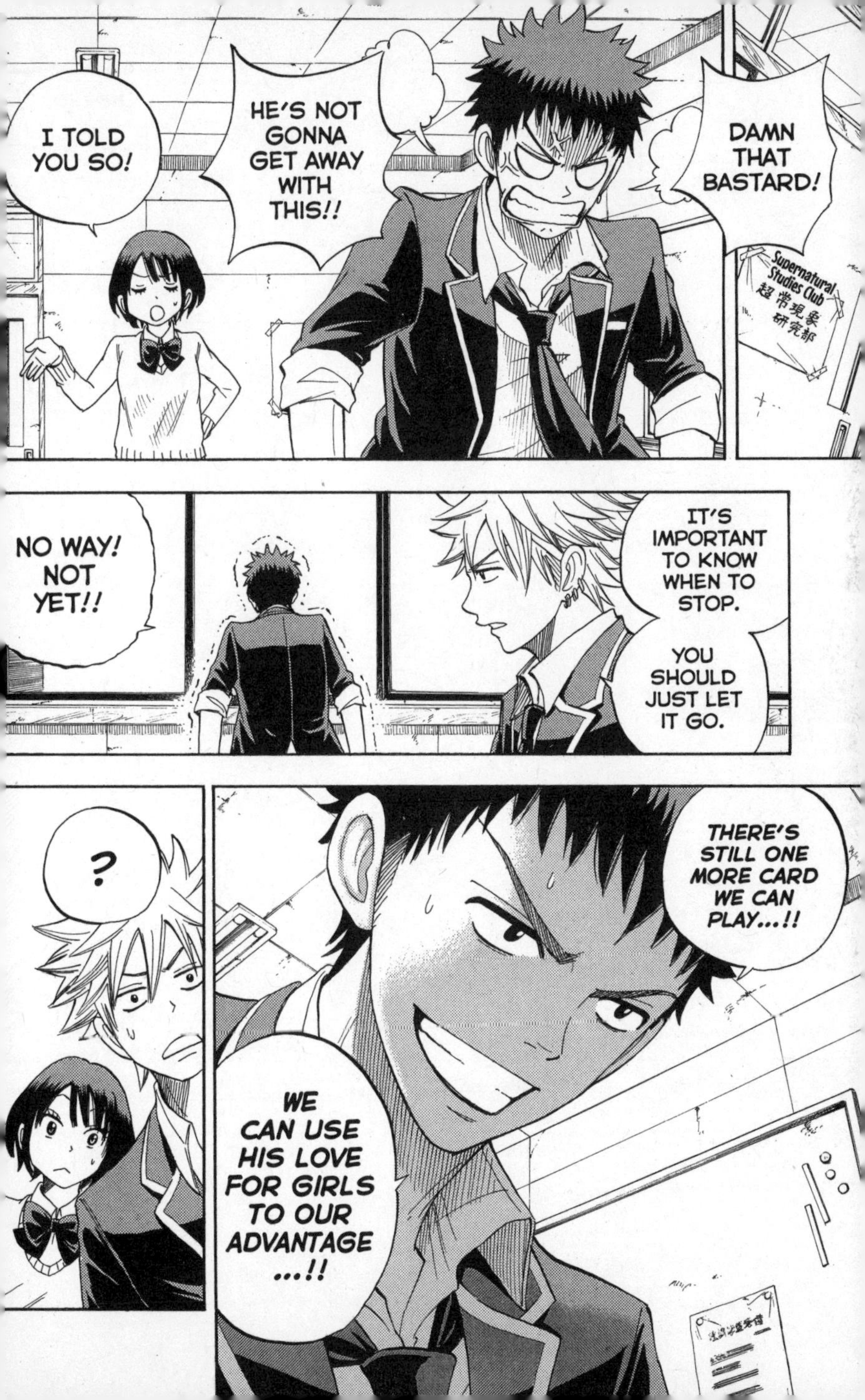
DAMN THAT BASTARD!
Supernatural Studies Club
超常現象研究部
HE'S NOT GONNA GET AWAY WITH THIS!!
I TOLD YOU SO!
IT'S IMPORTANT TO KNOW WHEN TO STOP.
YOU SHOULD JUST LET IT GO.
NO WAY! NOT YET!!
THERE'S STILL ONE MORE CARD WE CAN PLAY...!!
WE CAN USE HIS LOVE FOR GIRLS TO OUR ADVANTAGE ...!!
?

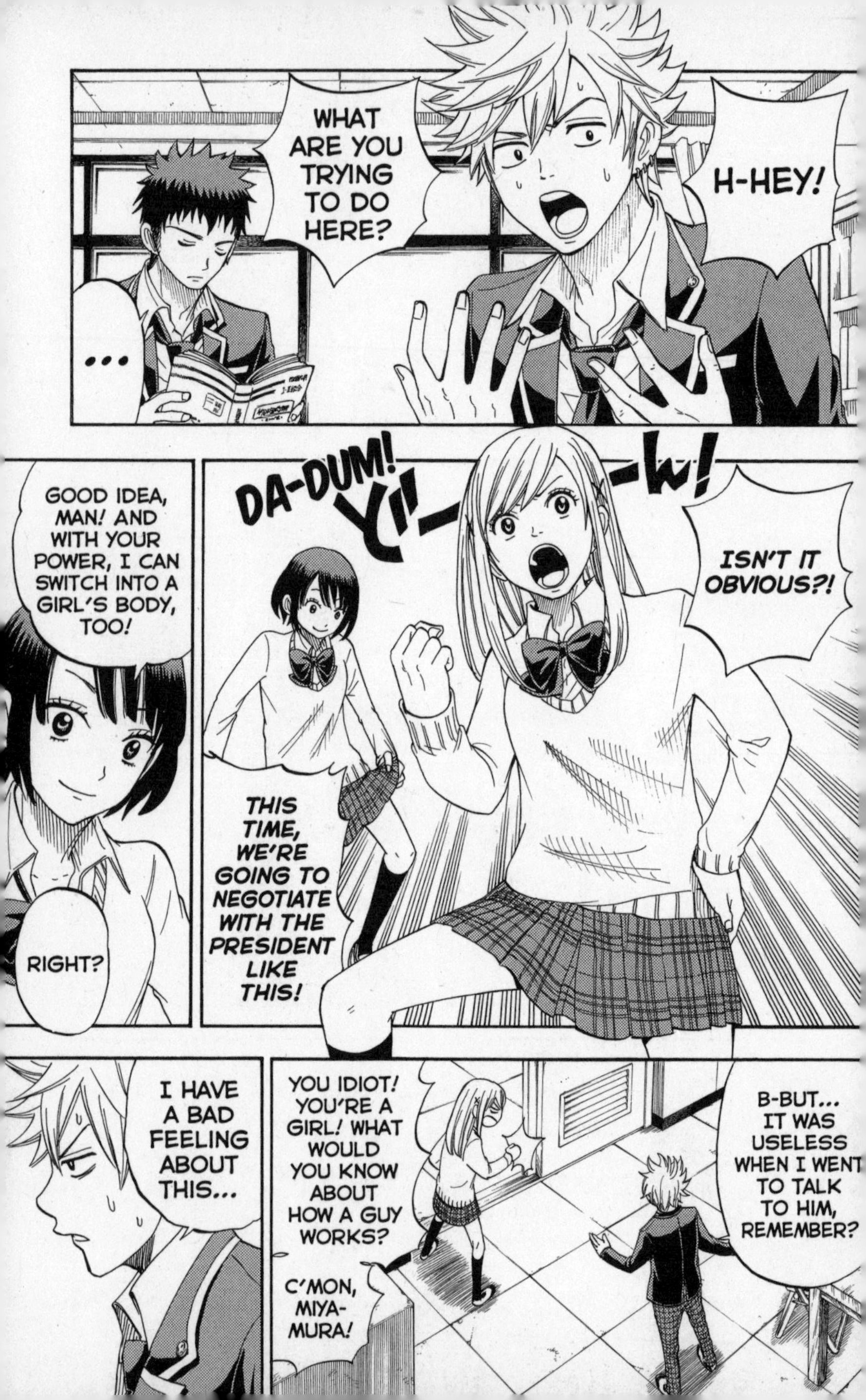
H-HEY!
WHAT ARE YOU TRYING TO DO HERE?
...
ISN'T IT OBVIOUS?!
DA-DUM!
THIS TIME, WE'RE GOING TO NEGOTIATE WITH THE PRESIDENT LIKE THIS!
GOOD IDEA, MAN! AND WITH YOUR POWER, I CAN SWITCH INTO A GIRL'S BODY, TOO!
RIGHT?
B-BUT... IT WAS USELESS WHEN I WENT TO TALK TO HIM, REMEMBER?
YOU IDIOT! YOU'RE A GIRL! WHAT WOULD YOU KNOW ABOUT HOW A GUY WORKS?
C'MON, MIYAMURA!
I HAVE A BAD FEELING ABOUT THIS...

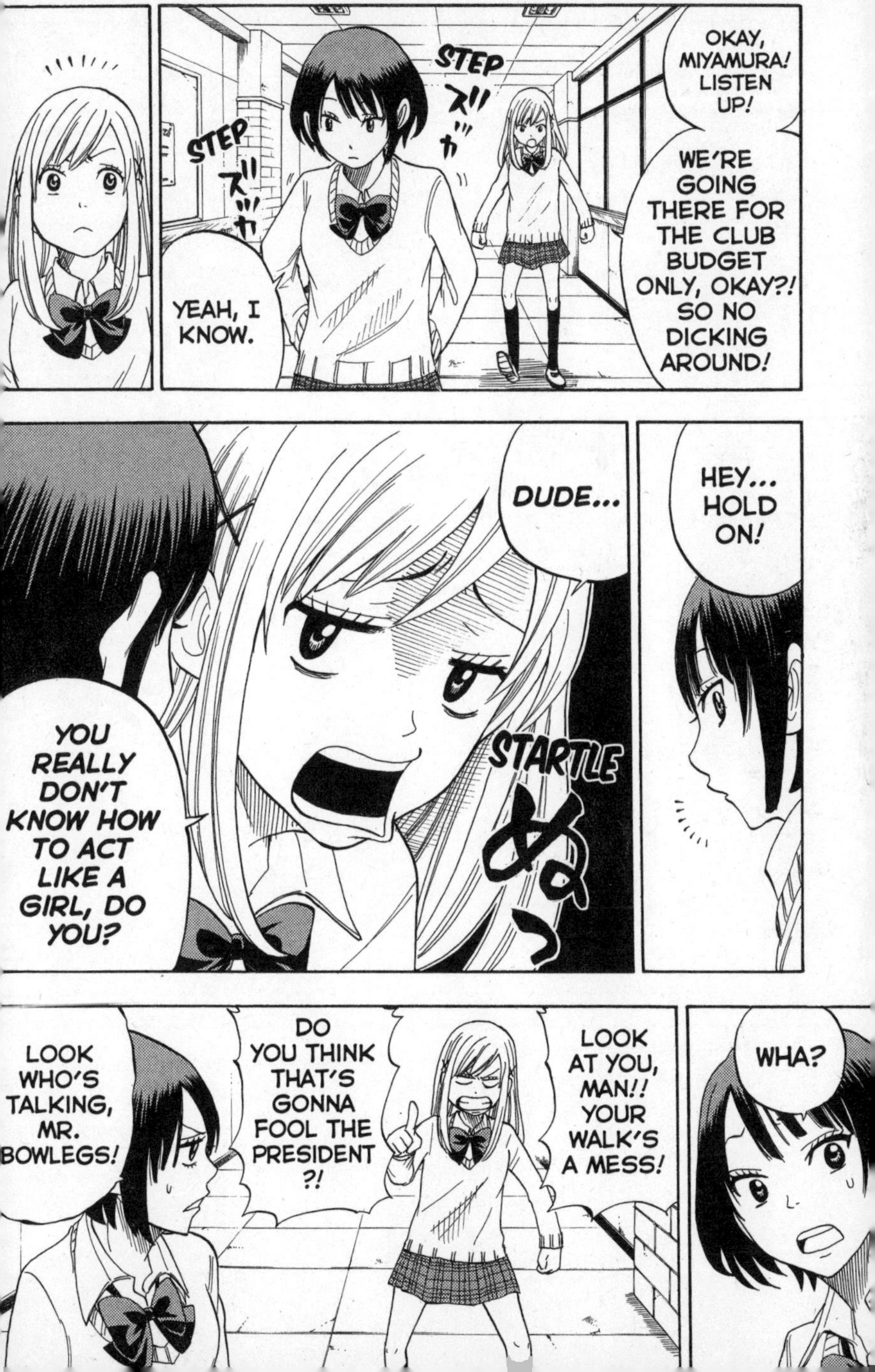

OKAY, MIYAMURA! LISTEN UP!
WE'RE GOING THERE FOR THE CLUB BUDGET ONLY, OKAY?! SO NO DICKING AROUND!
STEP ズッ ガ
STEP ズッ ガ
YEAH, I KNOW.
HEY... HOLD ON!
DUDE...
STARTLE ぬっ
YOU REALLY DON'T KNOW HOW TO ACT LIKE A GIRL, DO YOU?
WHA?
LOOK AT YOU, MAN!! YOUR WALK'S A MESS!
DO YOU THINK THAT'S GONNA FOOL THE PRESIDENT?!
LOOK WHO'S TALKING, MR. BOWLEGS!

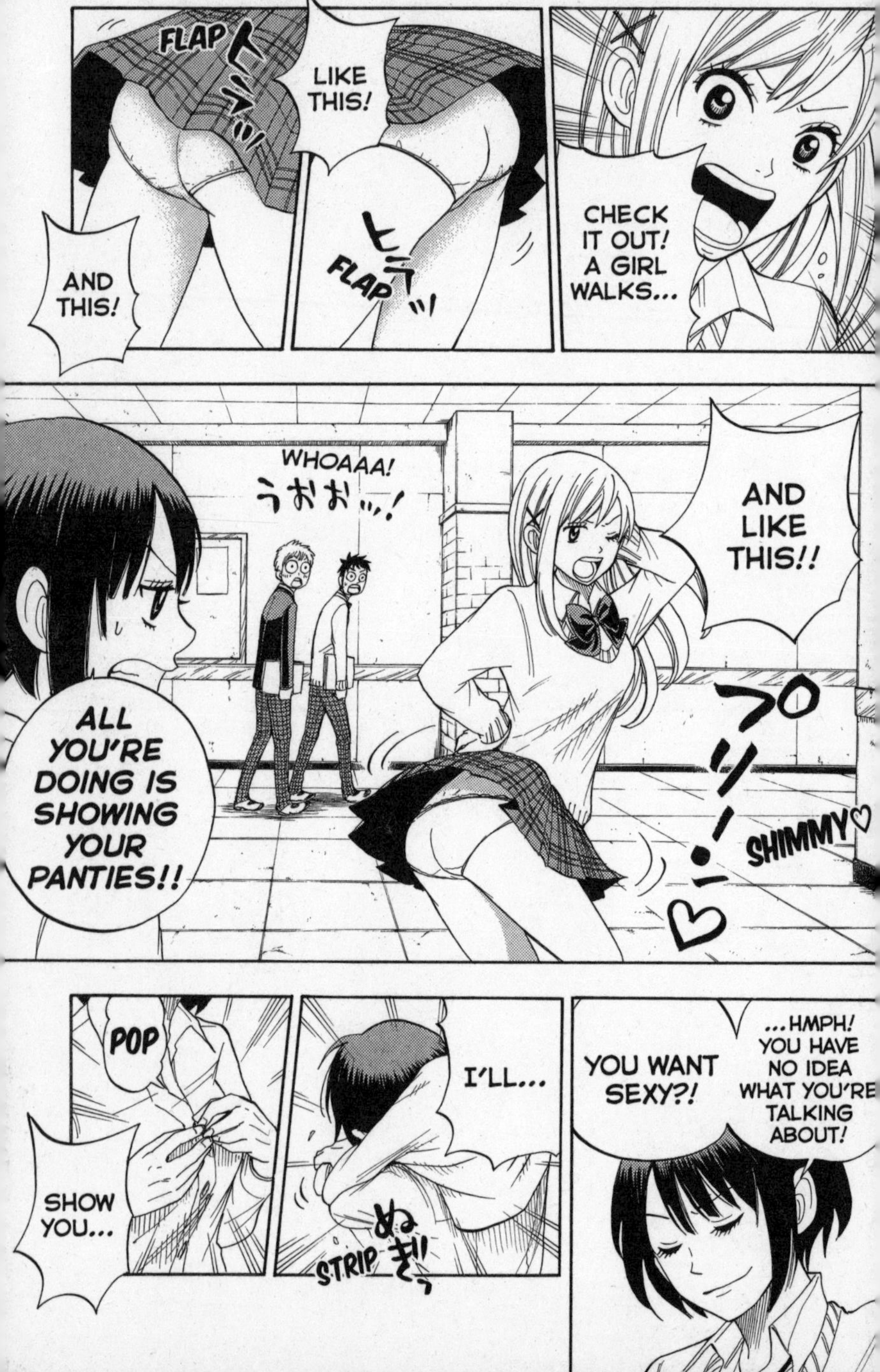

CHECK IT OUT! A GIRL WALKS...
LIKE THIS!
FLAP
ヒラッ
FLAP
ヒラッ
AND THIS!
AND LIKE THIS!!
SHIMMY♡
WHOAAA!
うおおっ…!
ALL YOU'RE DOING IS SHOWING YOUR PANTIES!!
...HMPH! YOU HAVE NO IDEA WHAT YOU'RE TALKING ABOUT!
YOU WANT SEXY?!
I'LL...
STRIP
ぬぎっ
POP
SHOW YOU...

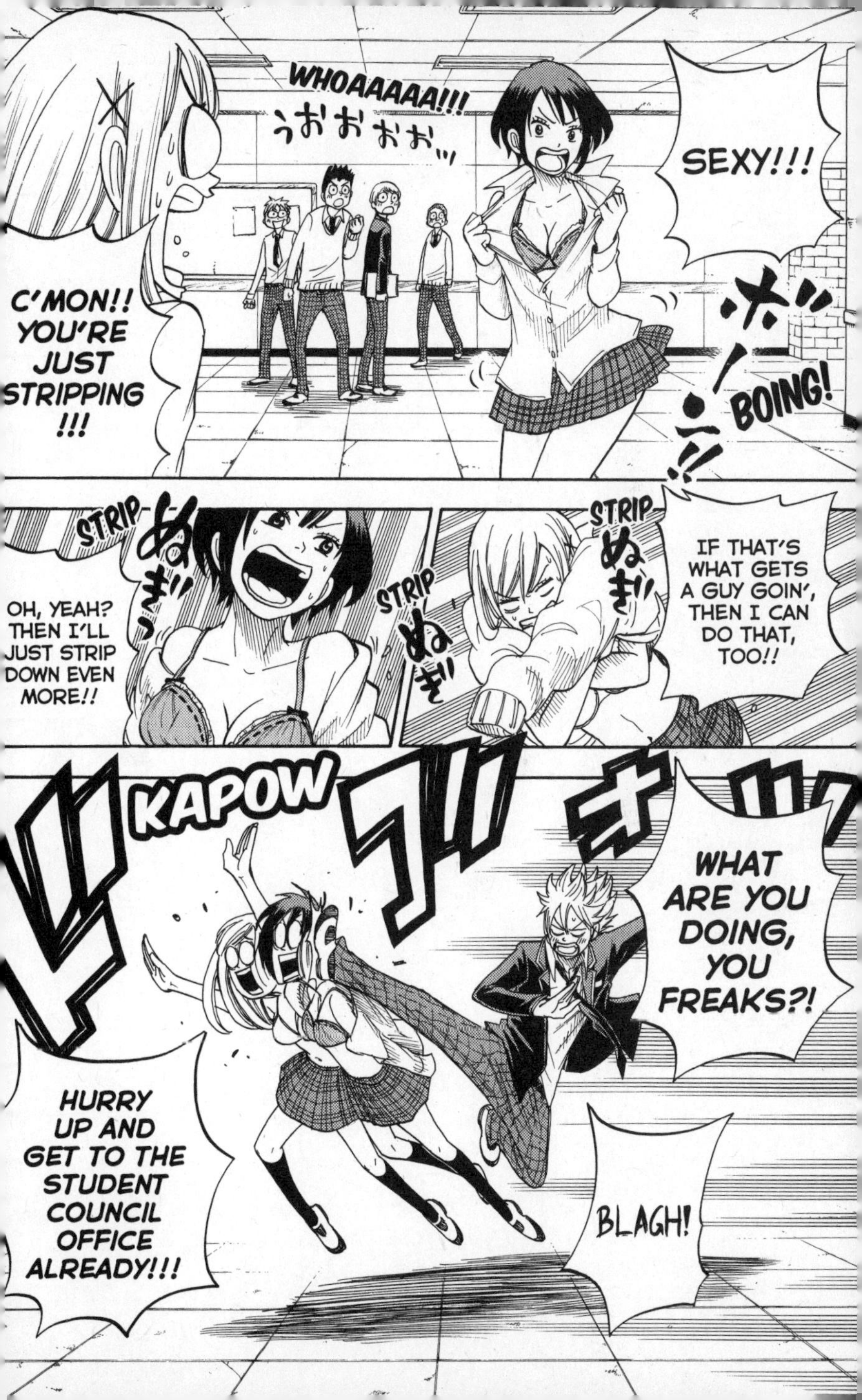
SEXY!!!
ボン!!
BOING!
WHOAAAAA!!!
うおおおおッ
C'MON!! YOU'RE JUST STRIPPING!!!
STRIP
ぬぎ
IF THAT'S WHAT GETS A GUY GOIN', THEN I CAN DO THAT, TOO!!
STRIP
ぬぎ
STRIP
ぬぎっ
OH, YEAH? THEN I'LL JUST STRIP DOWN EVEN MORE!!
WHAT ARE YOU DOING, YOU FREAKS?!
ドゴオッ
KAPOW
BLAGH!
HURRY UP AND GET TO THE STUDENT COUNCIL OFFICE ALREADY!!!

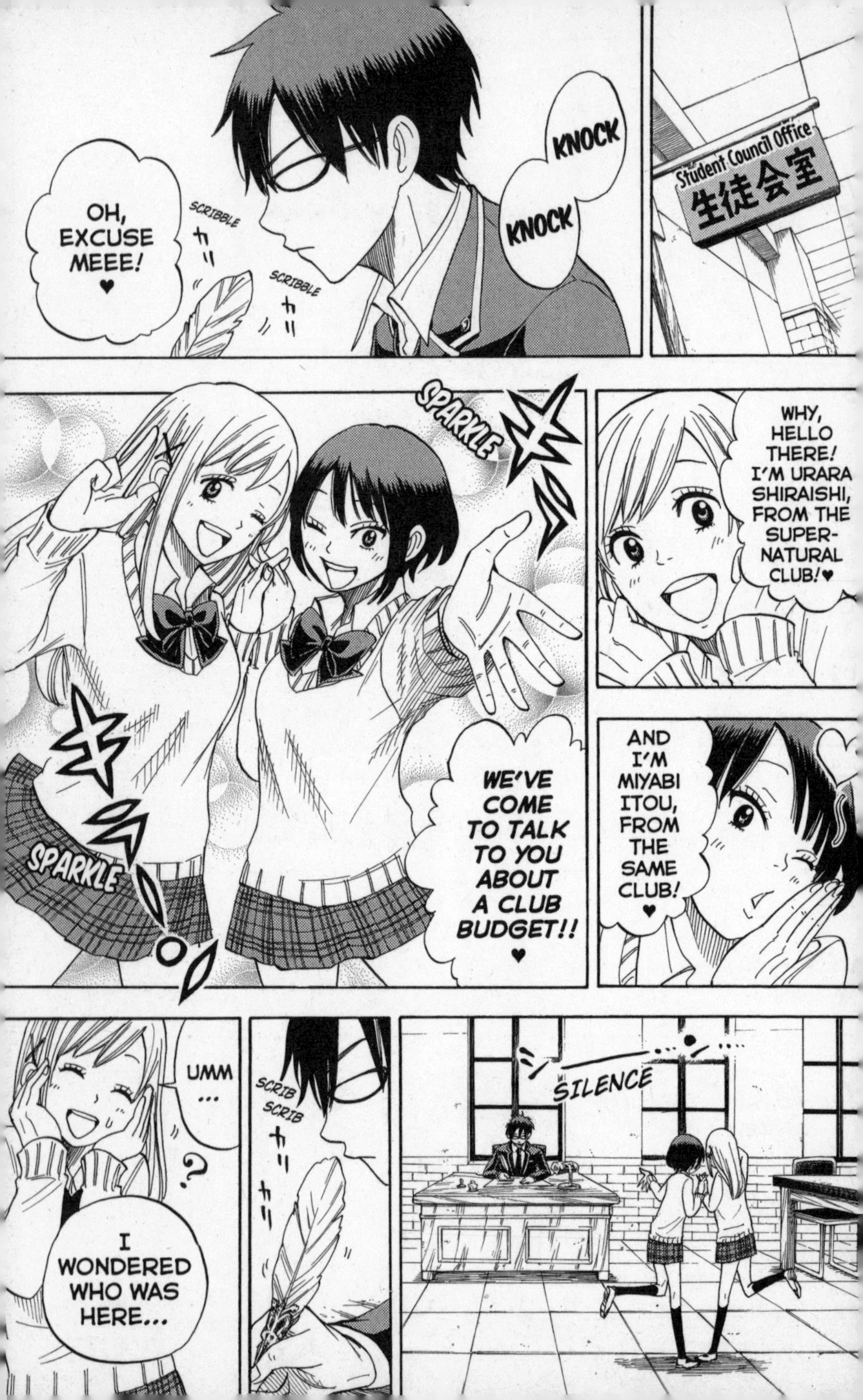
Student Council Office
生徒会室
KNOCK
KNOCK
SCRIBBLE
カリ
OH, EXCUSE MEEE! ♥
SCRIBBLE
カリ
WHY, HELLO THERE! I'M URARA SHIRAISHI, FROM THE SUPER-NATURAL CLUB! ♥
AND I'M MIYABI ITOU, FROM THE SAME CLUB! ♥
SPARKLE
WE'VE COME TO TALK TO YOU ABOUT A CLUB BUDGET!! ♥
SPARKLE
SILENCE
SCRIB
SCRIB
カリ
カリ
UMM...
?
I WONDERED WHO WAS HERE...

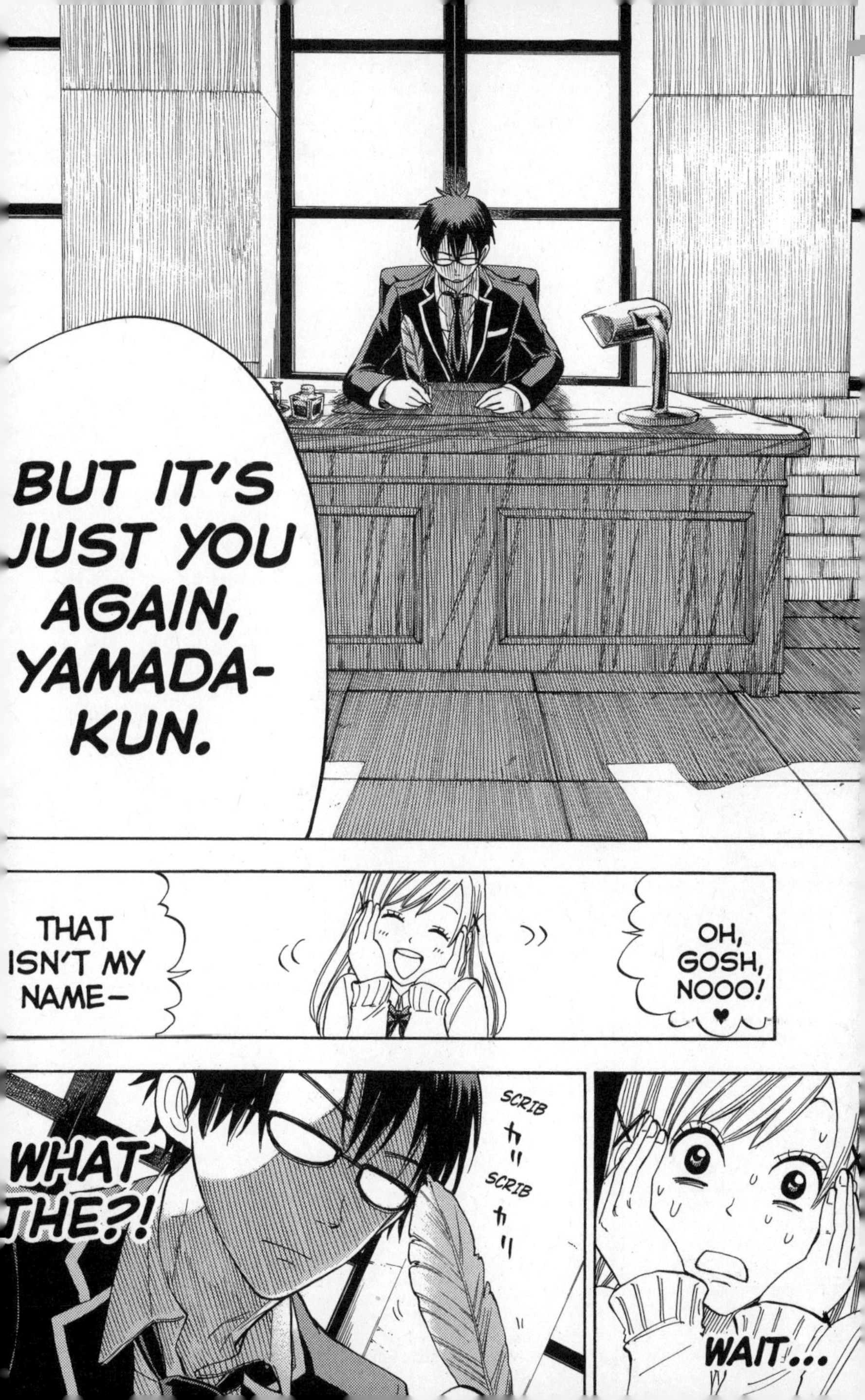
BUT IT'S JUST YOU AGAIN, YAMADA-KUN.
OH, GOSH, NOOO! ♥
THAT ISN'T MY NAME—
WAIT...
SCRIB
SCRIB
WHAT THE?!

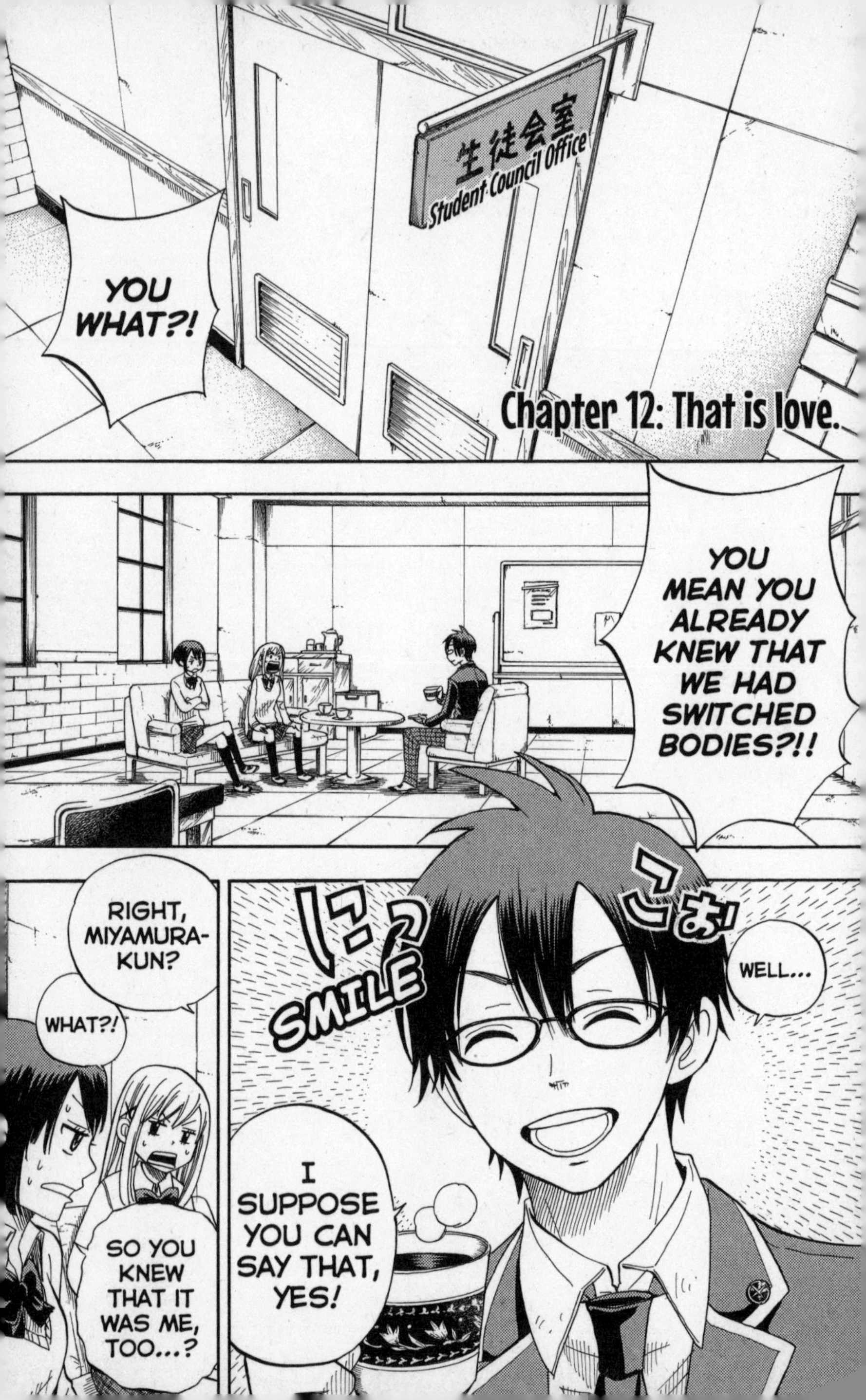
生徒会室
Student Council Office
YOU WHAT?!
Chapter 12: That is love.
YOU MEAN YOU ALREADY KNEW THAT WE HAD SWITCHED BODIES?!!
にっこぉ
SMILE
WELL...
I SUPPOSE YOU CAN SAY THAT, YES!
RIGHT, MIYAMURA-KUN?
WHAT?!
SO YOU KNEW THAT IT WAS ME, TOO...?

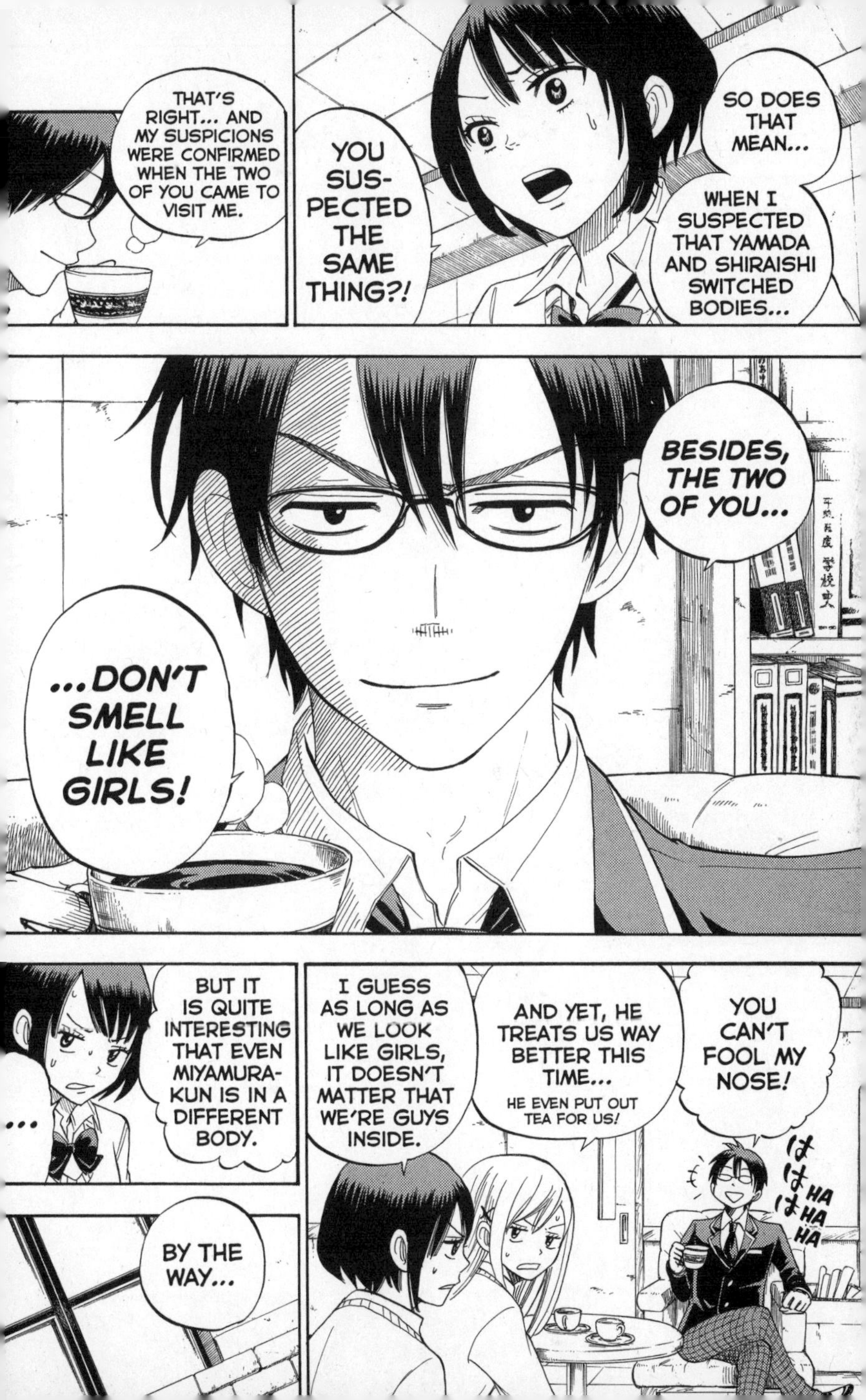
SO DOES THAT MEAN...
WHEN I SUSPECTED THAT YAMADA AND SHIRAISHI SWITCHED BODIES...
YOU SUSPECTED THE SAME THING?!
THAT'S RIGHT... AND MY SUSPICIONS WERE CONFIRMED WHEN THE TWO OF YOU CAME TO VISIT ME.
BESIDES, THE TWO OF YOU...
...DON'T SMELL LIKE GIRLS!
YOU CAN'T FOOL MY NOSE!
ははは
HA HA HA
AND YET, HE TREATS US WAY BETTER THIS TIME...
HE EVEN PUT OUT TEA FOR US!
I GUESS AS LONG AS WE LOOK LIKE GIRLS, IT DOESN'T MATTER THAT WE'RE GUYS INSIDE.
...
BUT IT IS QUITE INTERESTING THAT EVEN MIYAMURA-KUN IS IN A DIFFERENT BODY.
BY THE WAY...

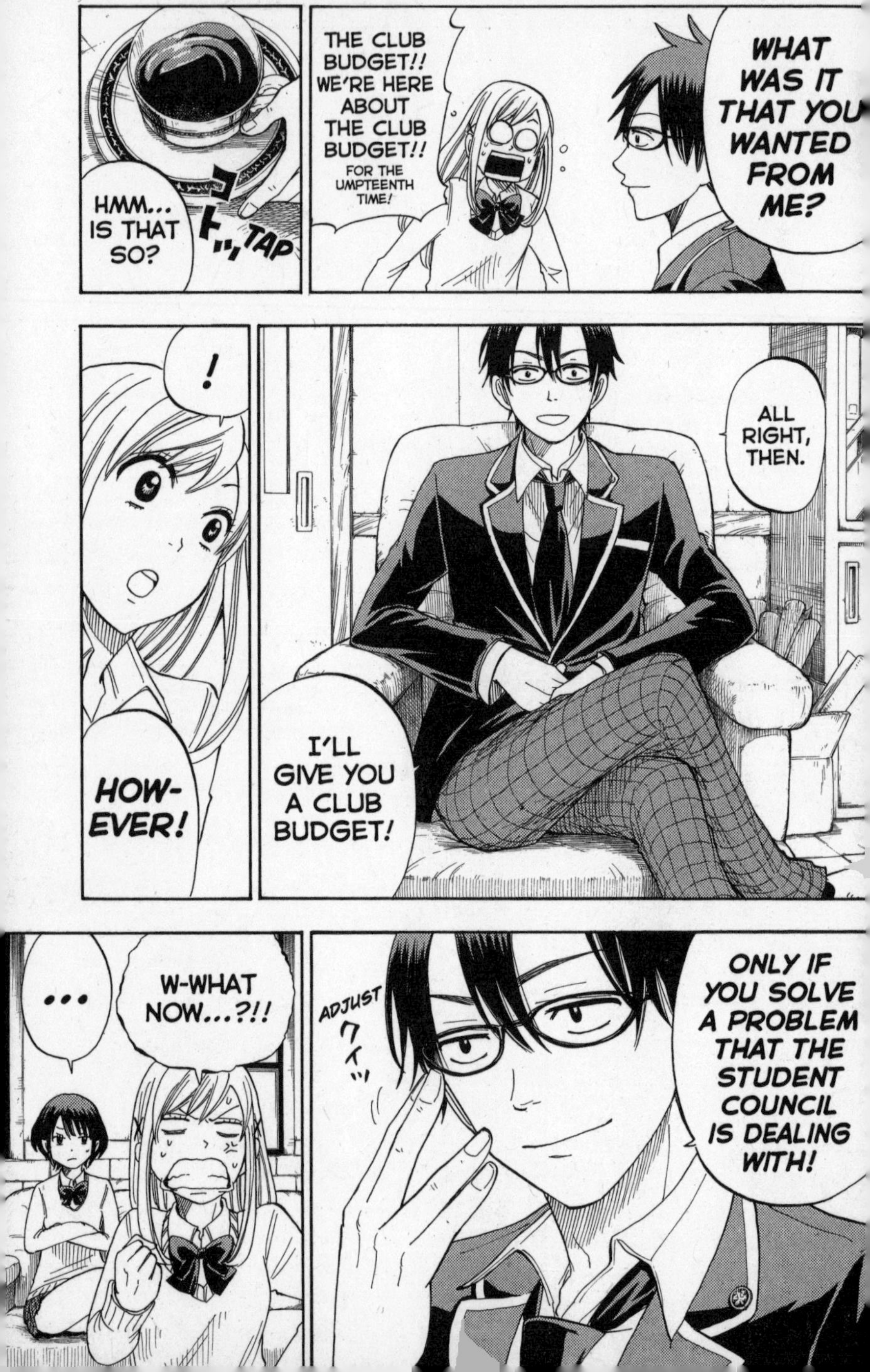
WHAT WAS IT THAT YOU WANTED FROM ME?
THE CLUB BUDGET!! WE'RE HERE ABOUT THE CLUB BUDGET!!
FOR THE UMPTEENTH TIME!
HMM... IS THAT SO?
TAP
ALL RIGHT, THEN.
I'LL GIVE YOU A CLUB BUDGET!
!
HOW-EVER!
ONLY IF YOU SOLVE A PROBLEM THAT THE STUDENT COUNCIL IS DEALING WITH!
ADJUST
W-WHAT NOW...?!!
...

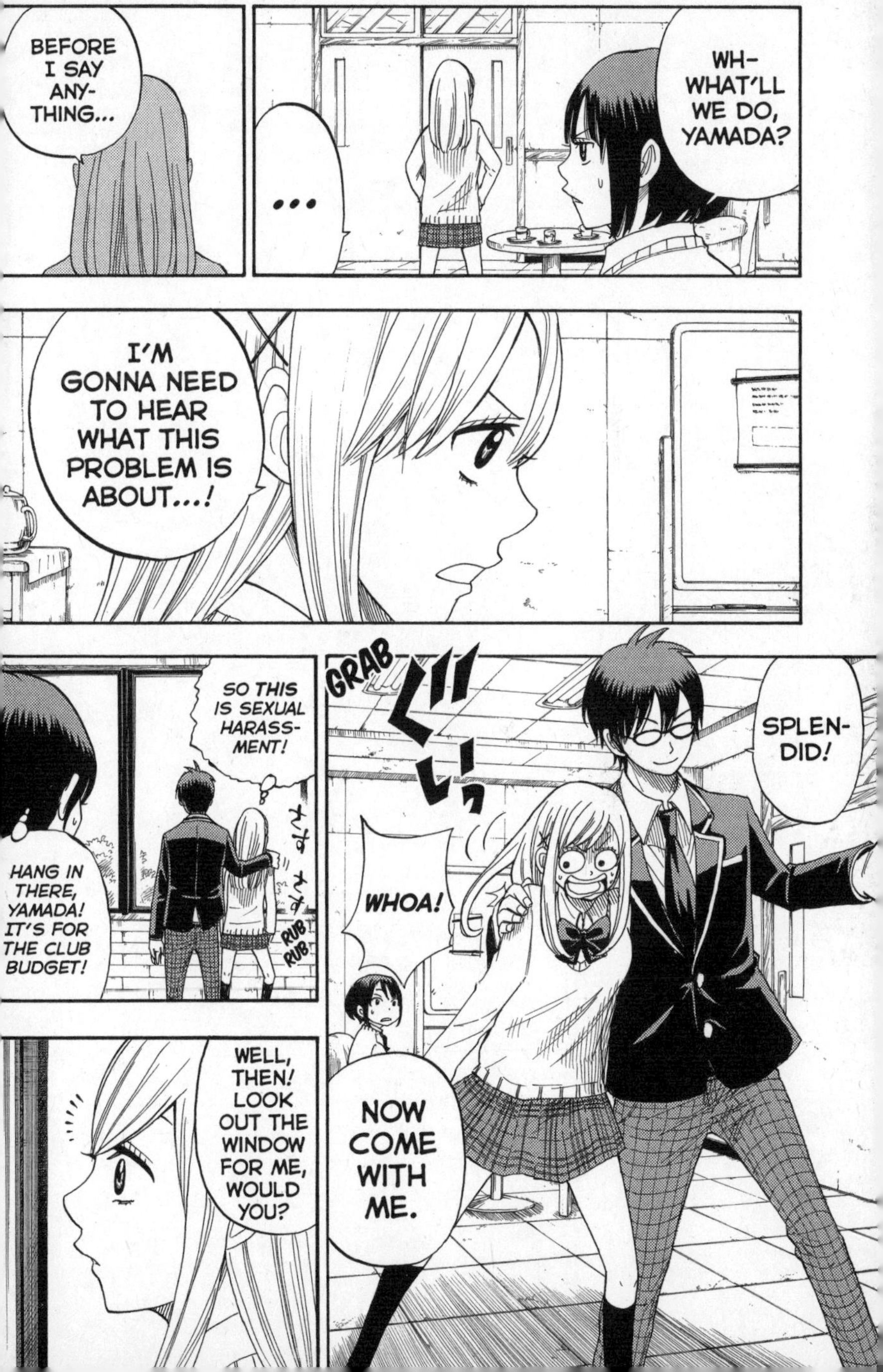
WH- WHAT'LL WE DO, YAMADA?
...
BEFORE I SAY ANYTHING...
I'M GONNA NEED TO HEAR WHAT THIS PROBLEM IS ABOUT...!
SPLENDID!
GRAB
WHOA!
NOW COME WITH ME.
SO THIS IS SEXUAL HARASSMENT!
RUB RUB
HANG IN THERE, YAMADA! IT'S FOR THE CLUB BUDGET!
WELL, THEN! LOOK OUT THE WINDOW FOR ME, WOULD YOU?

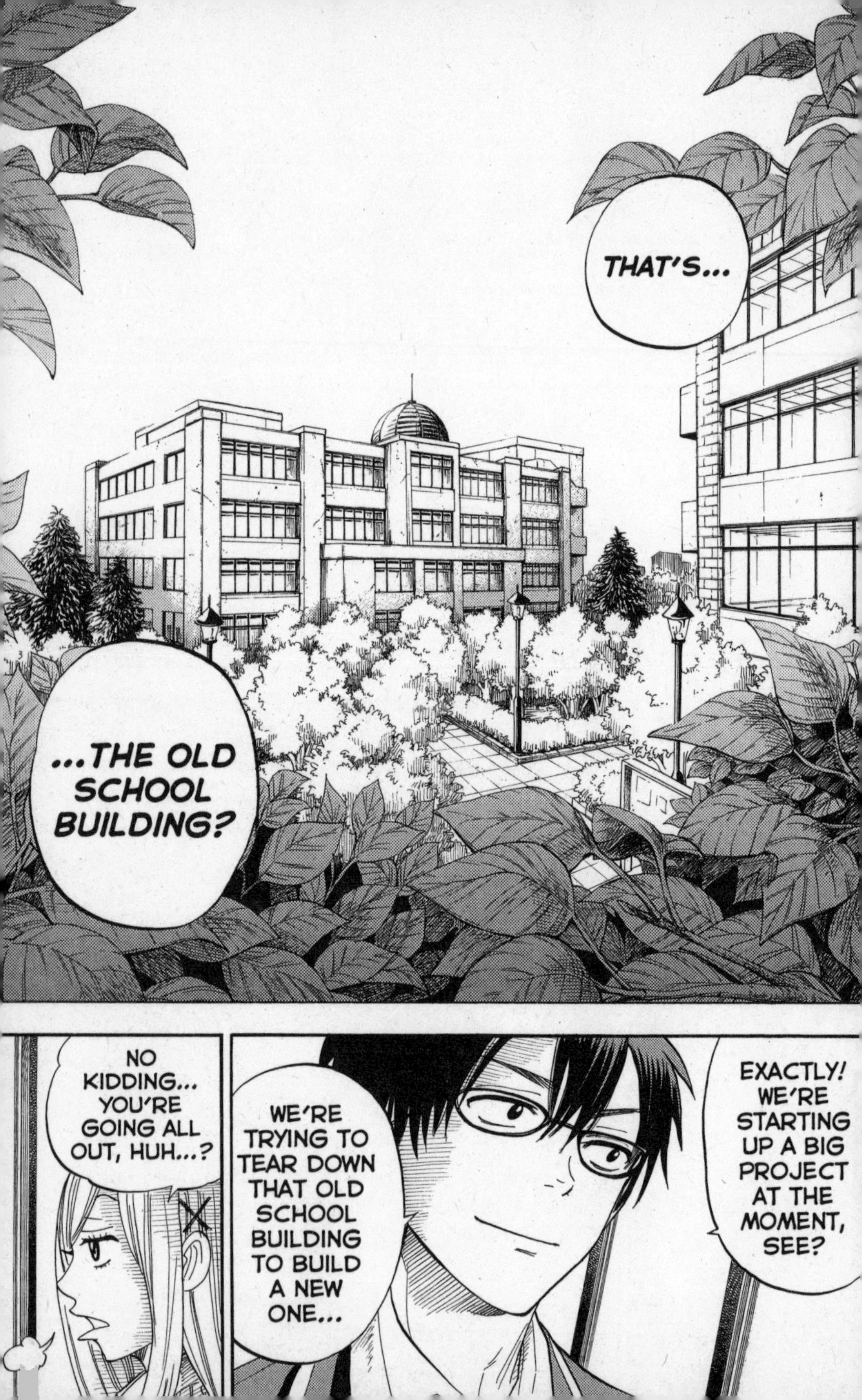
THAT'S...
...THE OLD SCHOOL BUILDING?
EXACTLY! WE'RE STARTING UP A BIG PROJECT AT THE MOMENT, SEE?
WE'RE TRYING TO TEAR DOWN THAT OLD SCHOOL BUILDING TO BUILD A NEW ONE...
NO KIDDING... YOU'RE GOING ALL OUT, HUH...?

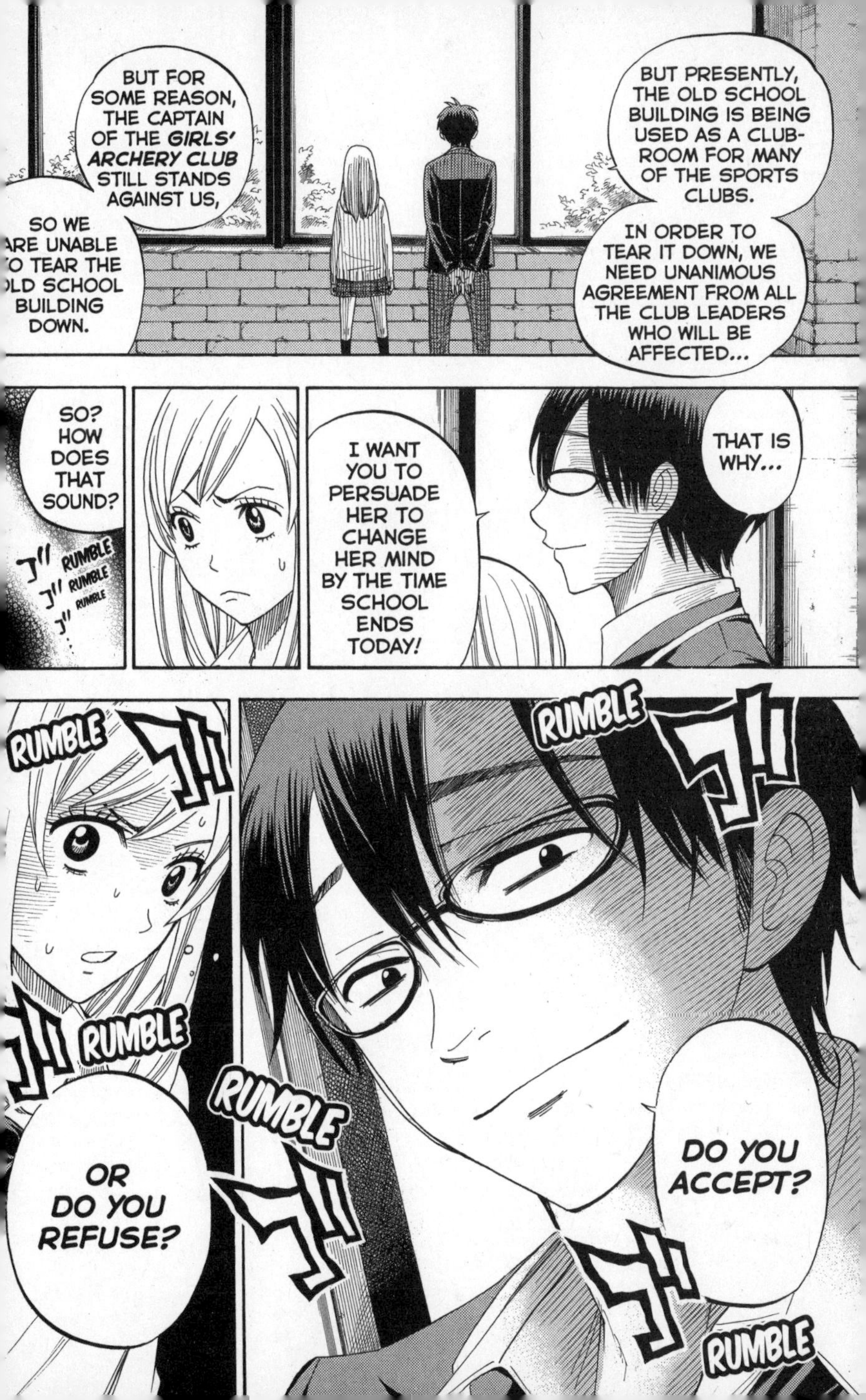
BUT PRESENTLY, THE OLD SCHOOL BUILDING IS BEING USED AS A CLUB-ROOM FOR MANY OF THE SPORTS CLUBS.
IN ORDER TO TEAR IT DOWN, WE NEED UNANIMOUS AGREEMENT FROM ALL THE CLUB LEADERS WHO WILL BE AFFECTED...
BUT FOR SOME REASON, THE CAPTAIN OF THE *GIRLS' ARCHERY CLUB* STILL STANDS AGAINST US,
SO WE ARE UNABLE TO TEAR THE OLD SCHOOL BUILDING DOWN.
THAT IS WHY...
I WANT YOU TO PERSUADE HER TO CHANGE HER MIND BY THE TIME SCHOOL ENDS TODAY!
SO? HOW DOES THAT SOUND?
RUMBLE
RUMBLE
RUMBLE
RUMBLE
DO YOU ACCEPT?
RUMBLE
RUMBLE
RUMBLE
RUMBLE
OR DO YOU REFUSE?

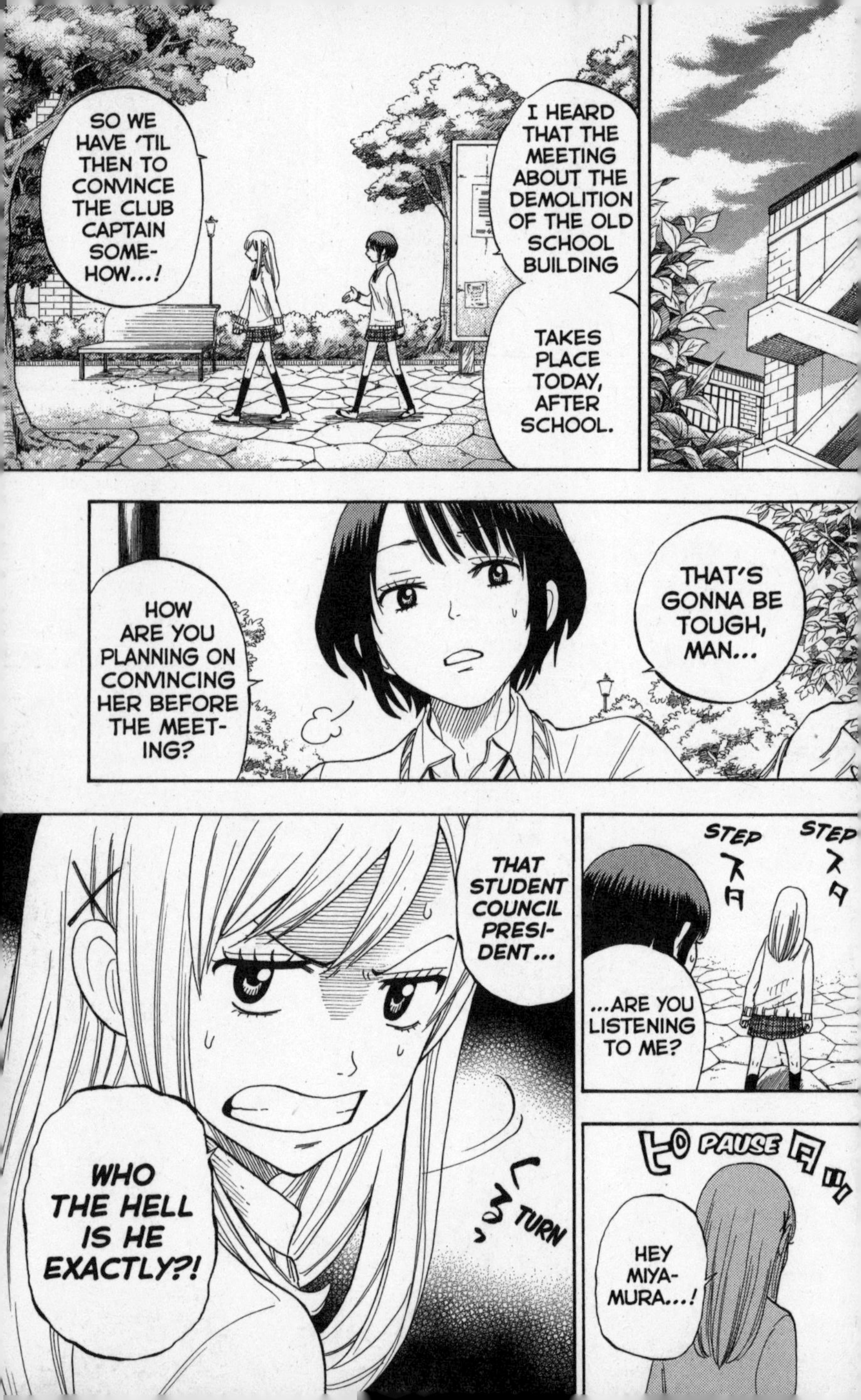
I HEARD THAT THE MEETING ABOUT THE DEMOLITION OF THE OLD SCHOOL BUILDING
TAKES PLACE TODAY, AFTER SCHOOL.
SO WE HAVE 'TIL THEN TO CONVINCE THE CLUB CAPTAIN SOMEHOW...!
THAT'S GONNA BE TOUGH, MAN...
HOW ARE YOU PLANNING ON CONVINCING HER BEFORE THE MEETING?
STEP
STEP
...ARE YOU LISTENING TO ME?
PAUSE
HEY MIYAMURA...!
THAT STUDENT COUNCIL PRESIDENT...
TURN
WHO THE HELL IS HE EXACTLY?!

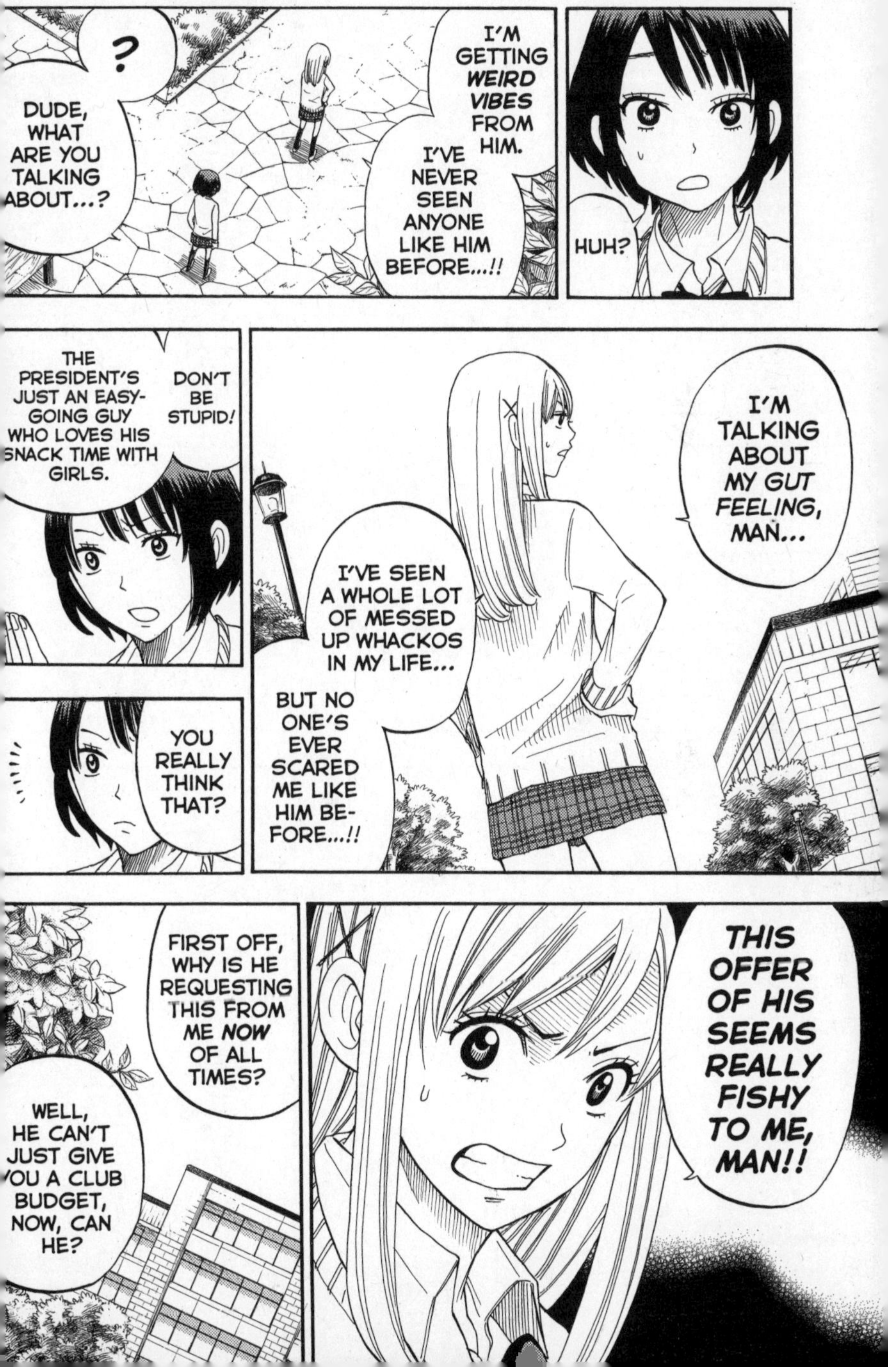
HUH?
I'M GETTING *WEIRD VIBES* FROM HIM.
I'VE NEVER SEEN ANYONE LIKE HIM BEFORE...!!
?
DUDE, WHAT ARE YOU TALKING ABOUT...?
I'M TALKING ABOUT *MY GUT* FEELING, MAN...
I'VE SEEN A WHOLE LOT OF MESSED UP WHACKOS IN MY LIFE...
BUT NO ONE'S EVER SCARED ME LIKE HIM BEFORE...!!
DON'T BE STUPID!
THE PRESIDENT'S JUST AN EASY-GOING GUY WHO LOVES HIS SNACK TIME WITH GIRLS.
YOU REALLY THINK THAT?
THIS OFFER OF HIS SEEMS REALLY FISHY TO ME, MAN!!
FIRST OFF, WHY IS HE REQUESTING THIS FROM ME *NOW* OF ALL TIMES?
WELL, HE CAN'T JUST GIVE YOU A CLUB BUDGET, NOW, CAN HE?

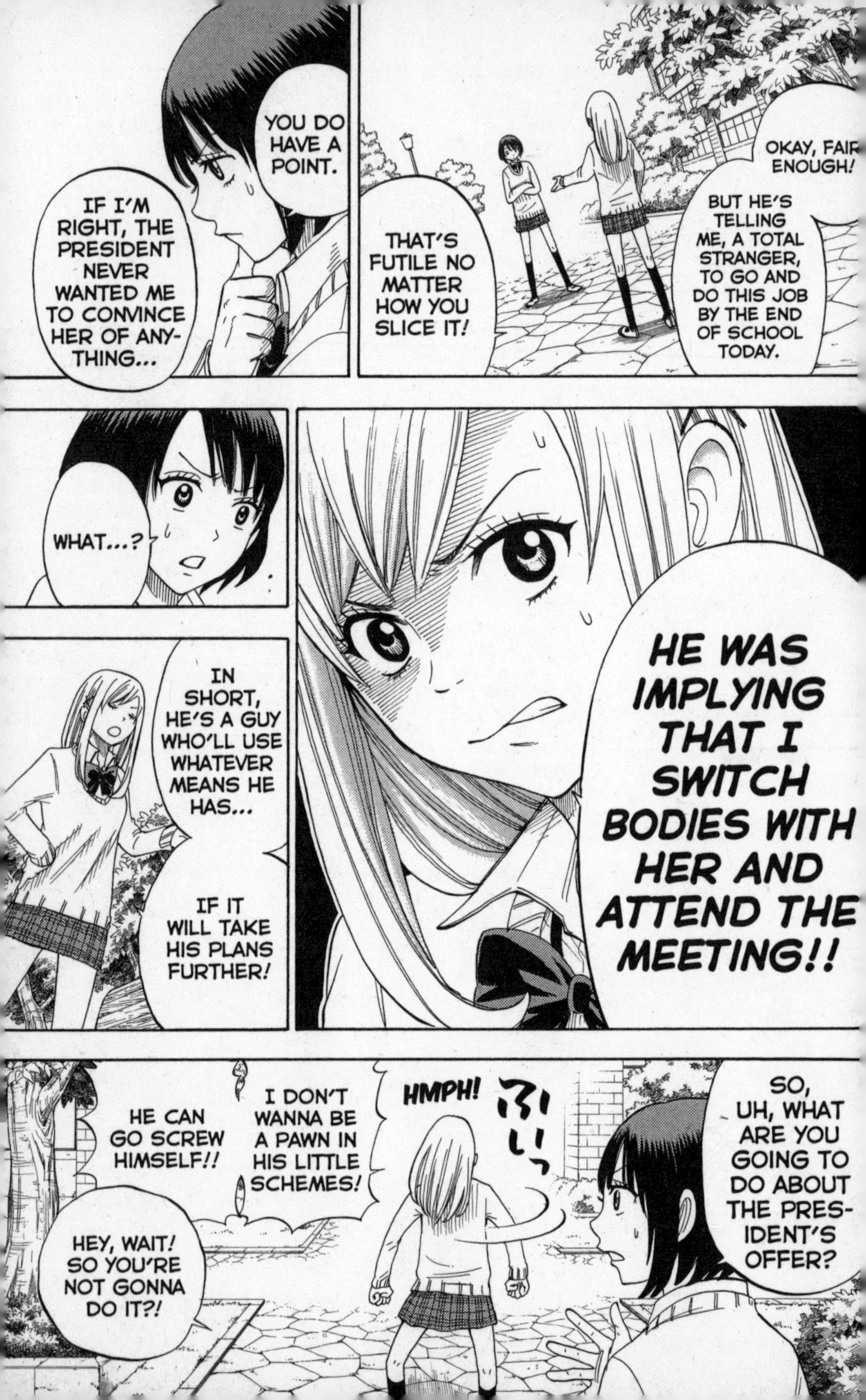
OKAY, FAIR ENOUGH!
BUT HE'S TELLING ME, A TOTAL STRANGER, TO GO AND DO THIS JOB BY THE END OF SCHOOL TODAY.
THAT'S FUTILE NO MATTER HOW YOU SLICE IT!
YOU DO HAVE A POINT.
IF I'M RIGHT, THE PRESIDENT NEVER WANTED ME TO CONVINCE HER OF ANYTHING...
HE WAS IMPLYING THAT I SWITCH BODIES WITH HER AND ATTEND THE MEETING!!
WHAT...?
IN SHORT, HE'S A GUY WHO'LL USE WHATEVER MEANS HE HAS...
IF IT WILL TAKE HIS PLANS FURTHER!
SO, UH, WHAT ARE YOU GOING TO DO ABOUT THE PRES-IDENT'S OFFER?
HMPH!
ふいっ
I DON'T WANNA BE A PAWN IN HIS LITTLE SCHEMES!
HE CAN GO SCREW HIMSELF!!
HEY, WAIT! SO YOU'RE NOT GONNA DO IT?!

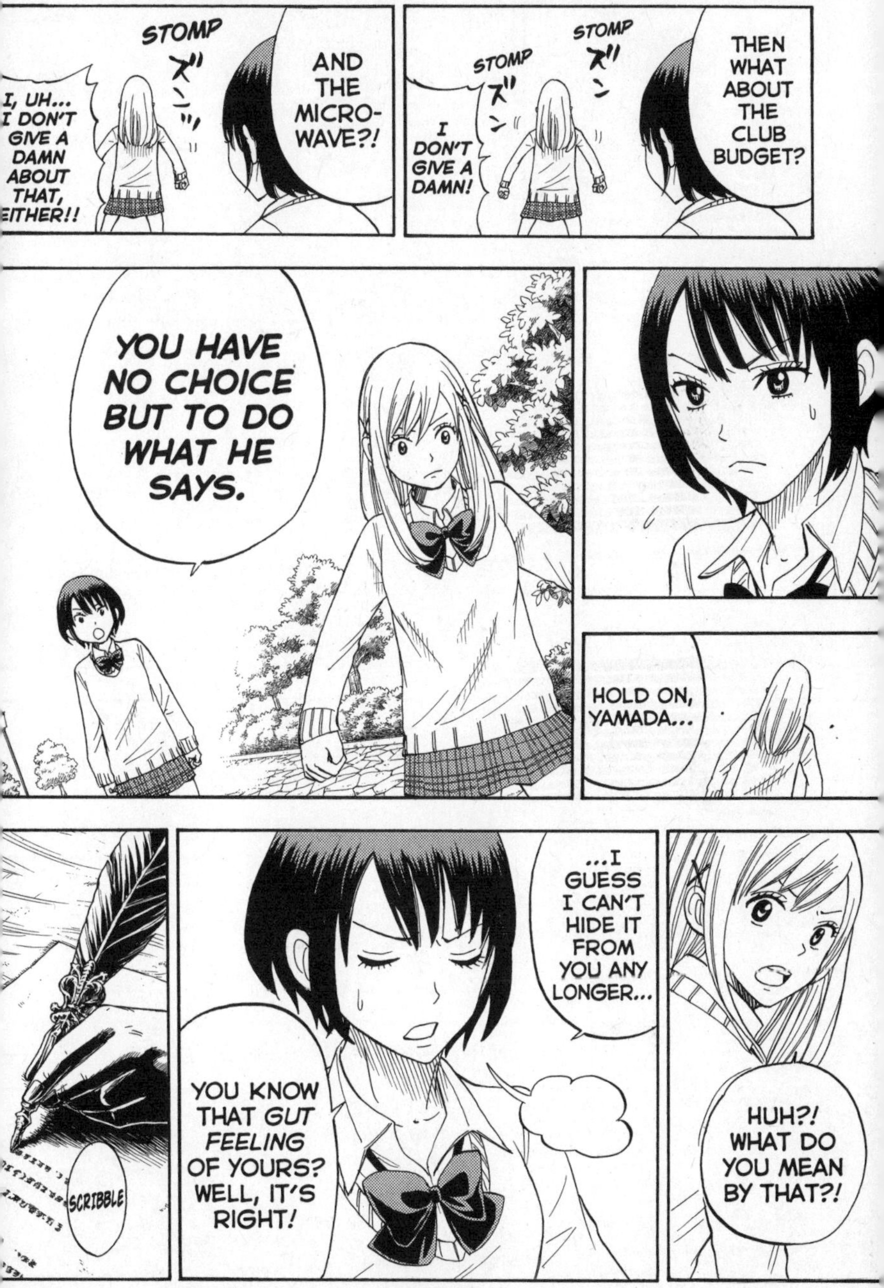
THEN WHAT ABOUT THE CLUB BUDGET?
STOMP
ズン
STOMP
ズン
I DON'T GIVE A DAMN!
AND THE MICRO-WAVE?!
STOMP
ズン
I, UH... I DON'T GIVE A DAMN ABOUT THAT, EITHER!!
HOLD ON, YAMADA...
YOU HAVE NO CHOICE BUT TO DO WHAT HE SAYS.
HUH?! WHAT DO YOU MEAN BY THAT?!
...I GUESS I CAN'T HIDE IT FROM YOU ANY LONGER...
YOU KNOW THAT *GUT* FEELING OF YOURS? WELL, IT'S RIGHT!
SCRIBBLE

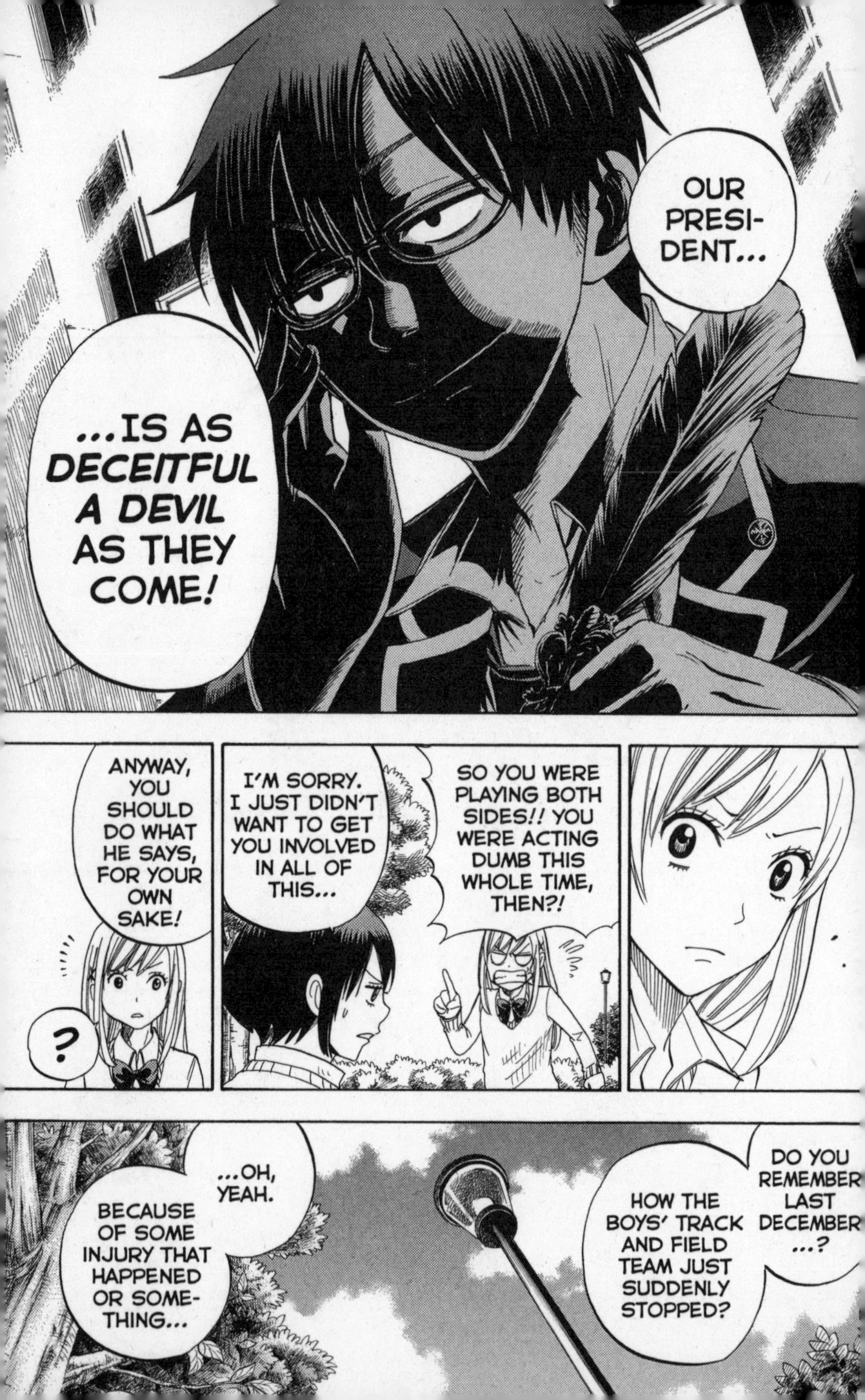
OUR PRESIDENT...
...IS AS DECEITFUL A DEVIL AS THEY COME!
SO YOU WERE PLAYING BOTH SIDES!! YOU WERE ACTING DUMB THIS WHOLE TIME, THEN?!
I'M SORRY. I JUST DIDN'T WANT TO GET YOU INVOLVED IN ALL OF THIS...
ANYWAY, YOU SHOULD DO WHAT HE SAYS, FOR YOUR OWN SAKE!
?
DO YOU REMEMBER LAST DECEMBER...?
HOW THE BOYS' TRACK AND FIELD TEAM JUST SUDDENLY STOPPED?
...OH, YEAH.
BECAUSE OF SOME INJURY THAT HAPPENED OR SOMETHING...

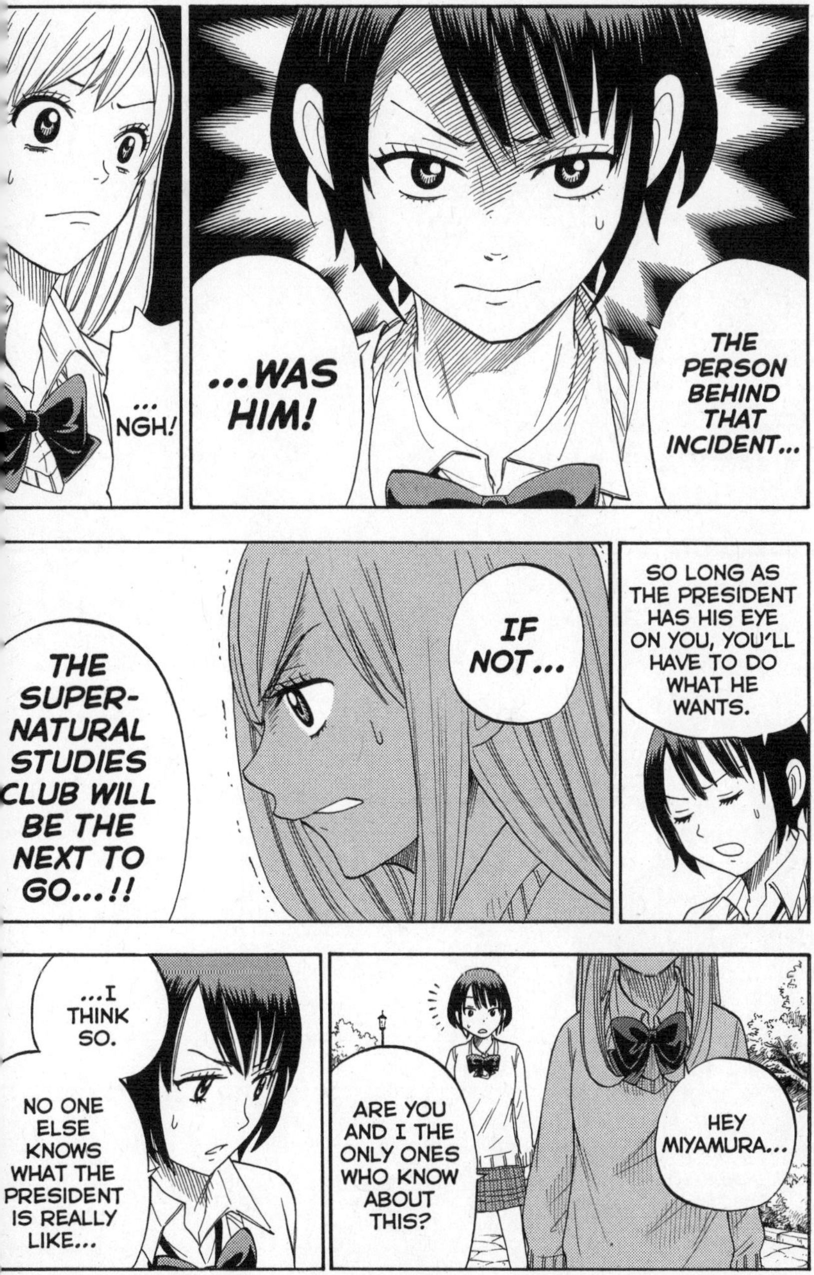
THE PERSON BEHIND THAT INCIDENT...
...WAS HIM!
...NGH!
SO LONG AS THE PRESIDENT HAS HIS EYE ON YOU, YOU'LL HAVE TO DO WHAT HE WANTS.
IF NOT...
THE SUPER-NATURAL STUDIES CLUB WILL BE THE NEXT TO GO...!!
HEY MIYAMURA...
ARE YOU AND I THE ONLY ONES WHO KNOW ABOUT THIS?
...I THINK SO.
NO ONE ELSE KNOWS WHAT THE PRESIDENT IS REALLY LIKE...

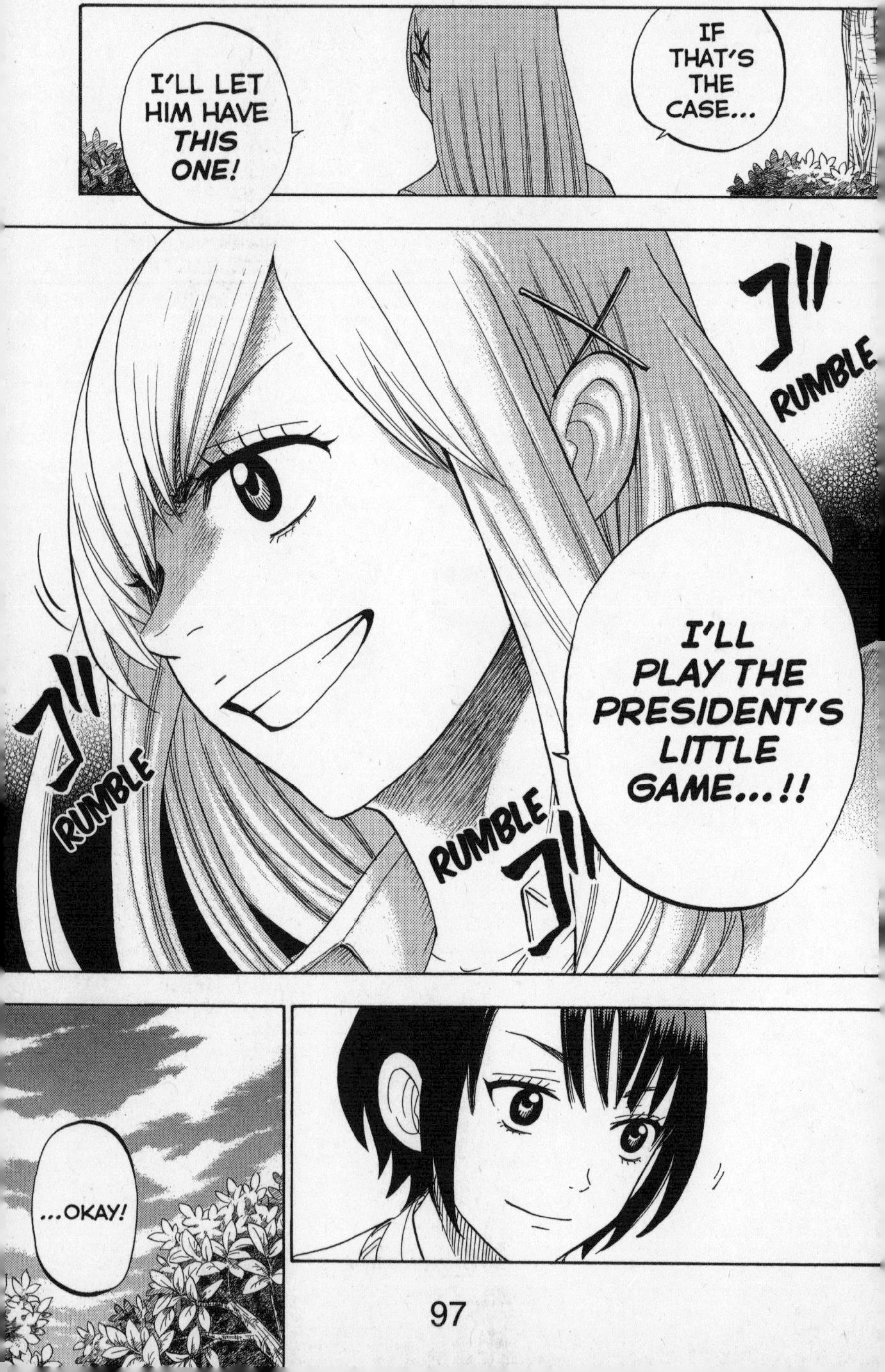
IF THAT'S THE CASE...
I'LL LET HIM HAVE THIS ONE!
RUMBLE
I'LL PLAY THE PRESIDENT'S LITTLE GAME...!!
RUMBLE
RUMBLE
...OKAY!

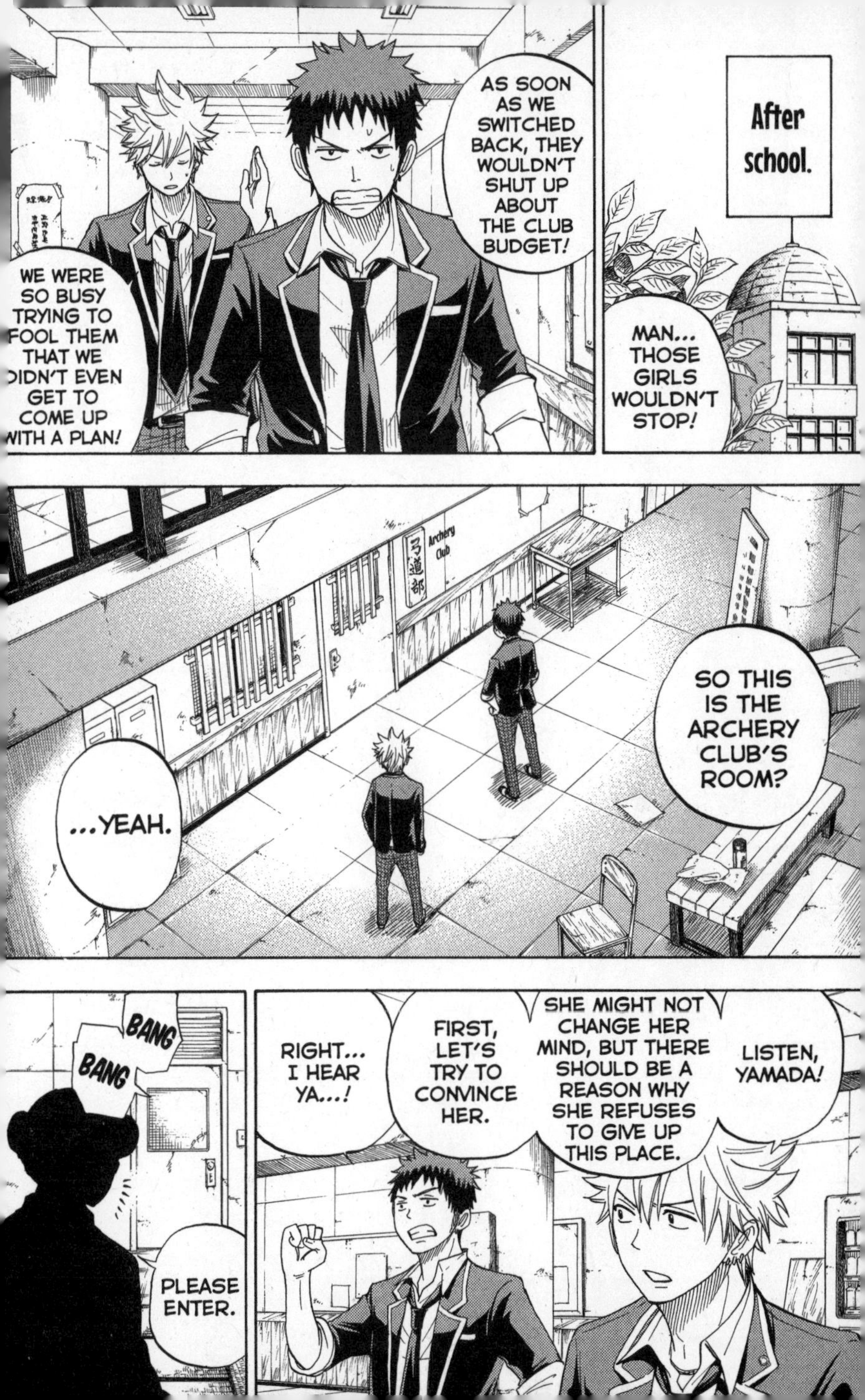
After school.
MAN... THOSE GIRLS WOULDN'T STOP!
AS SOON AS WE SWITCHED BACK, THEY WOULDN'T SHUT UP ABOUT THE CLUB BUDGET!
WE WERE SO BUSY TRYING TO FOOL THEM THAT WE DIDN'T EVEN GET TO COME UP WITH A PLAN!
弓道部
Archery Club
SO THIS IS THE ARCHERY CLUB'S ROOM?
...YEAH.
LISTEN, YAMADA!
SHE MIGHT NOT CHANGE HER MIND, BUT THERE SHOULD BE A REASON WHY SHE REFUSES TO GIVE UP THIS PLACE.
FIRST, LET'S TRY TO CONVINCE HER.
RIGHT... I HEAR YA...!
BANG
BANG
PLEASE ENTER.

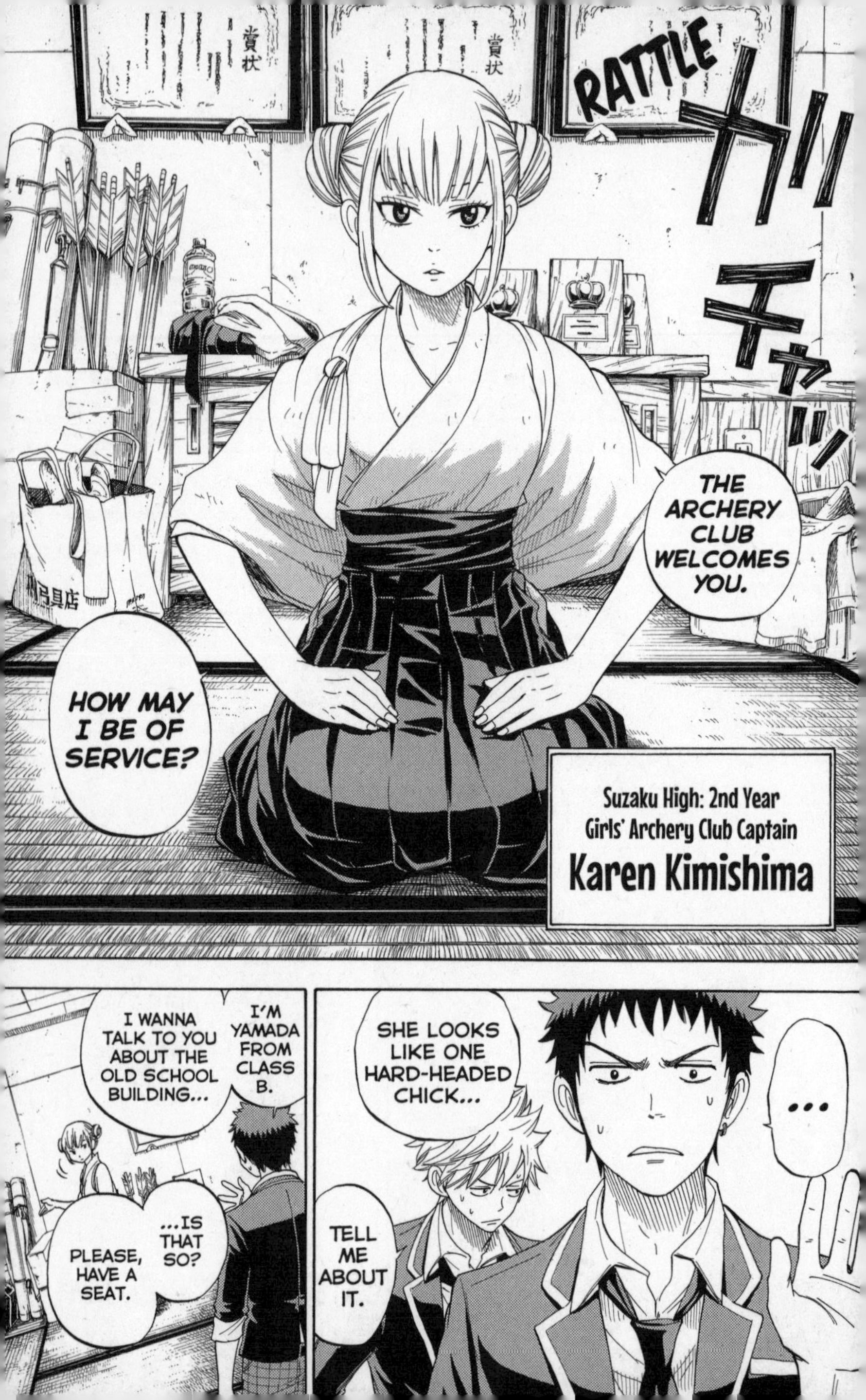
RATTLE
THE ARCHERY CLUB WELCOMES YOU.
HOW MAY I BE OF SERVICE?
Suzaku High: 2nd Year
Girls' Archery Club Captain
Karen Kimishima
...
SHE LOOKS LIKE ONE HARD-HEADED CHICK...
TELL ME ABOUT IT.
I'M YAMADA FROM CLASS B.
I WANNA TALK TO YOU ABOUT THE OLD SCHOOL BUILDING...
...IS THAT SO?
PLEASE, HAVE A SEAT.

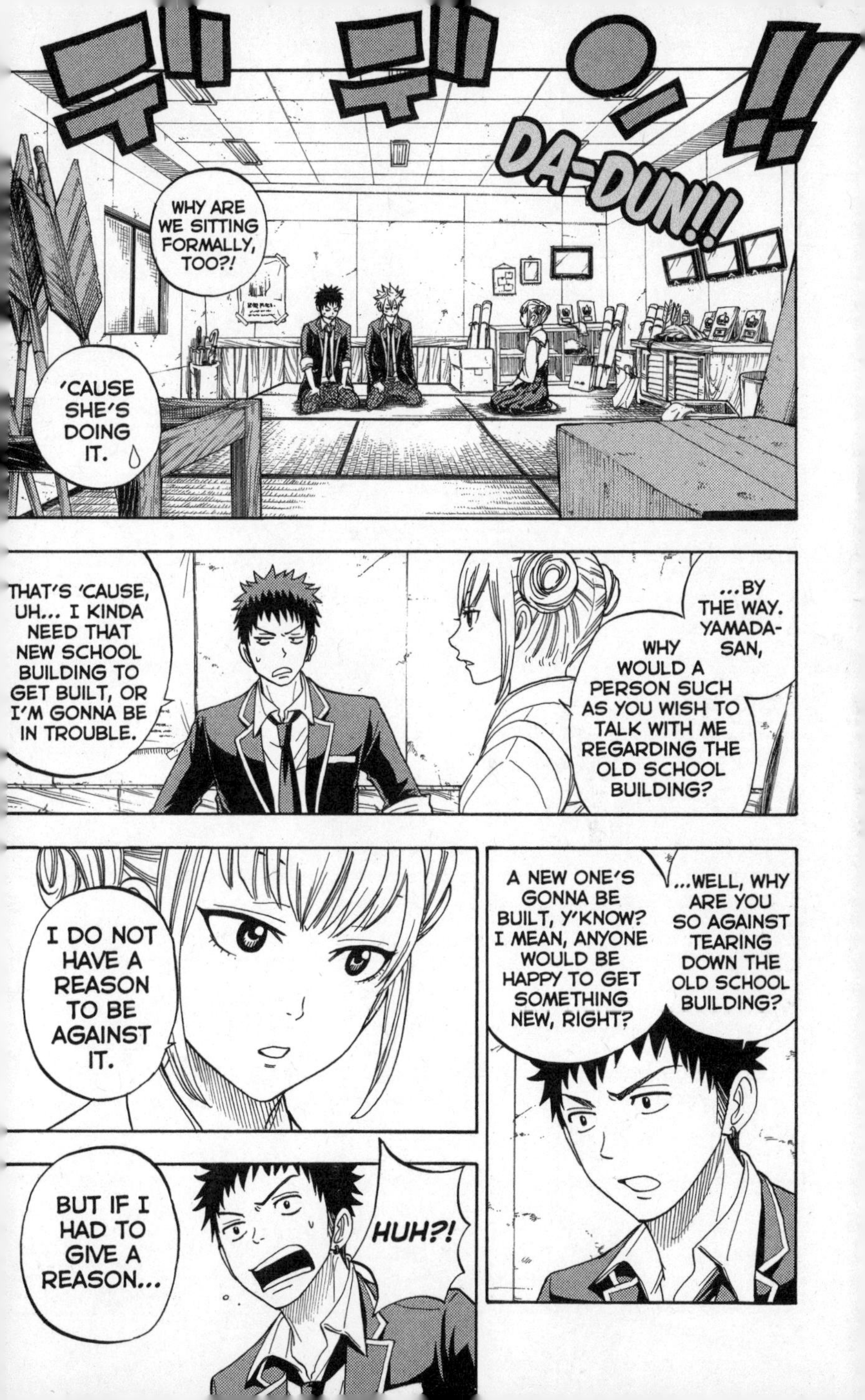
DA-DUN!!
WHY ARE WE SITTING FORMALLY, TOO?!
'CAUSE SHE'S DOING IT.
...BY THE WAY. YAMADA-SAN, WHY WOULD A PERSON SUCH AS YOU WISH TO TALK WITH ME REGARDING THE OLD SCHOOL BUILDING?
THAT'S 'CAUSE, UH... I KINDA NEED THAT NEW SCHOOL BUILDING TO GET BUILT, OR I'M GONNA BE IN TROUBLE.
...WELL, WHY ARE YOU SO AGAINST TEARING DOWN THE OLD SCHOOL BUILDING?
A NEW ONE'S GONNA BE BUILT, Y'KNOW? I MEAN, ANYONE WOULD BE HAPPY TO GET SOMETHING NEW, RIGHT?
I DO NOT HAVE A REASON TO BE AGAINST IT.
HUH?!
BUT IF I HAD TO GIVE A REASON...

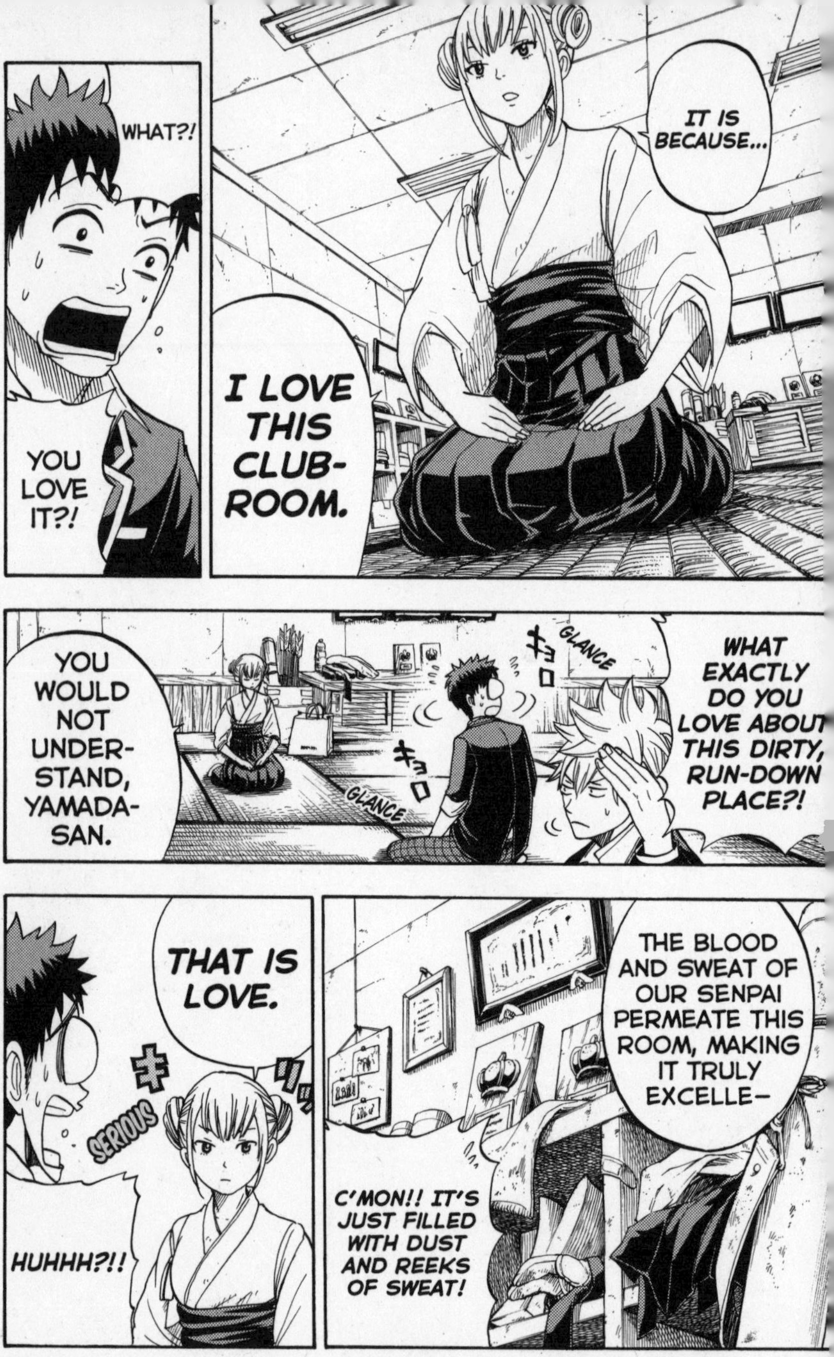
IT IS BECAUSE...
I LOVE THIS CLUB-ROOM.
WHAT?!
YOU LOVE IT?!
WHAT EXACTLY DO YOU LOVE ABOUT THIS DIRTY, RUN-DOWN PLACE?!
GLANCE
GLANCE
YOU WOULD NOT UNDER-STAND, YAMADA-SAN.
THE BLOOD AND SWEAT OF OUR SENPAI PERMEATE THIS ROOM, MAKING IT TRULY EXCELLE–
C'MON!! IT'S JUST FILLED WITH DUST AND REEKS OF SWEAT!
THAT IS LOVE.
SERIOUS
HUHHH?!!

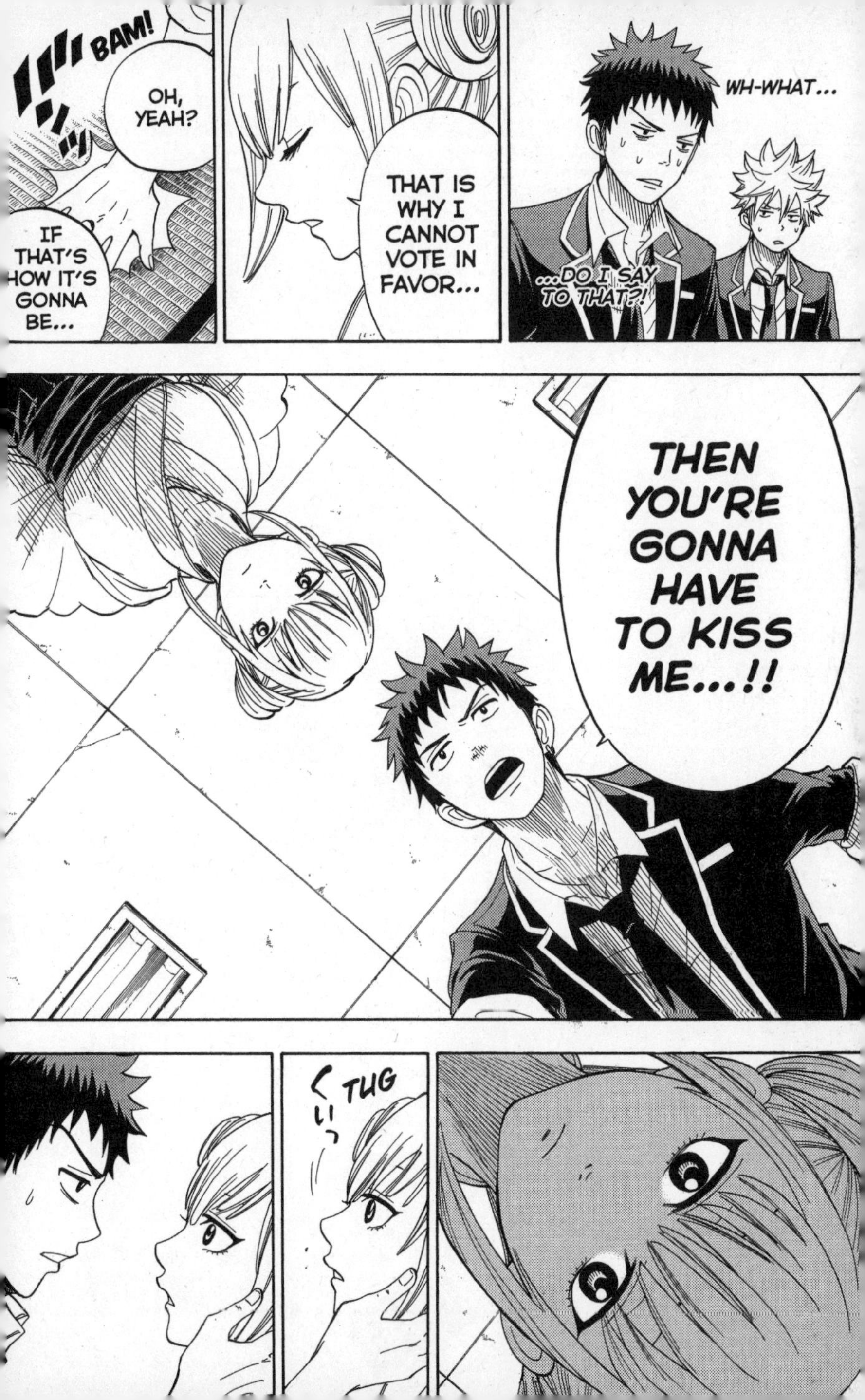
WH-WHAT...
...DO I SAY TO THAT?!
THAT IS WHY I CANNOT VOTE IN FAVOR...
BAM!
OH, YEAH?
IF THAT'S HOW IT'S GONNA BE...
THEN YOU'RE GONNA HAVE TO KISS ME...!!
くいっ
TUG

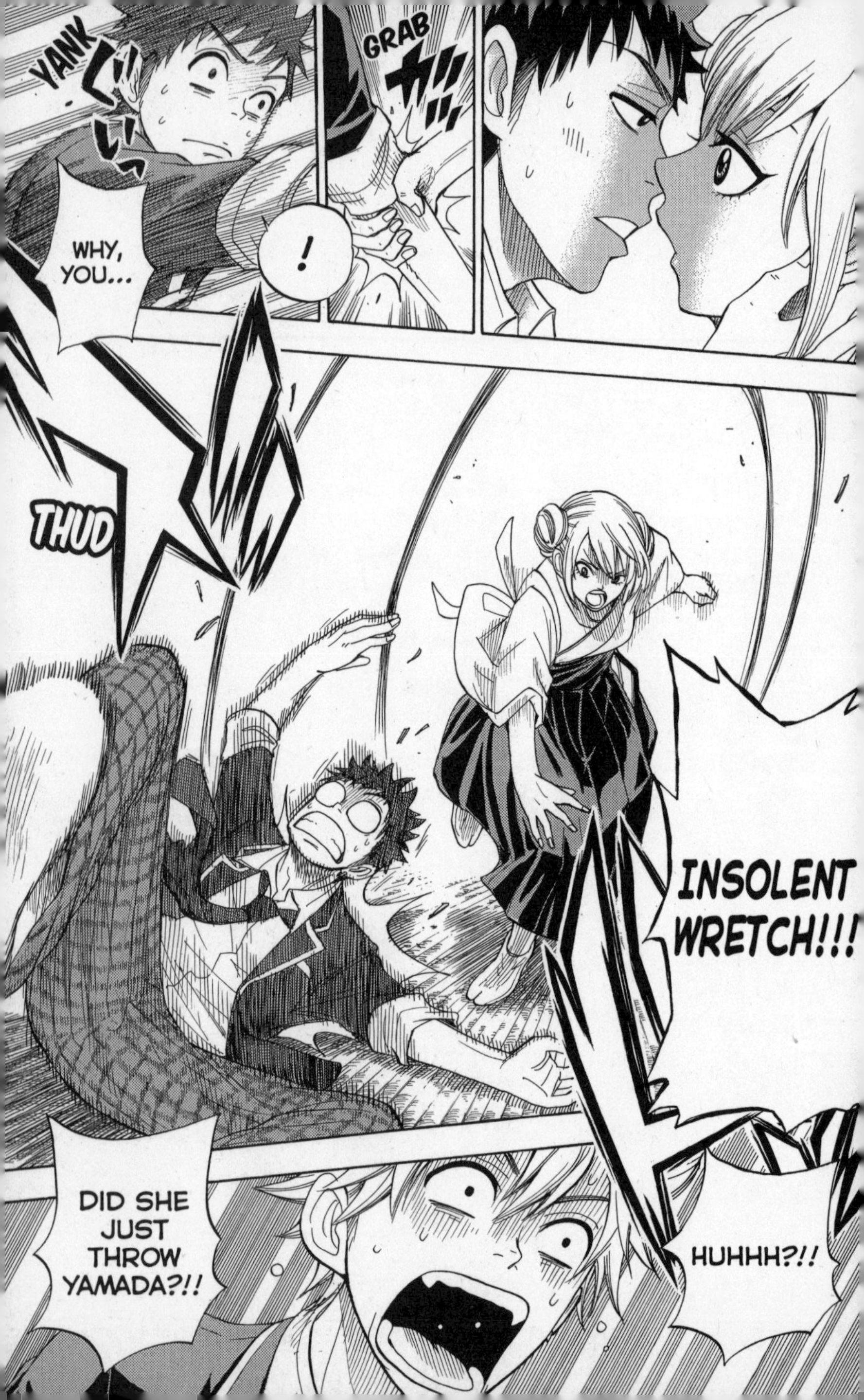
GRAB
!
YANK
WHY, YOU...
INSOLENT WRETCH!!!
THUD
HUHHH?!!
DID SHE JUST THROW YAMADA?!!

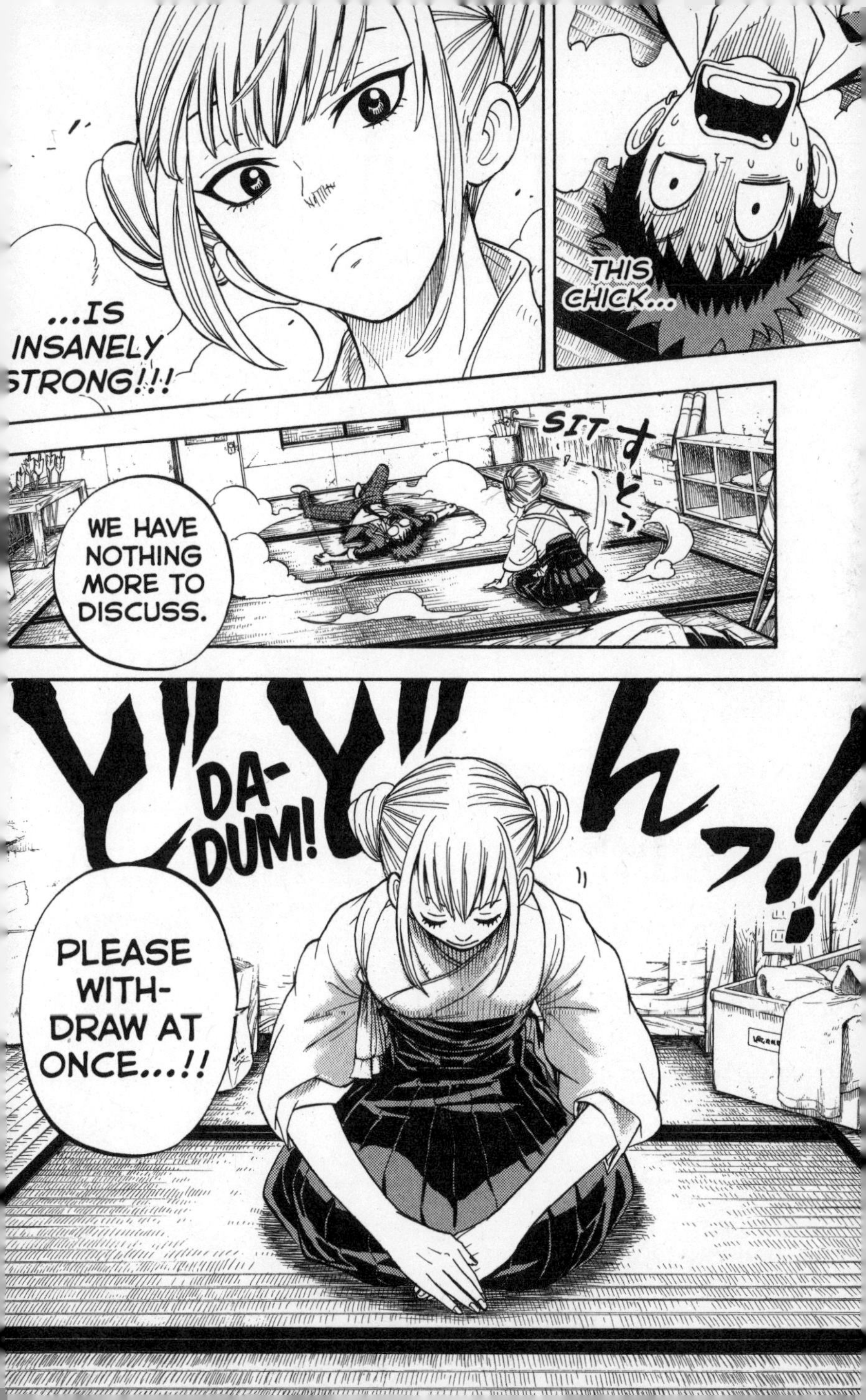
THIS CHICK...
...IS INSANELY STRONG!!!
SIT すとっ
WE HAVE NOTHING MORE TO DISCUSS.
DA-DUM!
PLEASE WITH-DRAW AT ONCE...!!

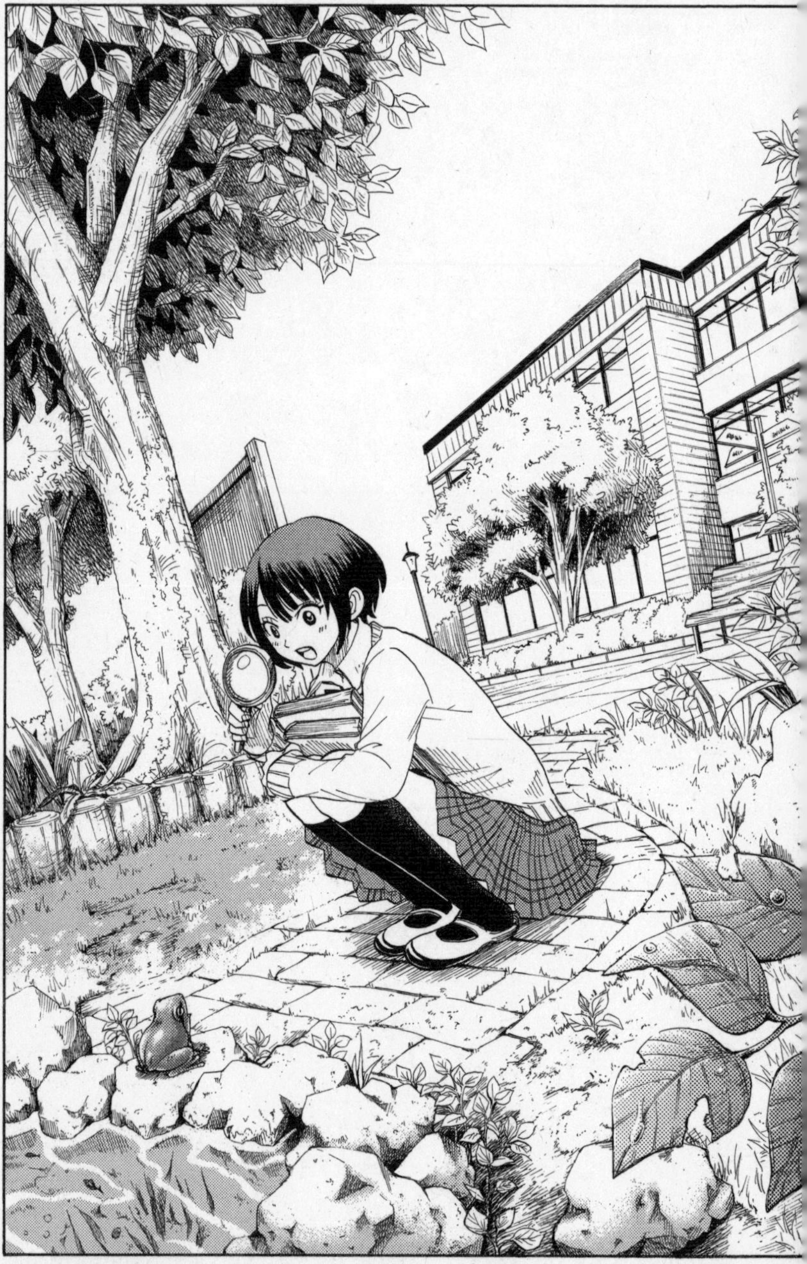

CHAPTER 13: I would like you to grant me this kiss!!

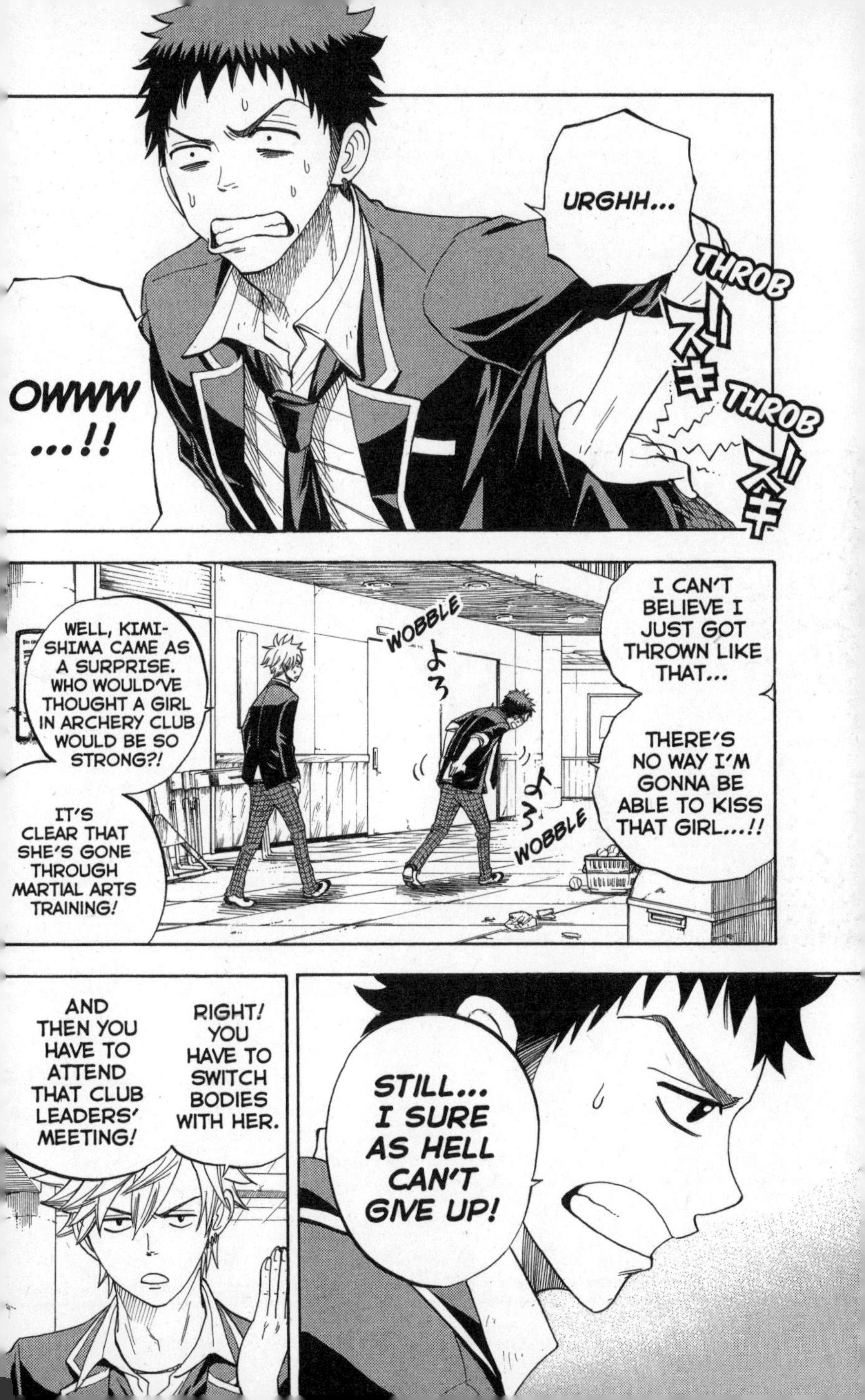
URGHH...
THROB
ズキ
THROB
ズキ
OWWW ...!!
I CAN'T BELIEVE I JUST GOT THROWN LIKE THAT...
THERE'S NO WAY I'M GONNA BE ABLE TO KISS THAT GIRL...!!
WOBBLE
よろ
WOBBLE
よろ
WELL, KIMI-SHIMA CAME AS A SURPRISE. WHO WOULD'VE THOUGHT A GIRL IN ARCHERY CLUB WOULD BE SO STRONG?!
IT'S CLEAR THAT SHE'S GONE THROUGH MARTIAL ARTS TRAINING!
STILL... I SURE AS HELL CAN'T GIVE UP!
RIGHT! YOU HAVE TO SWITCH BODIES WITH HER.
AND THEN YOU HAVE TO ATTEND THAT CLUB LEADERS' MEETING!

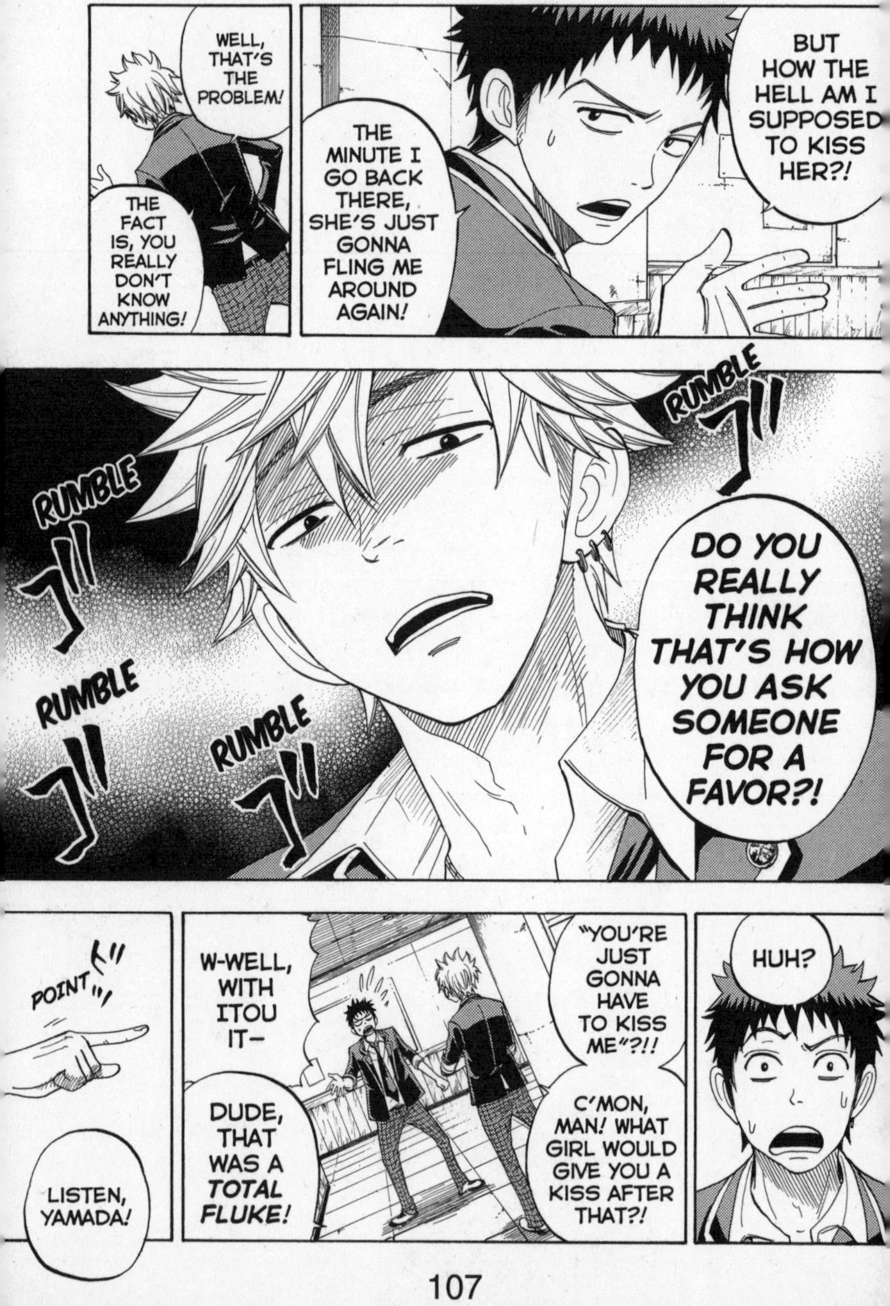
BUT HOW THE HELL AM I SUPPOSED TO KISS HER?!
THE MINUTE I GO BACK THERE, SHE'S JUST GONNA FLING ME AROUND AGAIN!
WELL, THAT'S THE PROBLEM!
THE FACT IS, YOU REALLY DON'T KNOW ANYTHING!
RUMBLE
DO YOU REALLY THINK THAT'S HOW YOU ASK SOMEONE FOR A FAVOR?!
RUMBLE
RUMBLE
RUMBLE
HUH?
"YOU'RE JUST GONNA HAVE TO KISS ME"?!!
W-WELL, WITH ITOU IT–
C'MON, MAN! WHAT GIRL WOULD GIVE YOU A KISS AFTER THAT?!
DUDE, THAT WAS A *TOTAL FLUKE!*
POINT
LISTEN, YAMADA!

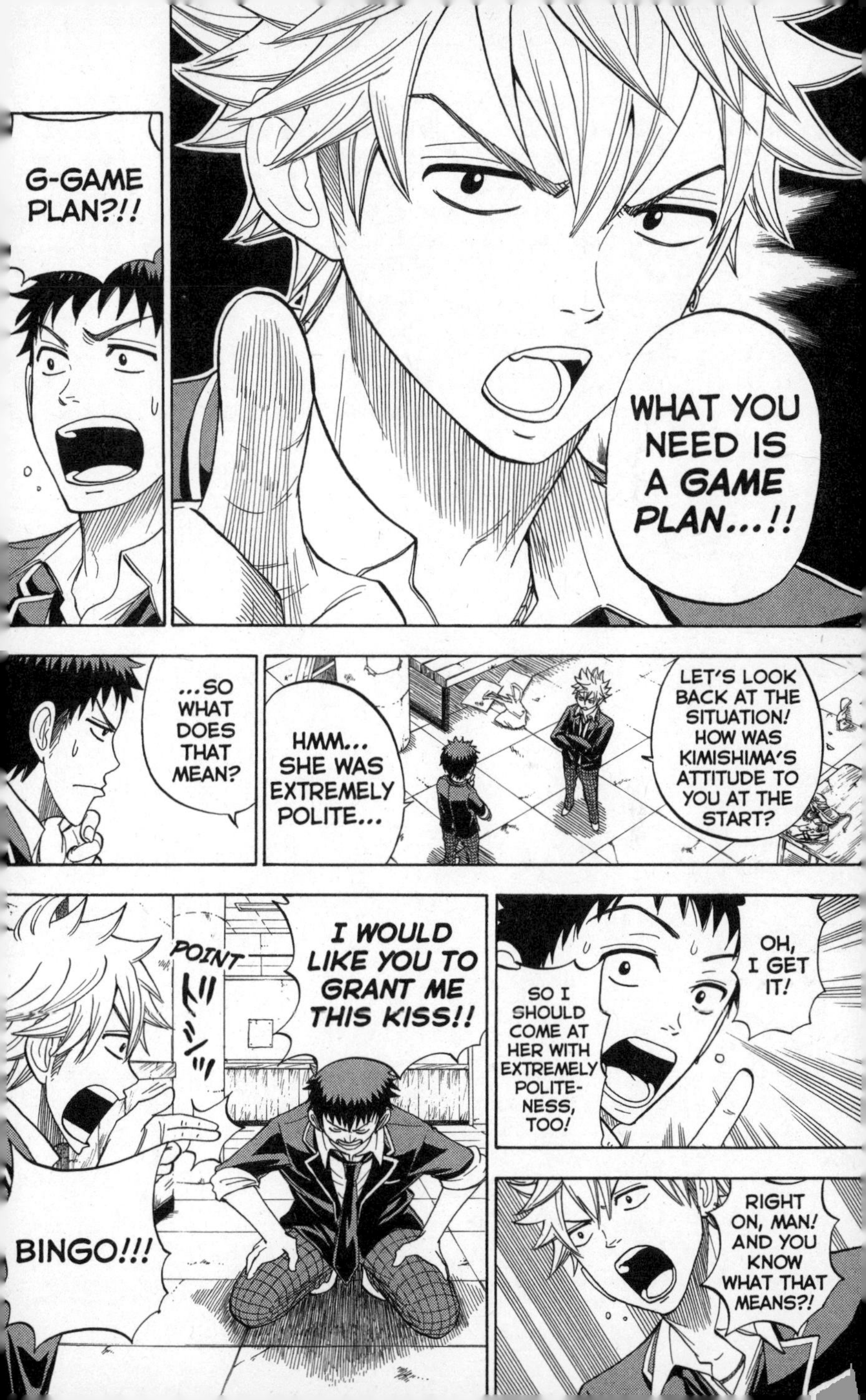
WHAT YOU NEED IS A GAME PLAN...!!
G-GAME PLAN?!!
LET'S LOOK BACK AT THE SITUATION! HOW WAS KIMISHIMA'S ATTITUDE TO YOU AT THE START?
HMM... SHE WAS EXTREMELY POLITE...
...SO WHAT DOES THAT MEAN?
OH, I GET IT!
SO I SHOULD COME AT HER WITH EXTREMELY POLITE-NESS, TOO!
RIGHT ON, MAN! AND YOU KNOW WHAT THAT MEANS?!
I WOULD LIKE YOU TO GRANT ME THIS KISS!!
POINT
BINGO!!!

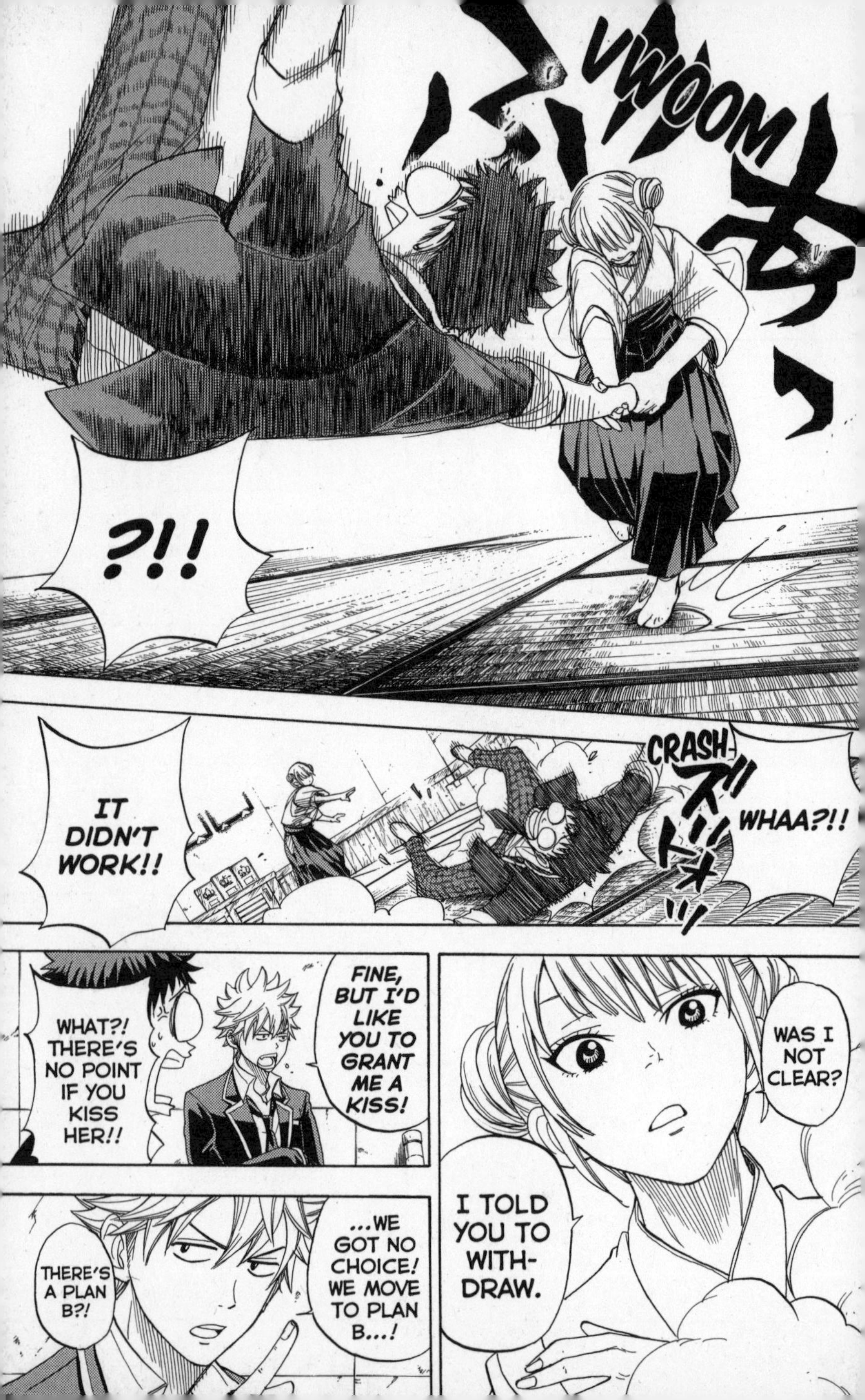
VWOOM
?!!
CRASH
WHAA?!!
IT DIDN'T WORK!!
WAS I NOT CLEAR?
I TOLD YOU TO WITH-DRAW.
FINE, BUT I'D LIKE YOU TO GRANT ME A KISS!
WHAT?! THERE'S NO POINT IF YOU KISS HER!!
...WE GOT NO CHOICE! WE MOVE TO PLAN B...!
THERE'S A PLAN B?!

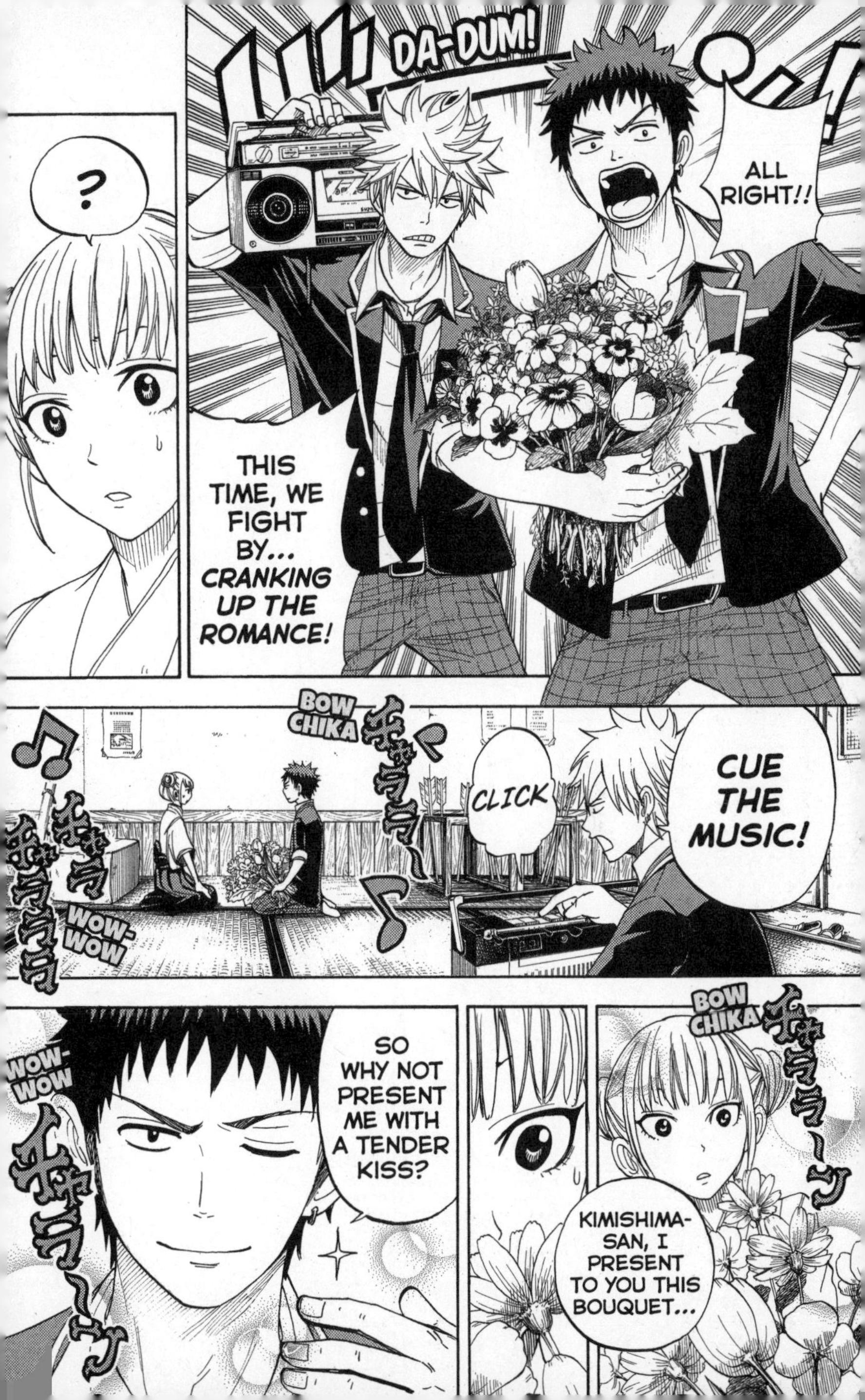
DA-DUM!
ALL RIGHT!!
THIS TIME, WE FIGHT BY... CRANKING UP THE ROMANCE!
?
CUE THE MUSIC!
CLICK
BOW CHIKA
WOW-WOW
BOW CHIKA
KIMISHIMA-SAN, I PRESENT TO YOU THIS BOUQUET...
WOW-WOW
SO WHY NOT PRESENT ME WITH A TENDER KISS?

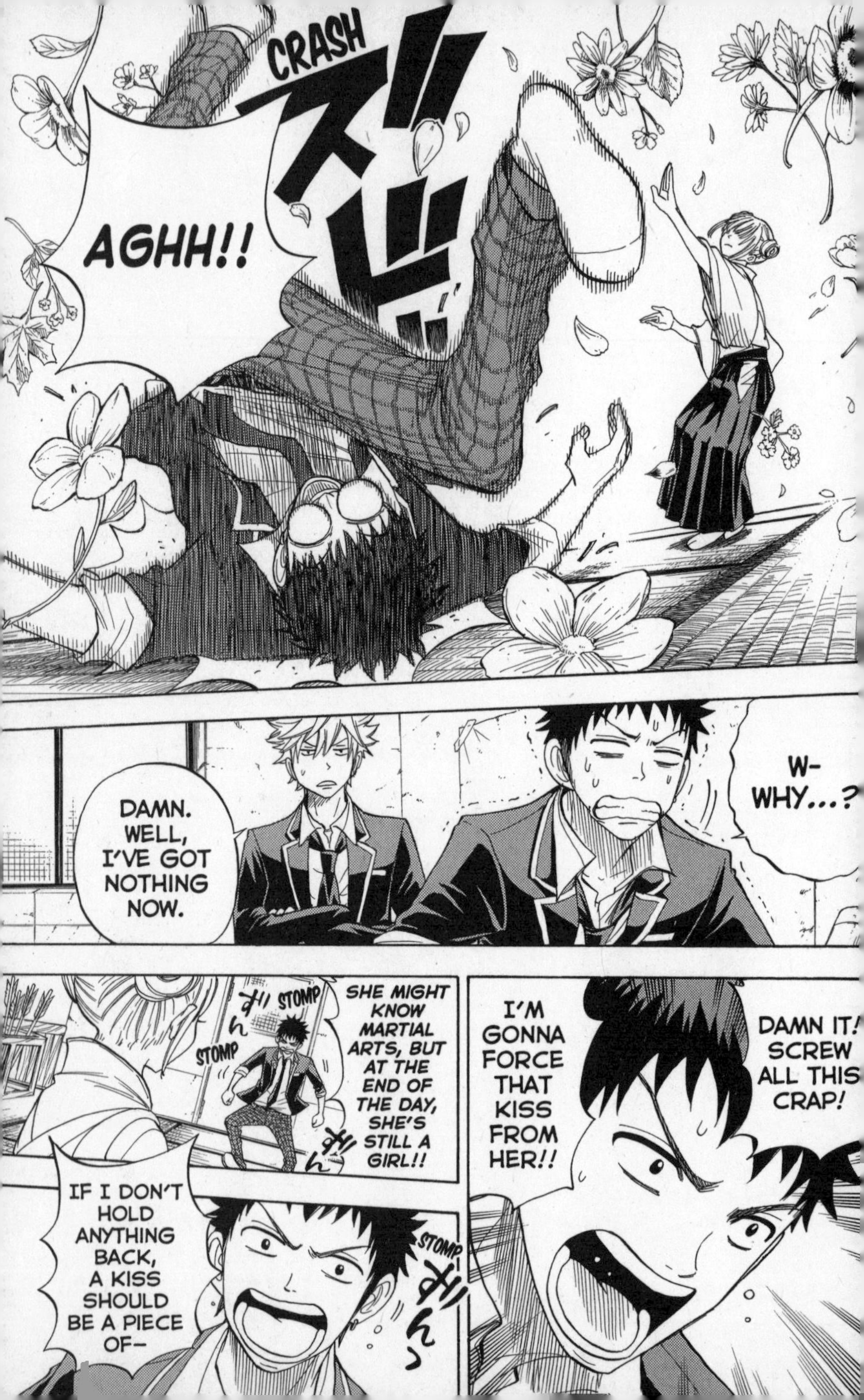
CRASH
AGHH!!
W- WHY...?
DAMN. WELL, I'VE GOT NOTHING NOW.
DAMN IT! SCREW ALL THIS CRAP!
I'M GONNA FORCE THAT KISS FROM HER!!
SHE MIGHT KNOW MARTIAL ARTS, BUT AT THE END OF THE DAY, SHE'S STILL A GIRL!!
STOMP
STOMP
IF I DON'T HOLD ANYTHING BACK, A KISS SHOULD BE A PIECE OF—
STOMP

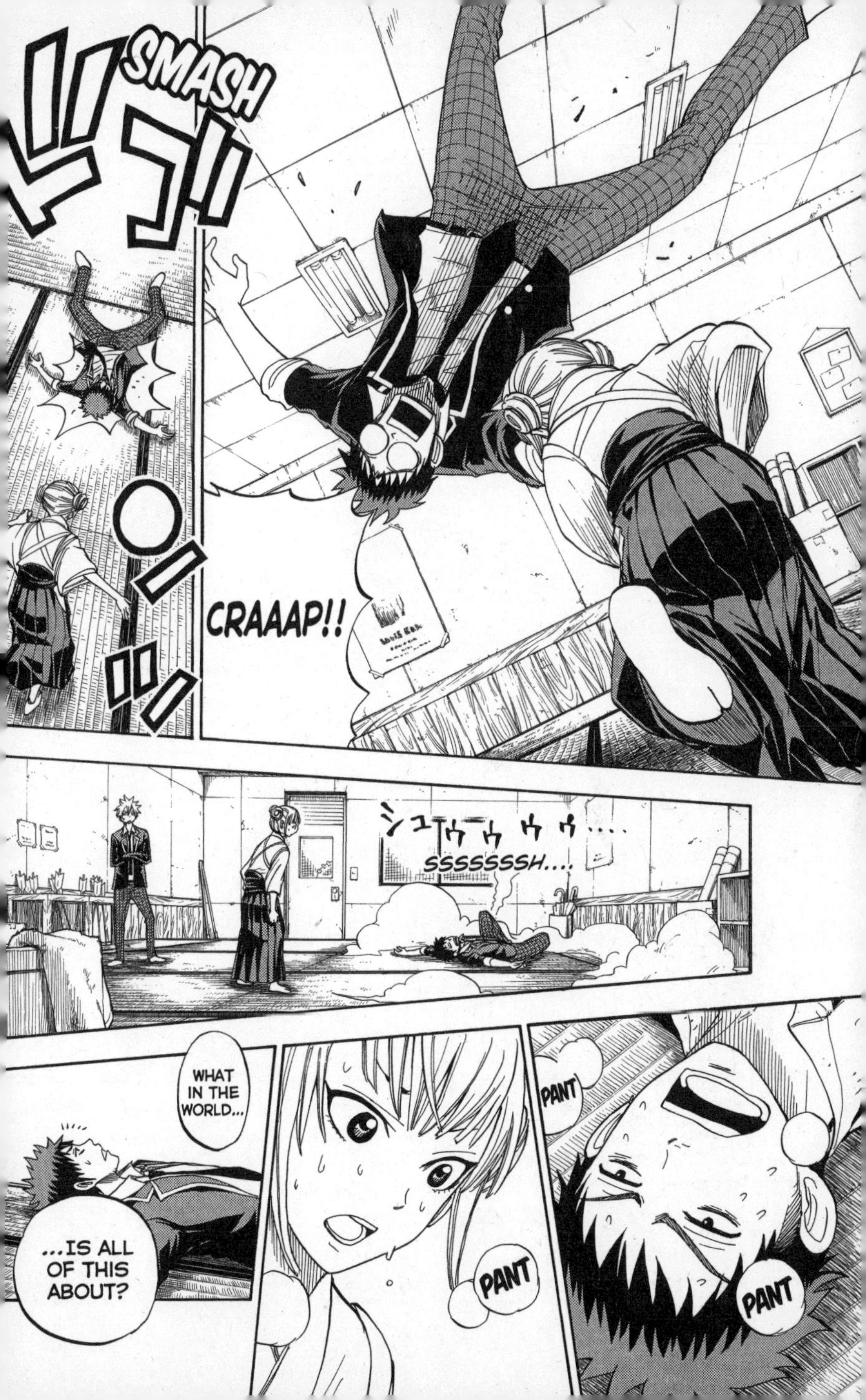
CRAAAP!!
SMASH
SSSSSSSH....
PANT
PANT
PANT
WHAT IN THE WORLD...
...IS ALL OF THIS ABOUT?

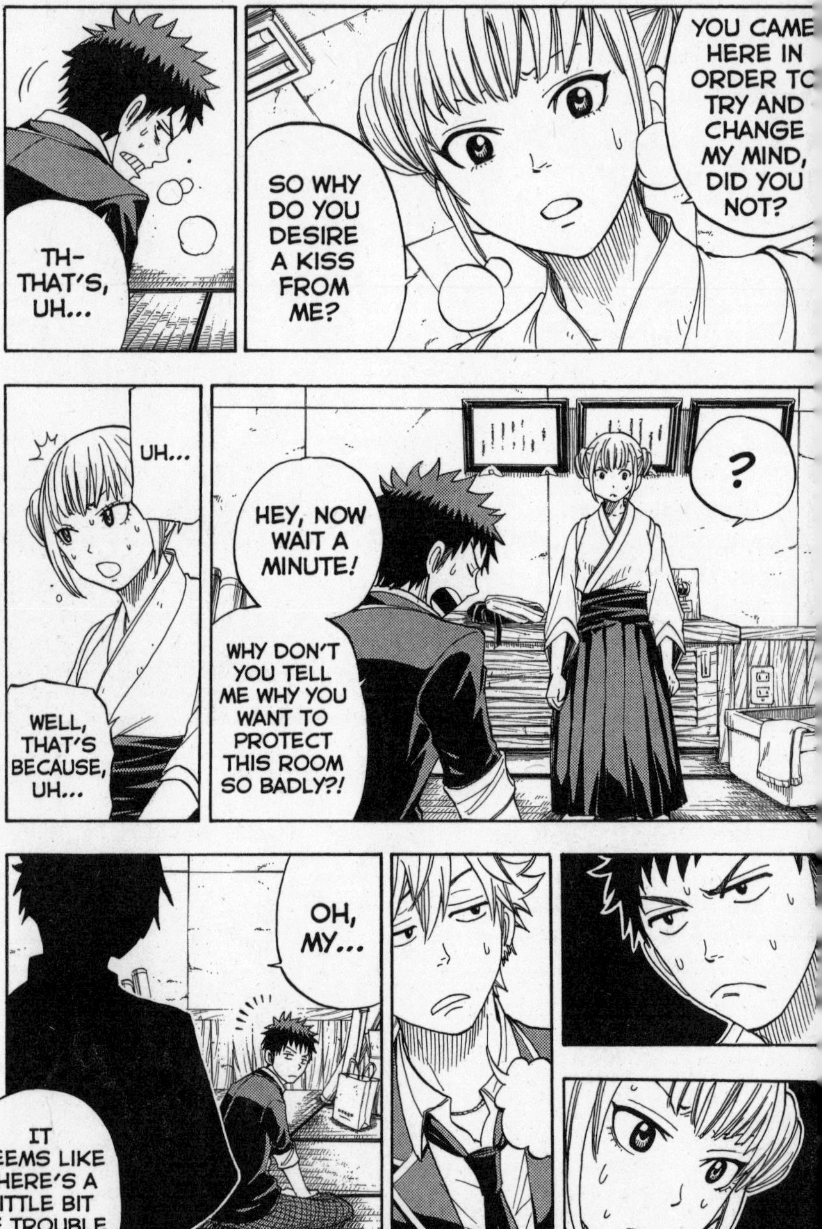
YOU CAME HERE IN ORDER TO TRY AND CHANGE MY MIND, DID YOU NOT?
SO WHY DO YOU DESIRE A KISS FROM ME?
TH- THAT'S, UH...
?
HEY, NOW WAIT A MINUTE!
WHY DON'T YOU TELL ME WHY YOU WANT TO PROTECT THIS ROOM SO BADLY?!
UH...
WELL, THAT'S BECAUSE, UH...
OH, MY...
IT SEEMS LIKE THERE'S A LITTLE BIT OF TROUBLE GOING ON HERE...

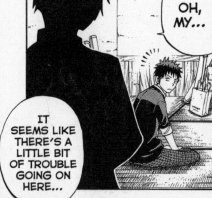

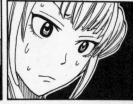

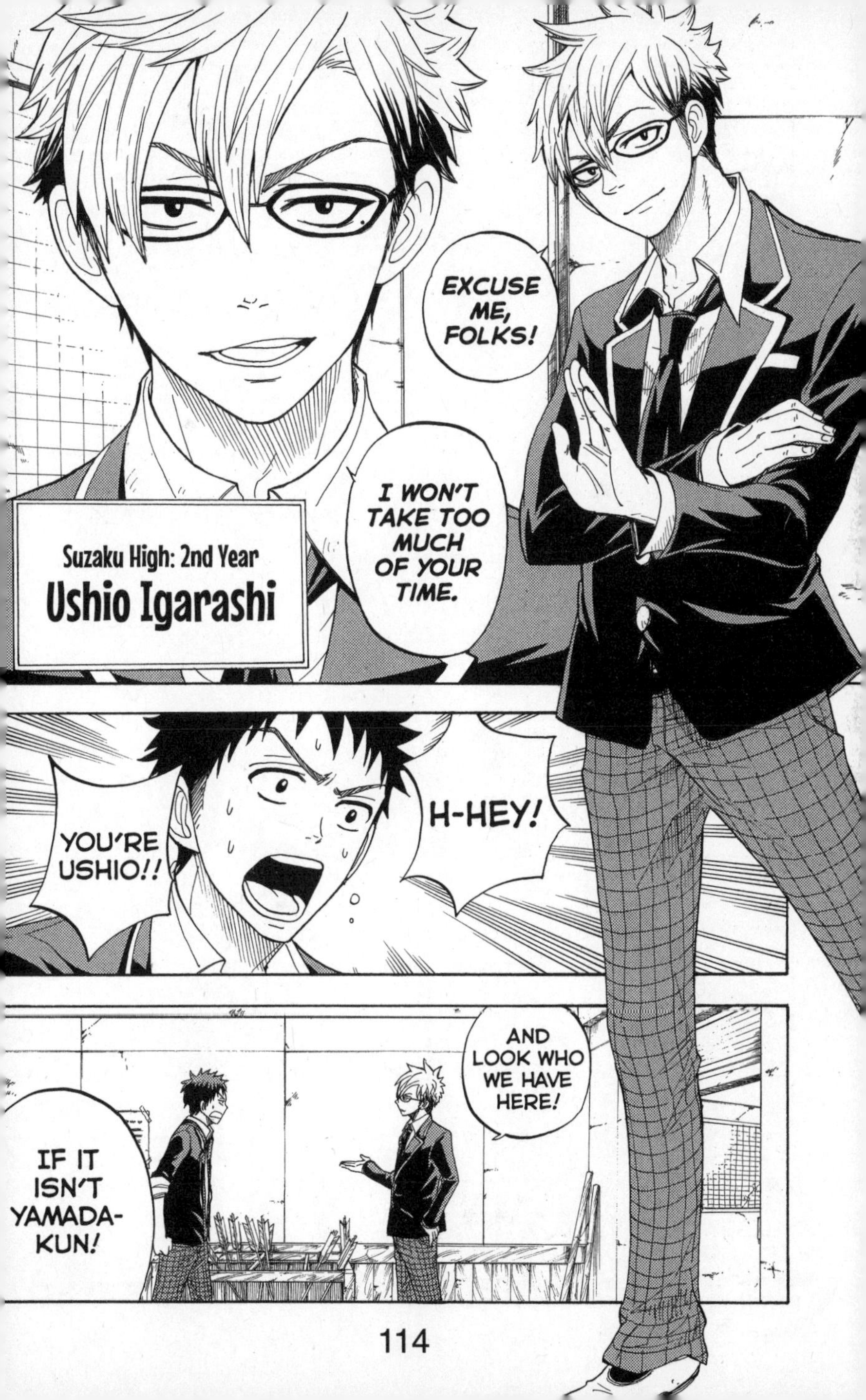
EXCUSE ME, FOLKS!
I WON'T TAKE TOO MUCH OF YOUR TIME.
Suzaku High: 2nd Year
Ushio Igarashi
H-HEY!
YOU'RE USHIO!!
AND LOOK WHO WE HAVE HERE!
IF IT ISN'T YAMADA-KUN!

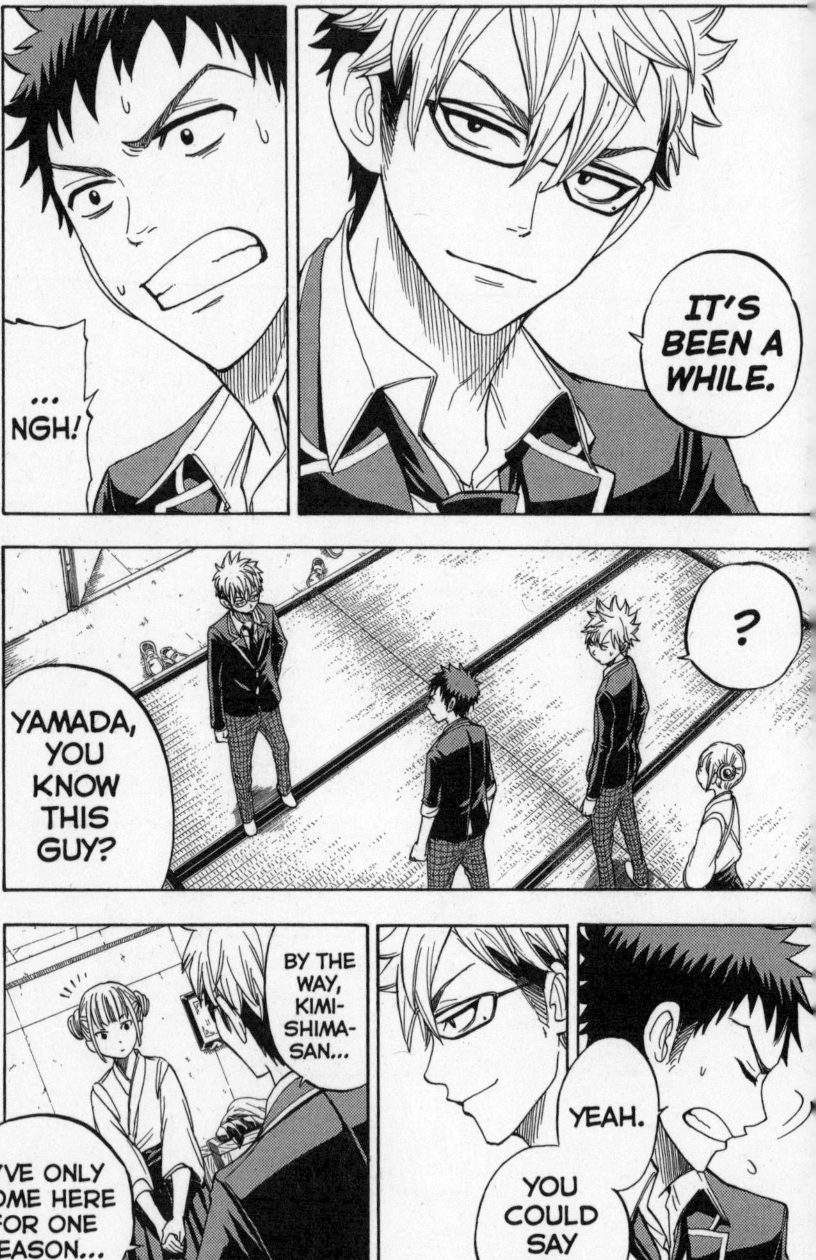
IT'S BEEN A WHILE.
... NGH!
?
YAMADA, YOU KNOW THIS GUY?
YEAH.
YOU COULD SAY THAT!
BY THE WAY, KIMI-SHIMA-SAN...
I'VE ONLY COME HERE FOR ONE REASON...

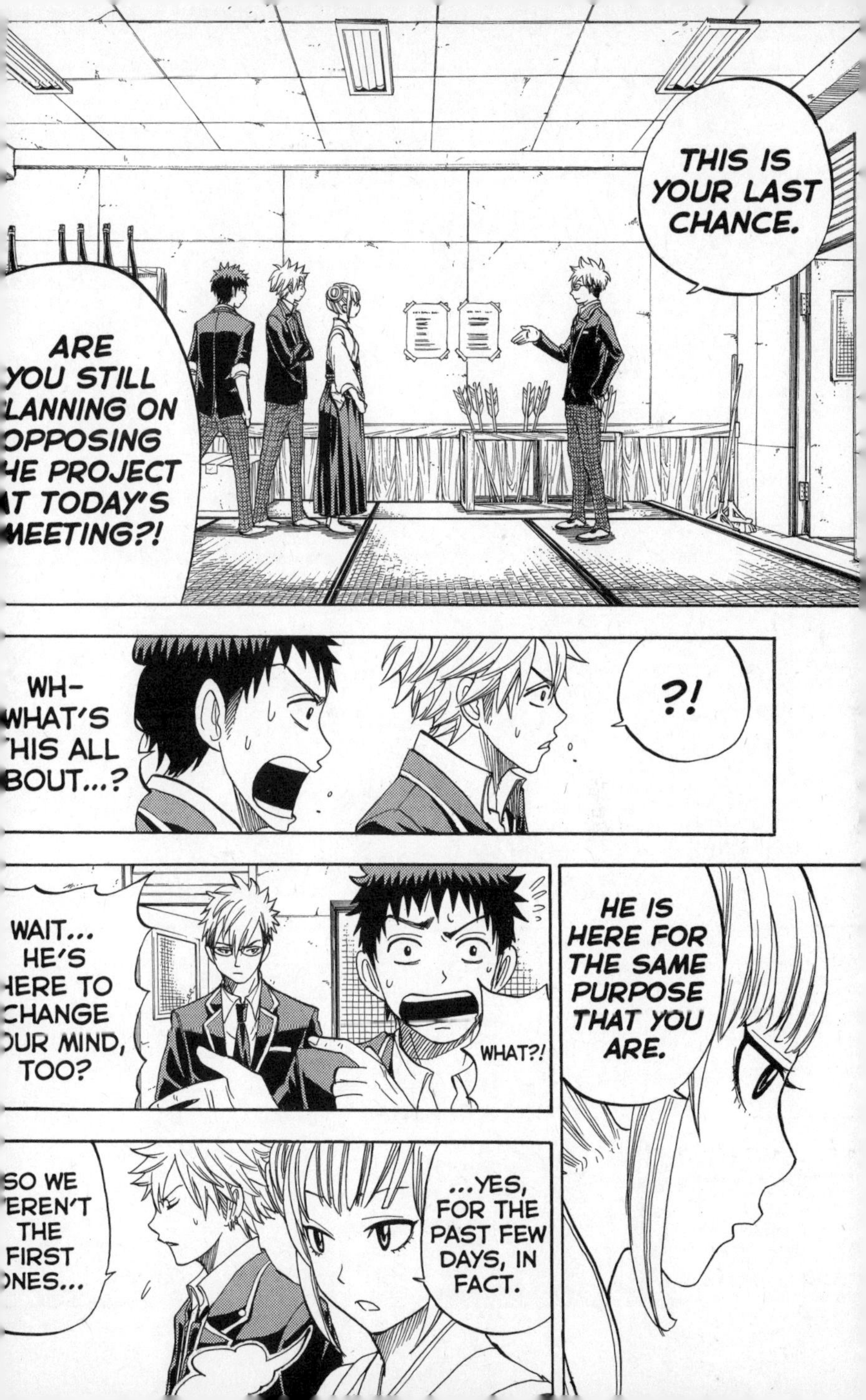
THIS IS YOUR LAST CHANCE.
ARE YOU STILL LANNING ON OPPOSING HE PROJECT T TODAY'S MEETING?!
?!
WH- WHAT'S HIS ALL BOUT...?
HE IS HERE FOR THE SAME PURPOSE THAT YOU ARE.
WHAT?!
WAIT... HE'S HERE TO CHANGE UR MIND, TOO?
...YES, FOR THE PAST FEW DAYS, IN FACT.
SO WE EREN'T THE FIRST NES...

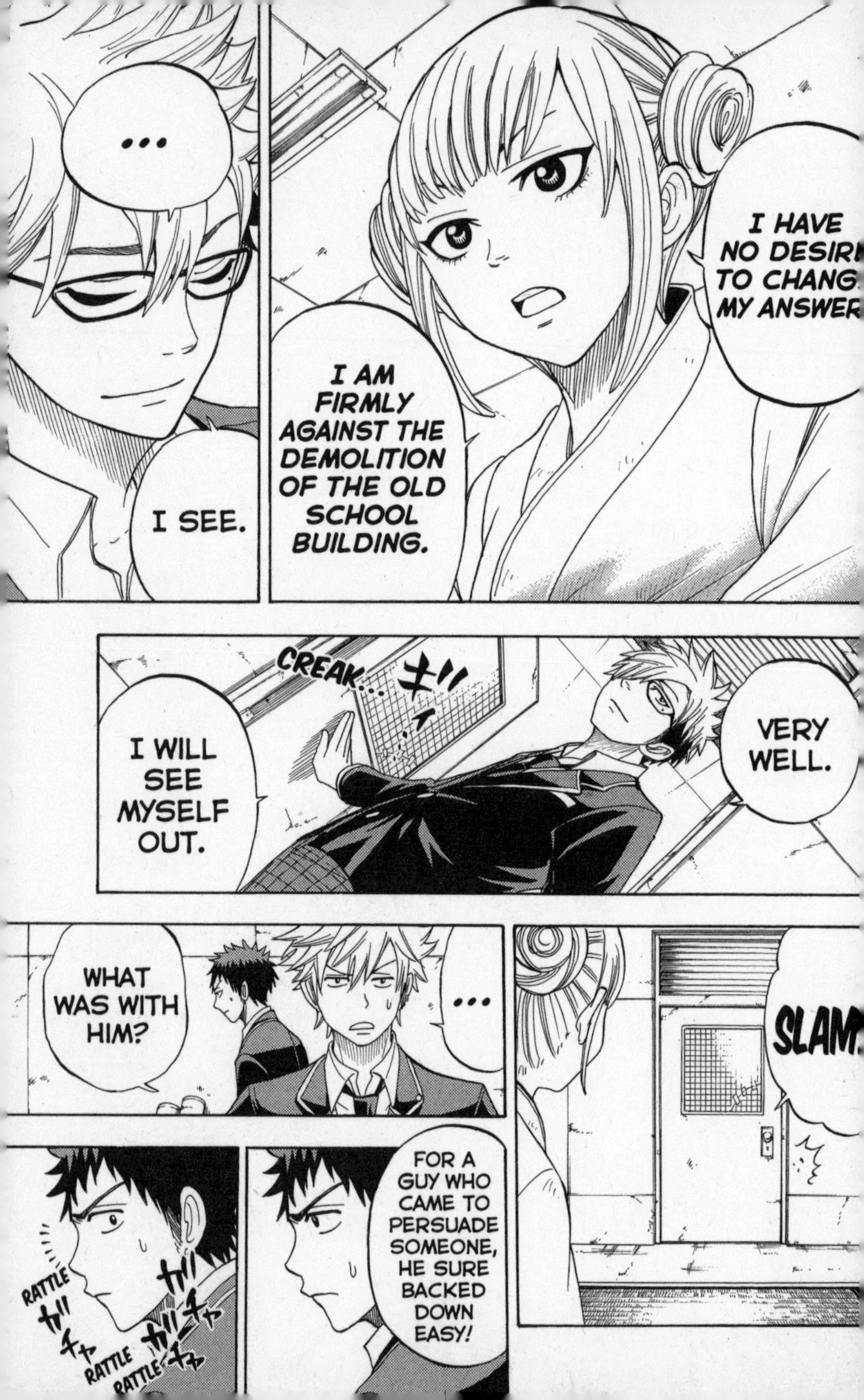
I HAVE NO DESIR TO CHANG MY ANSWER
I AM FIRMLY AGAINST THE DEMOLITION OF THE OLD SCHOOL BUILDING.
...
I SEE.
VERY WELL.
CREAK...
I WILL SEE MYSELF OUT.
SLAM
...
WHAT WAS WITH HIM?
FOR A GUY WHO CAME TO PERSUADE SOMEONE, HE SURE BACKED DOWN EASY!
RATTLE
RATTLE
RATTLE

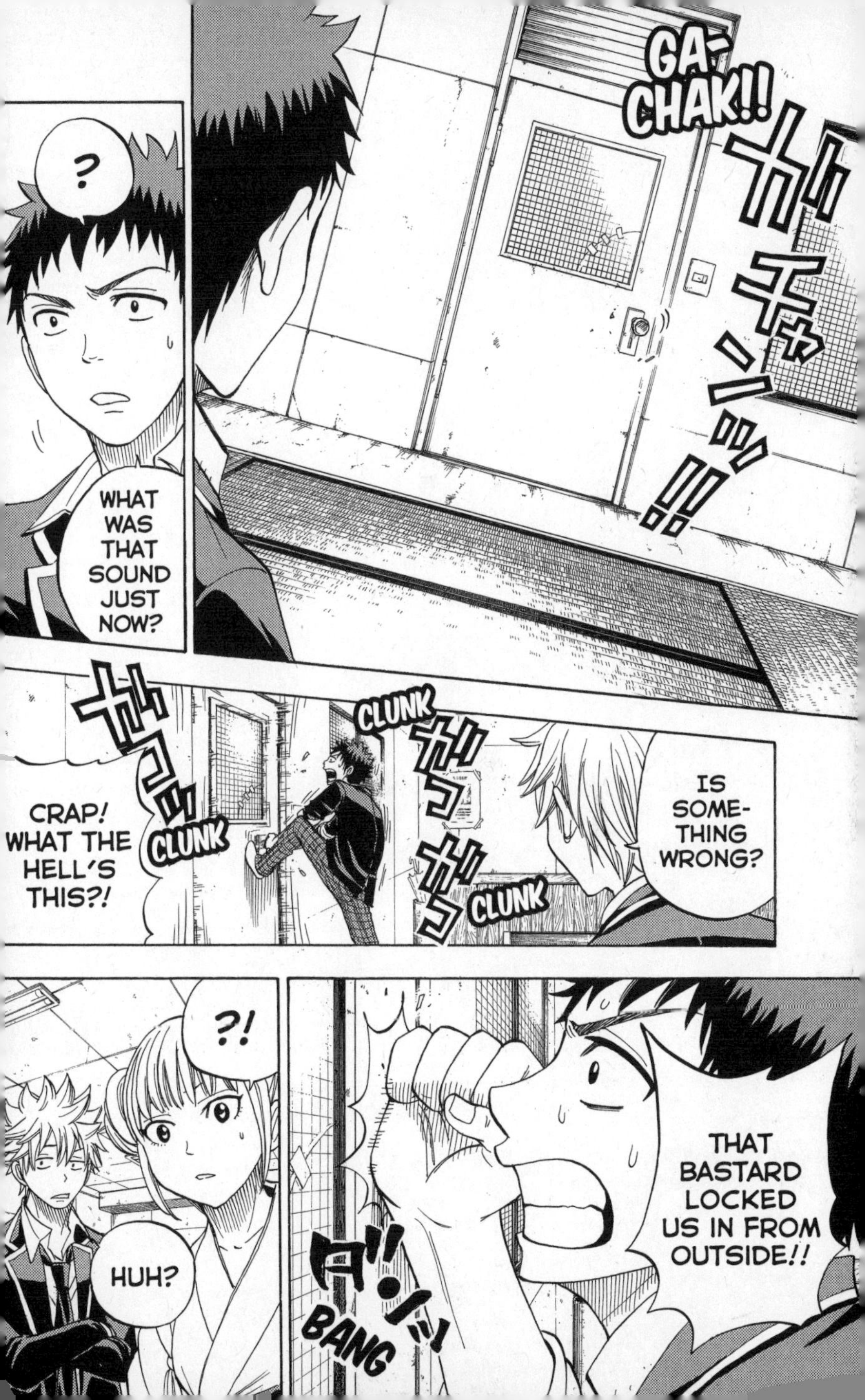
GA-CHAK!!
?
WHAT WAS THAT SOUND JUST NOW?
IS SOMETHING WRONG?
CLUNK
CLUNK
CLUNK
CRAP! WHAT THE HELL'S THIS?!
THAT BASTARD LOCKED US IN FROM OUTSIDE!!
BANG
?!
HUH?

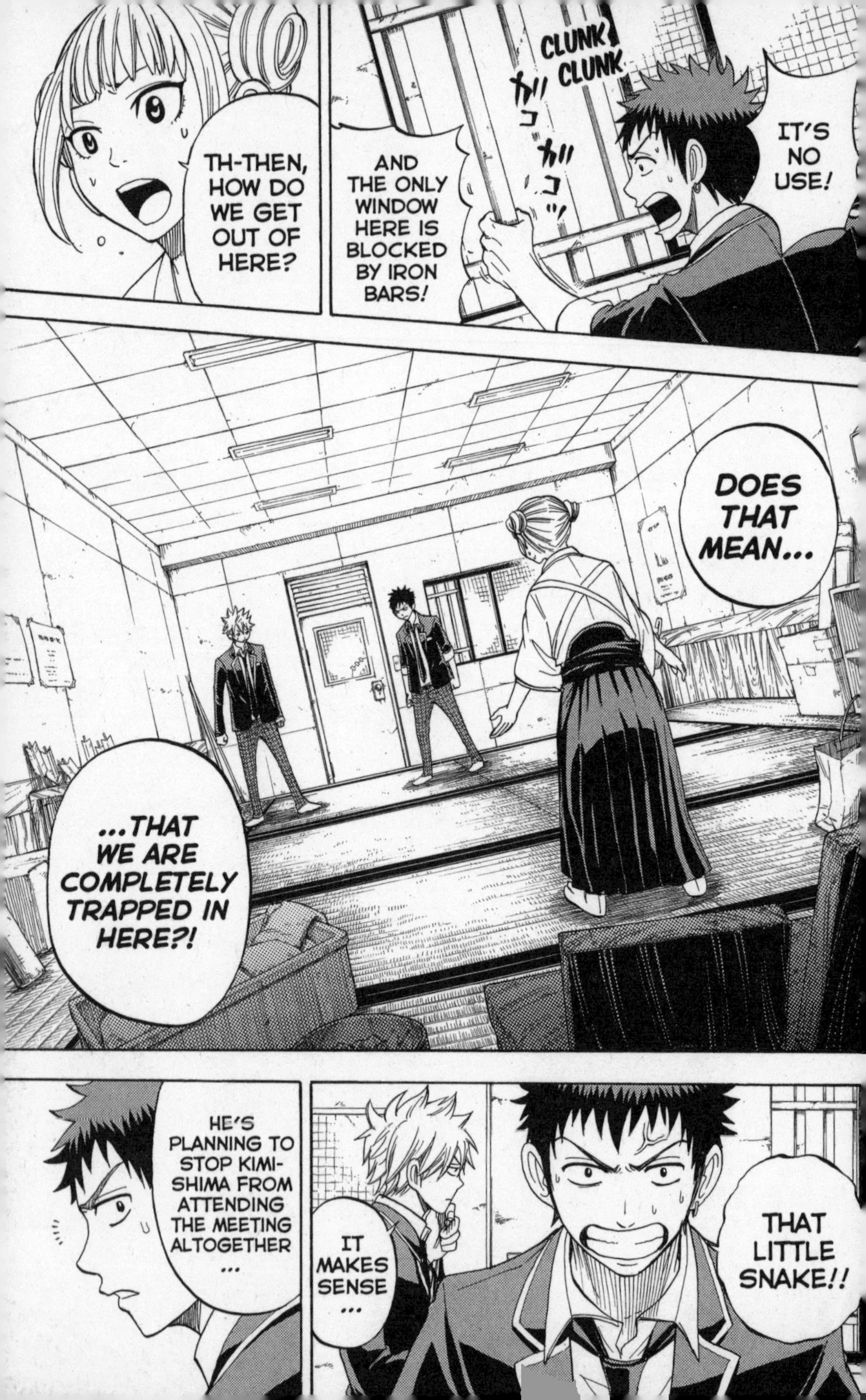
CLUNK CLUNK
IT'S NO USE!
AND THE ONLY WINDOW HERE IS BLOCKED BY IRON BARS!
TH-THEN, HOW DO WE GET OUT OF HERE?
DOES THAT MEAN...
...THAT WE ARE COMPLETELY TRAPPED IN HERE?!
THAT LITTLE SNAKE!!
IT MAKES SENSE ...
HE'S PLANNING TO STOP KIMI-SHIMA FROM ATTENDING THE MEETING ALTOGETHER ...

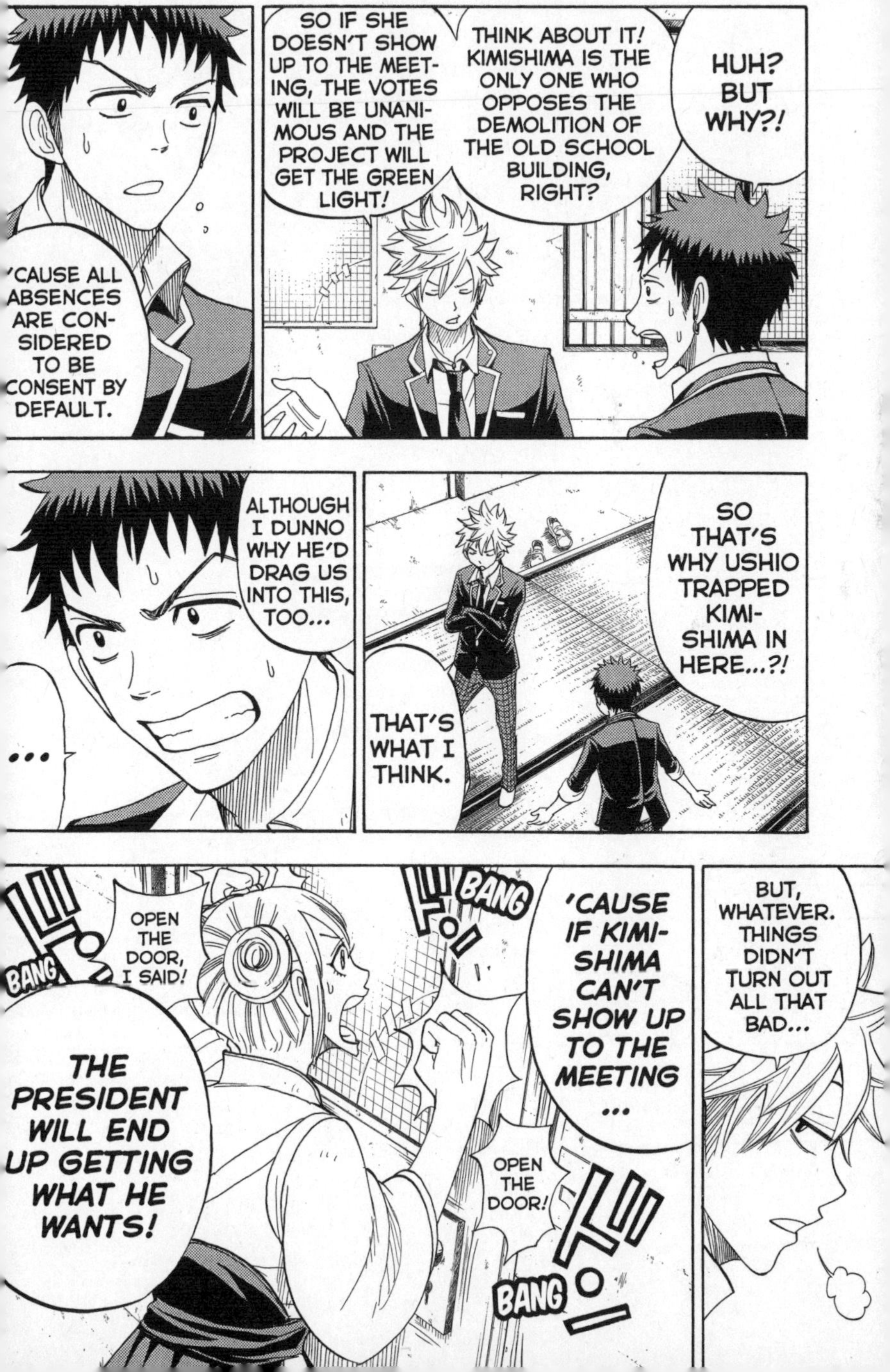
HUH? BUT WHY?!
THINK ABOUT IT! KIMISHIMA IS THE ONLY ONE WHO OPPOSES THE DEMOLITION OF THE OLD SCHOOL BUILDING, RIGHT?
SO IF SHE DOESN'T SHOW UP TO THE MEETING, THE VOTES WILL BE UNANIMOUS AND THE PROJECT WILL GET THE GREEN LIGHT!
'CAUSE ALL ABSENCES ARE CONSIDERED TO BE CONSENT BY DEFAULT.
SO THAT'S WHY USHIO TRAPPED KIMISHIMA IN HERE...?!
THAT'S WHAT I THINK.
ALTHOUGH I DUNNO WHY HE'D DRAG US INTO THIS, TOO...
...
BUT, WHATEVER. THINGS DIDN'T TURN OUT ALL THAT BAD...
BANG
'CAUSE IF KIMISHIMA CAN'T SHOW UP TO THE MEETING...
OPEN THE DOOR, I SAID!
BANG
THE PRESIDENT WILL END UP GETTING WHAT HE WANTS!
OPEN THE DOOR!
BANG

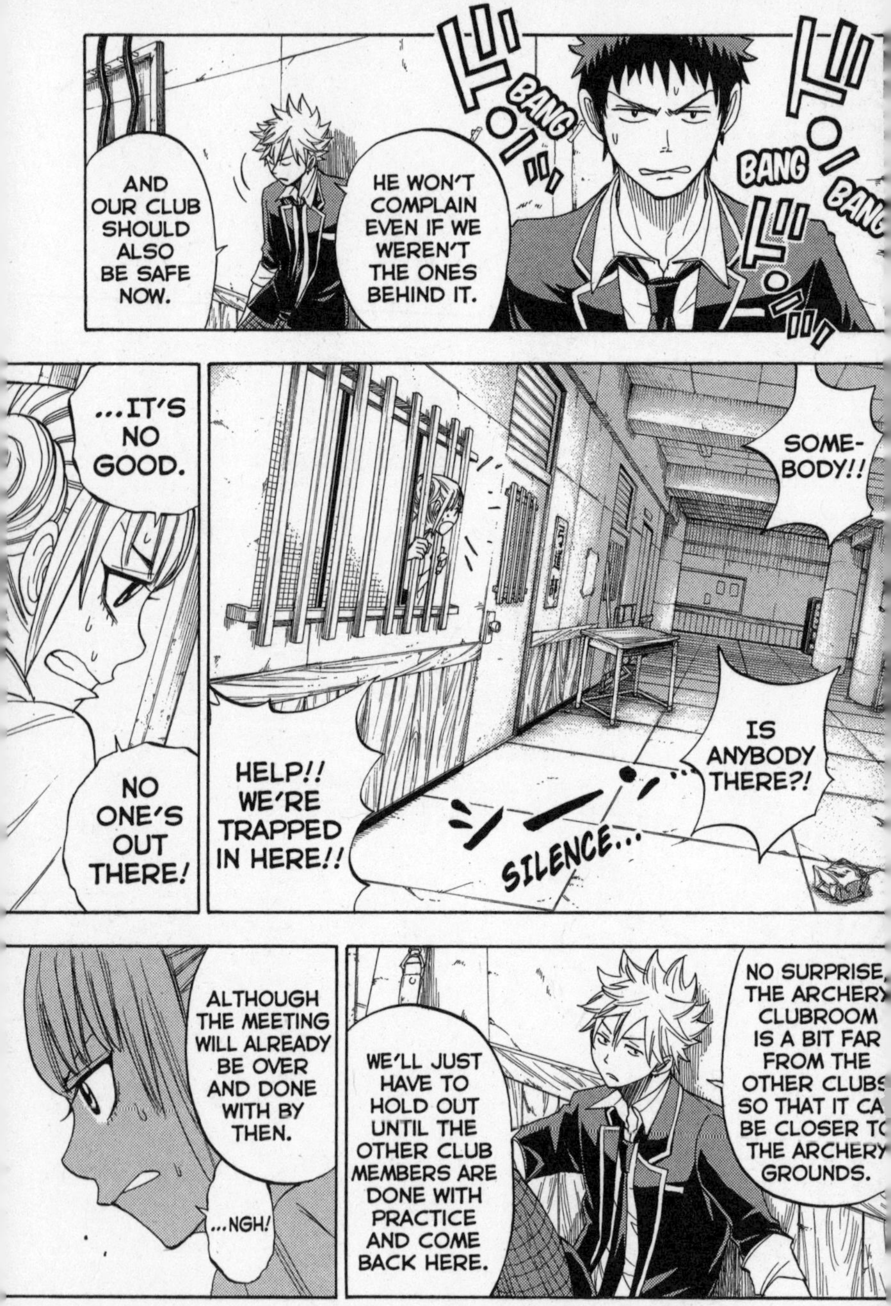
BANG
BANG
BANG
HE WON'T COMPLAIN EVEN IF WE WEREN'T THE ONES BEHIND IT.
AND OUR CLUB SHOULD ALSO BE SAFE NOW.
SOME-BODY!!
IS ANYBODY THERE?!
HELP!! WE'RE TRAPPED IN HERE!!
SILENCE...
...IT'S NO GOOD.
NO ONE'S OUT THERE!
NO SURPRISE, THE ARCHERY CLUBROOM IS A BIT FAR FROM THE OTHER CLUBS SO THAT IT CA BE CLOSER TO THE ARCHERY GROUNDS.
WE'LL JUST HAVE TO HOLD OUT UNTIL THE OTHER CLUB MEMBERS ARE DONE WITH PRACTICE AND COME BACK HERE.
ALTHOUGH THE MEETING WILL ALREADY BE OVER AND DONE WITH BY THEN.
...NGH!

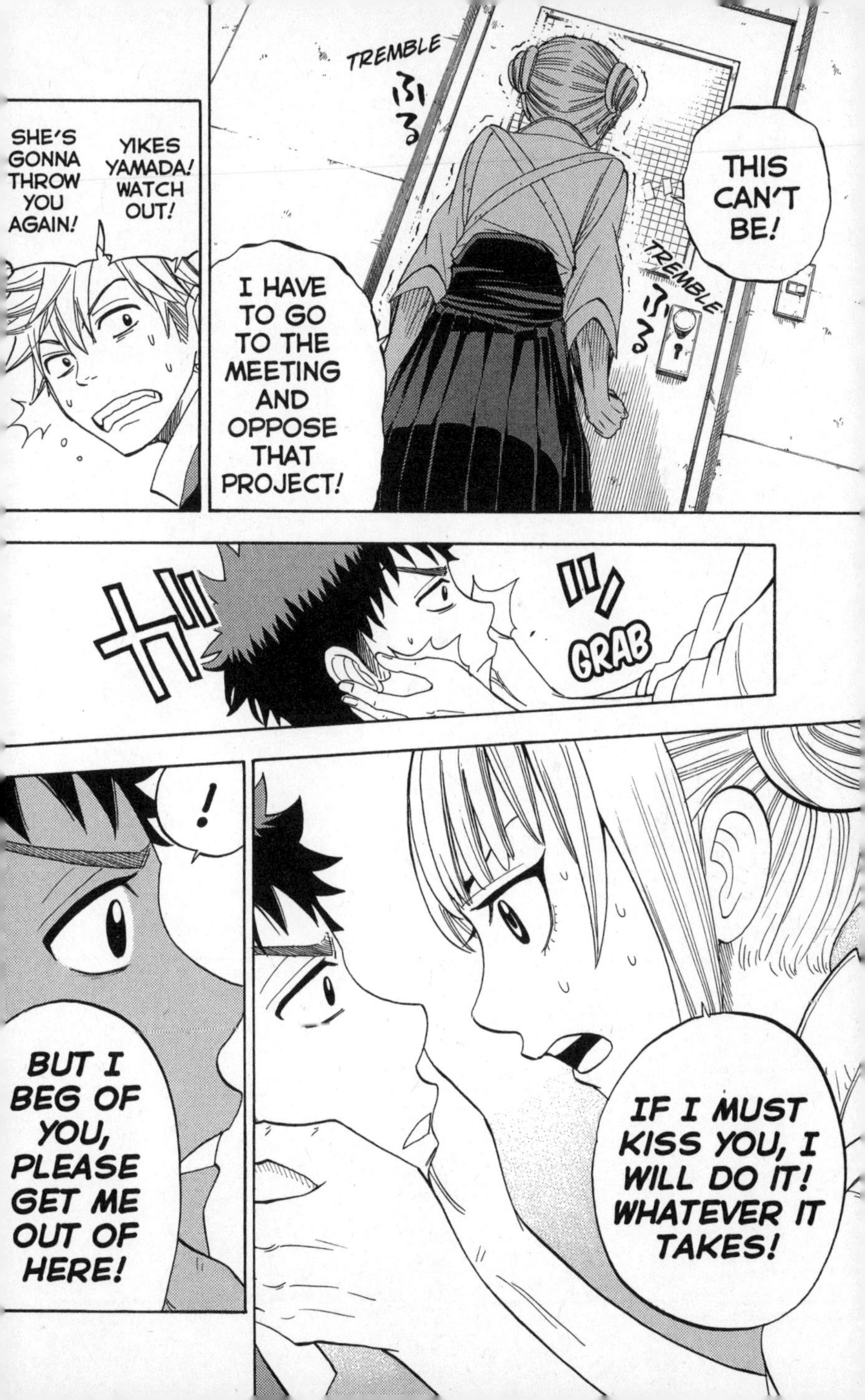
TREMBLE
ふる
THIS CAN'T BE!
TREMBLE
ふる
I HAVE TO GO TO THE MEETING AND OPPOSE THAT PROJECT!
YIKES YAMADA! WATCH OUT!
SHE'S GONNA THROW YOU AGAIN!
GRAB
IF I MUST KISS YOU, I WILL DO IT! WHATEVER IT TAKES!
!
BUT I BEG OF YOU, PLEASE GET ME OUT OF HERE!

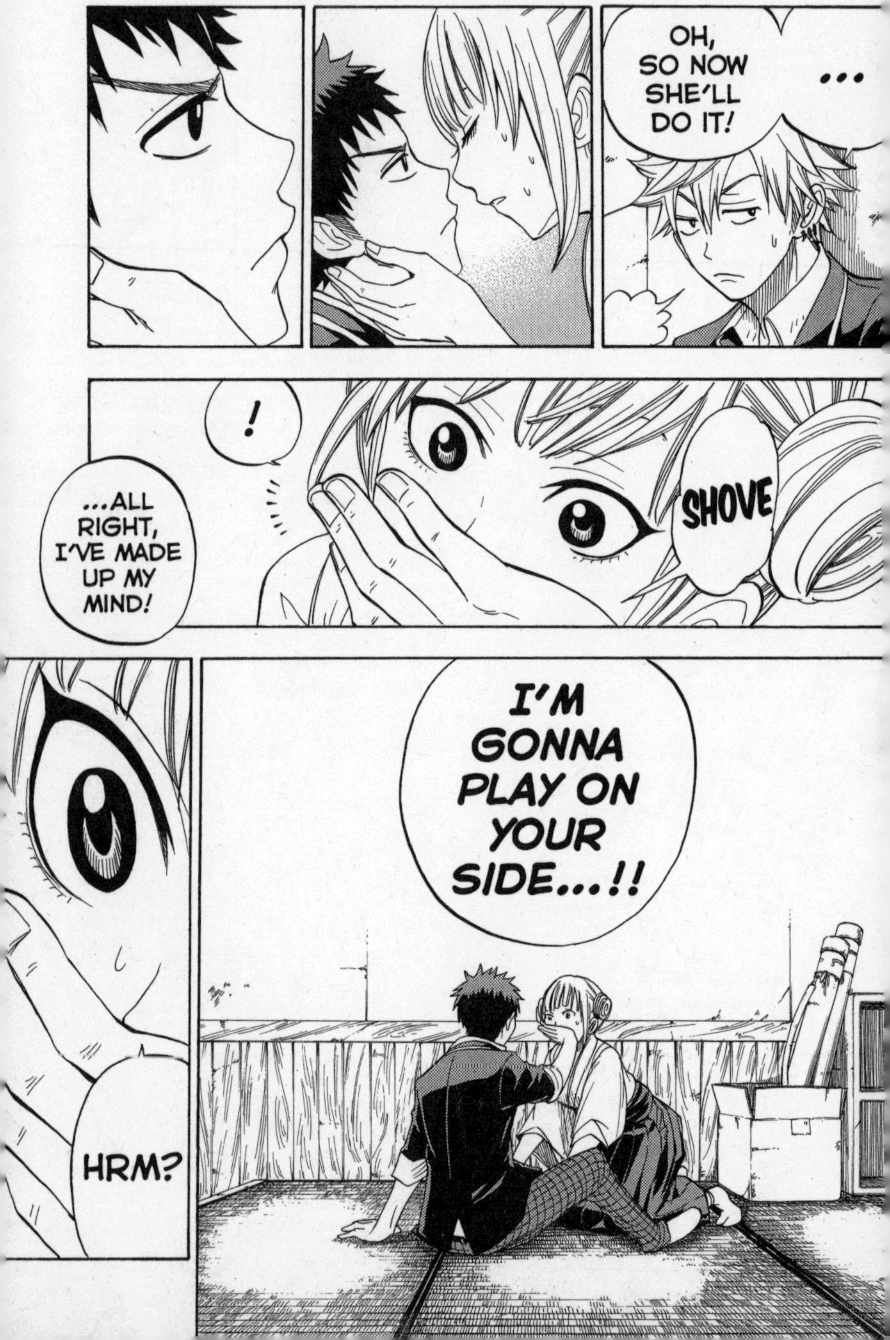
OH, SO NOW SHE'LL DO IT!
...
SHOVE
!
...ALL RIGHT, I'VE MADE UP MY MIND!
I'M GONNA PLAY ON YOUR SIDE...!!
HRM?

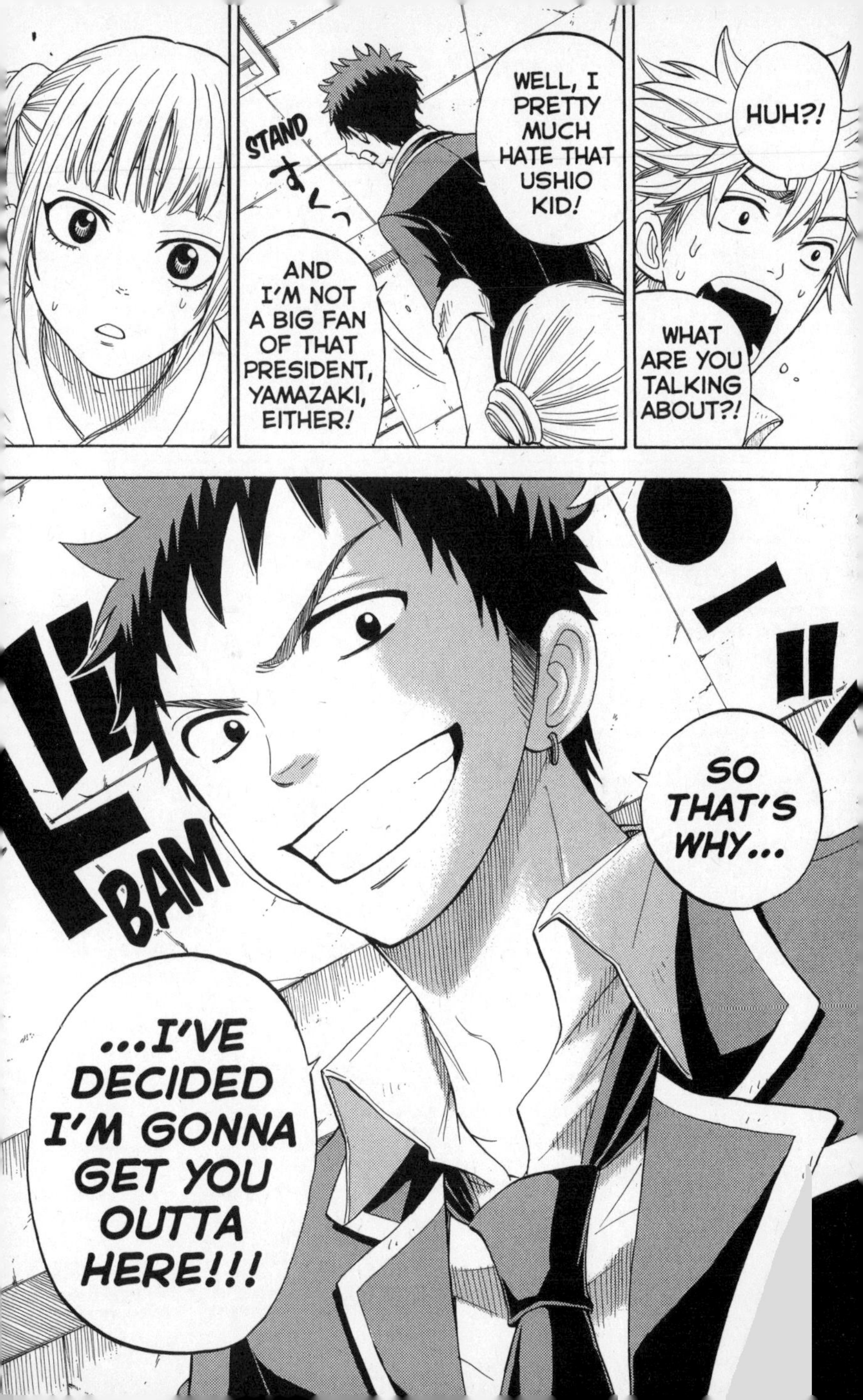

HUH?!
WHAT ARE YOU TALKING ABOUT?!
WELL, I PRETTY MUCH HATE THAT USHIO KID!
STAND
AND I'M NOT A BIG FAN OF THAT PRESIDENT, YAMAZAKI, EITHER!
SO THAT'S WHY...
BAM
...I'VE DECIDED I'M GONNA GET YOU OUTTA HERE!!!

CHAPTER 14: Shingi Ikkyu.

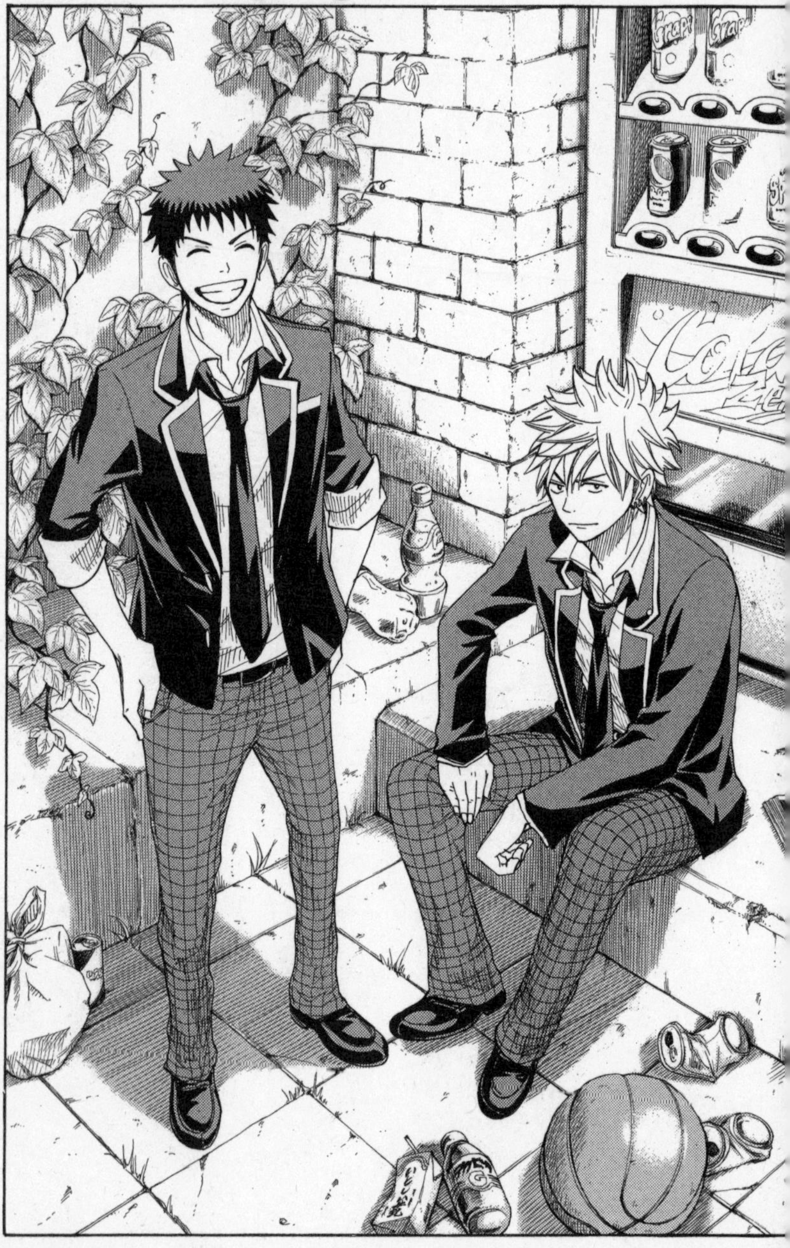

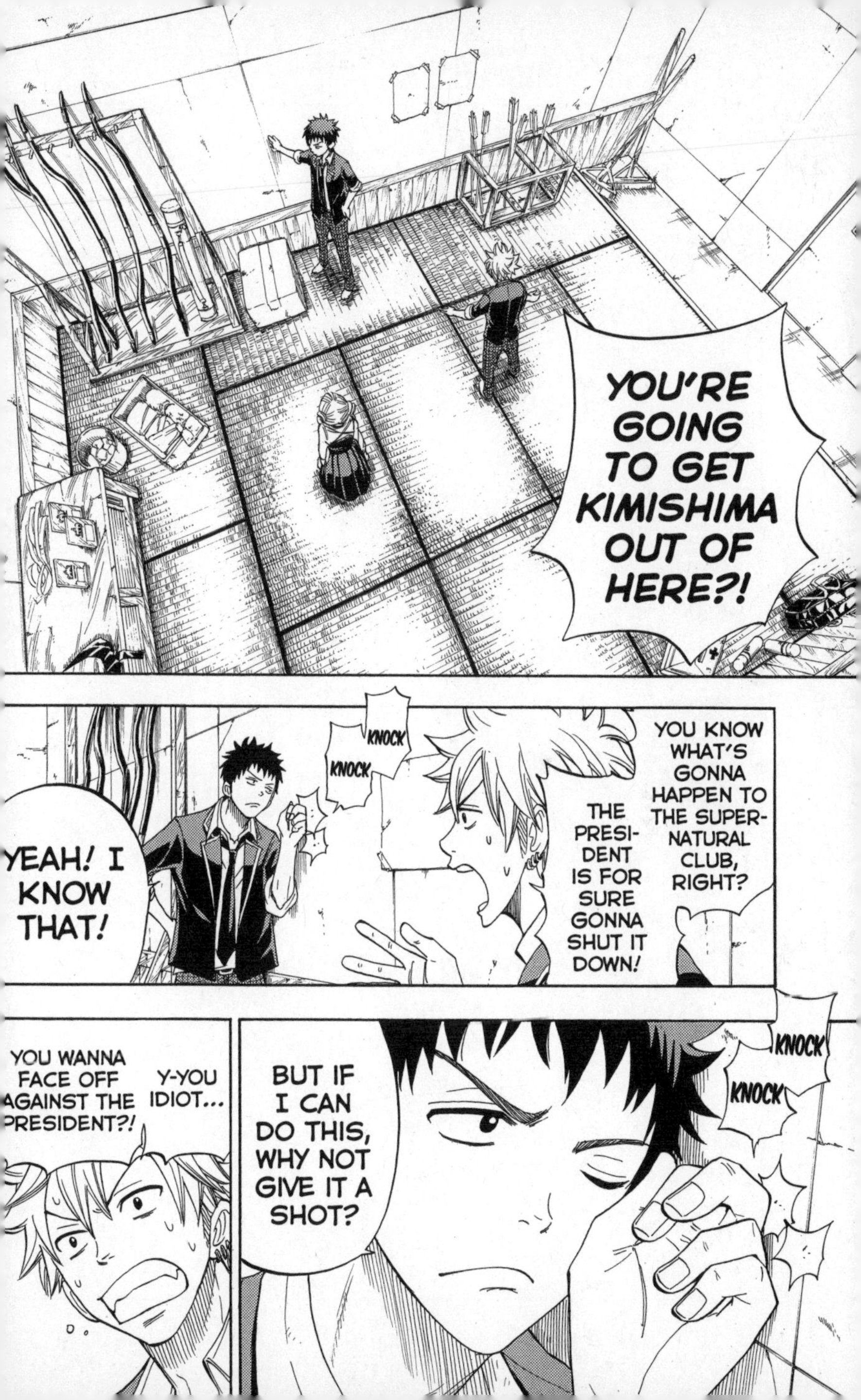
YOU'RE GOING TO GET KIMISHIMA OUT OF HERE?!
YOU KNOW WHAT'S GONNA HAPPEN TO THE SUPERNATURAL CLUB, RIGHT?
THE PRESIDENT IS FOR SURE GONNA SHUT IT DOWN!
KNOCK
KNOCK
YEAH! I KNOW THAT!
KNOCK
KNOCK
BUT IF I CAN DO THIS, WHY NOT GIVE IT A SHOT?
Y-YOU IDIOT...
YOU WANNA FACE OFF AGAINST THE PRESIDENT?!

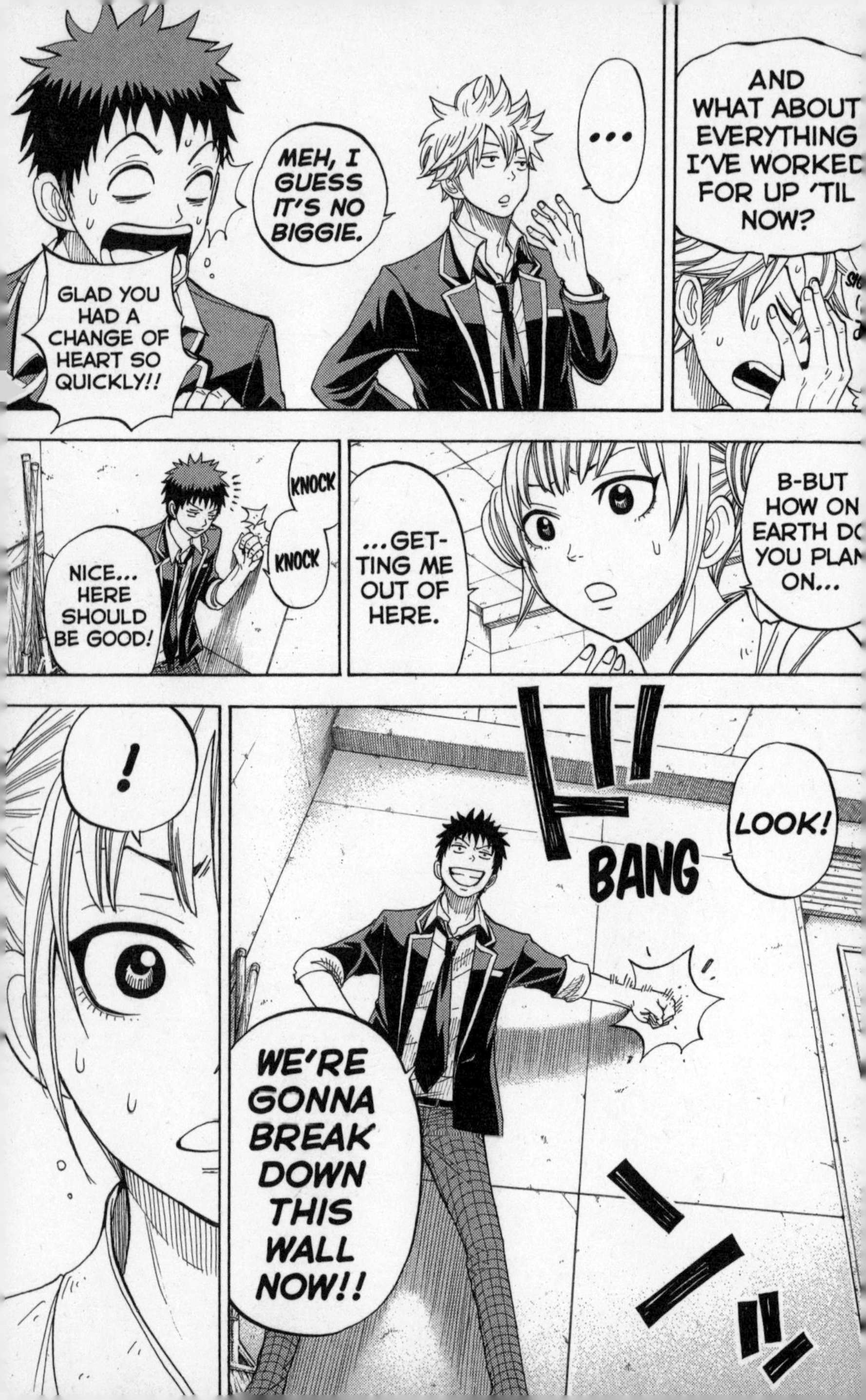
AND WHAT ABOUT EVERYTHING I'VE WORKED FOR UP 'TIL NOW?
...
MEH, I GUESS IT'S NO BIGGIE.
GLAD YOU HAD A CHANGE OF HEART SO QUICKLY!!
B-BUT HOW ON EARTH DO YOU PLAN ON...
...GETTING ME OUT OF HERE.
KNOCK
KNOCK
NICE... HERE SHOULD BE GOOD!
LOOK!
BANG
WE'RE GONNA BREAK DOWN THIS WALL NOW!!
!

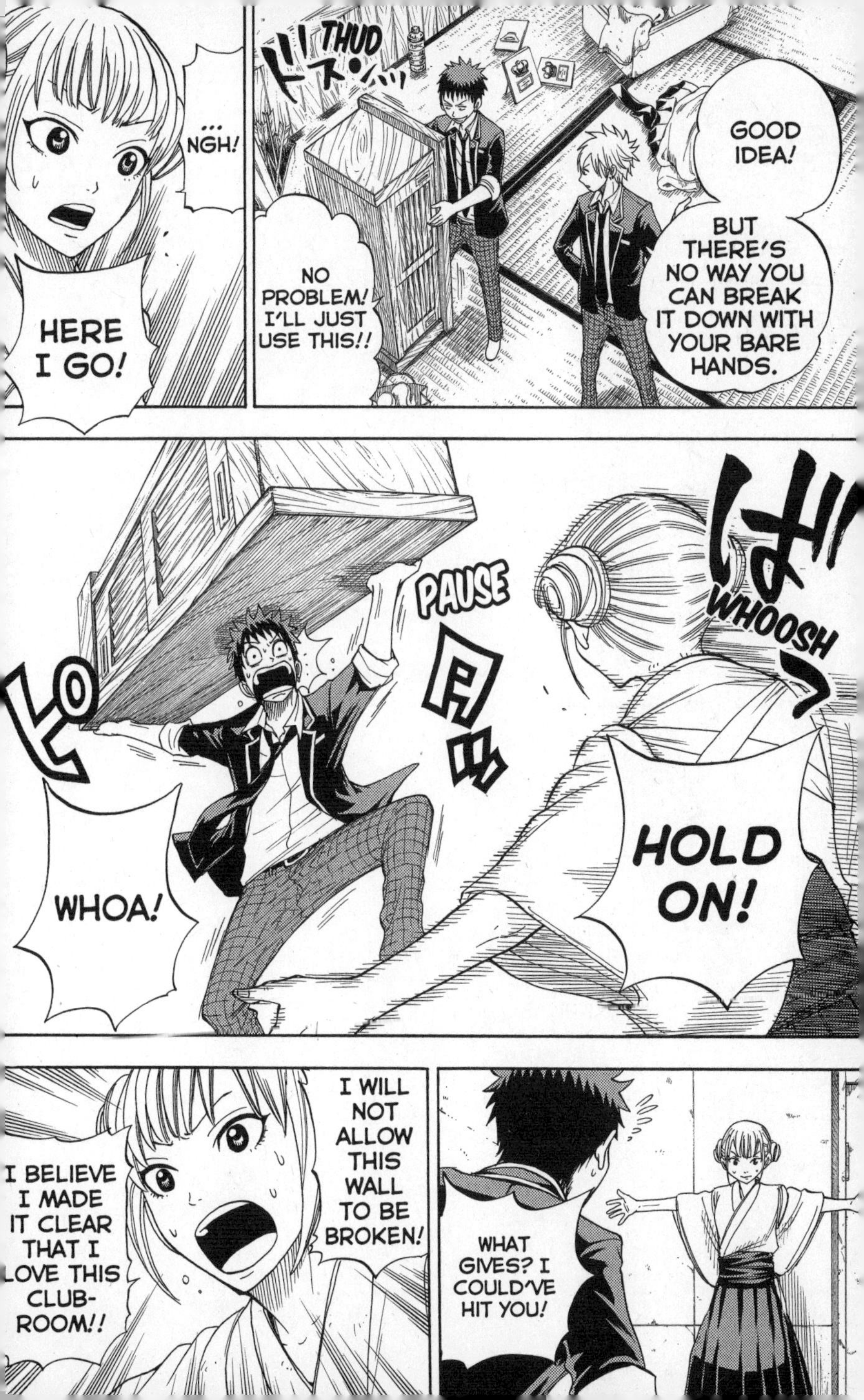
GOOD IDEA!
BUT THERE'S NO WAY YOU CAN BREAK IT DOWN WITH YOUR BARE HANDS.
ドスッ THUD
NO PROBLEM! I'LL JUST USE THIS!!
...NGH!
HERE I GO!
はっ WHOOSH
HOLD ON!
PAUSE
WHOA!
WHAT GIVES? I COULD'VE HIT YOU!
I WILL NOT ALLOW THIS WALL TO BE BROKEN!
I BELIEVE I MADE IT CLEAR THAT I LOVE THIS CLUB-ROOM!!

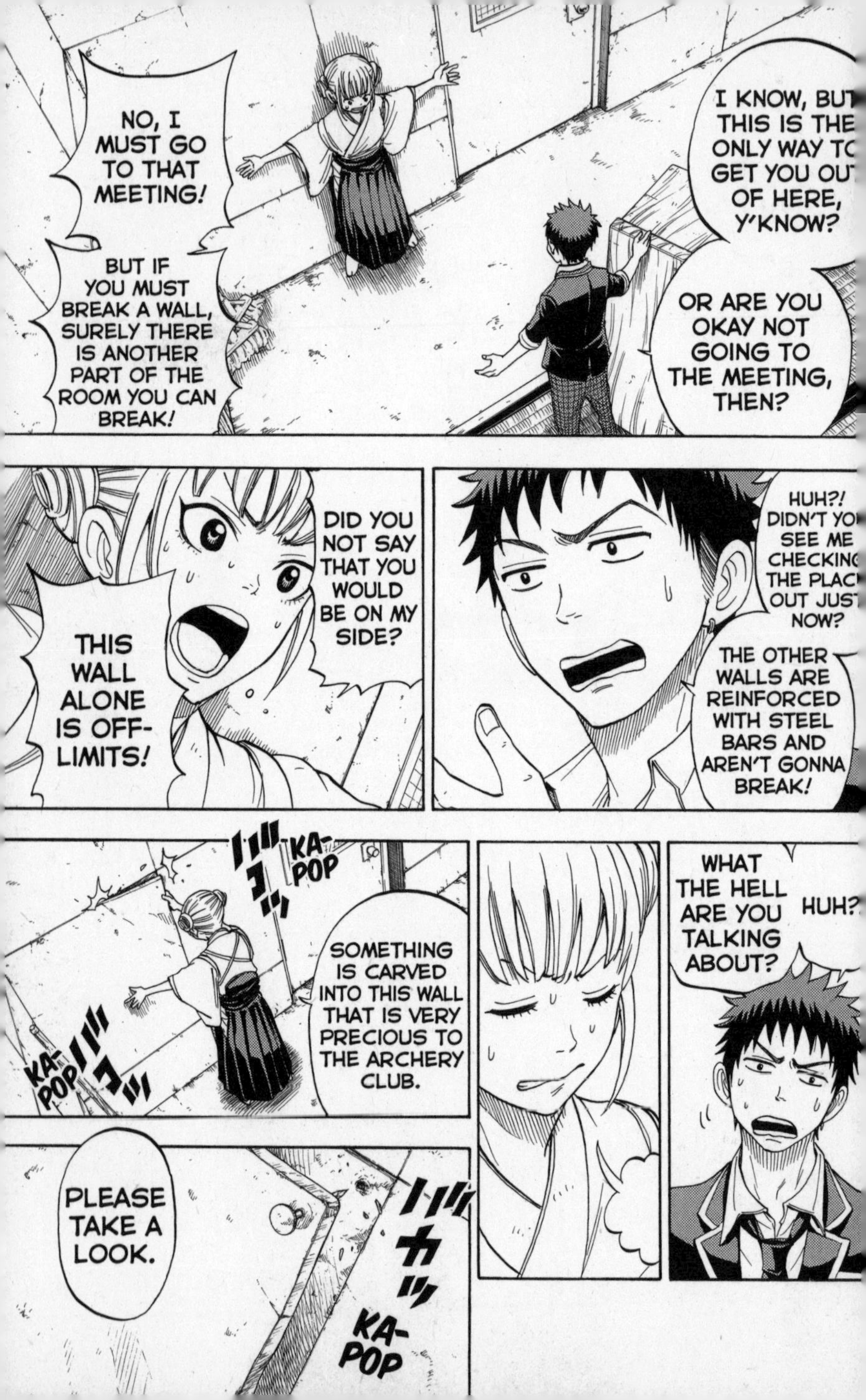
I KNOW, BUT THIS IS THE ONLY WAY TO GET YOU OUT OF HERE, Y'KNOW?
OR ARE YOU OKAY NOT GOING TO THE MEETING, THEN?
NO, I MUST GO TO THAT MEETING!
BUT IF YOU MUST BREAK A WALL, SURELY THERE IS ANOTHER PART OF THE ROOM YOU CAN BREAK!
HUH?! DIDN'T YOU SEE ME CHECKING THE PLACE OUT JUST NOW?
THE OTHER WALLS ARE REINFORCED WITH STEEL BARS AND AREN'T GONNA BREAK!
DID YOU NOT SAY THAT YOU WOULD BE ON MY SIDE?
THIS WALL ALONE IS OFF-LIMITS!
WHAT THE HELL ARE YOU TALKING ABOUT?
HUH?
KA-POP
SOMETHING IS CARVED INTO THIS WALL THAT IS VERY PRECIOUS TO THE ARCHERY CLUB.
KA-POP
PLEASE TAKE A LOOK.
KA-POP

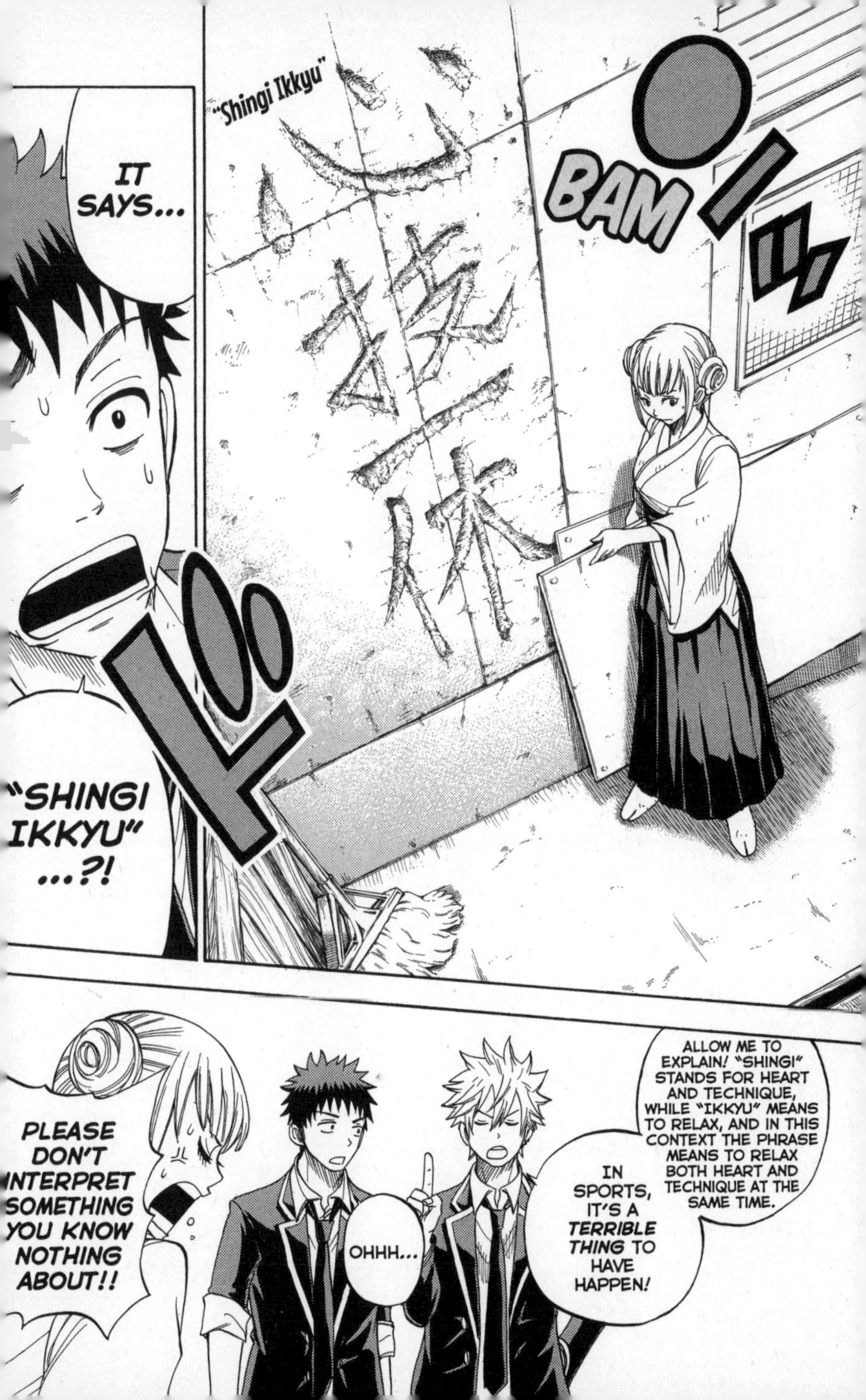
"Shingi Ikkyu"
BAM
IT SAYS...
"SHINGI IKKYU" ...?!
ALLOW ME TO EXPLAIN! "SHINGI" STANDS FOR HEART AND TECHNIQUE, WHILE "IKKYU" MEANS TO RELAX, AND IN THIS CONTEXT THE PHRASE MEANS TO RELAX BOTH HEART AND TECHNIQUE AT THE SAME TIME.
IN SPORTS, IT'S A *TERRIBLE THING* TO HAVE HAPPEN!
OHHH...
PLEASE DON'T INTERPRET SOMETHING YOU KNOW NOTHING ABOUT!!

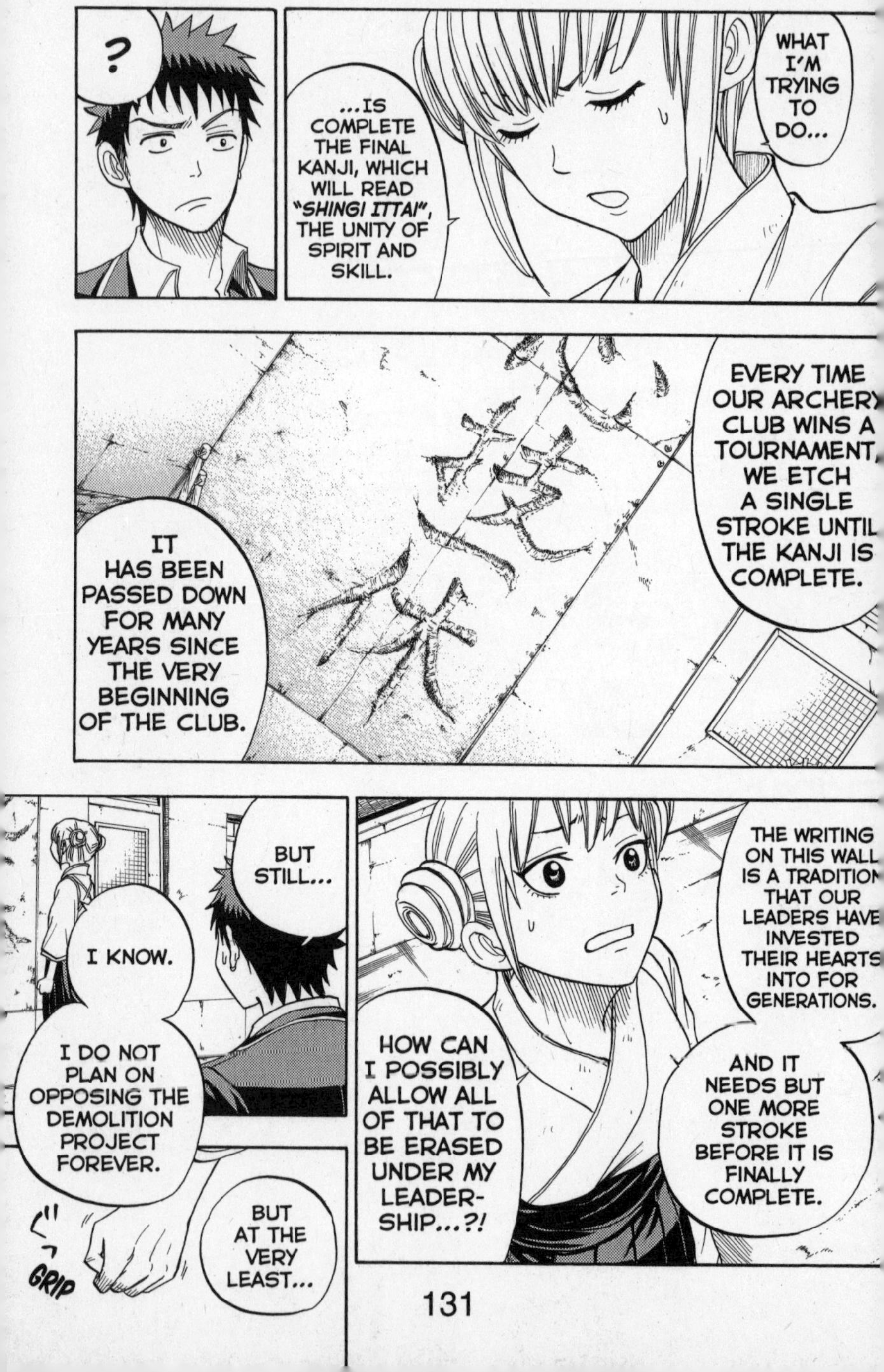
WHAT I'M TRYING TO DO...
...IS COMPLETE THE FINAL KANJI, WHICH WILL READ *"SHINGI ITTAI"*, THE UNITY OF SPIRIT AND SKILL.
?
EVERY TIME OUR ARCHERY CLUB WINS A TOURNAMENT, WE ETCH A SINGLE STROKE UNTIL THE KANJI IS COMPLETE.
IT HAS BEEN PASSED DOWN FOR MANY YEARS SINCE THE VERY BEGINNING OF THE CLUB.
THE WRITING ON THIS WALL IS A TRADITION THAT OUR LEADERS HAVE INVESTED THEIR HEARTS INTO FOR GENERATIONS.
AND IT NEEDS BUT ONE MORE STROKE BEFORE IT IS FINALLY COMPLETE.
HOW CAN I POSSIBLY ALLOW ALL OF THAT TO BE ERASED UNDER MY LEADER-SHIP...?!
BUT STILL...
I KNOW.
I DO NOT PLAN ON OPPOSING THE DEMOLITION PROJECT FOREVER.
GRIP
BUT AT THE VERY LEAST...

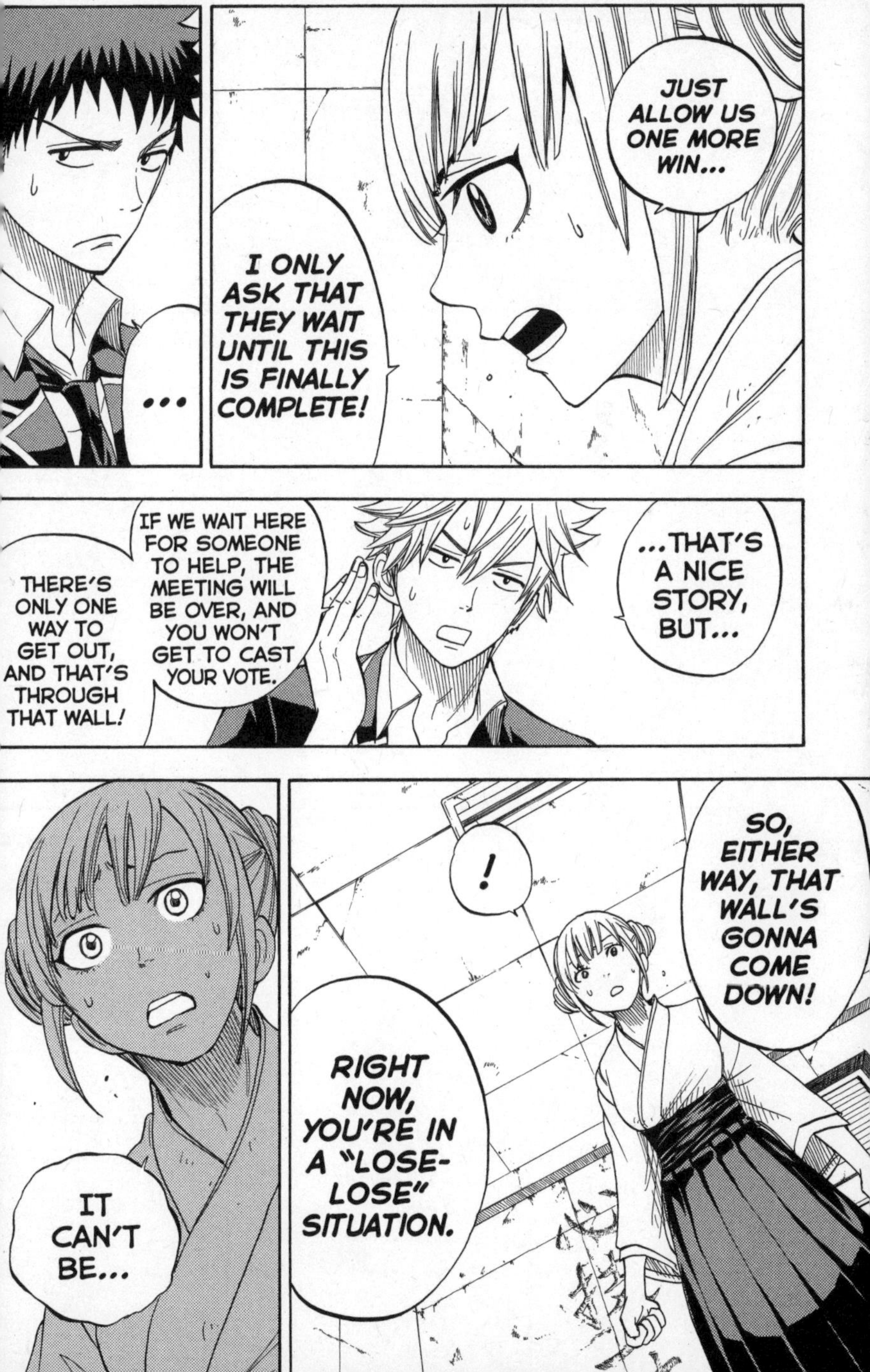
JUST ALLOW US ONE MORE WIN...
I ONLY ASK THAT THEY WAIT UNTIL THIS IS FINALLY COMPLETE!
...
...THAT'S A NICE STORY, BUT...
IF WE WAIT HERE FOR SOMEONE TO HELP, THE MEETING WILL BE OVER, AND YOU WON'T GET TO CAST YOUR VOTE.
THERE'S ONLY ONE WAY TO GET OUT, AND THAT'S THROUGH THAT WALL!
SO, EITHER WAY, THAT WALL'S GONNA COME DOWN!
!
RIGHT NOW, YOU'RE IN A "LOSE-LOSE" SITUATION.
IT CAN'T BE...

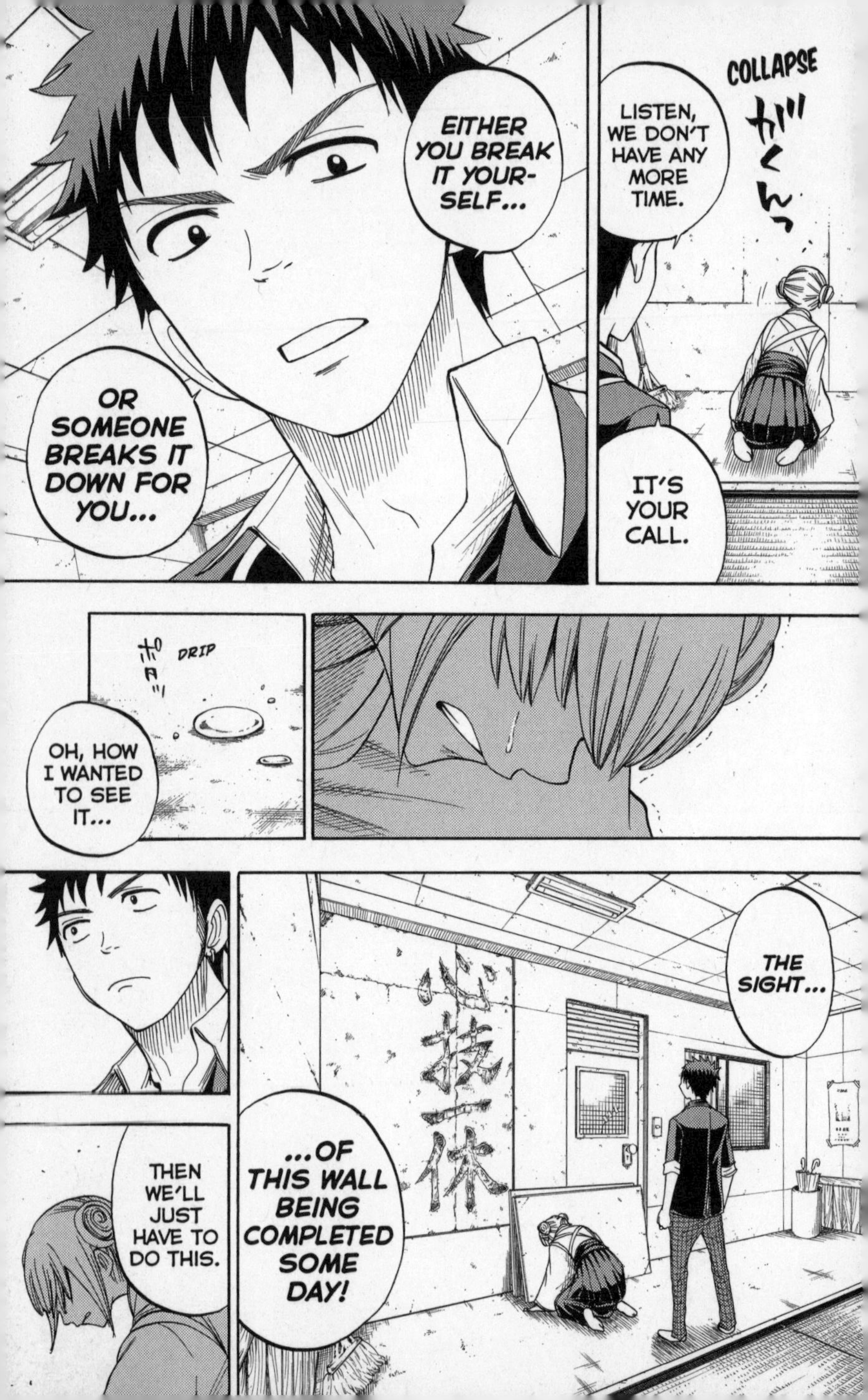
COLLAPSE
がくんっ
LISTEN, WE DON'T HAVE ANY MORE TIME.
IT'S YOUR CALL.
EITHER YOU BREAK IT YOUR-SELF...
OR SOMEONE BREAKS IT DOWN FOR YOU...
ポタッ
DRIP
OH, HOW I WANTED TO SEE IT...
THE SIGHT...
...OF THIS WALL BEING COMPLETED SOME DAY!
THEN WE'LL JUST HAVE TO DO THIS.

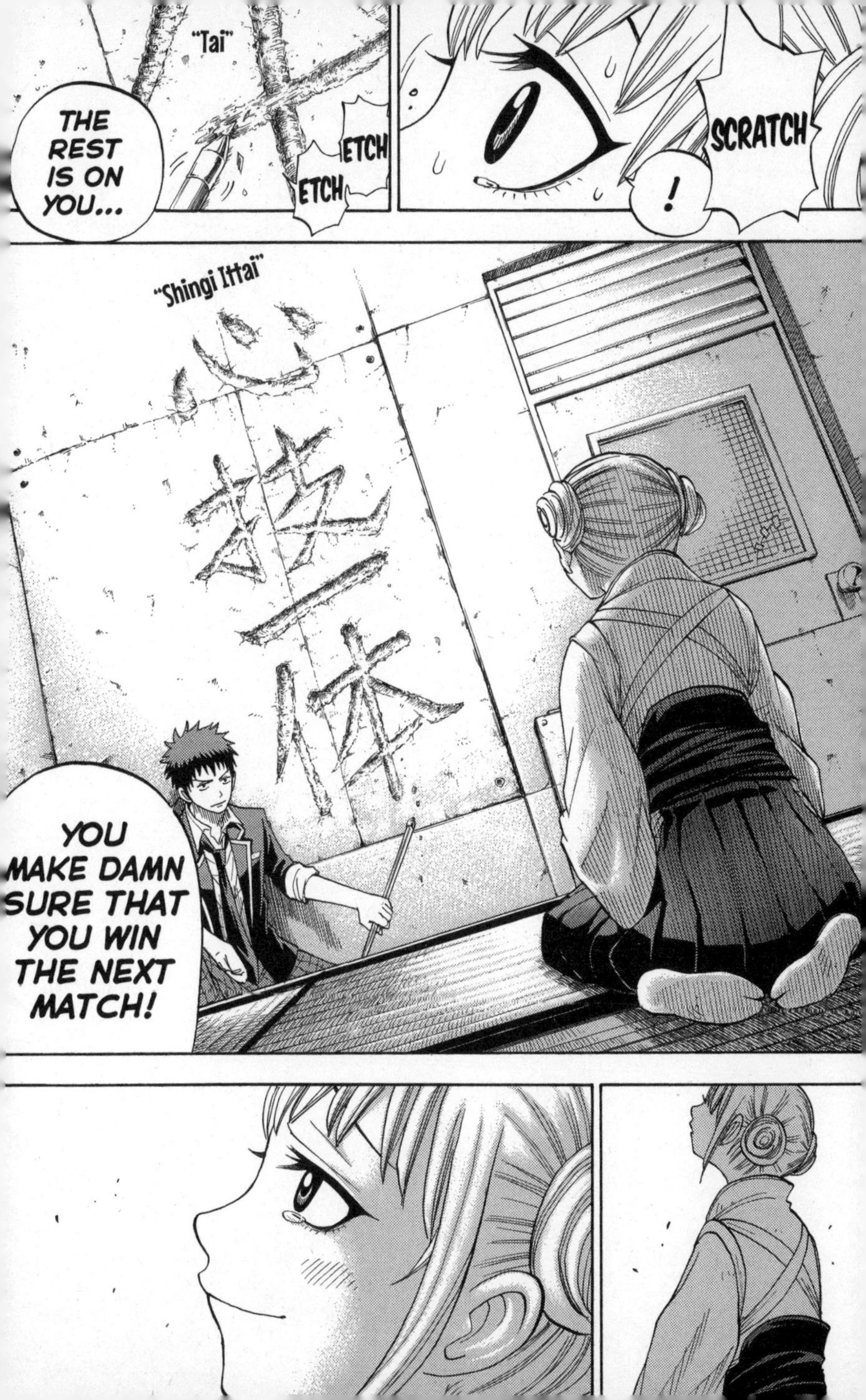
SCRATCH
!
"Tai"
ETCH
THE REST IS ON YOU...
ETCH
"Shingi Ittai"
YOU MAKE DAMN SURE THAT YOU WIN THE NEXT MATCH!

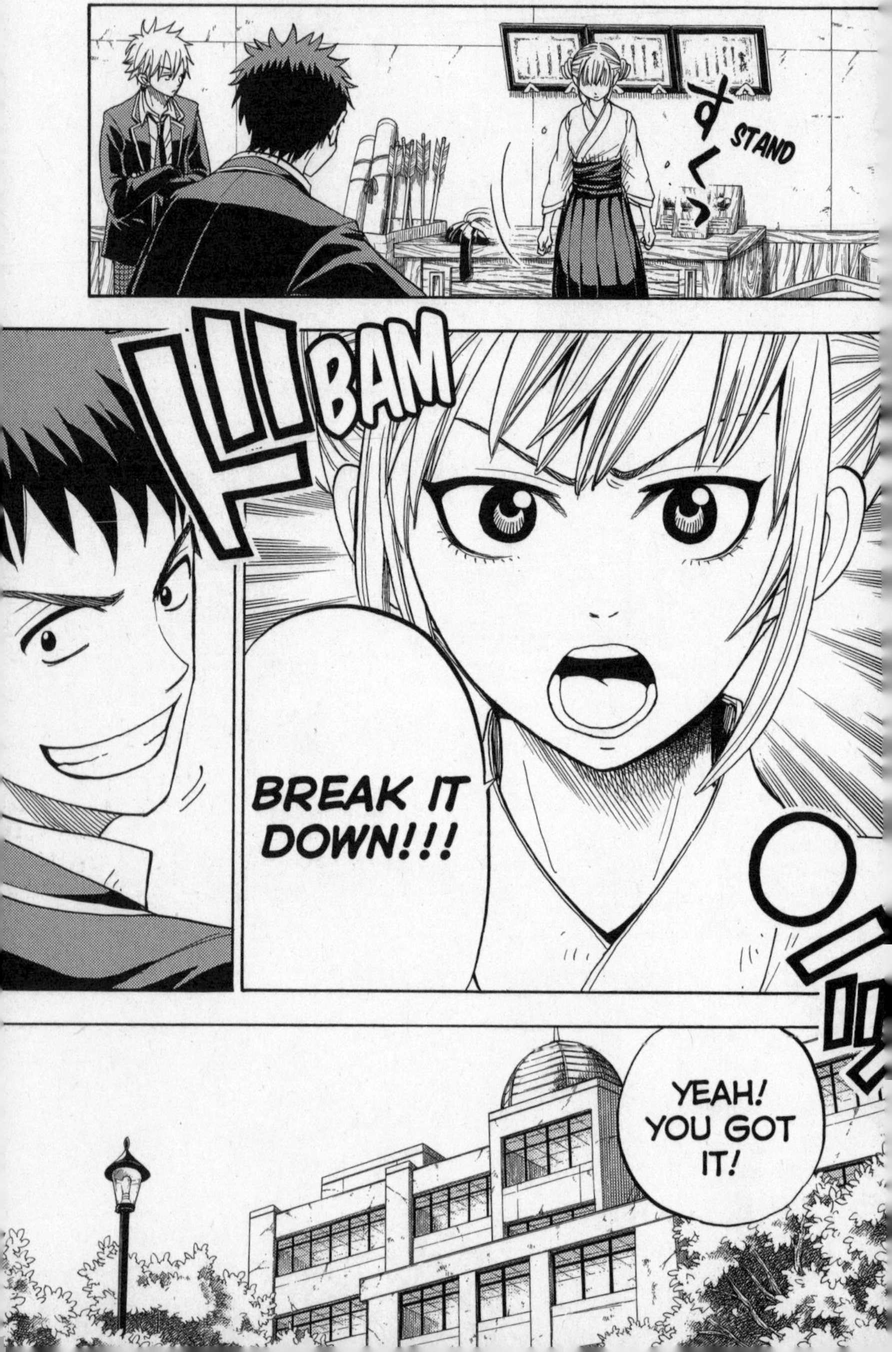
STAND
BREAK IT DOWN!!!
BAM
YEAH! YOU GOT IT!

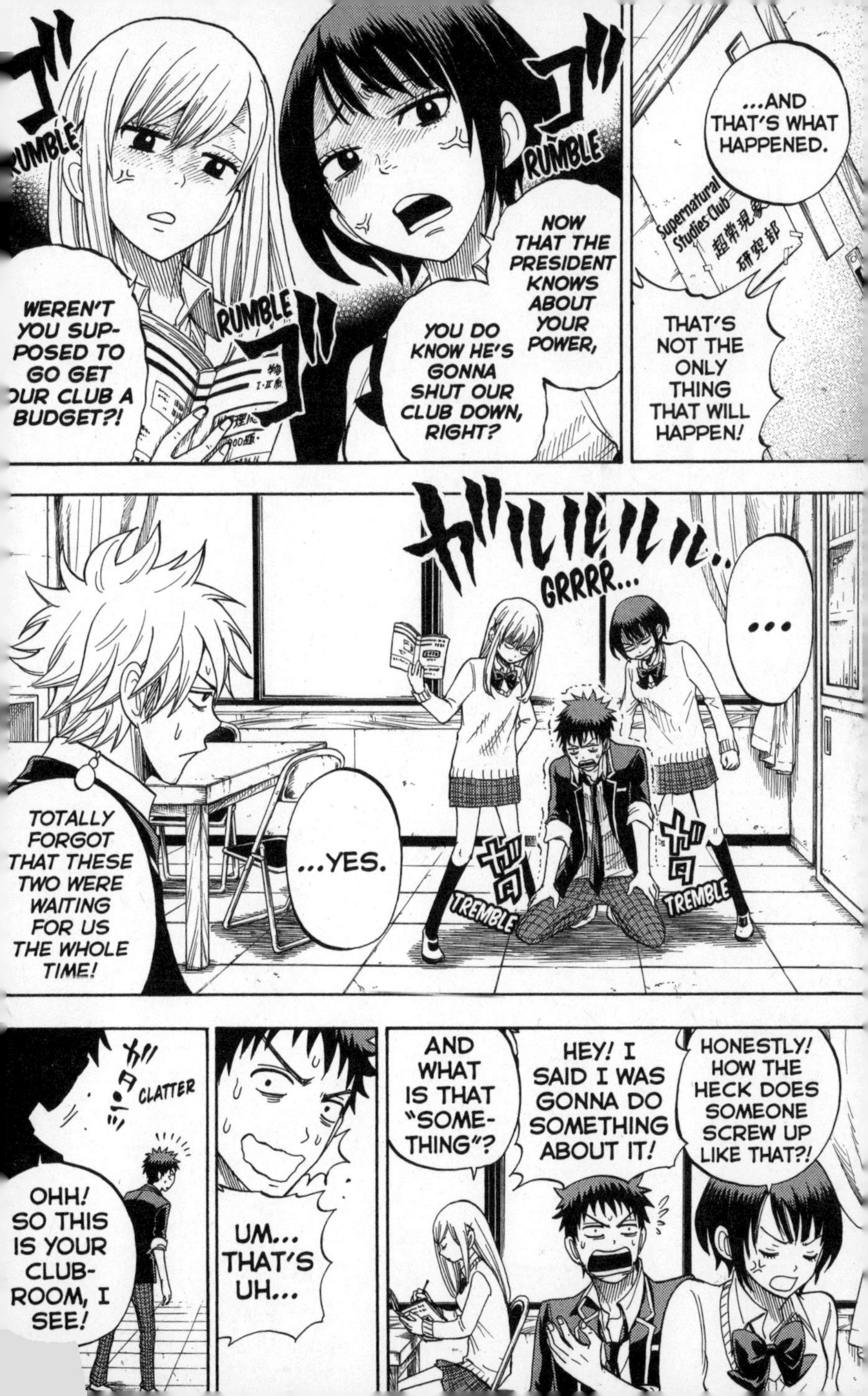
...AND THAT'S WHAT HAPPENED.
Supernatural Studies Club
超常現象研究部
THAT'S NOT THE ONLY THING THAT WILL HAPPEN!
RUMBLE
NOW THAT THE PRESIDENT KNOWS ABOUT YOUR POWER,
YOU DO KNOW HE'S GONNA SHUT OUR CLUB DOWN, RIGHT?
RUMBLE
RUMBLE
WEREN'T YOU SUP-POSED TO GO GET OUR CLUB A BUDGET?!
GRRRR...
...
...YES.
TREMBLE
TREMBLE
TOTALLY FORGOT THAT THESE TWO WERE WAITING FOR US THE WHOLE TIME!
HONESTLY! HOW THE HECK DOES SOMEONE SCREW UP LIKE THAT?!
HEY! I SAID I WAS GONNA DO SOMETHING ABOUT IT!
AND WHAT IS THAT "SOME-THING"?
UM... THAT'S UH...
CLATTER
OHH! SO THIS IS YOUR CLUB-ROOM, I SEE!

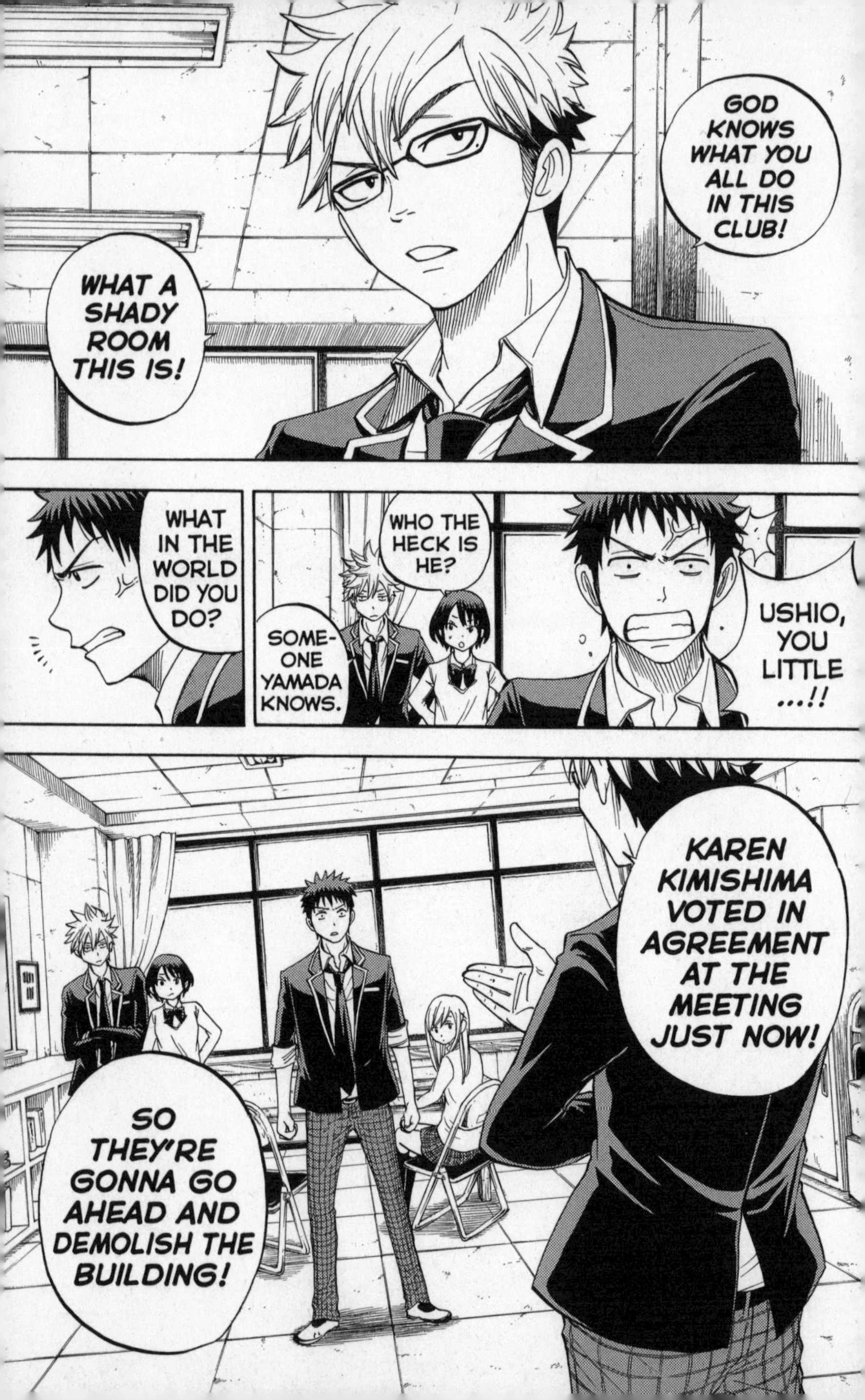
GOD KNOWS WHAT YOU ALL DO IN THIS CLUB!
WHAT A SHADY ROOM THIS IS!
USHIO, YOU LITTLE ...!!
WHO THE HECK IS HE?
SOME-ONE YAMADA KNOWS.
WHAT IN THE WORLD DID YOU DO?
KAREN KIMISHIMA VOTED IN AGREEMENT AT THE MEETING JUST NOW!
SO THEY'RE GONNA GO AHEAD AND DEMOLISH THE BUILDING!

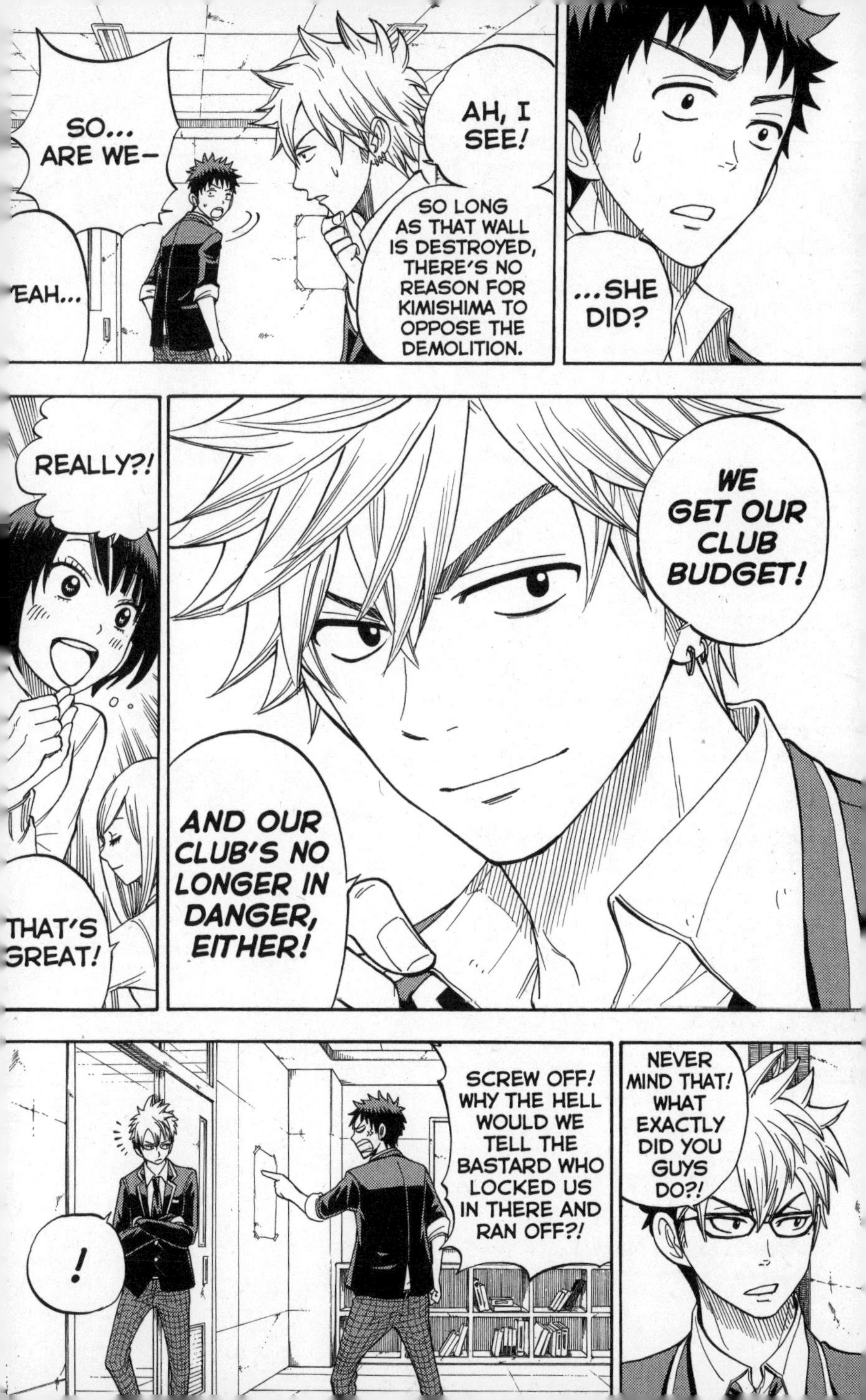
...SHE DID?
AH, I SEE!
SO LONG AS THAT WALL IS DESTROYED, THERE'S NO REASON FOR KIMISHIMA TO OPPOSE THE DEMOLITION.
SO... ARE WE–
EAH...
WE GET OUR CLUB BUDGET!
AND OUR CLUB'S NO LONGER IN DANGER, EITHER!
REALLY?!
THAT'S GREAT!
NEVER MIND THAT! WHAT EXACTLY DID YOU GUYS DO?!
SCREW OFF! WHY THE HELL WOULD WE TELL THE BASTARD WHO LOCKED US IN THERE AND RAN OFF?!
!

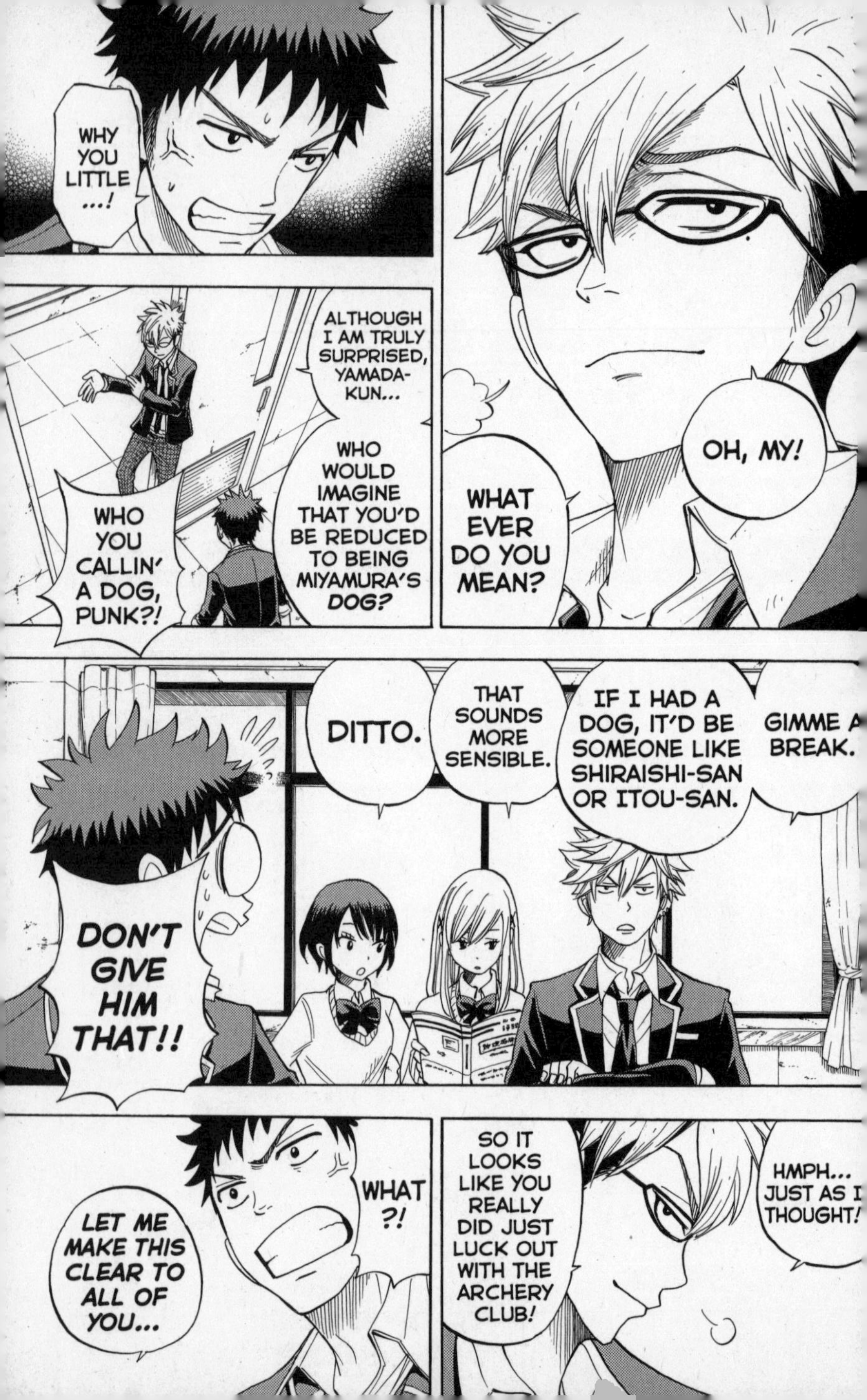
OH, MY!
WHAT EVER DO YOU MEAN?
WHY YOU LITTLE ...!
ALTHOUGH I AM TRULY SURPRISED, YAMADA-KUN...
WHO WOULD IMAGINE THAT YOU'D BE REDUCED TO BEING MIYAMURA'S *DOG?*
WHO YOU CALLIN' A DOG, PUNK?!
GIMME A BREAK.
IF I HAD A DOG, IT'D BE SOMEONE LIKE SHIRAISHI-SAN OR ITOU-SAN.
THAT SOUNDS MORE SENSIBLE.
DITTO.
DON'T GIVE HIM THAT!!
HMPH... JUST AS I THOUGHT!
SO IT LOOKS LIKE YOU REALLY DID JUST LUCK OUT WITH THE ARCHERY CLUB!
WHAT ?!
LET ME MAKE THIS CLEAR TO ALL OF YOU...

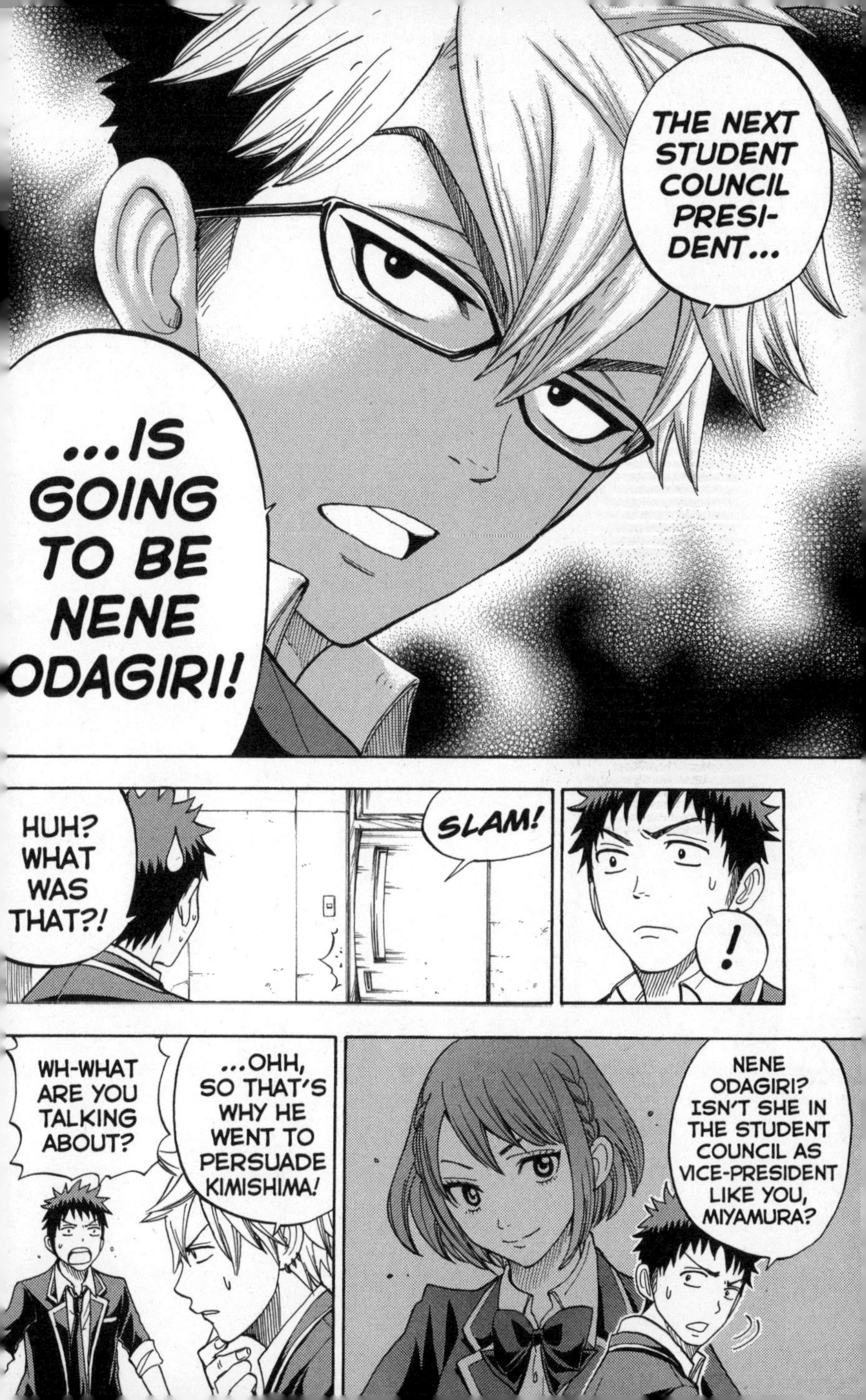
THE NEXT STUDENT COUNCIL PRESI-DENT...
...IS GOING TO BE NENE ODAGIRI!
!
SLAM!
HUH? WHAT WAS THAT?!
NENE ODAGIRI? ISN'T SHE IN THE STUDENT COUNCIL AS VICE-PRESIDENT LIKE YOU, MIYAMURA?
...OHH, SO THAT'S WHY HE WENT TO PERSUADE KIMISHIMA!
WH-WHAT ARE YOU TALKING ABOUT?

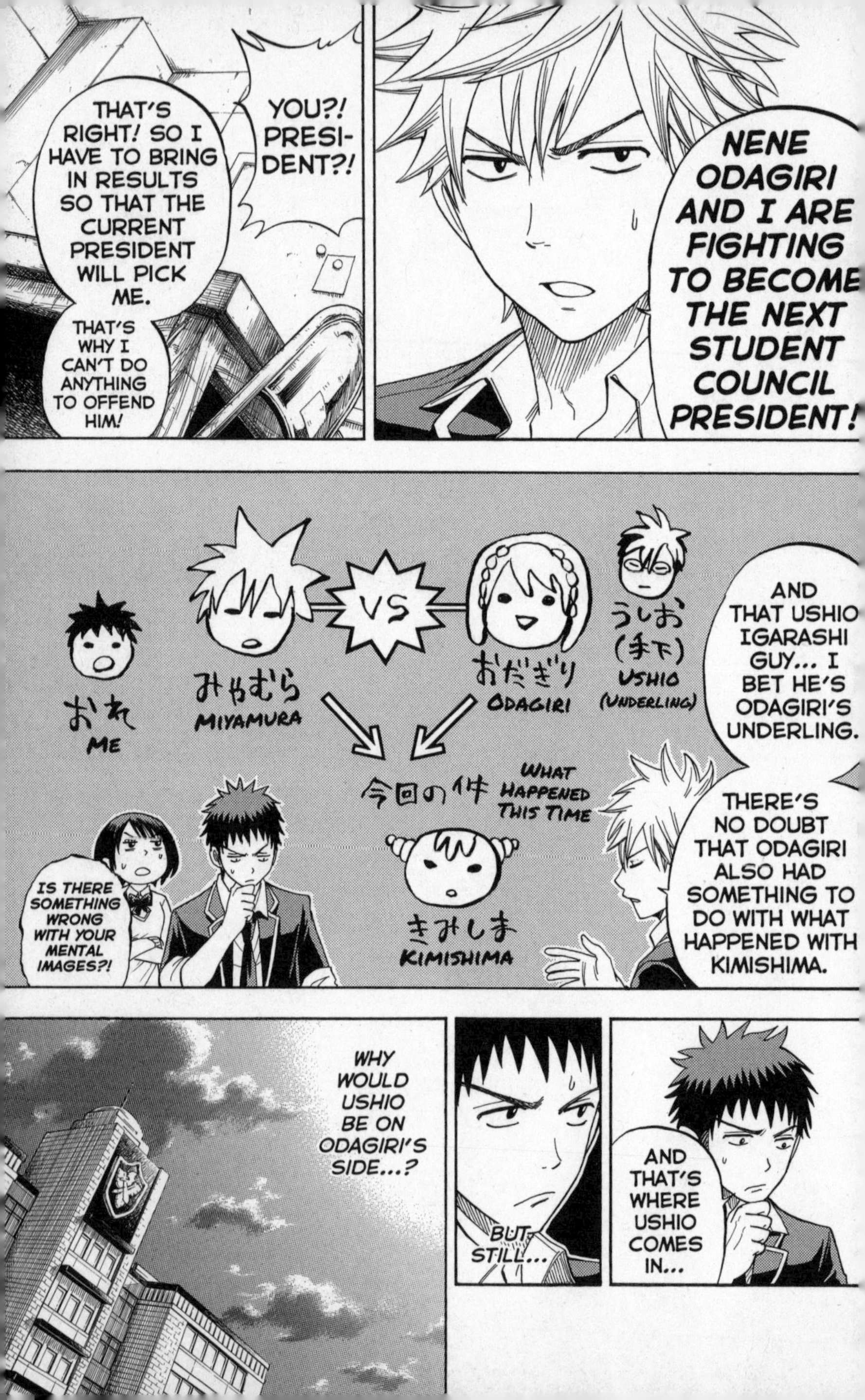
NENE ODAGIRI AND I ARE FIGHTING TO BECOME THE NEXT STUDENT COUNCIL PRESIDENT!
YOU?! PRESIDENT?!
THAT'S RIGHT! SO I HAVE TO BRING IN RESULTS SO THAT THE CURRENT PRESIDENT WILL PICK ME.
THAT'S WHY I CAN'T DO ANYTHING TO OFFEND HIM!
AND THAT USHIO IGARASHI GUY... I BET HE'S ODAGIRI'S UNDERLING.
うしお (手下)
USHIO (UNDERLING)
おだぎり
ODAGIRI
VS
みやむら
MIYAMURA
おれ
ME
今回の件
WHAT HAPPENED THIS TIME
きみしま
KIMISHIMA
THERE'S NO DOUBT THAT ODAGIRI ALSO HAD SOMETHING TO DO WITH WHAT HAPPENED WITH KIMISHIMA.
IS THERE SOMETHING WRONG WITH YOUR MENTAL IMAGES?!
AND THAT'S WHERE USHIO COMES IN...
BUT STILL...
WHY WOULD USHIO BE ON ODAGIRI'S SIDE...?

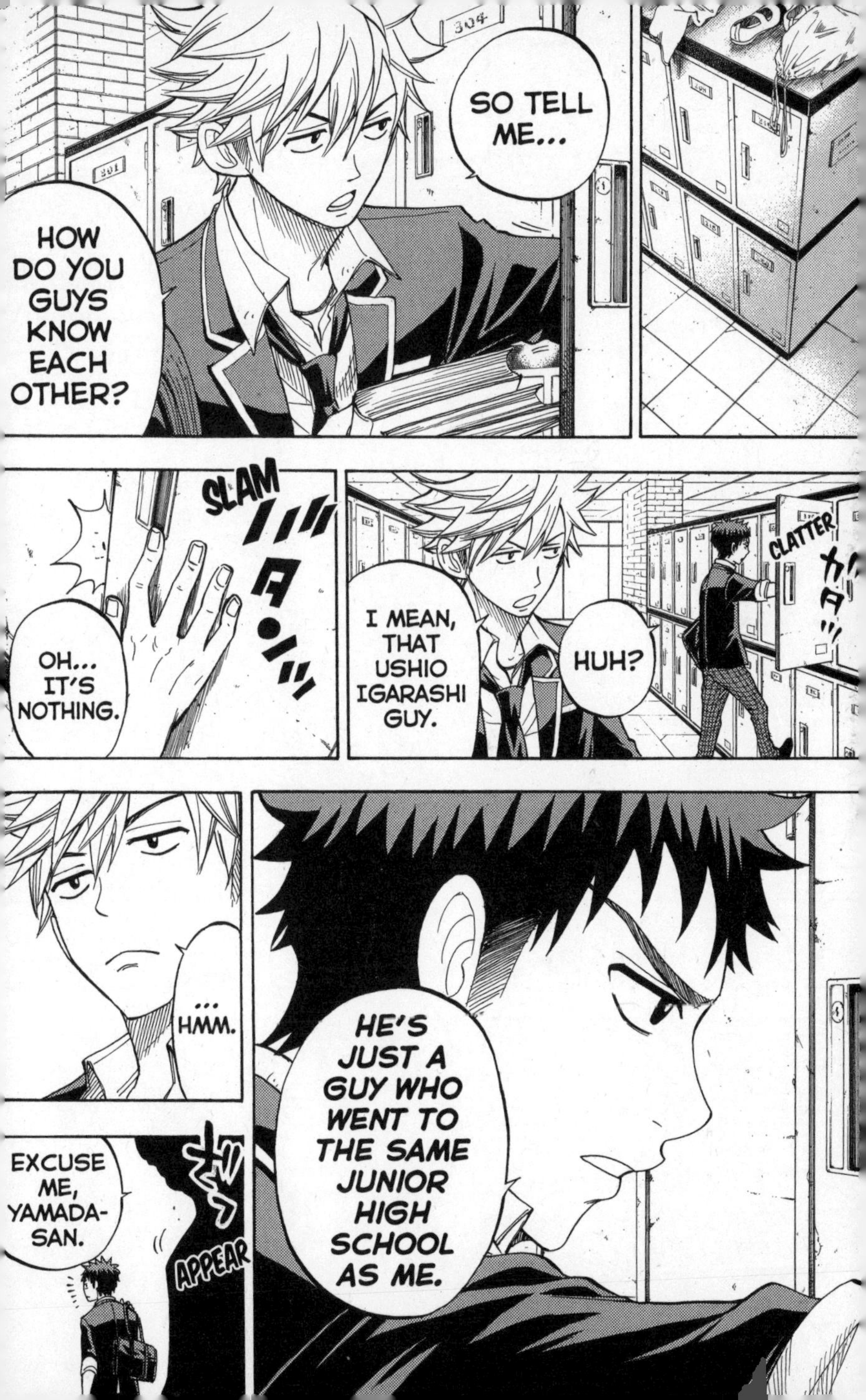
SO TELL ME...
HOW DO YOU GUYS KNOW EACH OTHER?
CLATTER
HUH?
I MEAN, THAT USHIO IGARASHI GUY.
SLAM
OH... IT'S NOTHING.
HE'S JUST A GUY WHO WENT TO THE SAME JUNIOR HIGH SCHOOL AS ME.
... HMM.
APPEAR
EXCUSE ME, YAMADA-SAN.

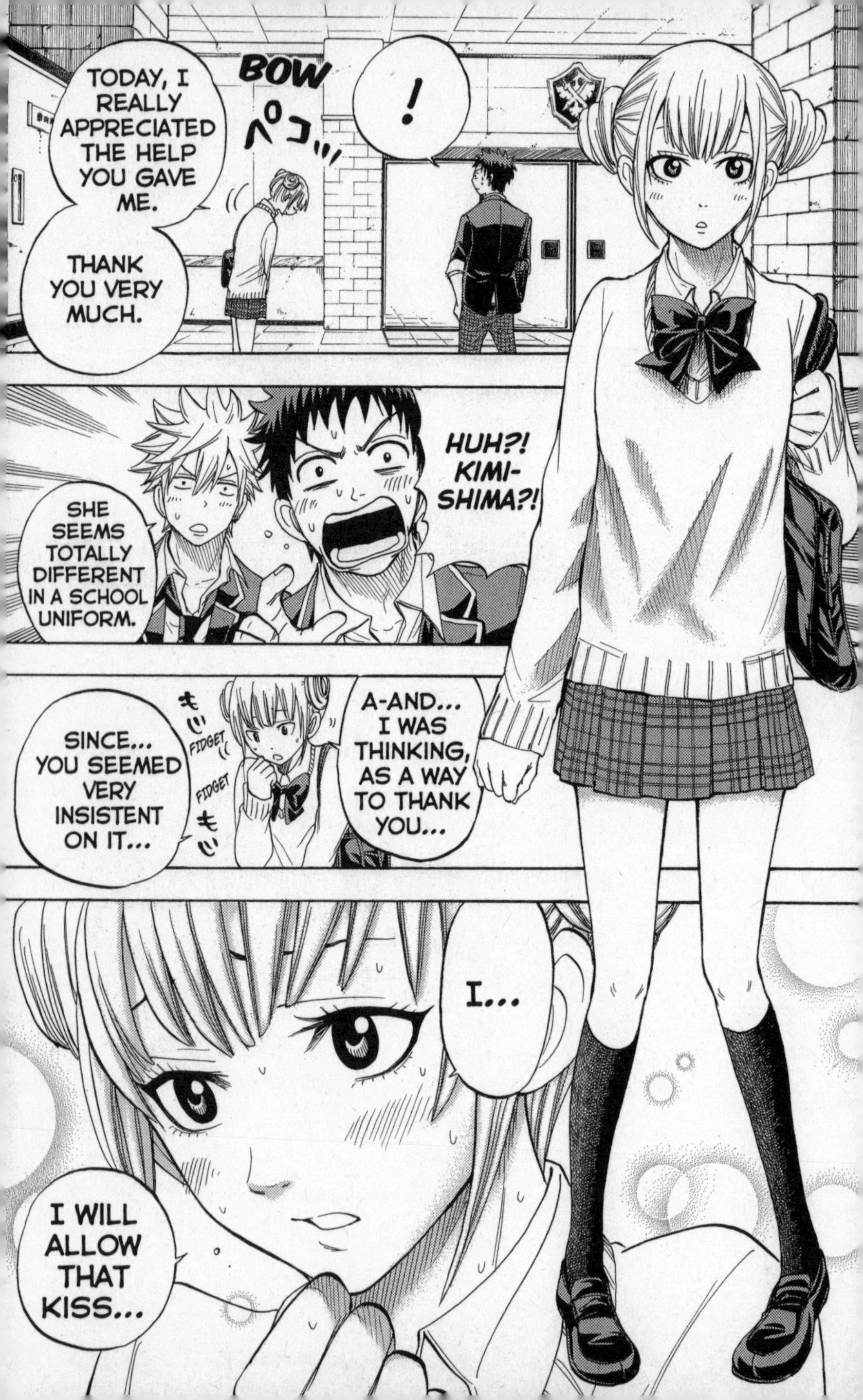
!
BOW
ペコッ
TODAY, I REALLY APPRECIATED THE HELP YOU GAVE ME.
THANK YOU VERY MUCH.
HUH?! KIMI-SHIMA?!
SHE SEEMS TOTALLY DIFFERENT IN A SCHOOL UNIFORM.
A-AND... I WAS THINKING, AS A WAY TO THANK YOU...
もじ FIDGET
もじ FIDGET
SINCE... YOU SEEMED VERY INSISTENT ON IT...
I...
I WILL ALLOW THAT KISS...

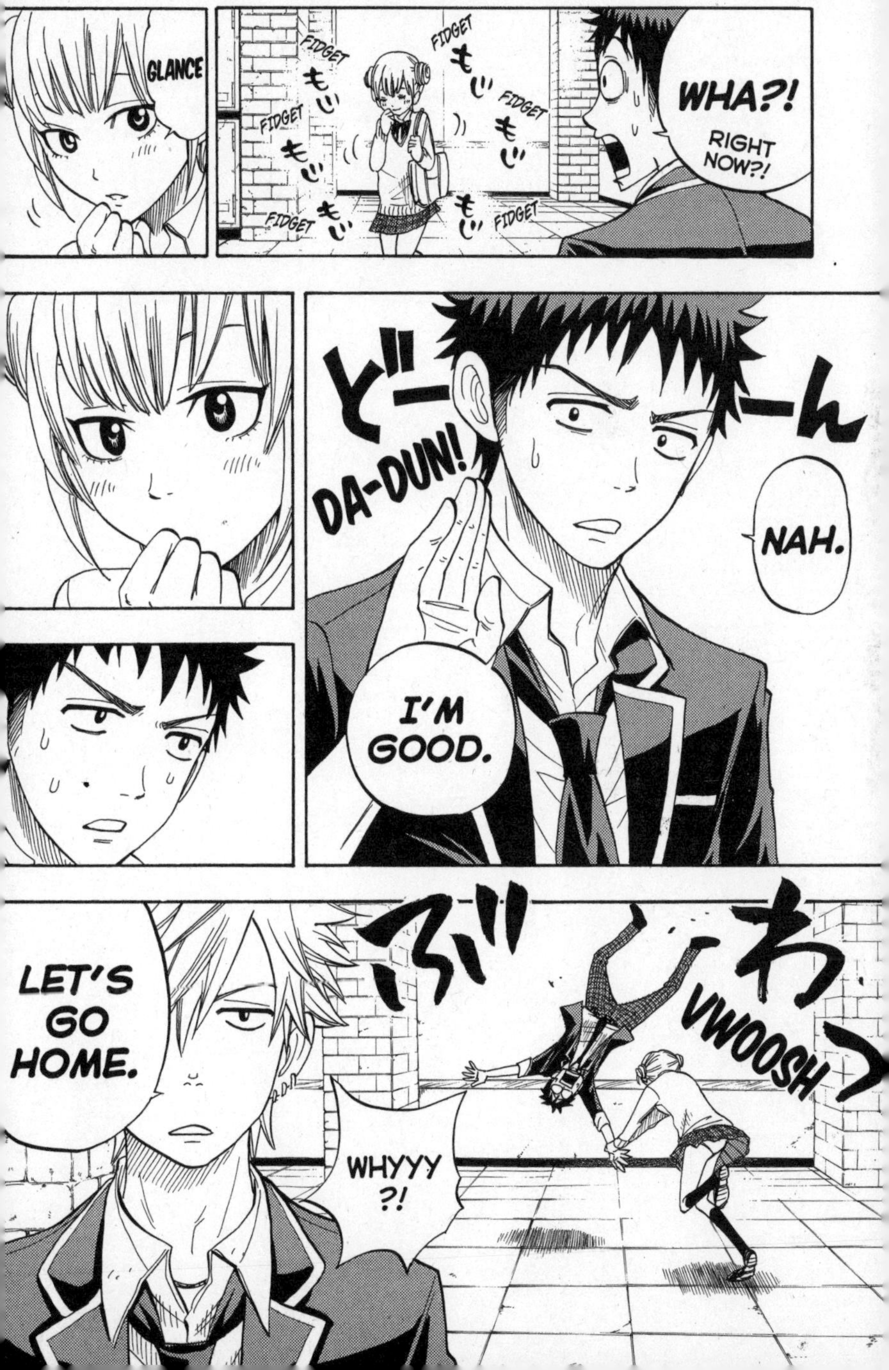

WHA?!
RIGHT NOW?!
FIDGET もじ
FIDGET もじ
FIDGET もじ
FIDGET もじ
FIDGET もじ
FIDGET もじ
GLANCE
どーーん
DA-DUN!
NAH.
I'M GOOD.
ぶわっ
VWOOSH
LET'S GO HOME.
WHYYY ?!

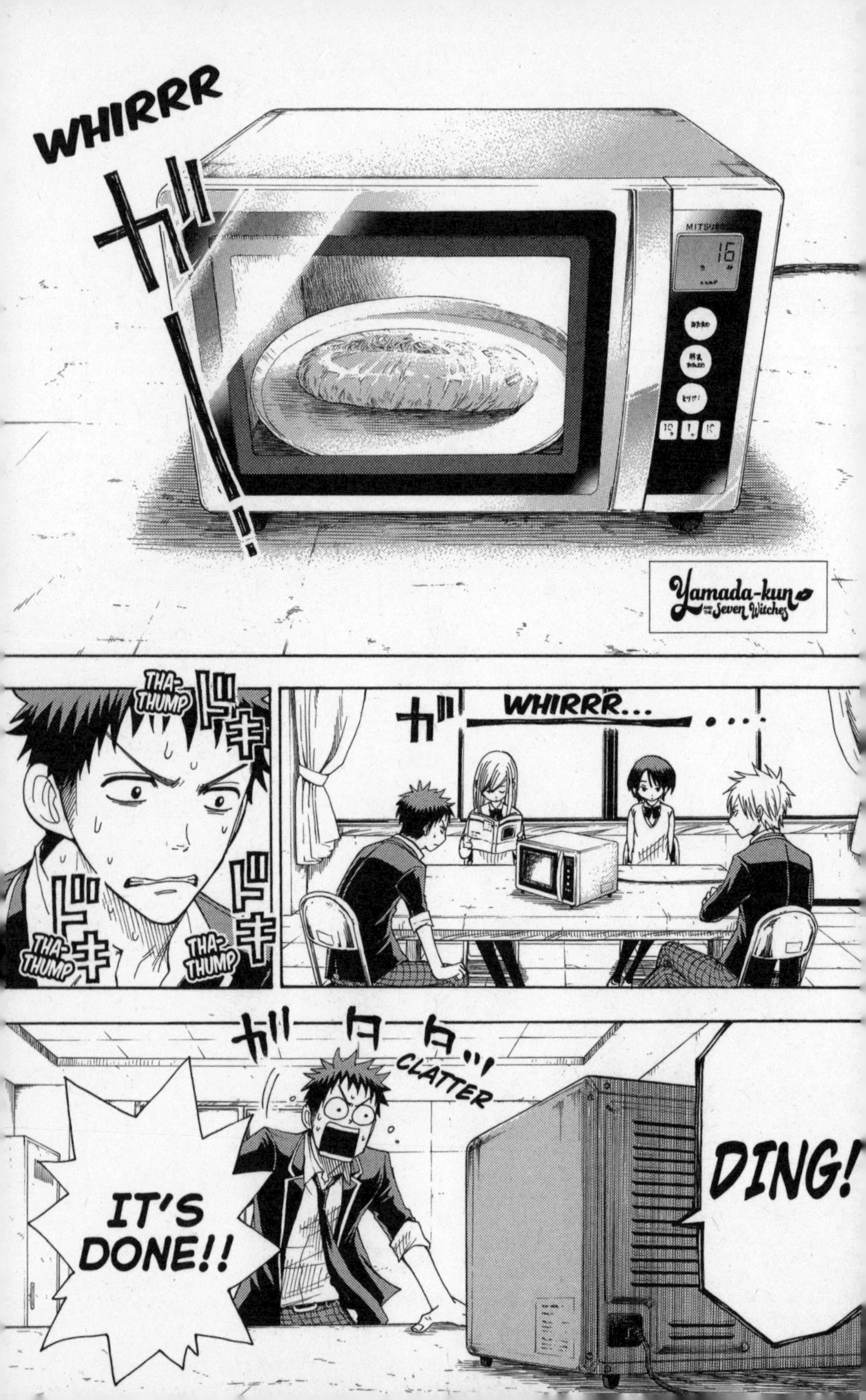
WHIRRR
ガー
Yamada-kun and the Seven Witches
ガー
WHIRRR...
....
THA-THUMP
ドキ
ドキ
THA-THUMP
ドキ
THA-THUMP
DING!
ガタタッ
CLATTER
IT'S DONE!!

Chapter 15: Oh...my...god!

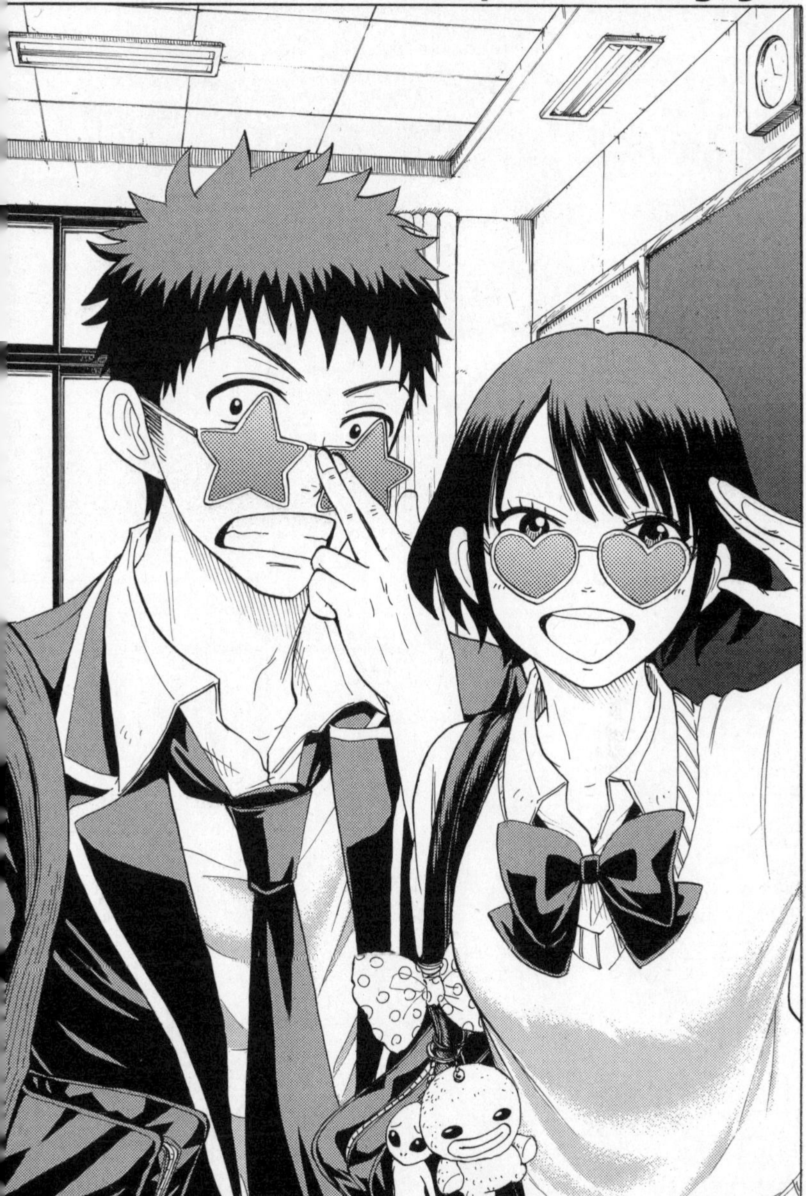

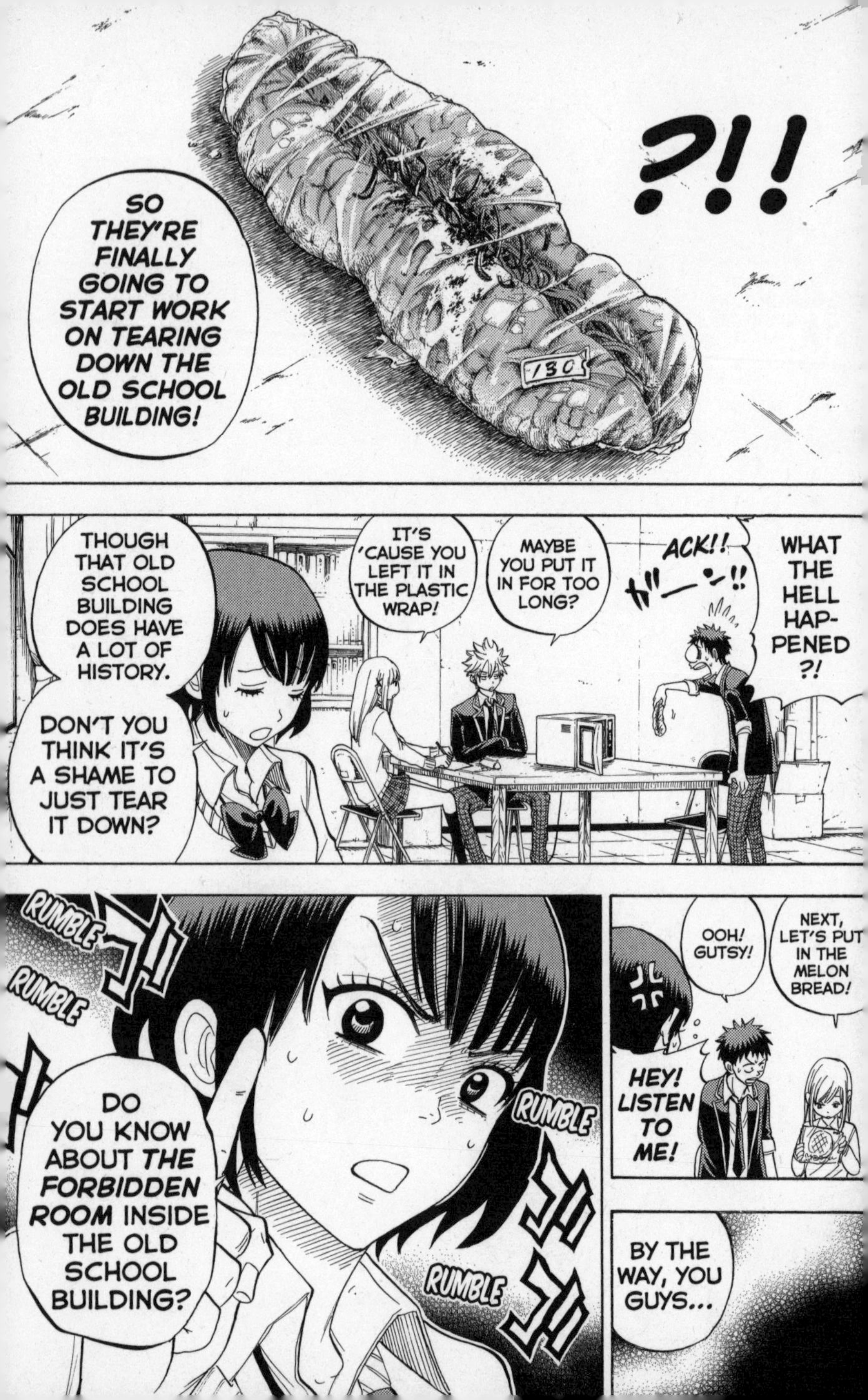
?!!
SO THEY'RE FINALLY GOING TO START WORK ON TEARING DOWN THE OLD SCHOOL BUILDING!
130
WHAT THE HELL HAP-PENED?!
ACK!!
ガーン!!
MAYBE YOU PUT IT IN FOR TOO LONG?
IT'S 'CAUSE YOU LEFT IT IN THE PLASTIC WRAP!
THOUGH THAT OLD SCHOOL BUILDING DOES HAVE A LOT OF HISTORY.
DON'T YOU THINK IT'S A SHAME TO JUST TEAR IT DOWN?
NEXT, LET'S PUT IN THE MELON BREAD!
OOH! GUTSY!
HEY! LISTEN TO ME!
BY THE WAY, YOU GUYS...
RUMBLE
RUMBLE
RUMBLE
RUMBLE
DO YOU KNOW ABOUT THE FORBIDDEN ROOM INSIDE THE OLD SCHOOL BUILDING?

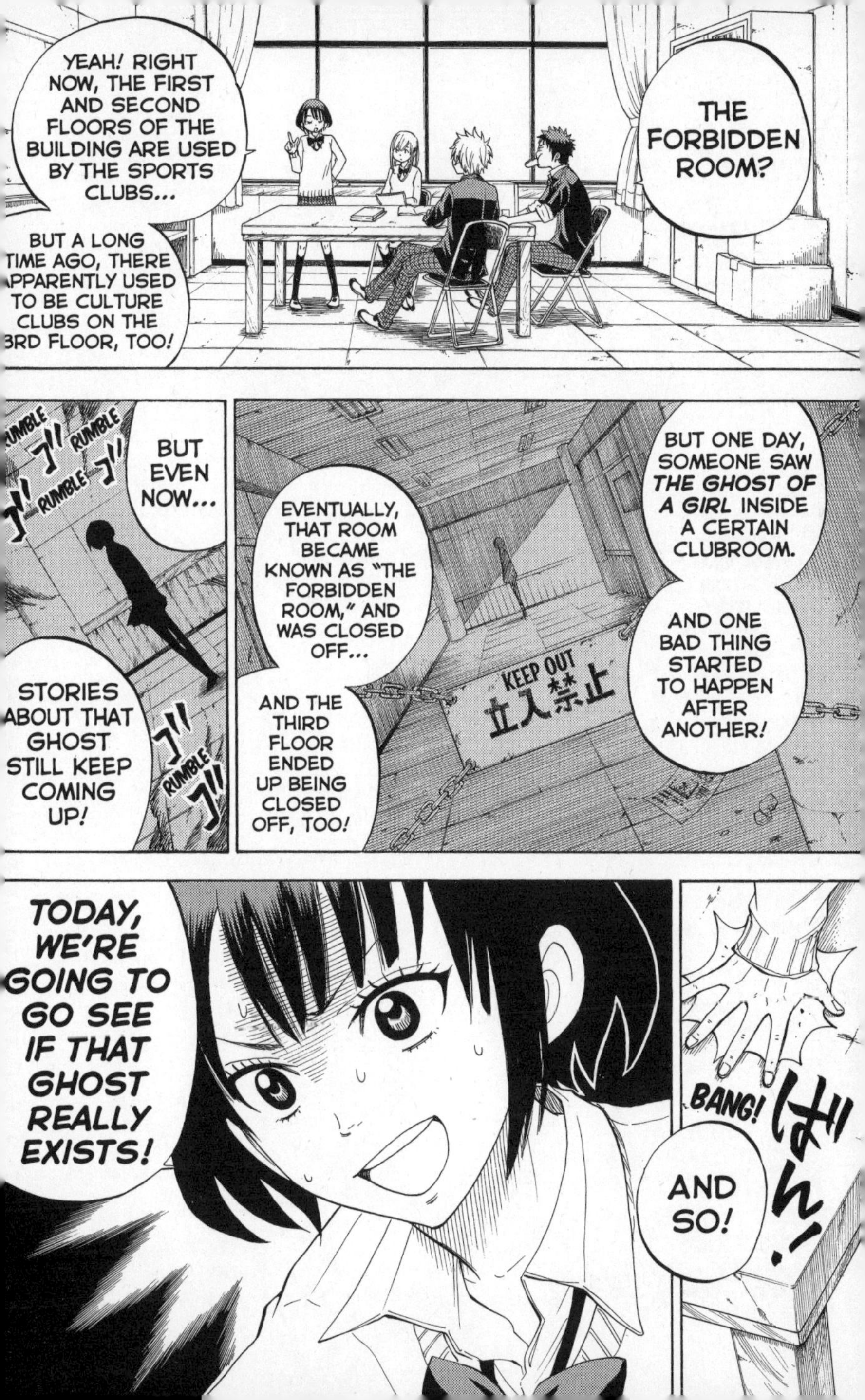
THE FORBIDDEN ROOM?
YEAH! RIGHT NOW, THE FIRST AND SECOND FLOORS OF THE BUILDING ARE USED BY THE SPORTS CLUBS...
BUT A LONG TIME AGO, THERE APPARENTLY USED TO BE CULTURE CLUBS ON THE 3RD FLOOR, TOO!
BUT ONE DAY, SOMEONE SAW *THE GHOST OF A GIRL* INSIDE A CERTAIN CLUBROOM.
AND ONE BAD THING STARTED TO HAPPEN AFTER ANOTHER!
EVENTUALLY, THAT ROOM BECAME KNOWN AS "THE FORBIDDEN ROOM," AND WAS CLOSED OFF...
KEEP OUT
立入禁止
AND THE THIRD FLOOR ENDED UP BEING CLOSED OFF, TOO!
RUMBLE ゴ RUMBLE ゴ RUMBLE ゴ RUMBLE ゴ
BUT EVEN NOW...
STORIES ABOUT THAT GHOST STILL KEEP COMING UP!
ゴ RUMBLE ゴ
BANG! ばん!
AND SO!
TODAY, WE'RE GOING TO GO SEE IF THAT GHOST REALLY EXISTS!

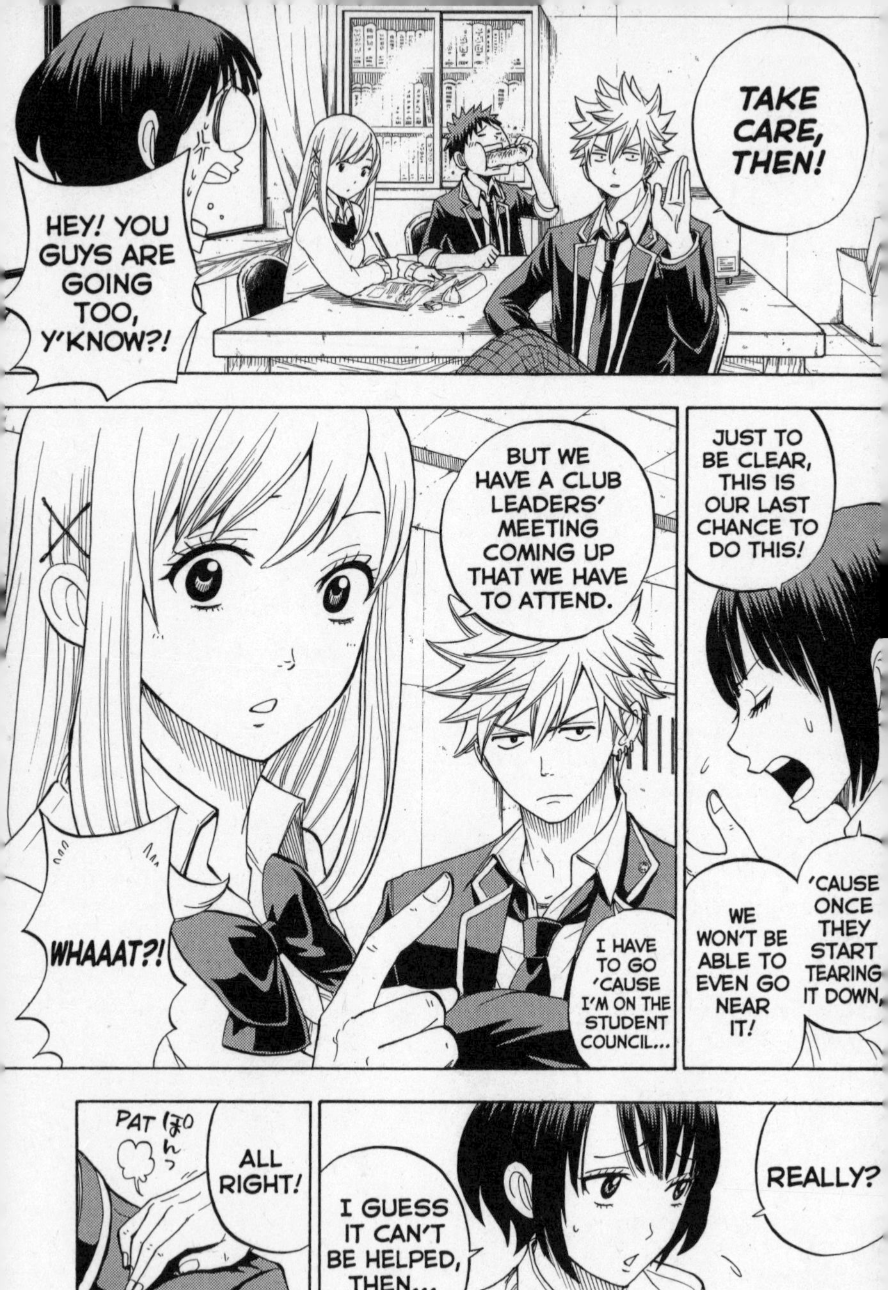
TAKE CARE, THEN!
HEY! YOU GUYS ARE GOING TOO, Y'KNOW?!
JUST TO BE CLEAR, THIS IS OUR LAST CHANCE TO DO THIS!
'CAUSE ONCE THEY START TEARING IT DOWN,
WE WON'T BE ABLE TO EVEN GO NEAR IT!
BUT WE HAVE A CLUB LEADERS' MEETING COMING UP THAT WE HAVE TO ATTEND.
I HAVE TO GO 'CAUSE I'M ON THE STUDENT COUNCIL...
WHAAAT?!
REALLY?
I GUESS IT CAN'T BE HELPED, THEN...
ALL RIGHT!
PAT ぽんっ

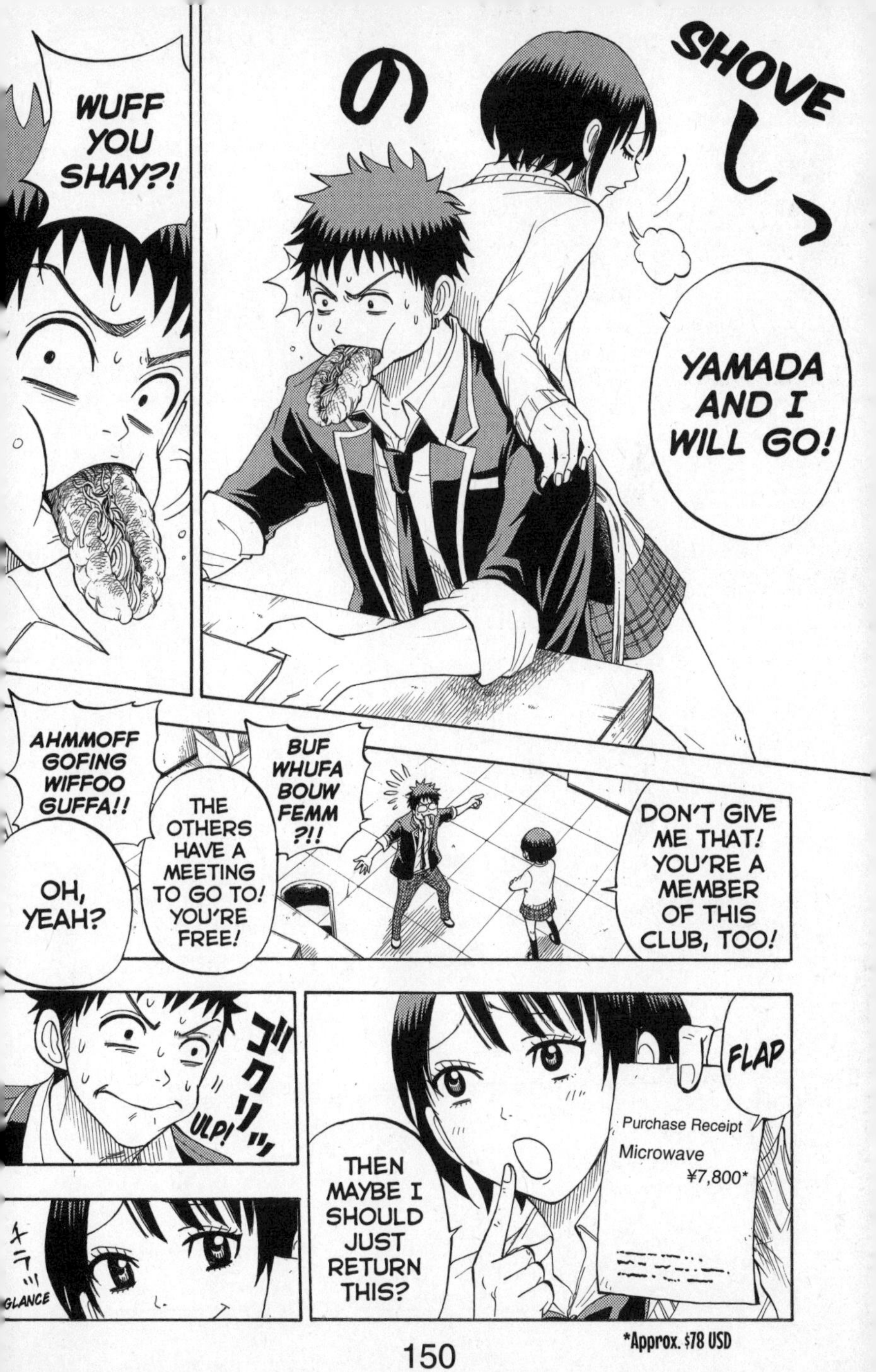
SHOVE
の
し
YAMADA AND I WILL GO!
WUFF YOU SHAY?!
DON'T GIVE ME THAT! YOU'RE A MEMBER OF THIS CLUB, TOO!
BUF WHUFA BOUW FEMM?!!
THE OTHERS HAVE A MEETING TO GO TO! YOU'RE FREE!
AHMMOFF GOFING WIFFOO GUFFA!!
OH, YEAH?
FLAP
Purchase Receipt
Microwave
¥7,800*
THEN MAYBE I SHOULD JUST RETURN THIS?
ゴクリッ
ULP!
GLANCE

*Approx. $78 USD

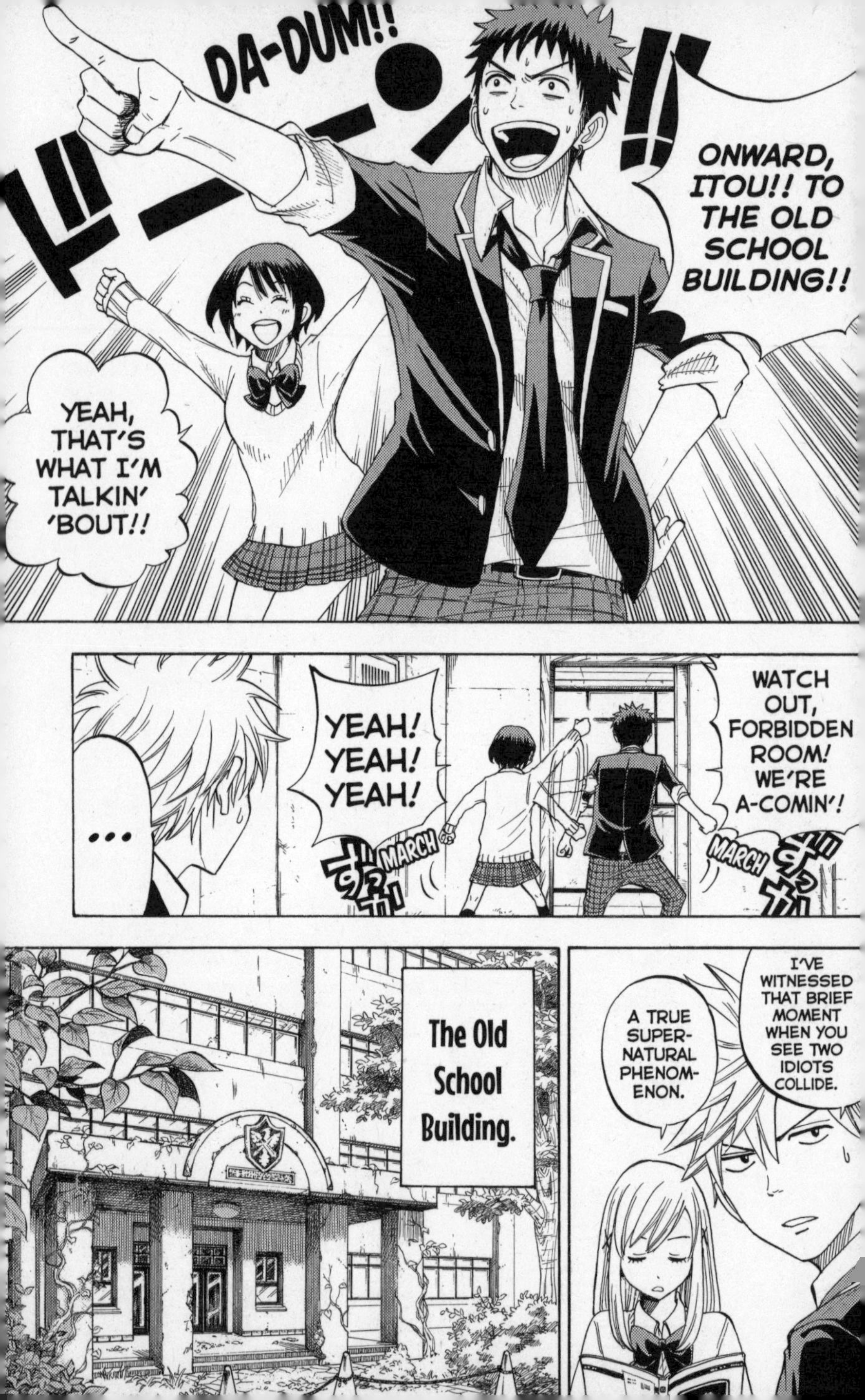
DA-DUM!!
ONWARD, ITOU!! TO THE OLD SCHOOL BUILDING!!
YEAH, THAT'S WHAT I'M TALKIN' 'BOUT!!
WATCH OUT, FORBIDDEN ROOM! WE'RE A-COMIN'!
MARCH
YEAH! YEAH! YEAH!
MARCH
...
I'VE WITNESSED THAT BRIEF MOMENT WHEN YOU SEE TWO IDIOTS COLLIDE.
A TRUE SUPER-NATURAL PHENOM-ENON.
The Old School Building.

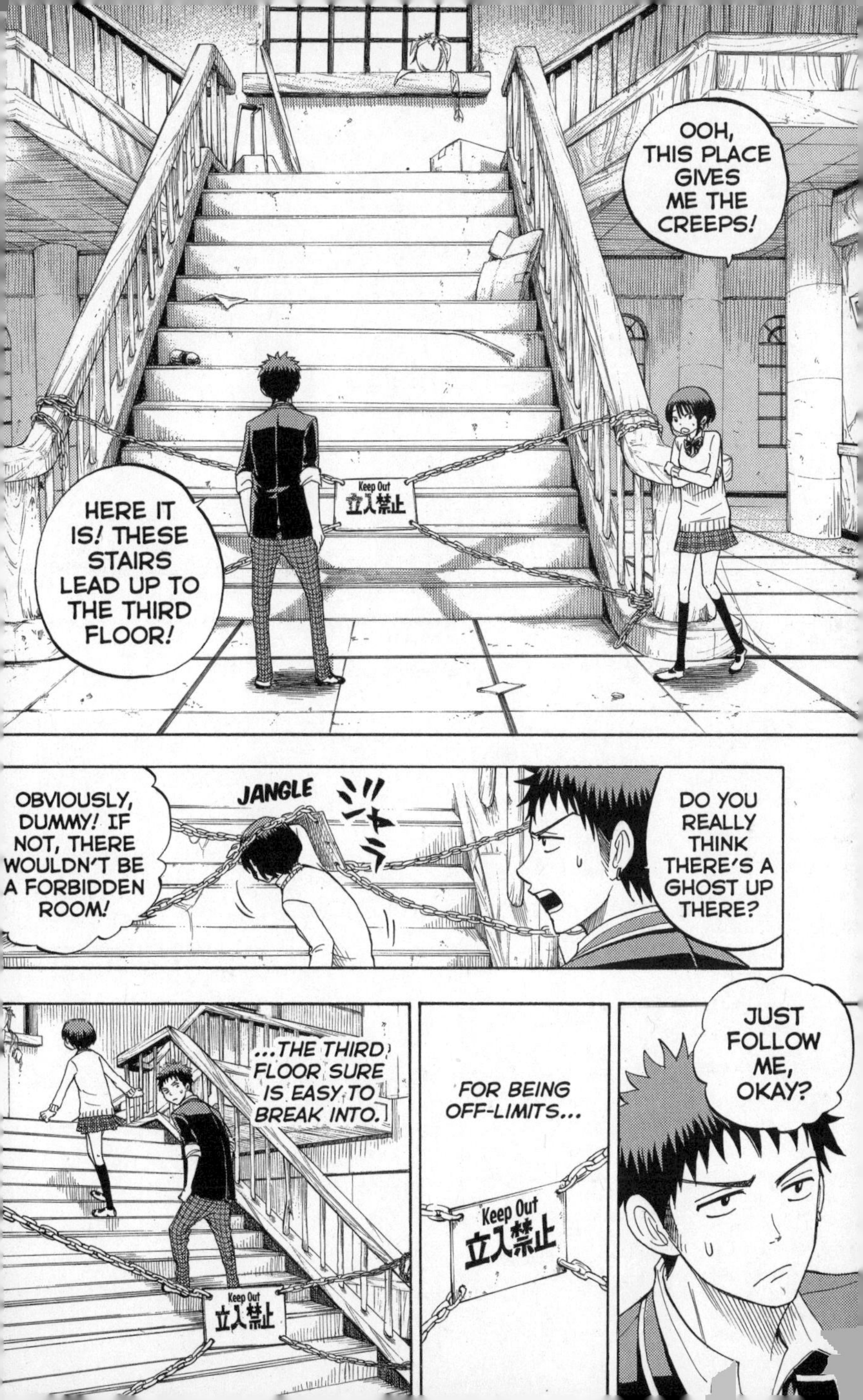
OOH, THIS PLACE GIVES ME THE CREEPS!
Keep Out 立入禁止
HERE IT IS! THESE STAIRS LEAD UP TO THE THIRD FLOOR!
DO YOU REALLY THINK THERE'S A GHOST UP THERE?
JANGLE
ジャラ
OBVIOUSLY, DUMMY! IF NOT, THERE WOULDN'T BE A FORBIDDEN ROOM!
JUST FOLLOW ME, OKAY?
Keep Out 立入禁止
FOR BEING OFF-LIMITS...
...THE THIRD FLOOR SURE IS EASY TO BREAK INTO.
Keep Out 立入禁止

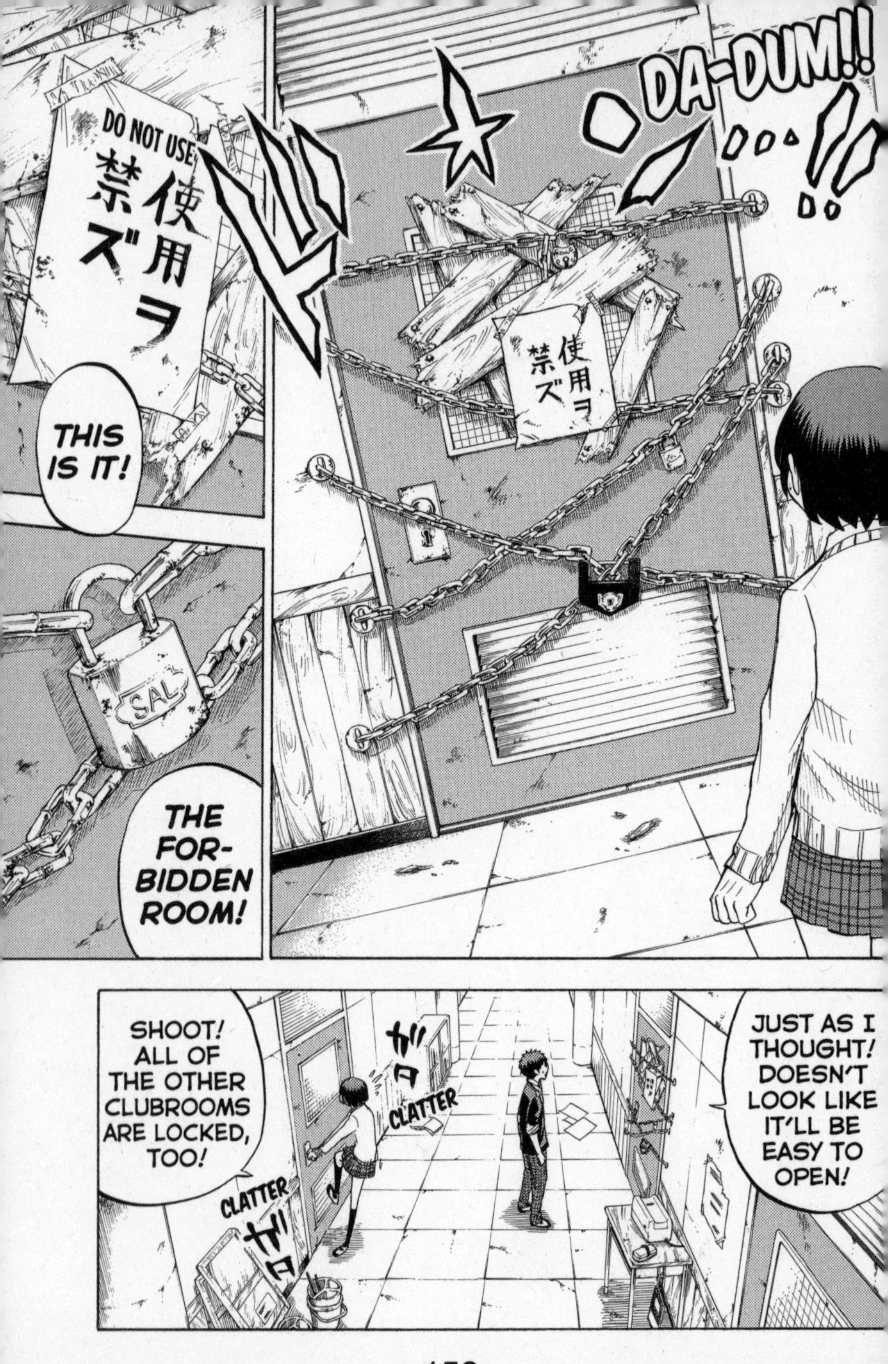
DA-DUM!!
使用ヲ禁ズ
DO NOT USE
使用ヲ禁ズ
THIS IS IT!
SAL
THE FOR-BIDDEN ROOM!
JUST AS I THOUGHT! DOESN'T LOOK LIKE IT'LL BE EASY TO OPEN!
ガタ
CLATTER
SHOOT! ALL OF THE OTHER CLUBROOMS ARE LOCKED, TOO!
CLATTER
ガタ

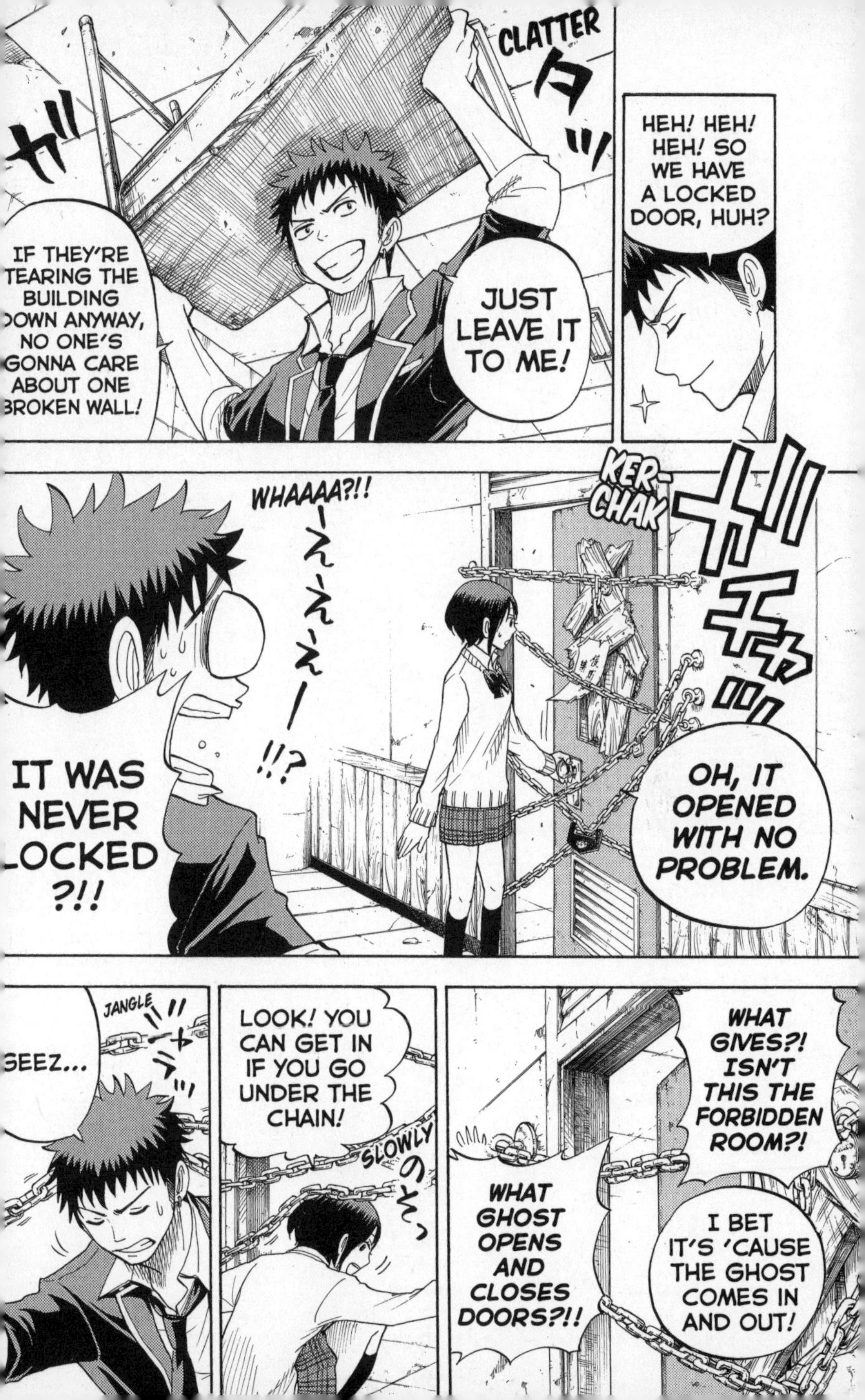
HEH! HEH! HEH! SO WE HAVE A LOCKED DOOR, HUH?
CLATTER
JUST LEAVE IT TO ME!
IF THEY'RE TEARING THE BUILDING DOWN ANYWAY, NO ONE'S GONNA CARE ABOUT ONE BROKEN WALL!
KER-CHAK
OH, IT OPENED WITH NO PROBLEM.
WHAAAA?!!
IT WAS NEVER LOCKED ?!!
WHAT GIVES?! ISN'T THIS THE FORBIDDEN ROOM?!
I BET IT'S 'CAUSE THE GHOST COMES IN AND OUT!
WHAT GHOST OPENS AND CLOSES DOORS?!!
LOOK! YOU CAN GET IN IF YOU GO UNDER THE CHAIN!
SLOWLY
JANGLE
GEEZ...

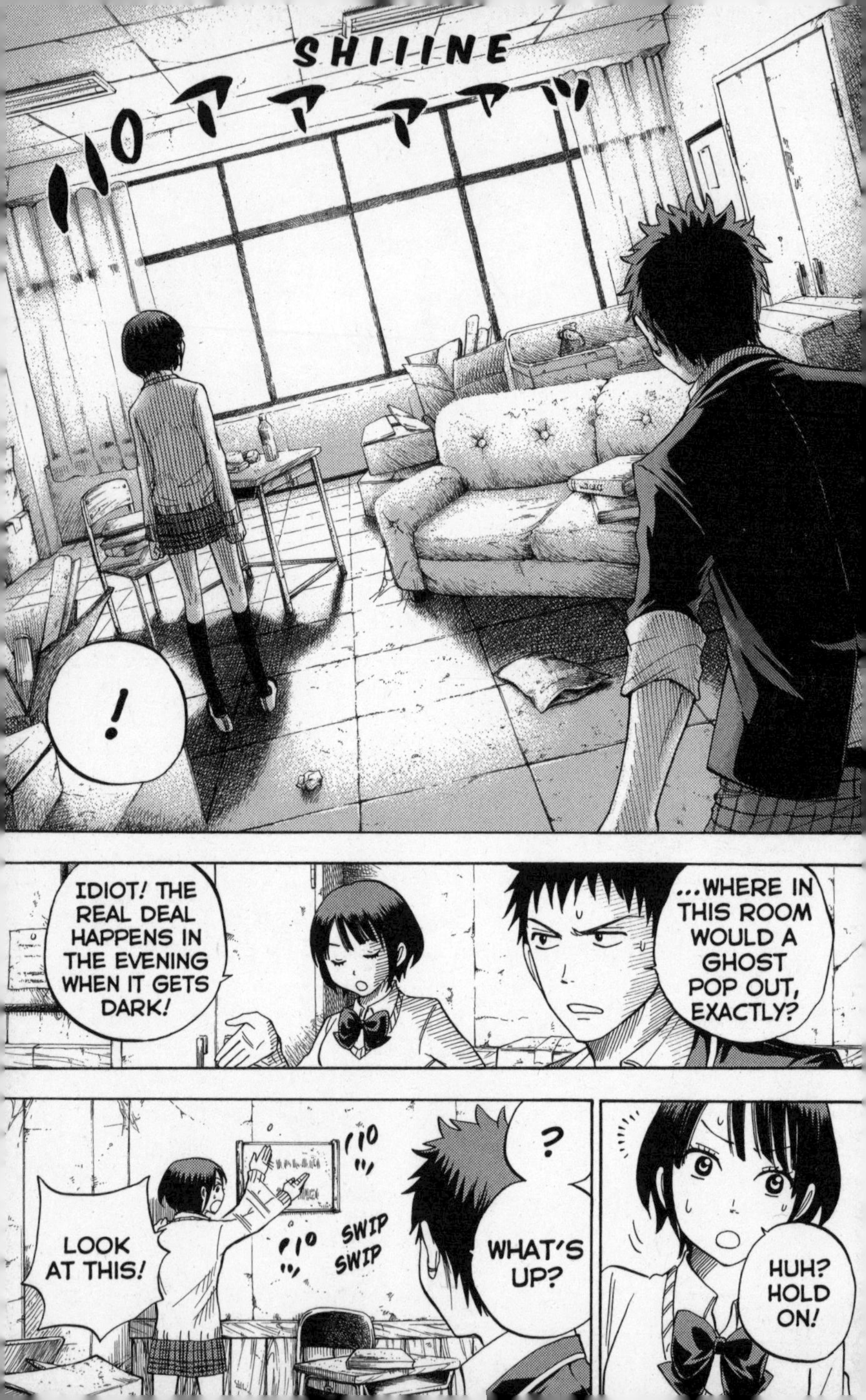
SHIIINE
!
...WHERE IN THIS ROOM WOULD A GHOST POP OUT, EXACTLY?
IDIOT! THE REAL DEAL HAPPENS IN THE EVENING WHEN IT GETS DARK!
HUH? HOLD ON!
?
WHAT'S UP?
SWIP SWIP
LOOK AT THIS!

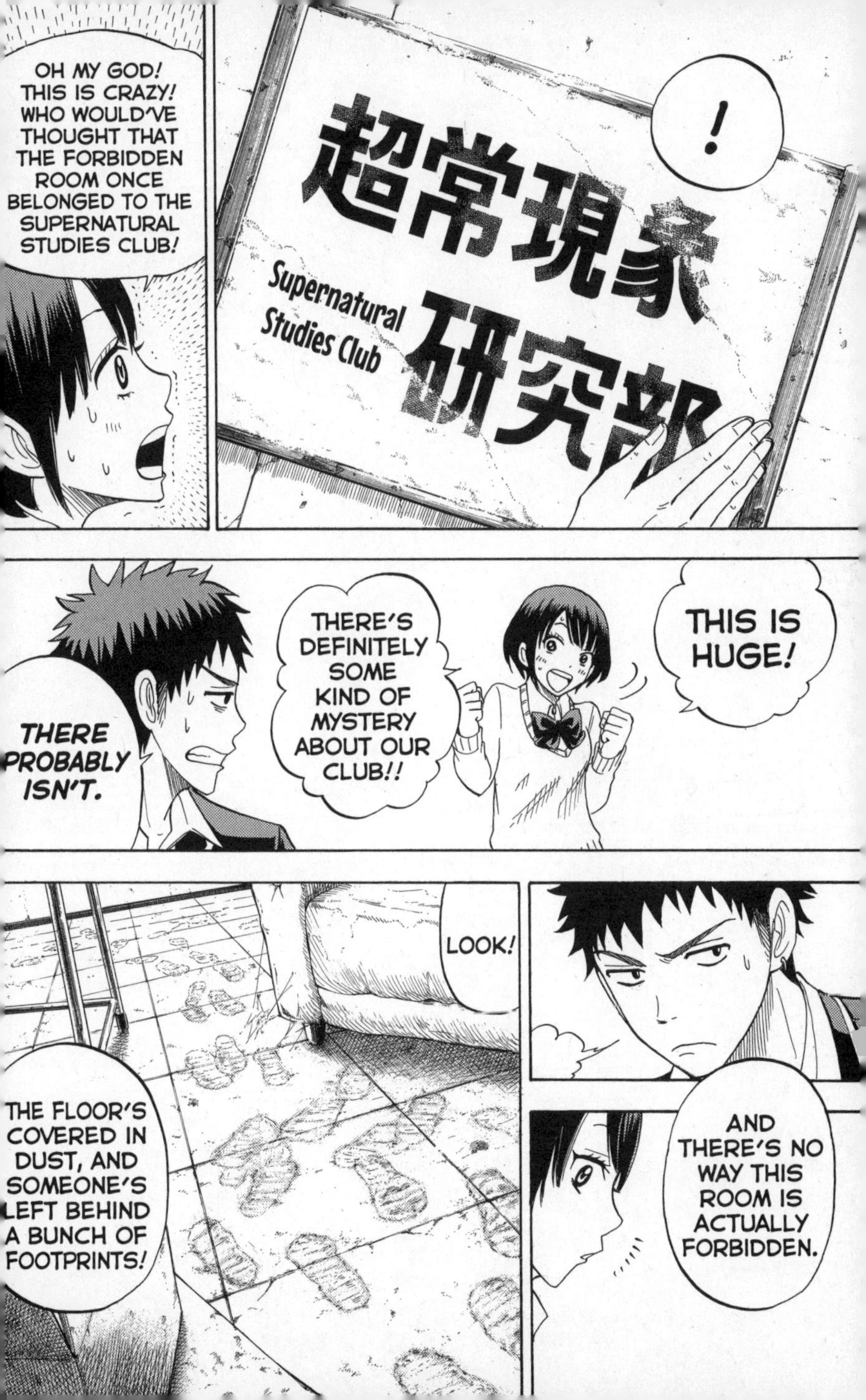
!
超常現象研究部
Supernatural Studies Club
OH MY GOD! THIS IS CRAZY! WHO WOULD'VE THOUGHT THAT THE FORBIDDEN ROOM ONCE BELONGED TO THE SUPERNATURAL STUDIES CLUB!
THIS IS HUGE!
THERE'S DEFINITELY SOME KIND OF MYSTERY ABOUT OUR CLUB!!
THERE PROBABLY ISN'T.
LOOK!
AND THERE'S NO WAY THIS ROOM IS ACTUALLY FORBIDDEN.
THE FLOOR'S COVERED IN DUST, AND SOMEONE'S LEFT BEHIND A BUNCH OF FOOTPRINTS!

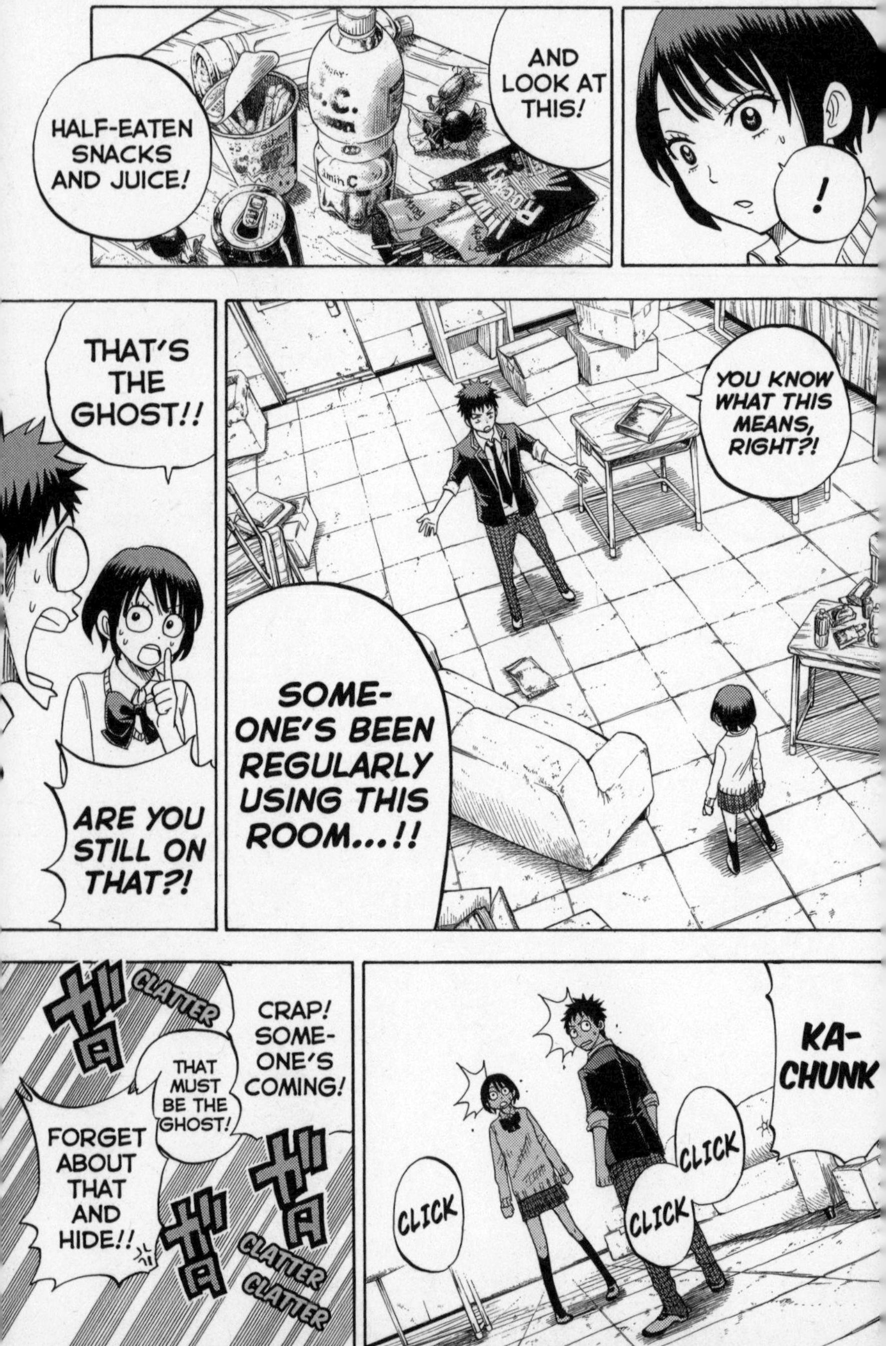
!
AND LOOK AT THIS!
HALF-EATEN SNACKS AND JUICE!
YOU KNOW WHAT THIS MEANS, RIGHT?!
SOME-ONE'S BEEN REGULARLY USING THIS ROOM...!!
THAT'S THE GHOST!!
ARE YOU STILL ON THAT?!
KA-CHUNK
CLICK
CLICK
CLICK
CLATTER
CRAP! SOME-ONE'S COMING!
THAT MUST BE THE GHOST!
FORGET ABOUT THAT AND HIDE!!
CLATTER
CLATTER

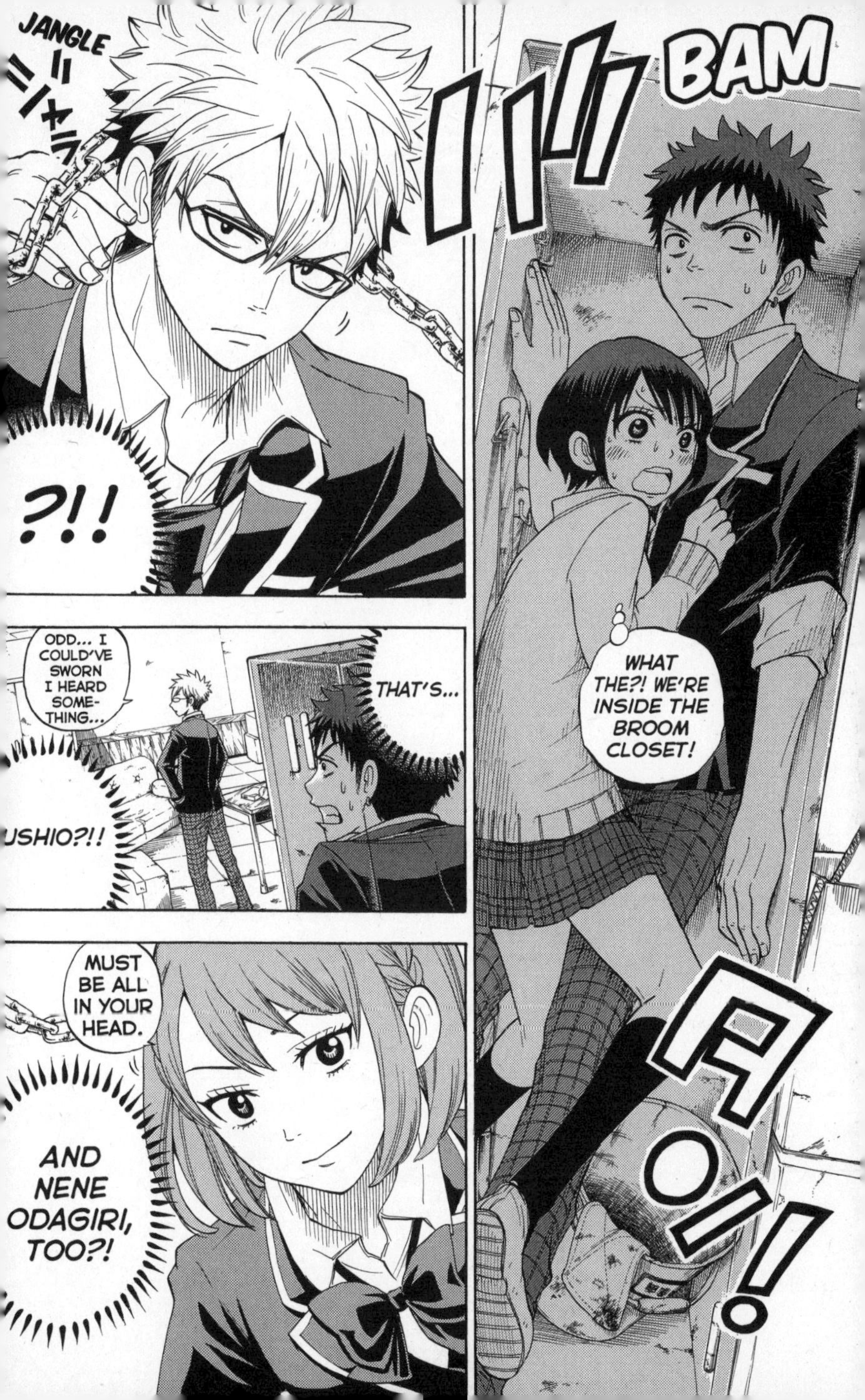
BAM
WHAT THE?! WE'RE INSIDE THE BROOM CLOSET!
JANGLE
?!!
THAT'S...
ODD... I COULD'VE SWORN I HEARD SOMETHING...
USHIO?!!
MUST BE ALL IN YOUR HEAD.
AND NENE ODAGIRI, TOO?!

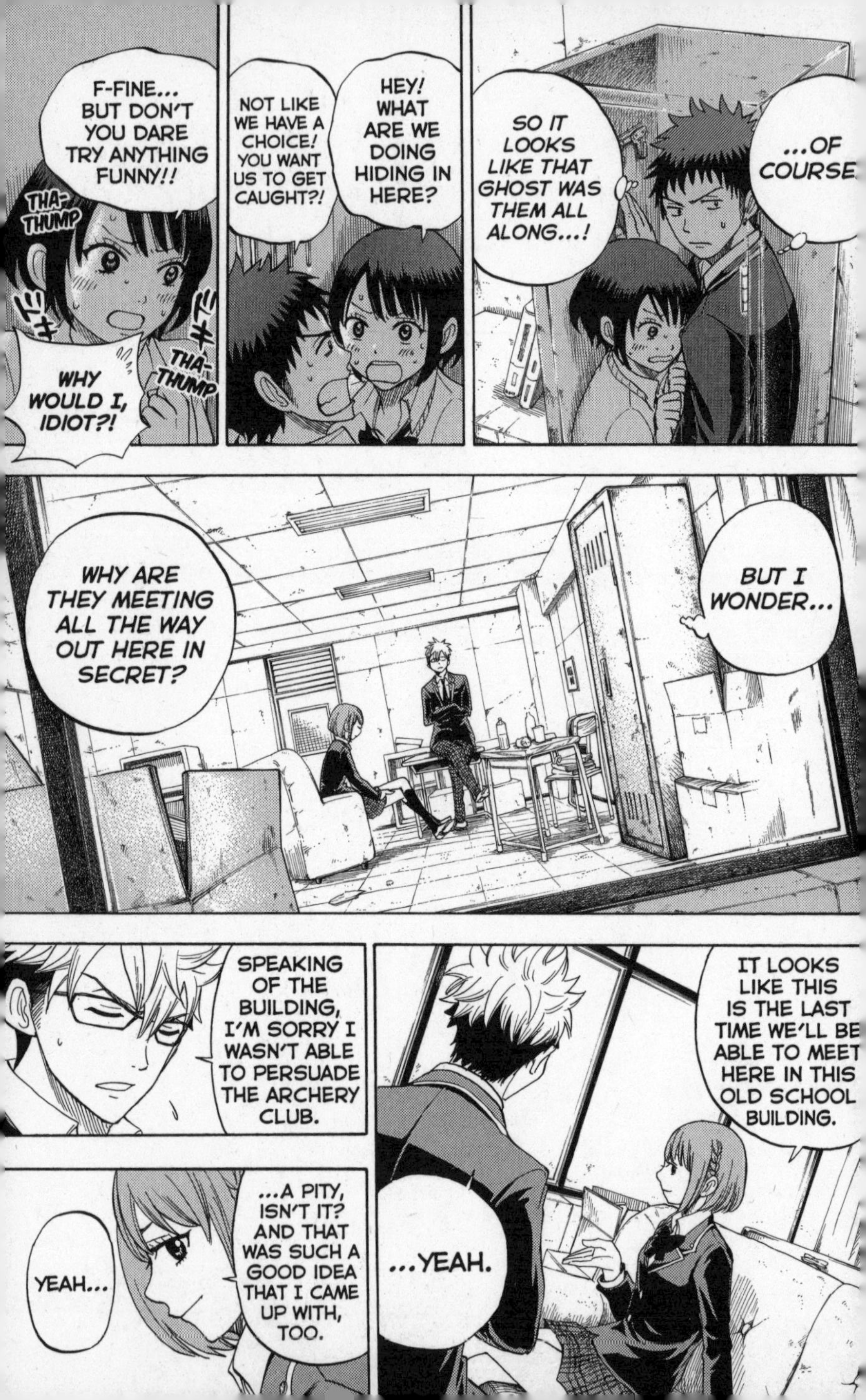
...OF COURSE.
SO IT LOOKS LIKE THAT GHOST WAS THEM ALL ALONG...!
HEY! WHAT ARE WE DOING HIDING IN HERE?
NOT LIKE WE HAVE A CHOICE! YOU WANT US TO GET CAUGHT?!
F-FINE... BUT DON'T YOU DARE TRY ANYTHING FUNNY!!
THA-THUMP
ドキ
ドキ
THA-THUMP
WHY WOULD I, IDIOT?!
BUT I WONDER...
WHY ARE THEY MEETING ALL THE WAY OUT HERE IN SECRET?
IT LOOKS LIKE THIS IS THE LAST TIME WE'LL BE ABLE TO MEET HERE IN THIS OLD SCHOOL BUILDING.
...YEAH.
SPEAKING OF THE BUILDING, I'M SORRY I WASN'T ABLE TO PERSUADE THE ARCHERY CLUB.
...A PITY, ISN'T IT? AND THAT WAS SUCH A GOOD IDEA THAT I CAME UP WITH, TOO.
YEAH...

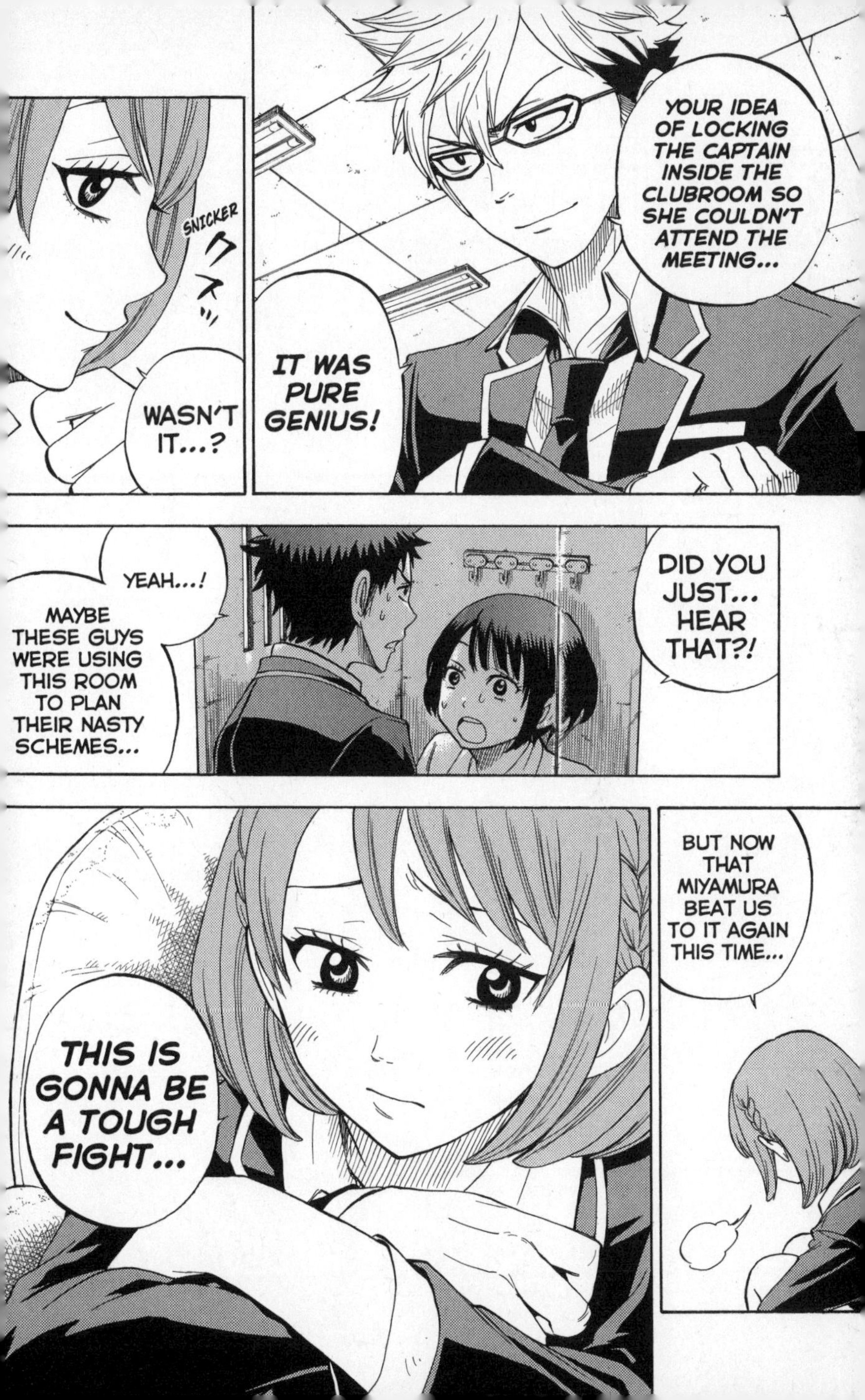
YOUR IDEA OF LOCKING THE CAPTAIN INSIDE THE CLUBROOM SO SHE COULDN'T ATTEND THE MEETING...
IT WAS PURE GENIUS!
SNICKER
クスッ
WASN'T IT...?
DID YOU JUST... HEAR THAT?!
YEAH...!
MAYBE THESE GUYS WERE USING THIS ROOM TO PLAN THEIR NASTY SCHEMES...
BUT NOW THAT MIYAMURA BEAT US TO IT AGAIN THIS TIME...
THIS IS GONNA BE A TOUGH FIGHT...

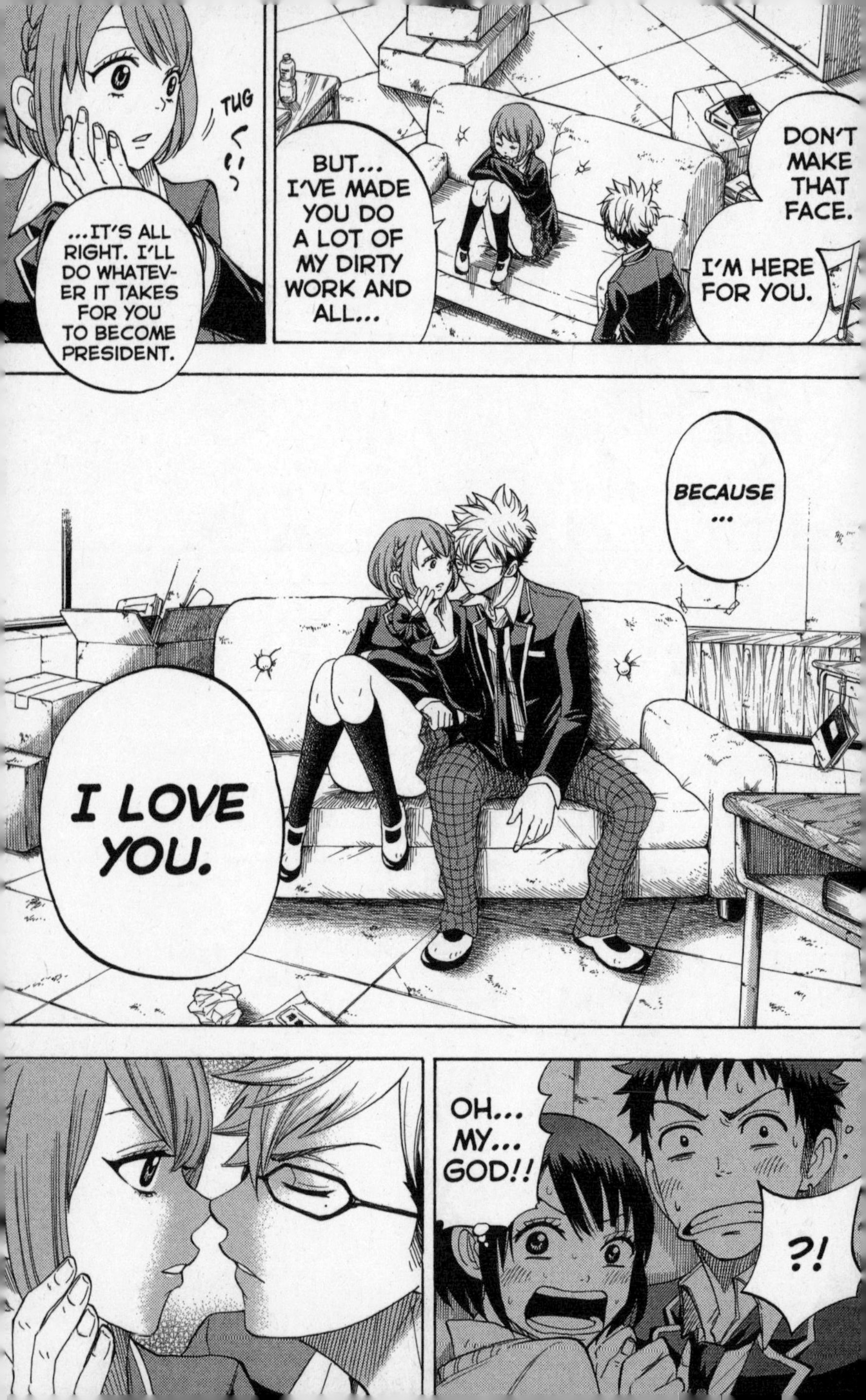

DON'T MAKE THAT FACE.
I'M HERE FOR YOU.
BUT... I'VE MADE YOU DO A LOT OF MY DIRTY WORK AND ALL...
TUG
...IT'S ALL RIGHT. I'LL DO WHATEVER IT TAKES FOR YOU TO BECOME PRESIDENT.
BECAUSE...
I LOVE YOU.
OH... MY... GOD!!
?!

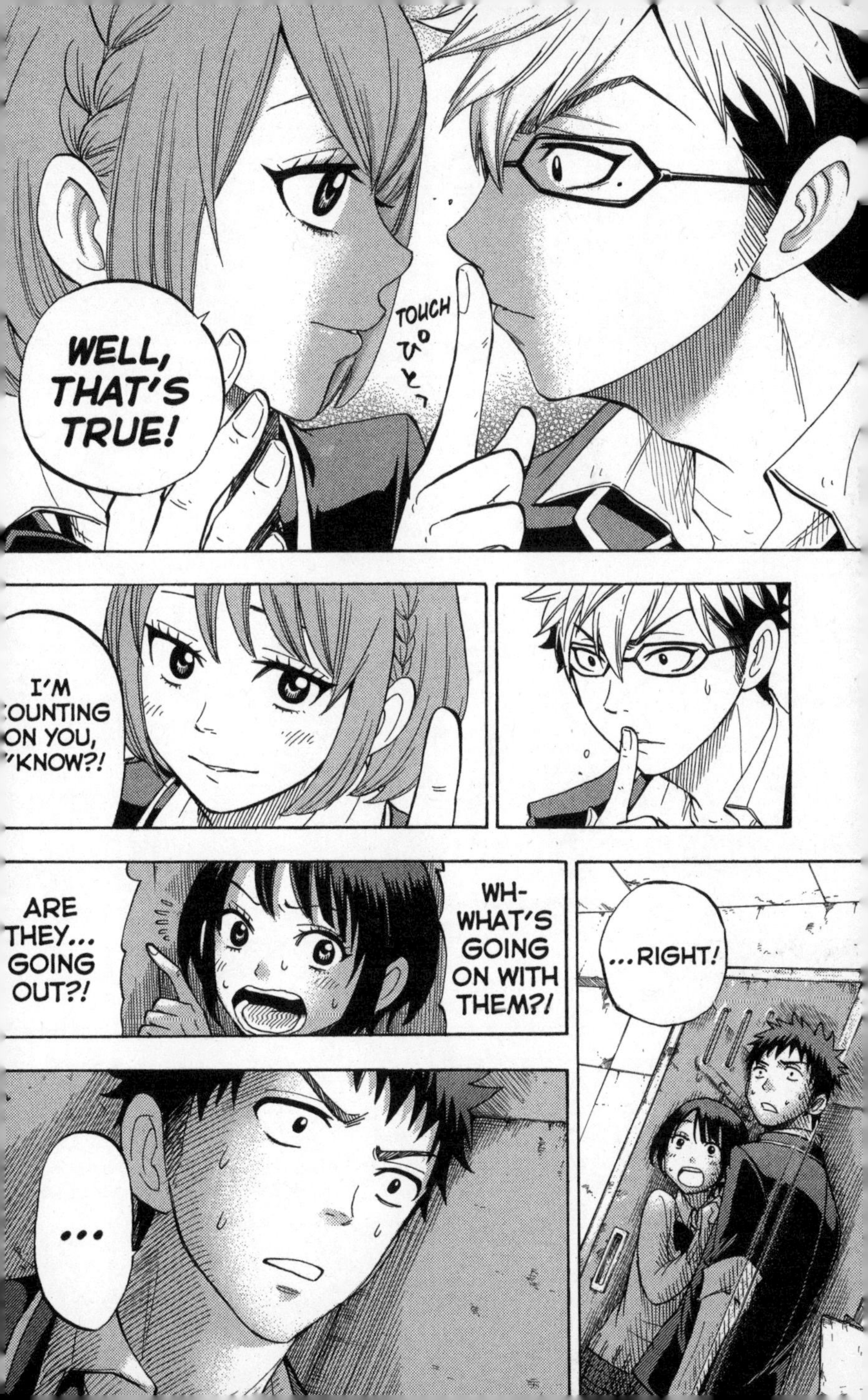
TOUCH
ぴとっ
WELL, THAT'S TRUE!
I'M COUNTING ON YOU, Y'KNOW?!
...RIGHT!
WH- WHAT'S GOING ON WITH THEM?!
ARE THEY... GOING OUT?!
...

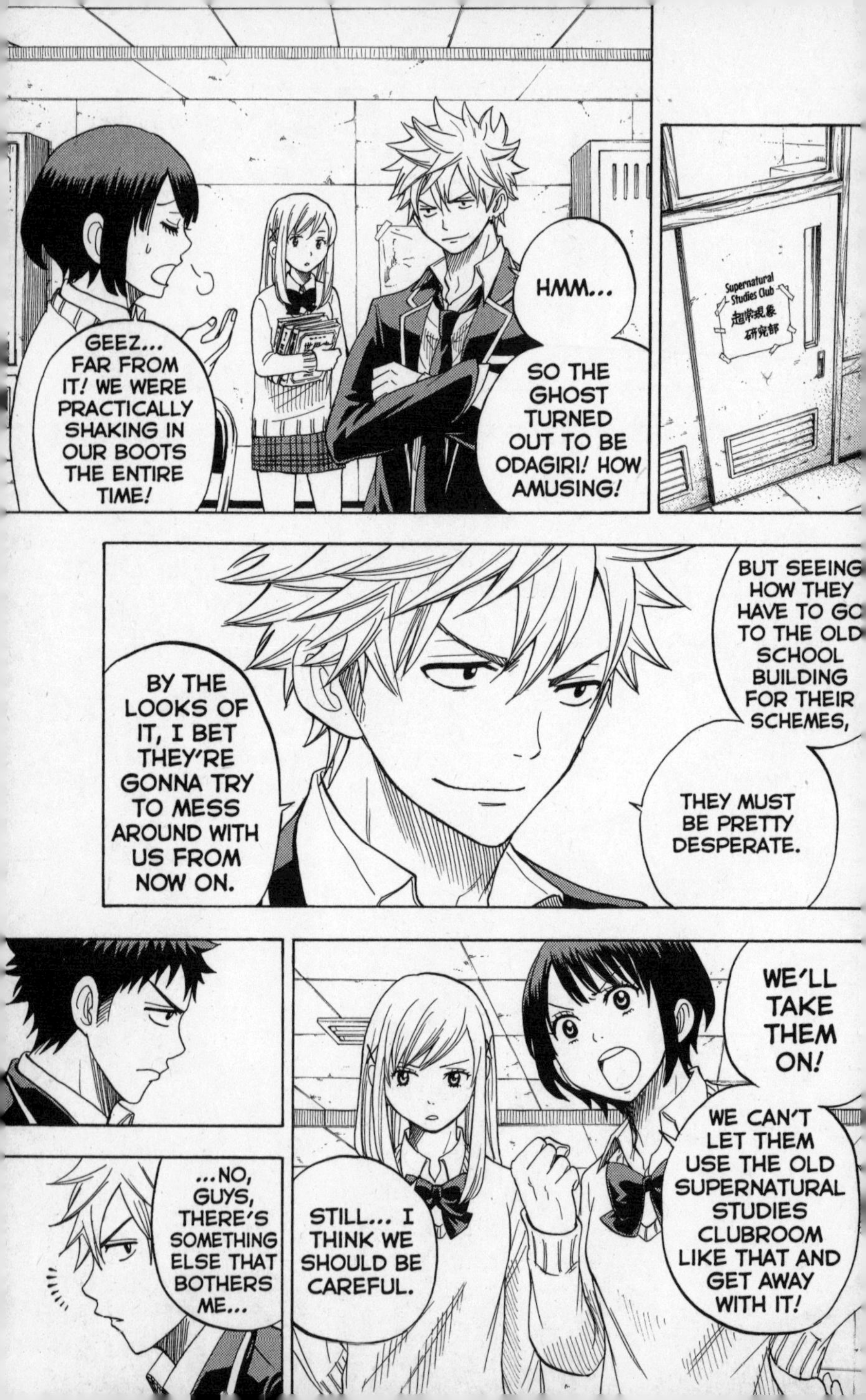
Supernatural Studies Club
超常現象研究部
HMM...
SO THE GHOST TURNED OUT TO BE ODAGIRI! HOW AMUSING!
GEEZ... FAR FROM IT! WE WERE PRACTICALLY SHAKING IN OUR BOOTS THE ENTIRE TIME!
BUT SEEING HOW THEY HAVE TO GO TO THE OLD SCHOOL BUILDING FOR THEIR SCHEMES,
THEY MUST BE PRETTY DESPERATE.
BY THE LOOKS OF IT, I BET THEY'RE GONNA TRY TO MESS AROUND WITH US FROM NOW ON.
WE'LL TAKE THEM ON!
WE CAN'T LET THEM USE THE OLD SUPERNATURAL STUDIES CLUBROOM LIKE THAT AND GET AWAY WITH IT!
STILL... I THINK WE SHOULD BE CAREFUL.
...NO, GUYS, THERE'S SOMETHING ELSE THAT BOTHERS ME...

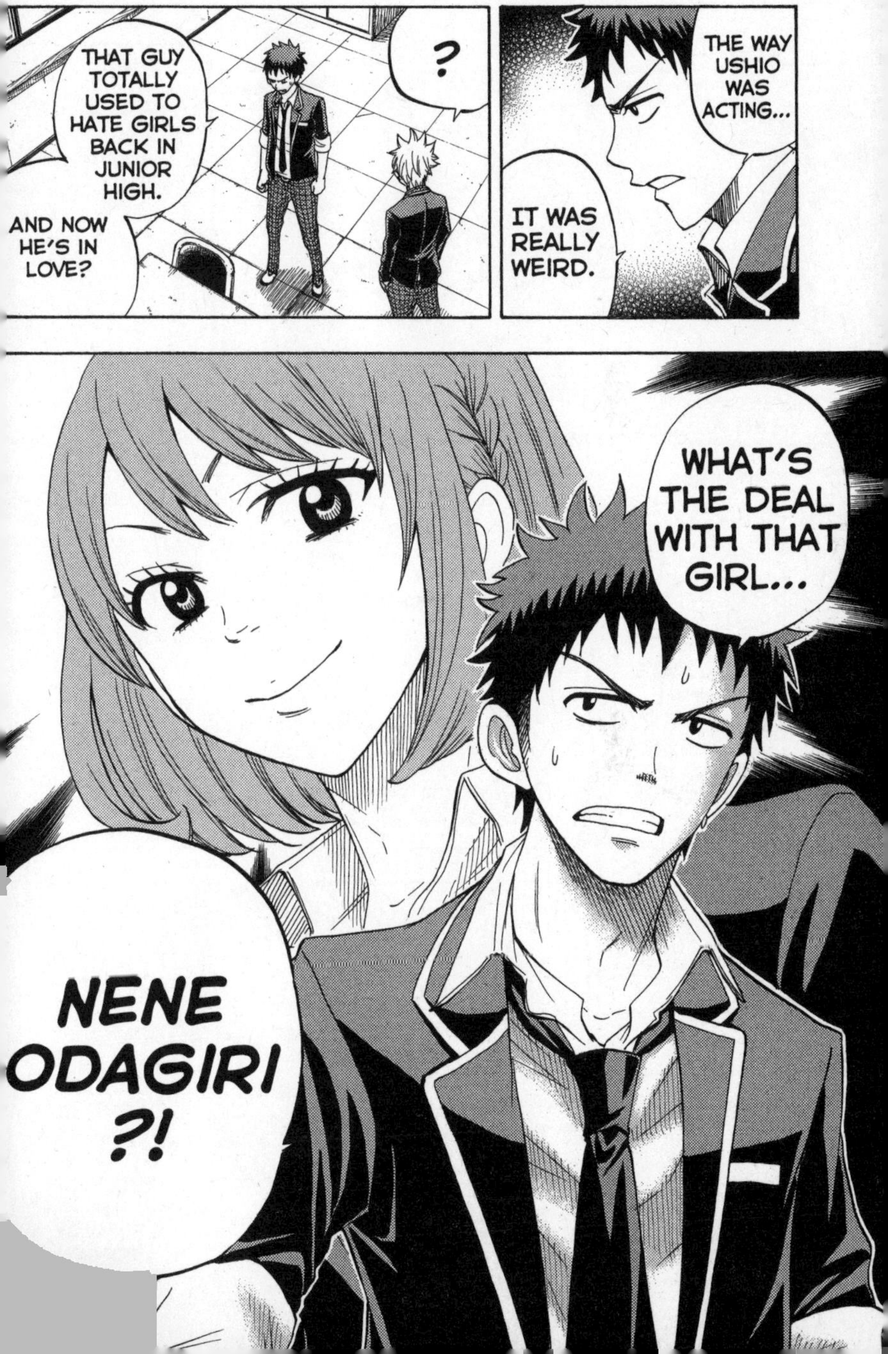
THE WAY USHIO WAS ACTING...
IT WAS REALLY WEIRD.
?
THAT GUY TOTALLY USED TO HATE GIRLS BACK IN JUNIOR HIGH.
AND NOW HE'S IN LOVE?
WHAT'S THE DEAL WITH THAT GIRL...
NENE ODAGIRI ?!

Chapter 16: They're sooo soft! ♥

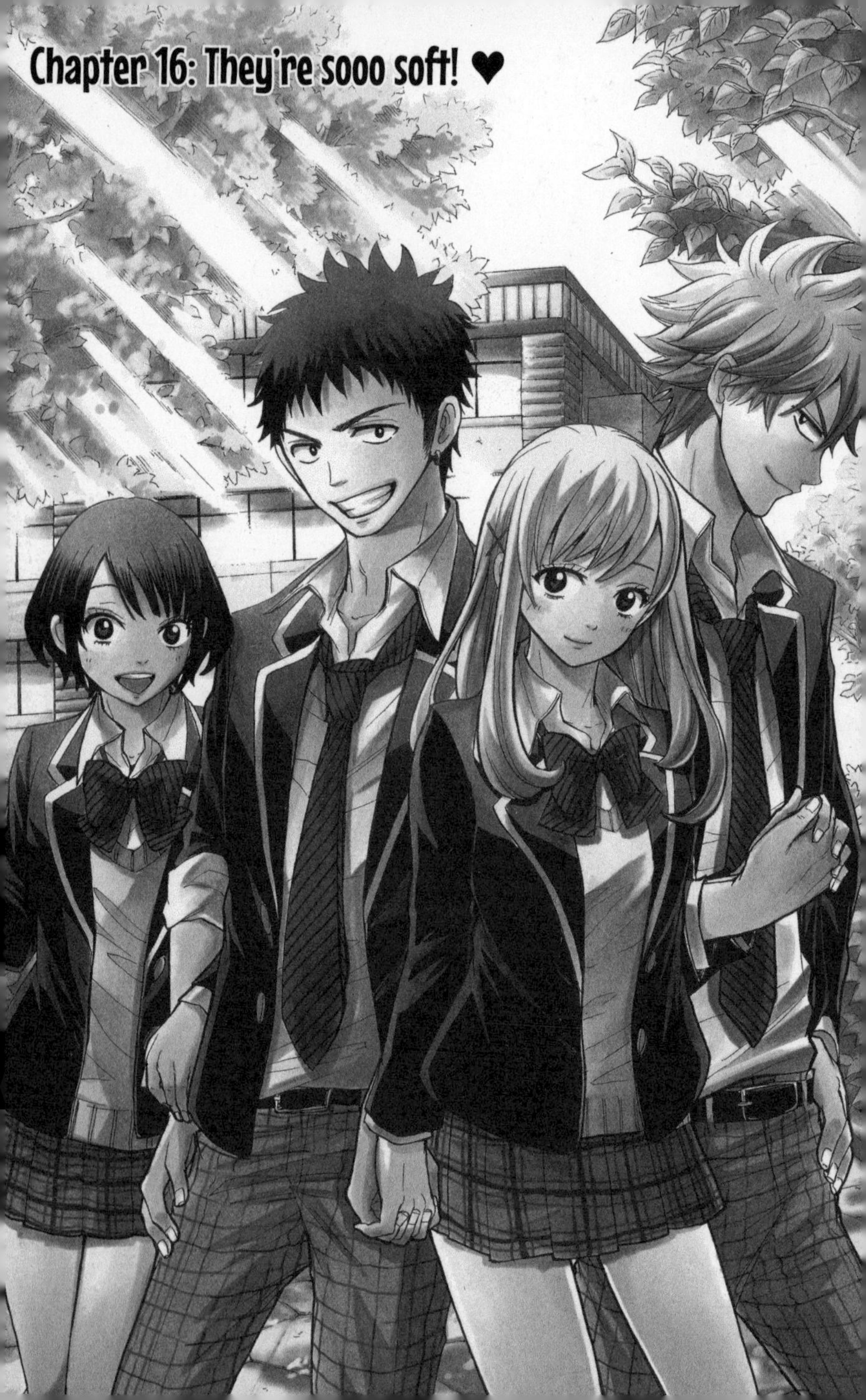

Yamada-kun
AND THE
Seven Witches

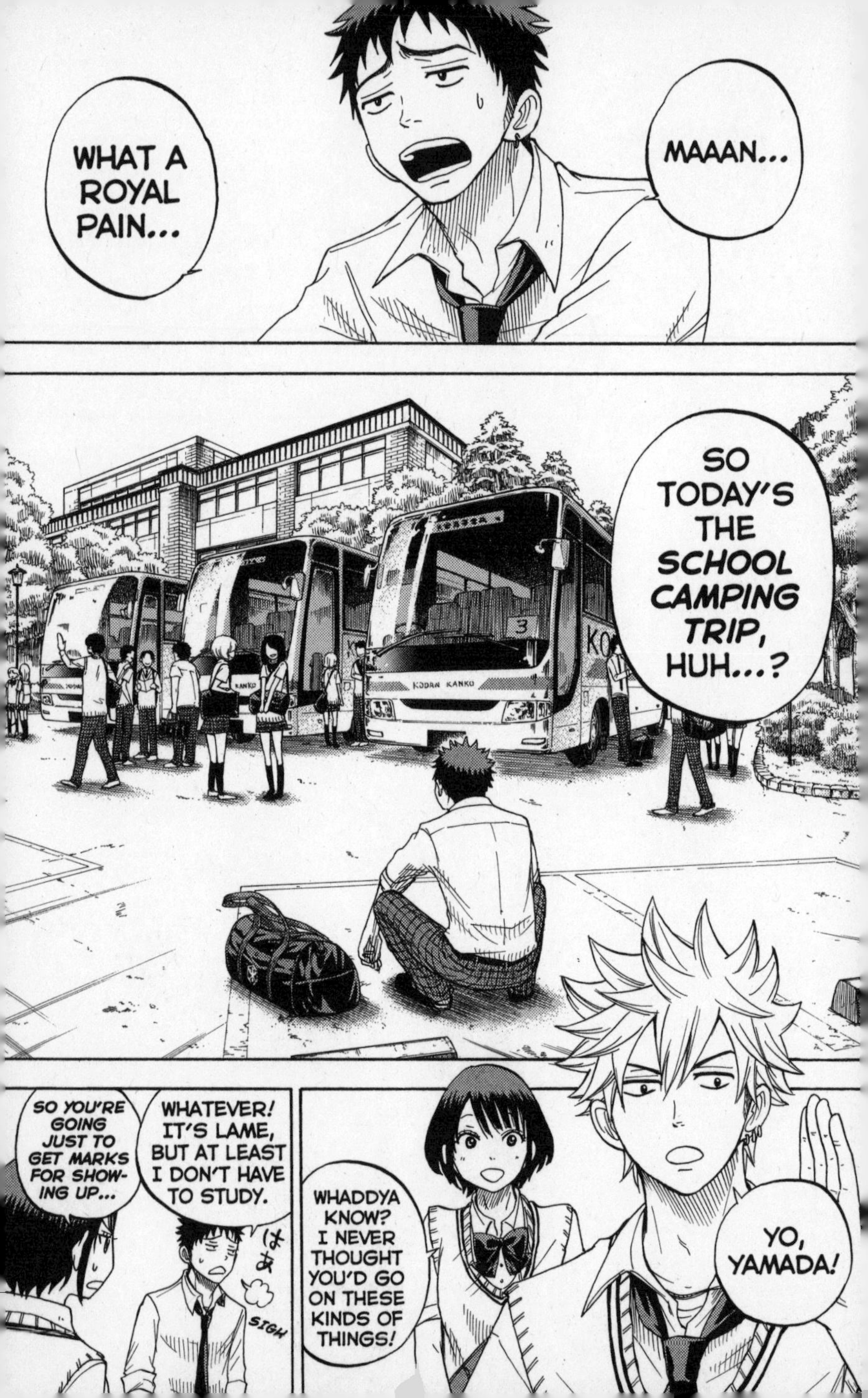
MAAAN...
WHAT A ROYAL PAIN...
SO TODAY'S THE SCHOOL CAMPING TRIP, HUH...?
YO, YAMADA!
WHADDYA KNOW? I NEVER THOUGHT YOU'D GO ON THESE KINDS OF THINGS!
WHATEVER! IT'S LAME, BUT AT LEAST I DON'T HAVE TO STUDY.
はぁ
SIGH
SO YOU'RE GOING JUST TO GET MARKS FOR SHOW-ING UP...

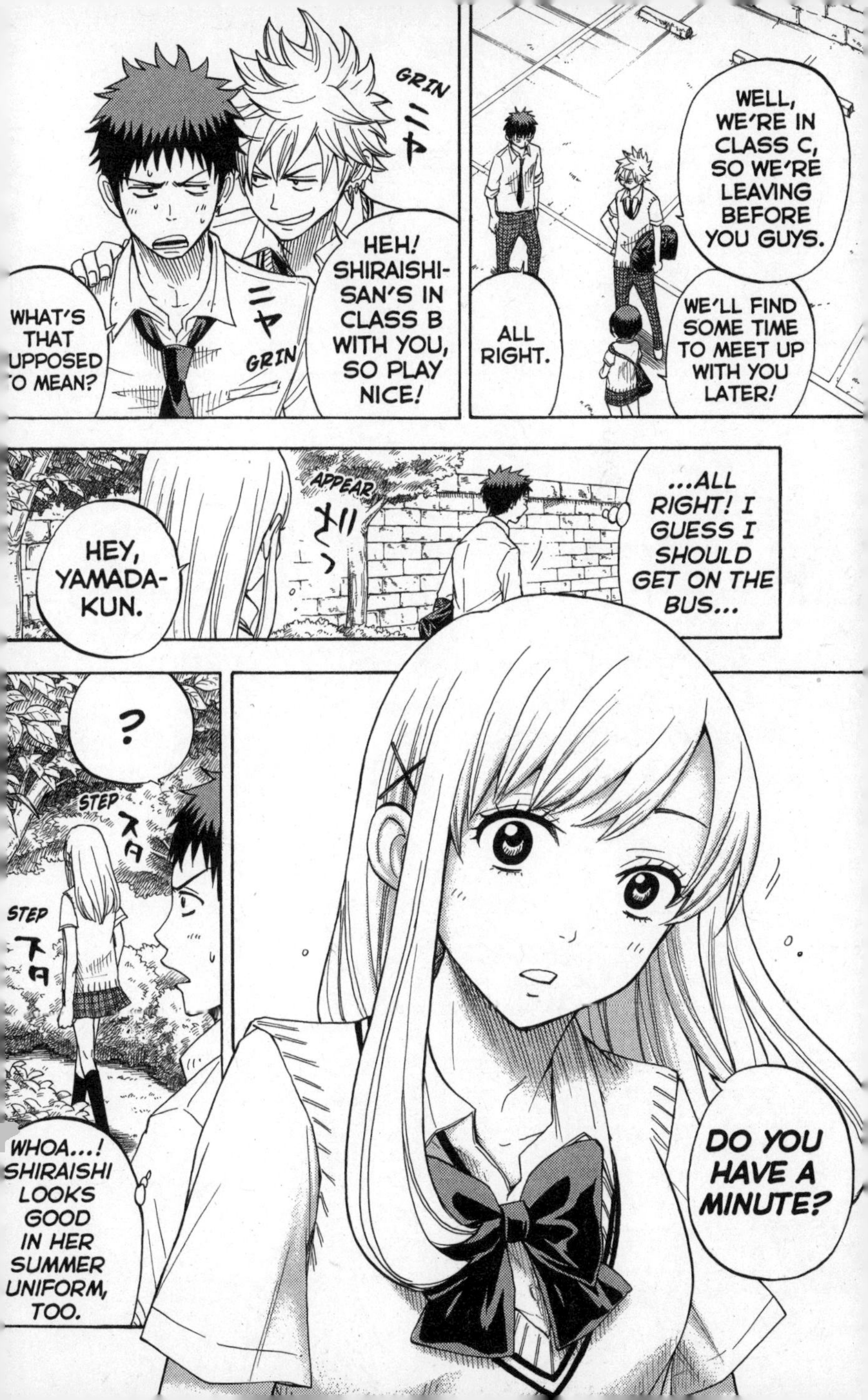
WELL, WE'RE IN CLASS C, SO WE'RE LEAVING BEFORE YOU GUYS.
WE'LL FIND SOME TIME TO MEET UP WITH YOU LATER!
ALL RIGHT.
GRIN
ニヤ
HEH! SHIRAISHI-SAN'S IN CLASS B WITH YOU, SO PLAY NICE!
ニヤ
GRIN
WHAT'S THAT UPPOSED 'O MEAN?
...ALL RIGHT! I GUESS I SHOULD GET ON THE BUS...
APPEAR
HEY, YAMADA-KUN.
DO YOU HAVE A MINUTE?
?
STEP
スタ
STEP
スタ
WHOA...! SHIRAISHI LOOKS GOOD IN HER SUMMER UNIFORM, TOO.

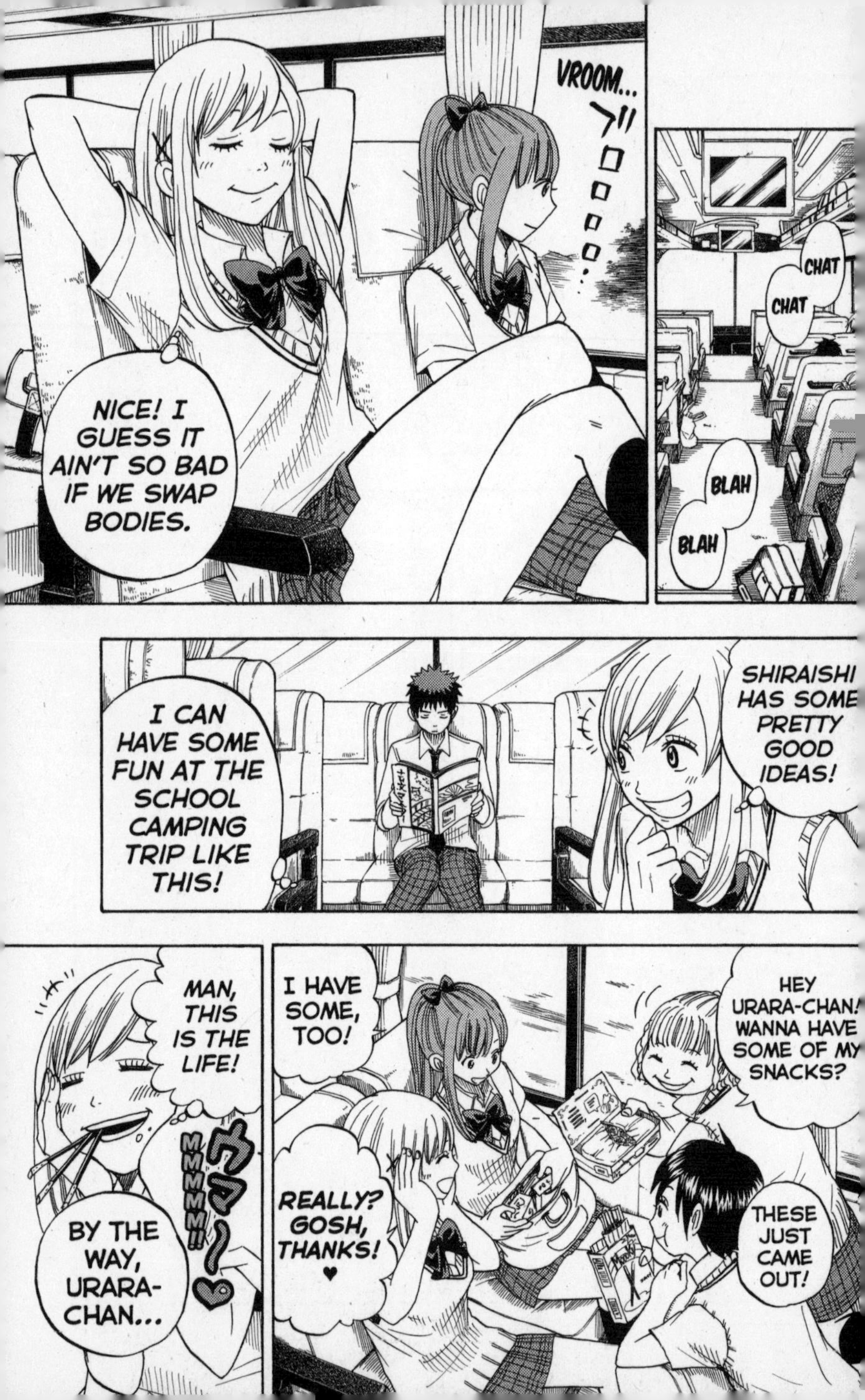
CHAT
CHAT
BLAH
BLAH
VROOM...
NICE! I GUESS IT AIN'T SO BAD IF WE SWAP BODIES.
SHIRAISHI HAS SOME PRETTY GOOD IDEAS!
I CAN HAVE SOME FUN AT THE SCHOOL CAMPING TRIP LIKE THIS!
HEY URARA-CHAN! WANNA HAVE SOME OF MY SNACKS?
THESE JUST CAME OUT!
I HAVE SOME, TOO!
REALLY? GOSH, THANKS! ♥
MAN, THIS IS THE LIFE!
MMMMM!!
BY THE WAY, URARA-CHAN...

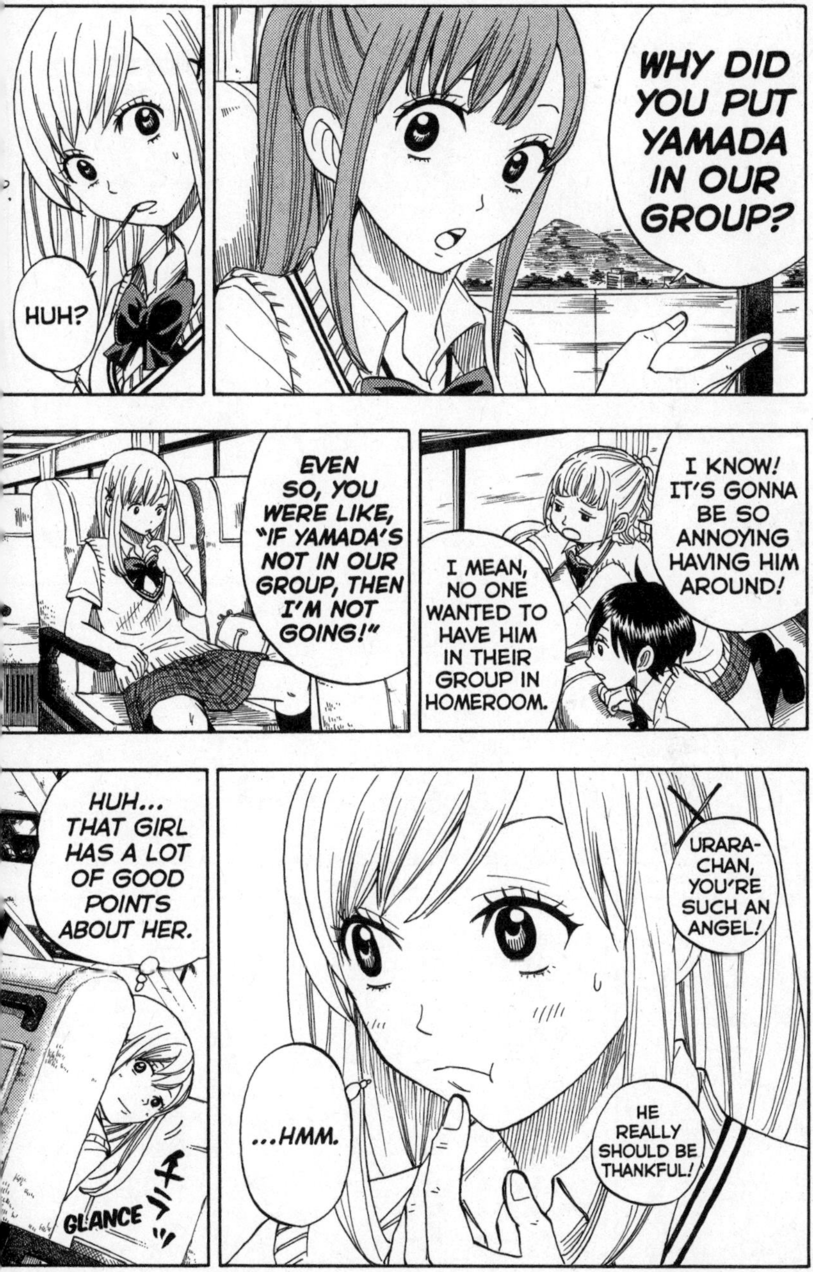
WHY DID YOU PUT YAMADA IN OUR GROUP?
HUH?
I KNOW! IT'S GONNA BE SO ANNOYING HAVING HIM AROUND!
I MEAN, NO ONE WANTED TO HAVE HIM IN THEIR GROUP IN HOMEROOM.
EVEN SO, YOU WERE LIKE, "IF YAMADA'S NOT IN OUR GROUP, THEN I'M NOT GOING!"
URARA-CHAN, YOU'RE SUCH AN ANGEL!
HE REALLY SHOULD BE THANKFUL!
...HMM.
HUH... THAT GIRL HAS A LOT OF GOOD POINTS ABOUT HER.
チラッ
GLANCE

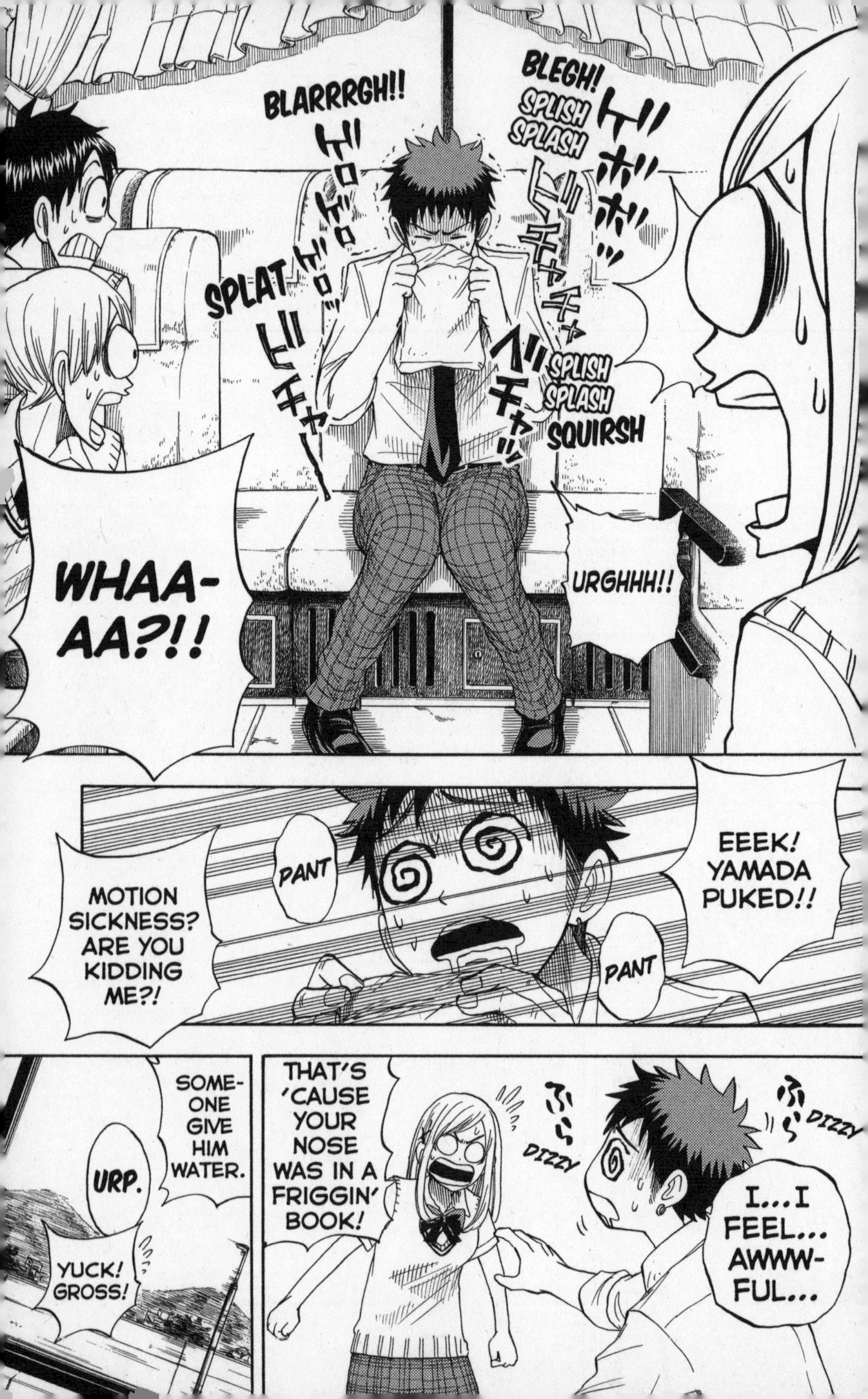
BLEGH!
SPLISH SPLASH
SPLISH SPLASH SQUIRSH
URGHHH!!
BLARRRGH!!
SPLAT
WHAA-AA?!!
EEEK! YAMADA PUKED!!
PANT
PANT
MOTION SICKNESS? ARE YOU KIDDING ME?!
ふら DIZZY
I...I FEEL... AWWW-FUL...
ふら DIZZY
THAT'S 'CAUSE YOUR NOSE WAS IN A FRIGGIN' BOOK!
SOME-ONE GIVE HIM WATER.
URP.
YUCK! GROSS!

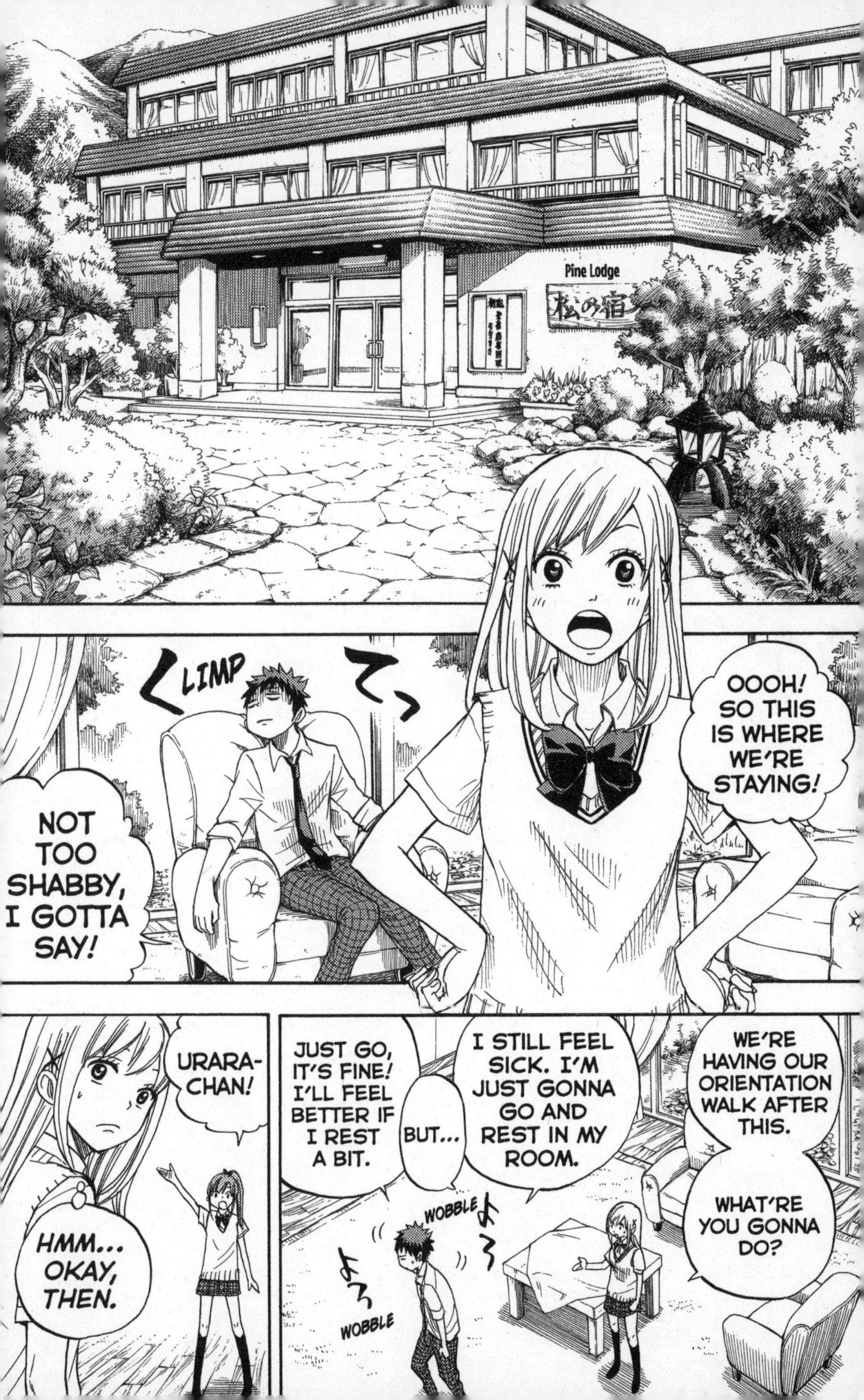

Pine Lodge
松の宿
OOOH! SO THIS IS WHERE WE'RE STAYING!
LIMP
NOT TOO SHABBY, I GOTTA SAY!
WE'RE HAVING OUR ORIENTATION WALK AFTER THIS.
WHAT'RE YOU GONNA DO?
I STILL FEEL SICK. I'M JUST GONNA GO AND REST IN MY ROOM.
BUT...
JUST GO, IT'S FINE! I'LL FEEL BETTER IF I REST A BIT.
WOBBLE
WOBBLE
URARA-CHAN!
HMM... OKAY, THEN.

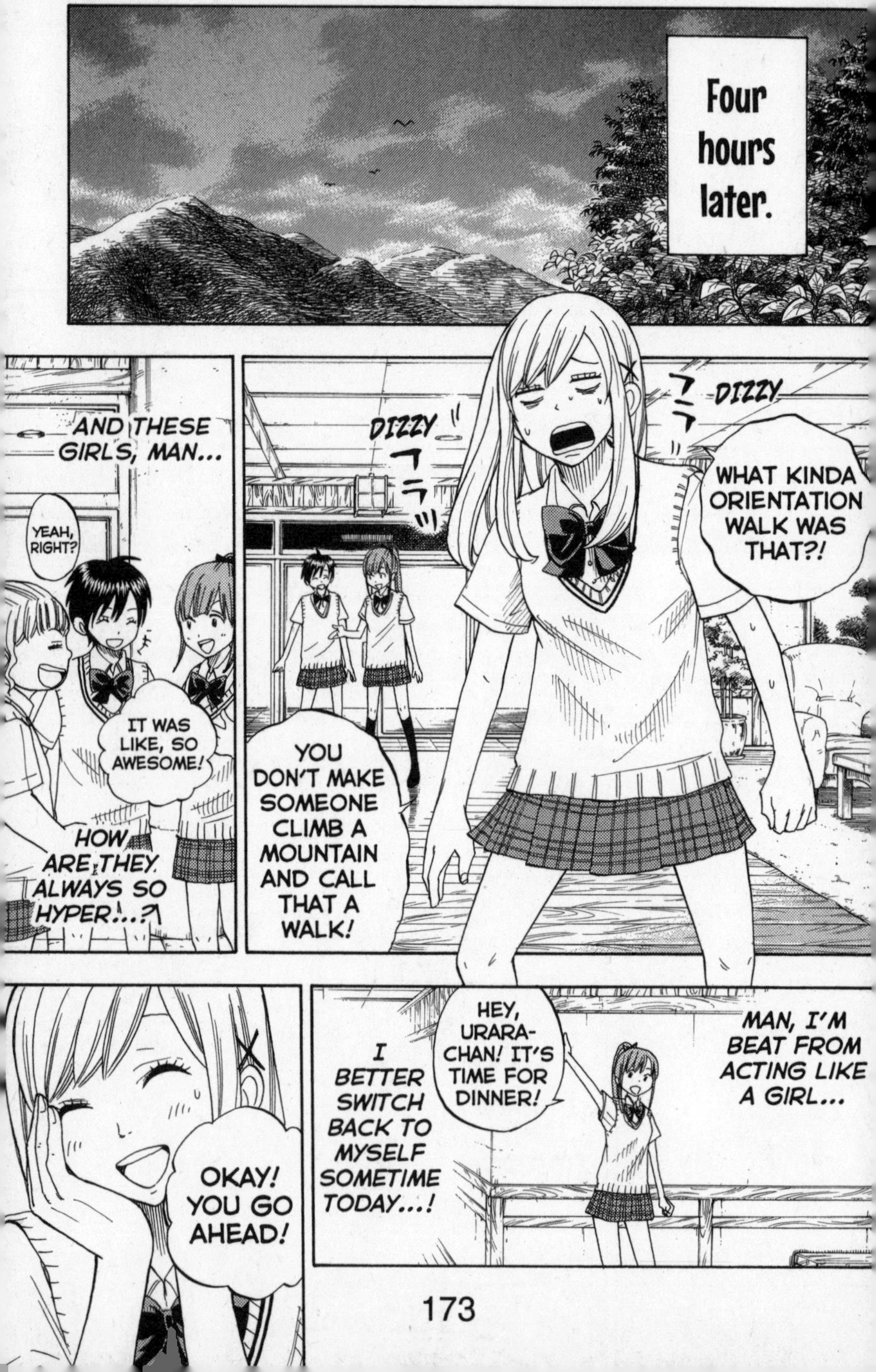
Four hours later.
DIZZY
WHAT KINDA ORIENTATION WALK WAS THAT?!
DIZZY
YOU DON'T MAKE SOMEONE CLIMB A MOUNTAIN AND CALL THAT A WALK!
AND THESE GIRLS, MAN...
YEAH, RIGHT?
IT WAS LIKE, SO AWESOME!
HOW ARE THEY ALWAYS SO HYPER...?!
MAN, I'M BEAT FROM ACTING LIKE A GIRL...
HEY, URARA-CHAN! IT'S TIME FOR DINNER!
I BETTER SWITCH BACK TO MYSELF SOMETIME TODAY...!
OKAY! YOU GO AHEAD!

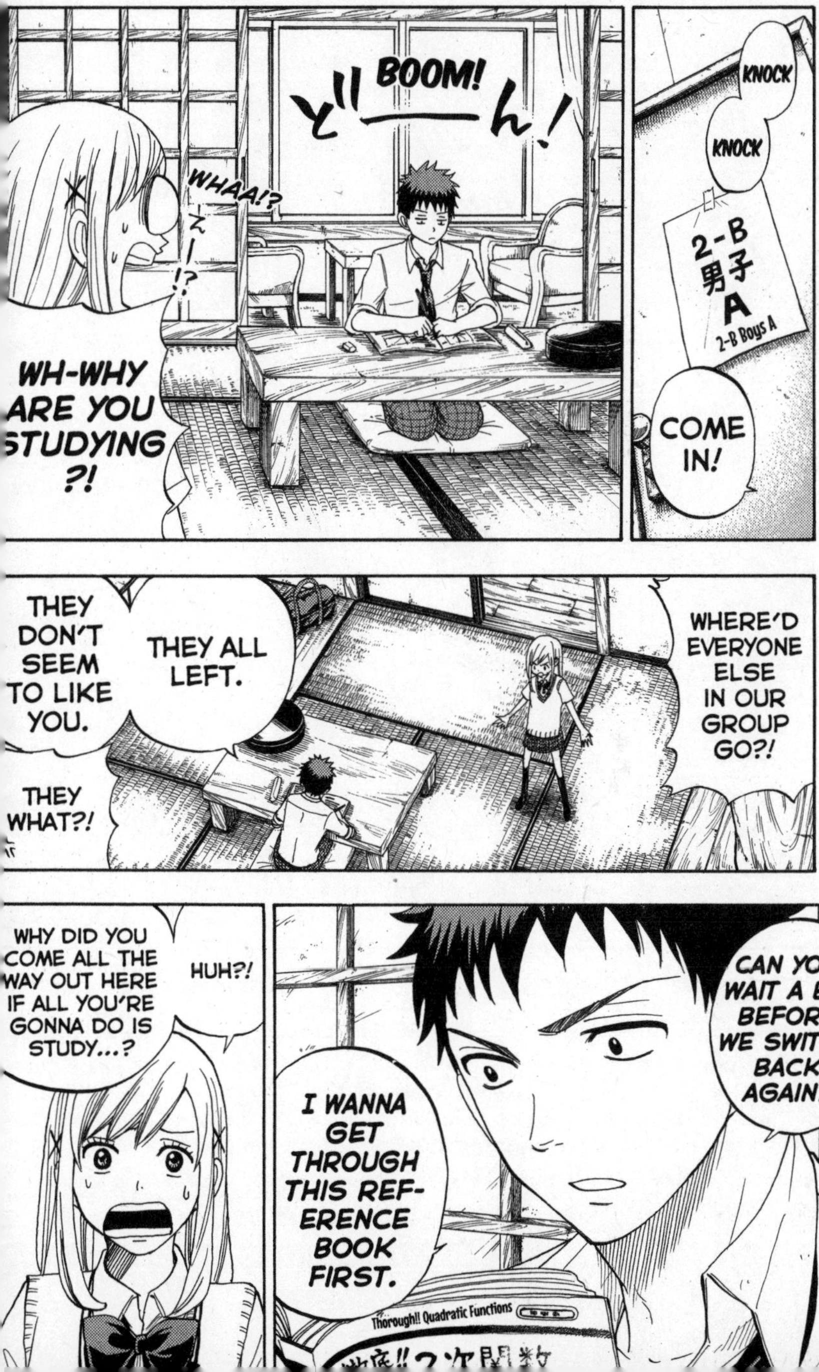
KNOCK
KNOCK
2-B 男子 A
2-B Boys A
COME IN!
BOOM!
どーーん!
WHAA!?
えー!?
WH-WHY ARE YOU STUDYING?!
WHERE'D EVERYONE ELSE IN OUR GROUP GO?!
THEY ALL LEFT.
THEY DON'T SEEM TO LIKE YOU.
THEY WHAT?!
CAN YOU WAIT A BIT BEFORE WE SWITCH BACK AGAIN?
I WANNA GET THROUGH THIS REFERENCE BOOK FIRST.
Thorough!! Quadratic Functions
HUH?!
WHY DID YOU COME ALL THE WAY OUT HERE IF ALL YOU'RE GONNA DO IS STUDY...?

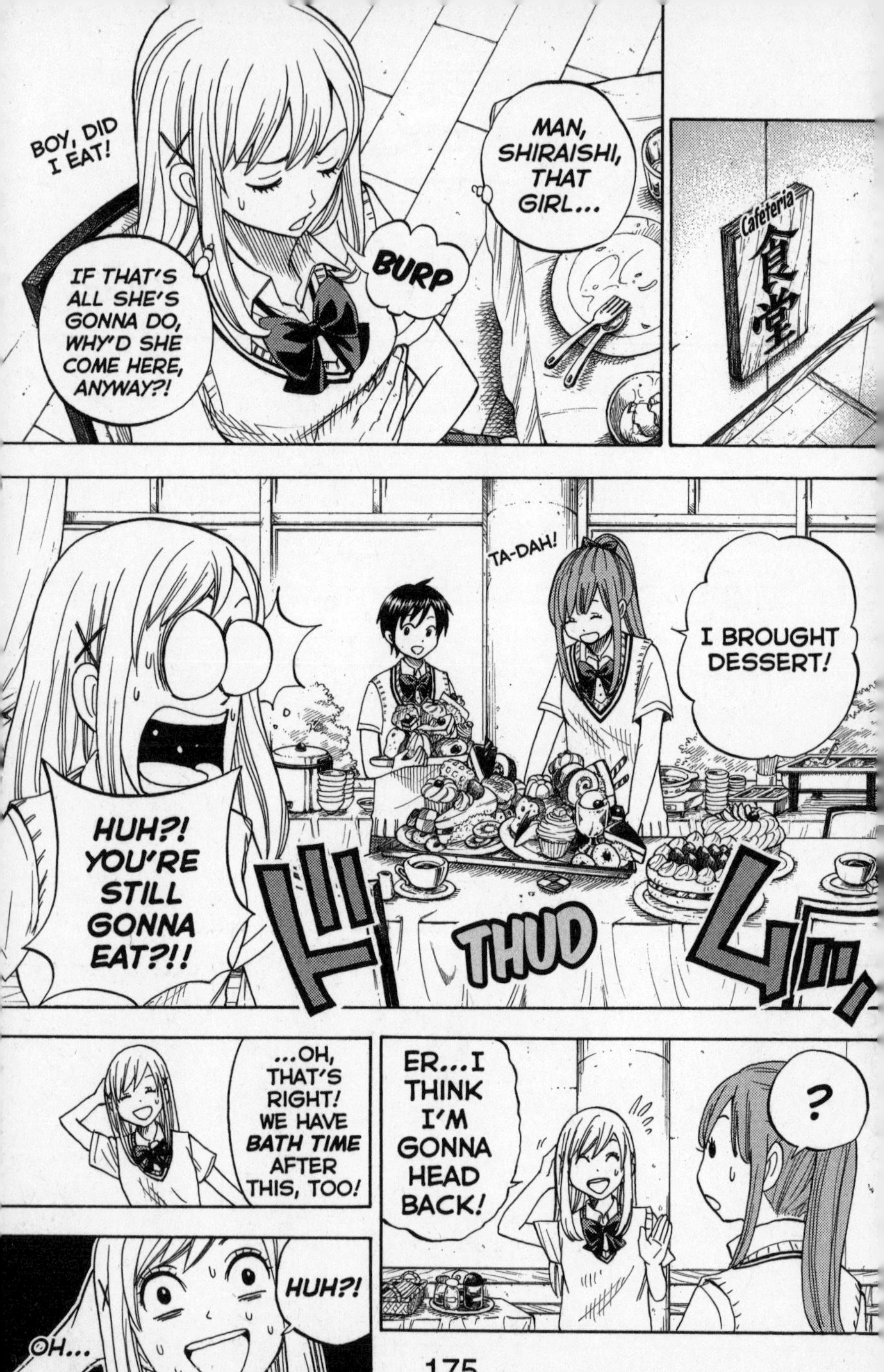
Cafeteria
食堂
MAN, SHIRAISHI, THAT GIRL...
BURP
BOY, DID I EAT!
IF THAT'S ALL SHE'S GONNA DO, WHY'D SHE COME HERE, ANYWAY?!
I BROUGHT DESSERT!
TA-DAH!
THUD
HUH?! YOU'RE STILL GONNA EAT?!!
?
ER...I THINK I'M GONNA HEAD BACK!
...OH, THAT'S RIGHT! WE HAVE *BATH TIME* AFTER THIS, TOO!
HUH?!
OH...

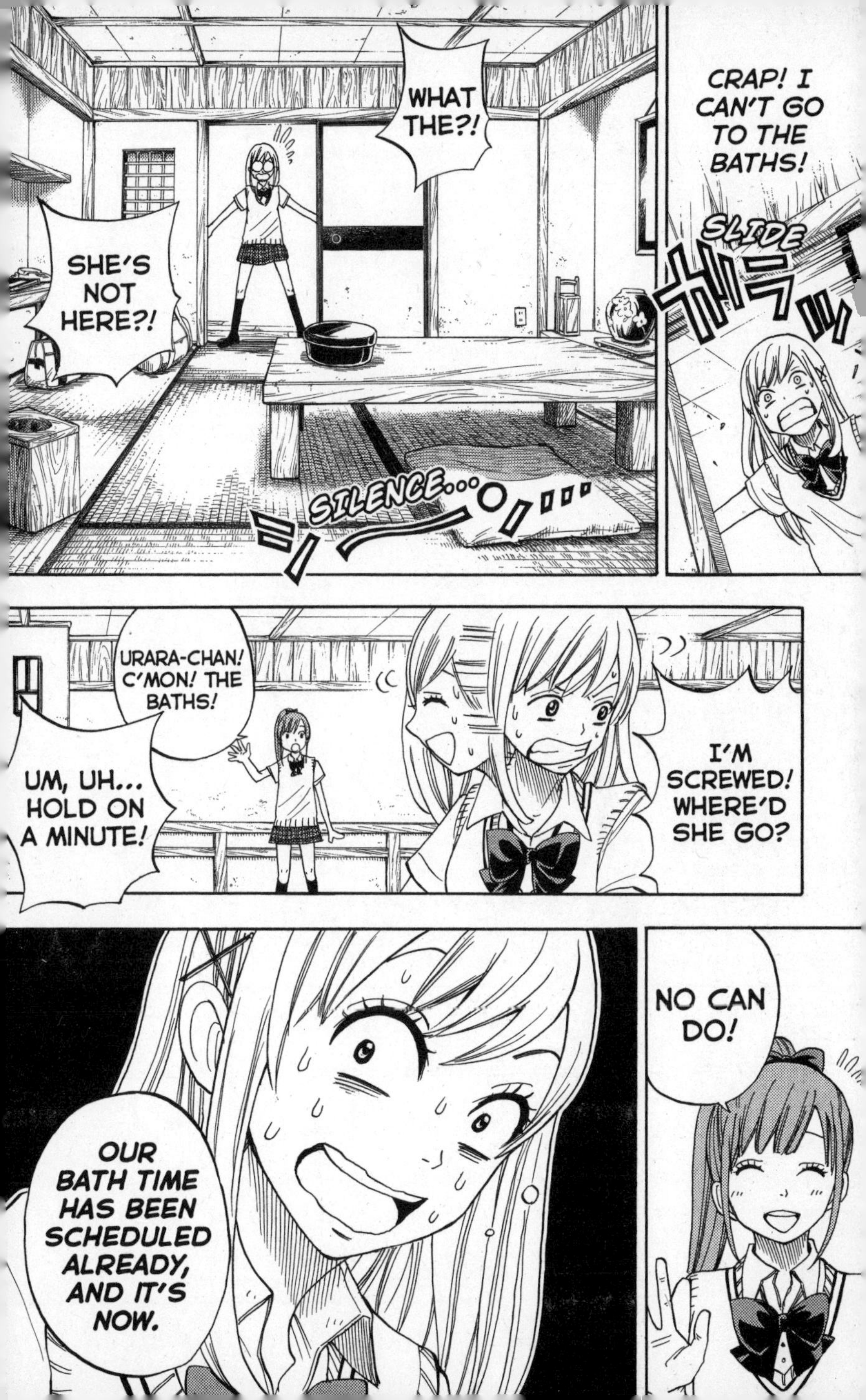
CRAP! I CAN'T GO TO THE BATHS!
SLIDE
WHAT THE?!
SHE'S NOT HERE?!
SILENCE...
I'M SCREWED! WHERE'D SHE GO?
URARA-CHAN! C'MON! THE BATHS!
UM, UH... HOLD ON A MINUTE!
NO CAN DO!
OUR BATH TIME HAS BEEN SCHEDULED ALREADY, AND IT'S NOW.

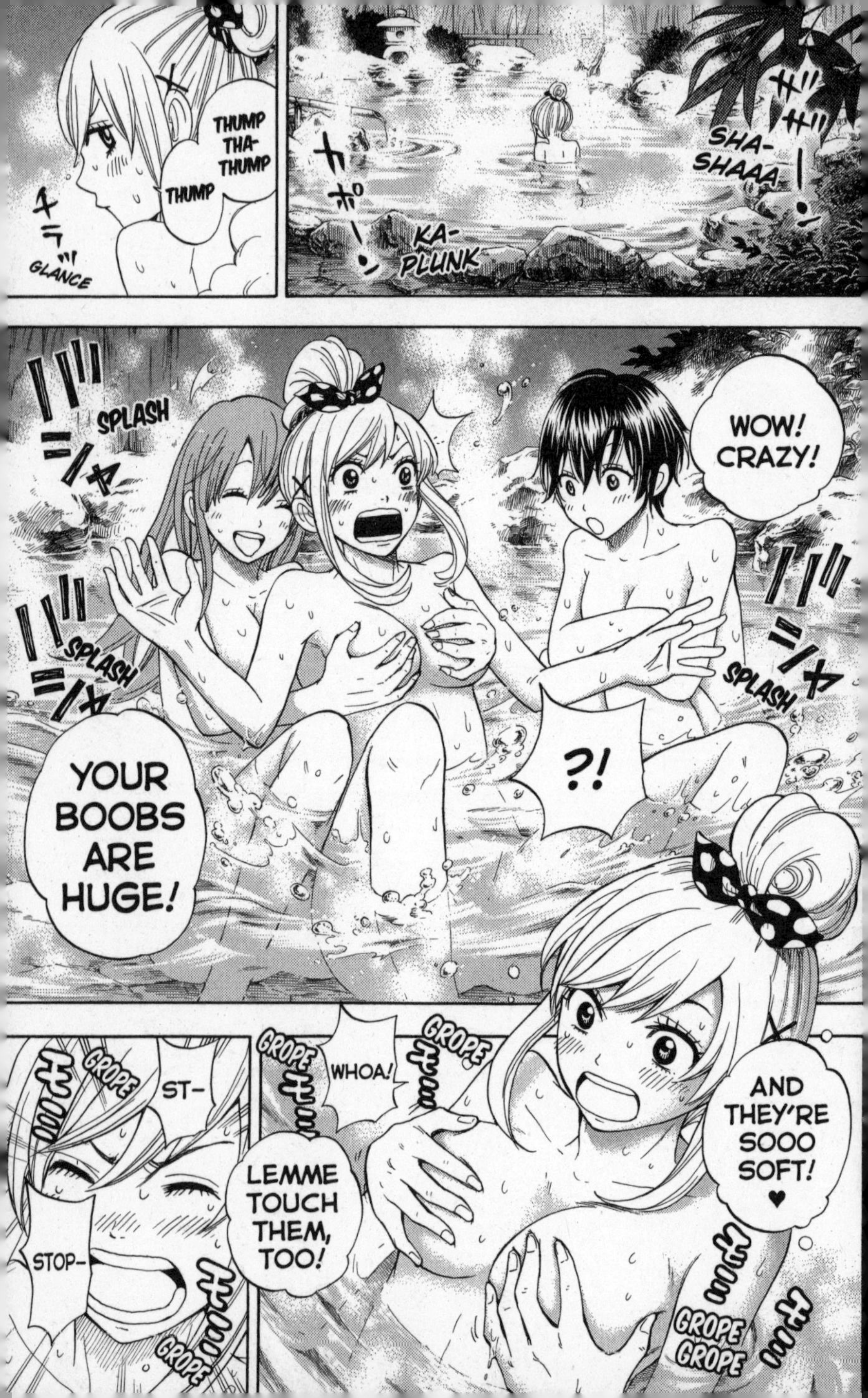
SHA-SHAAA
KA-PLUNK
THUMP THA-THUMP
THUMP
GLANCE
WOW! CRAZY!
SPLASH
?!
SPLASH
SPLASH
YOUR BOOBS ARE HUGE!
AND THEY'RE SOOO SOFT! ♥
GROPE GROPE
GROPE
WHOA!
GROPE
LEMME TOUCH THEM, TOO!
GROPE
ST-
STOP-
GROPE

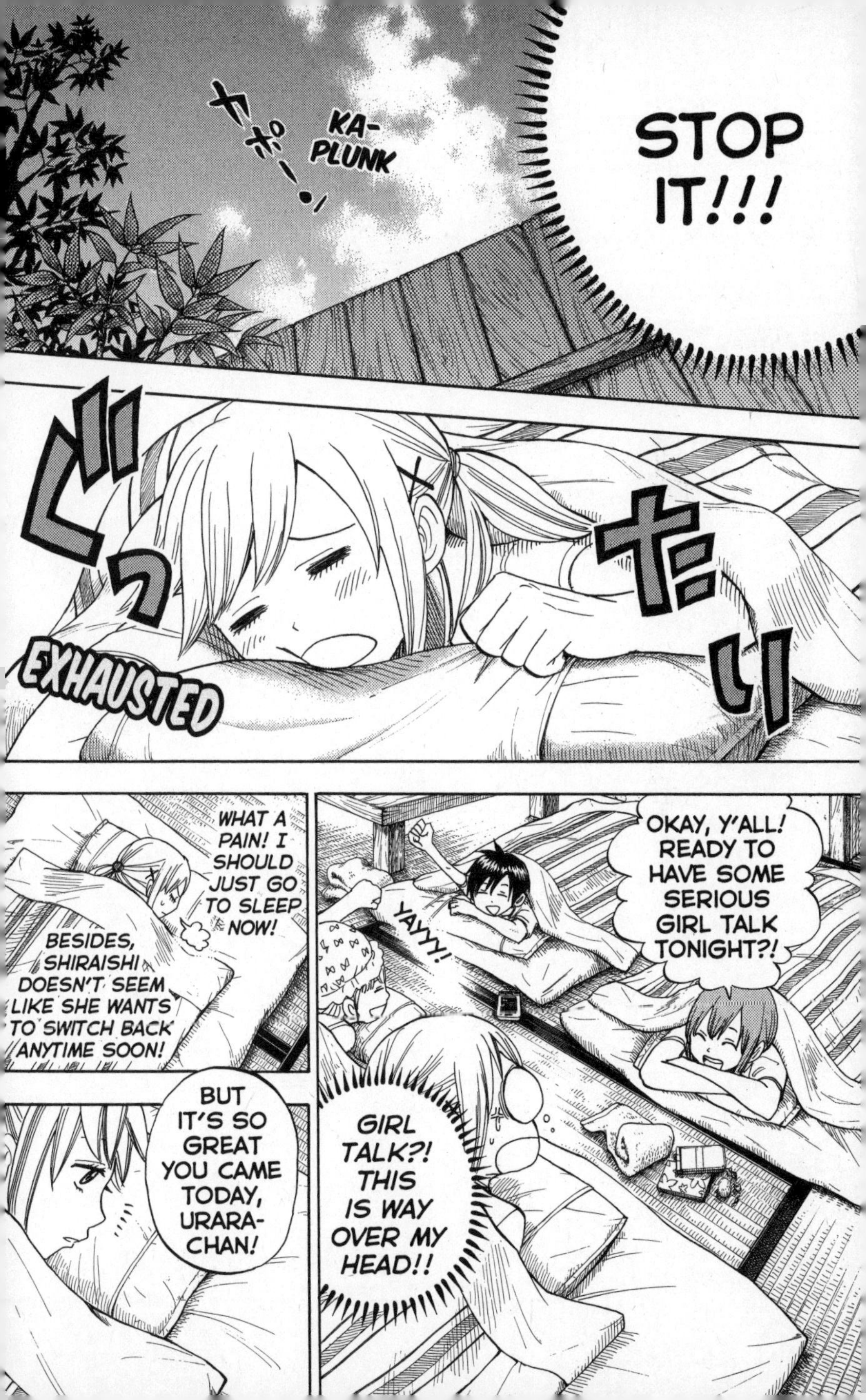
STOP IT!!!
KA-PLUNK
EXHAUSTED
OKAY, Y'ALL! READY TO HAVE SOME SERIOUS GIRL TALK TONIGHT?!
YAYYY!
WHAT A PAIN! I SHOULD JUST GO TO SLEEP NOW!
BESIDES, SHIRAISHI DOESN'T SEEM LIKE SHE WANTS TO SWITCH BACK ANYTIME SOON!
GIRL TALK?! THIS IS WAY OVER MY HEAD!!
BUT IT'S SO GREAT YOU CAME TODAY, URARA-CHAN!

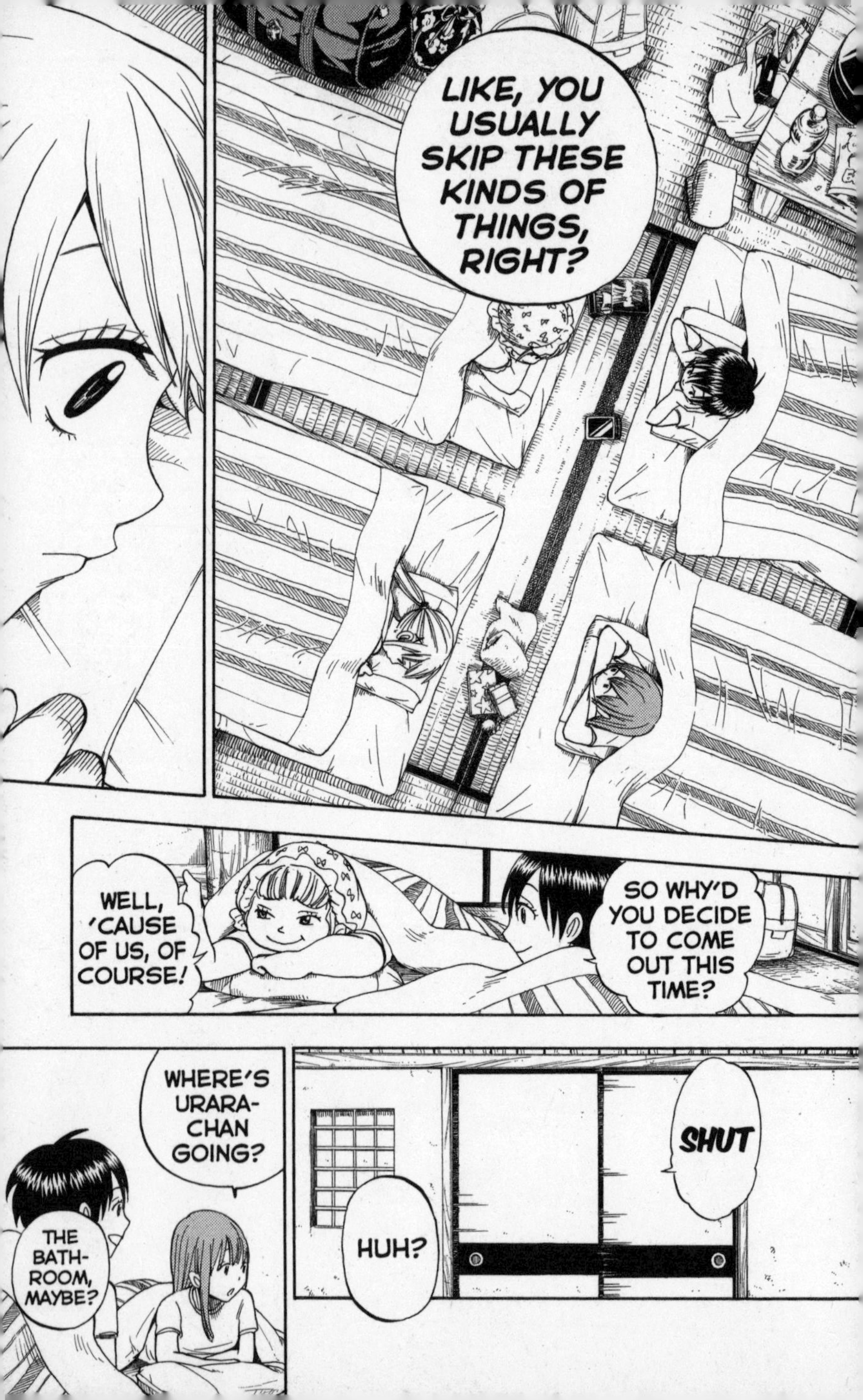
LIKE, YOU USUALLY SKIP THESE KINDS OF THINGS, RIGHT?
SO WHY'D YOU DECIDE TO COME OUT THIS TIME?
WELL, 'CAUSE OF US, OF COURSE!
SHUT
HUH?
WHERE'S URARA-CHAN GOING?
THE BATH-ROOM, MAYBE?

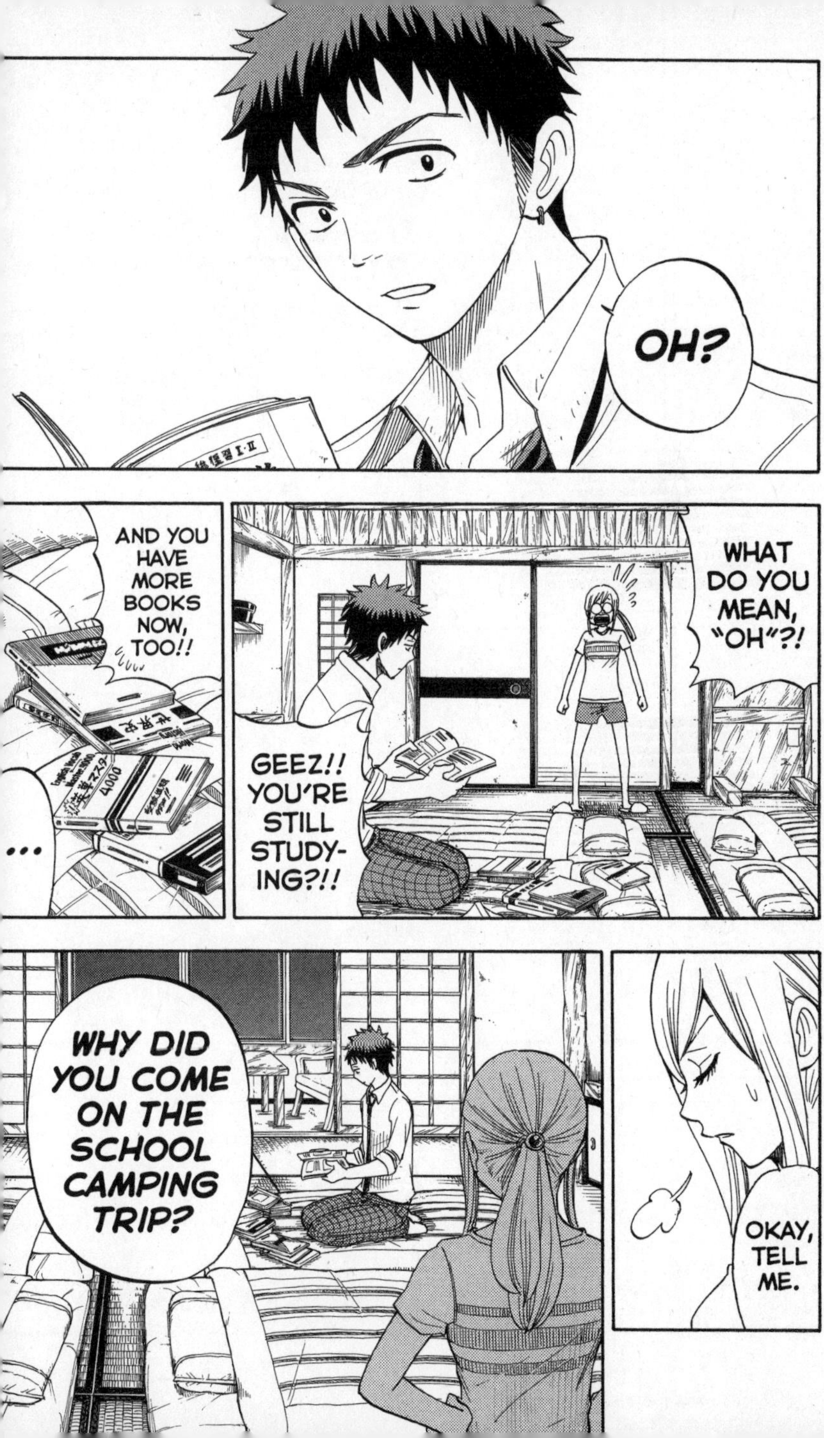
OH?
WHAT DO YOU MEAN, "OH"?!
GEEZ!! YOU'RE STILL STUDYING?!!
AND YOU HAVE MORE BOOKS NOW, TOO!!
...
OKAY, TELL ME.
WHY DID YOU COME ON THE SCHOOL CAMPING TRIP?

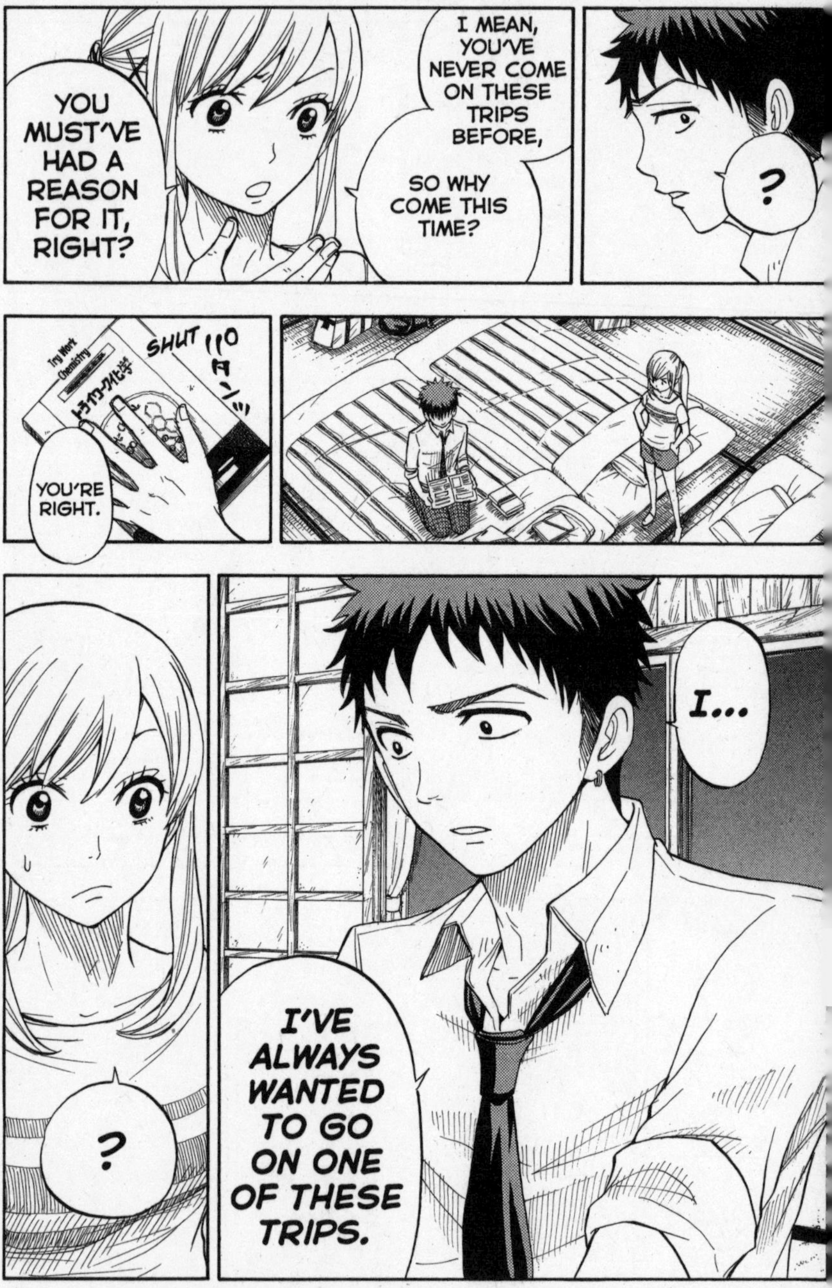
?
I MEAN, YOU'VE NEVER COME ON THESE TRIPS BEFORE,
SO WHY COME THIS TIME?
YOU MUST'VE HAD A REASON FOR IT, RIGHT?
SHUT
Try Work Chemistry
YOU'RE RIGHT.
I...
I'VE ALWAYS WANTED TO GO ON ONE OF THESE TRIPS.
?

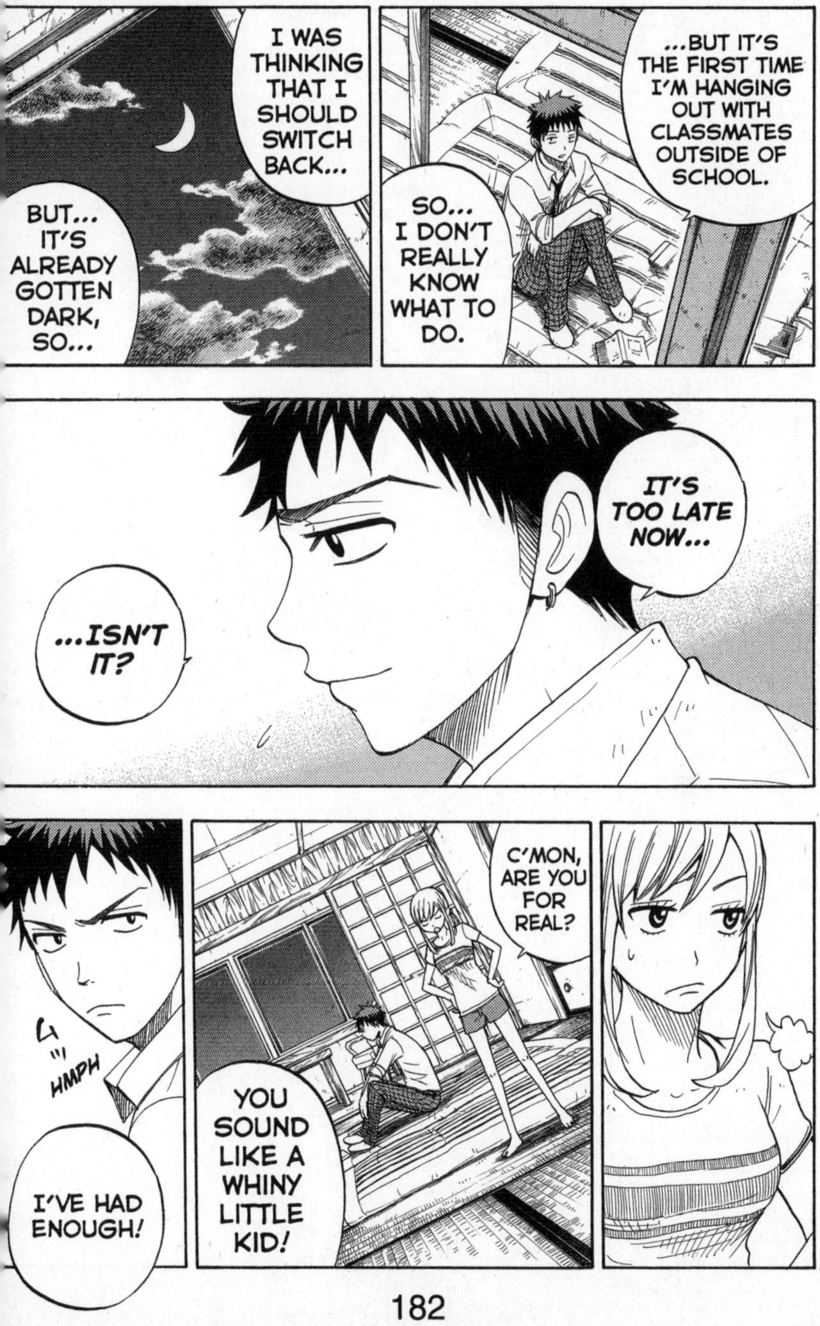
...BUT IT'S THE FIRST TIME I'M HANGING OUT WITH CLASSMATES OUTSIDE OF SCHOOL.
SO... I DON'T REALLY KNOW WHAT TO DO.
I WAS THINKING THAT I SHOULD SWITCH BACK...
BUT... IT'S ALREADY GOTTEN DARK, SO...
IT'S TOO LATE NOW...
...ISN'T IT?
C'MON, ARE YOU FOR REAL?
YOU SOUND LIKE A WHINY LITTLE KID!
HMPH
I'VE HAD ENOUGH!

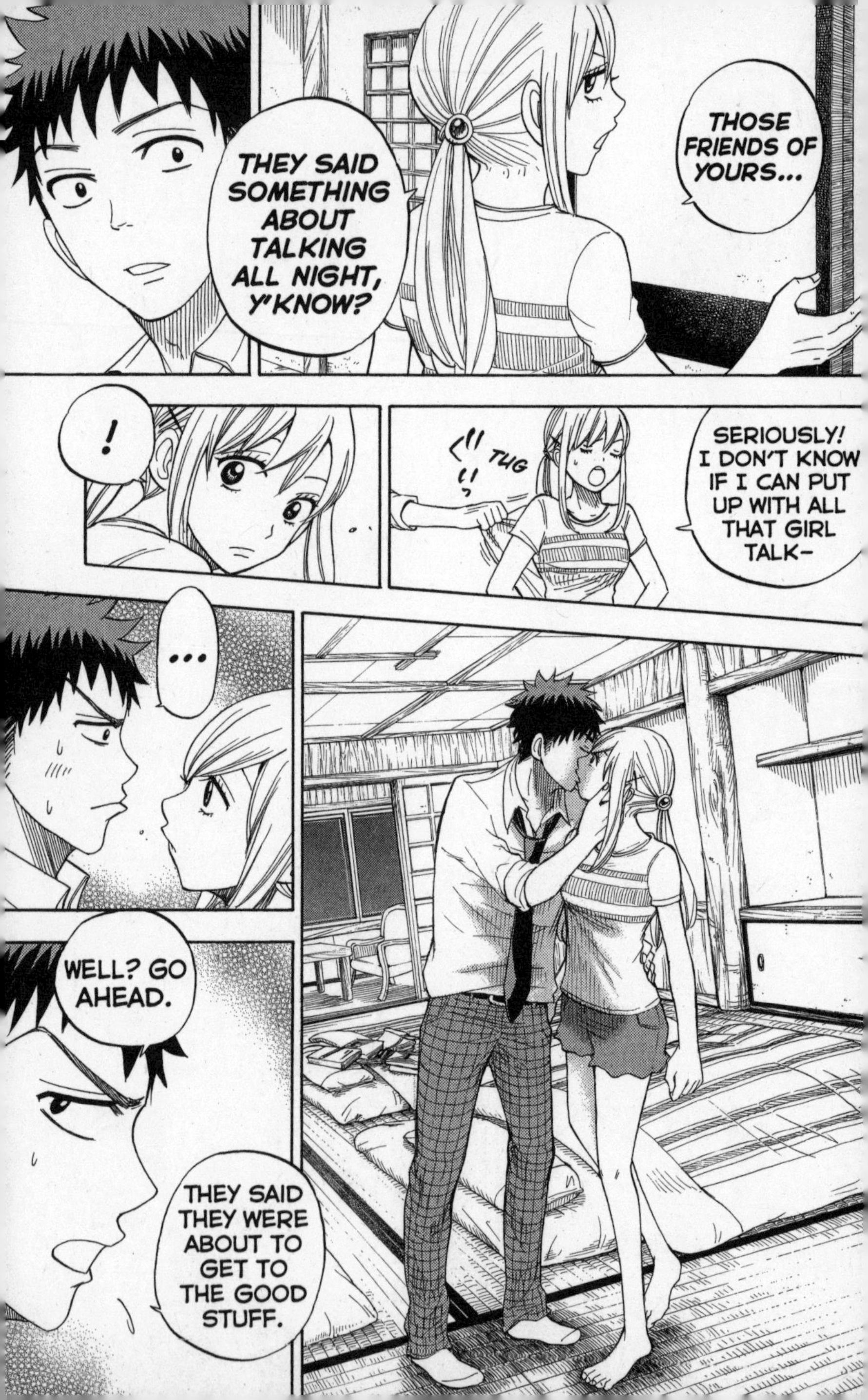
THOSE FRIENDS OF YOURS...
THEY SAID SOMETHING ABOUT TALKING ALL NIGHT, Y'KNOW?
SERIOUSLY! I DON'T KNOW IF I CAN PUT UP WITH ALL THAT GIRL TALK-
TUG
!
...
WELL? GO AHEAD.
THEY SAID THEY WERE ABOUT TO GET TO THE GOOD STUFF.

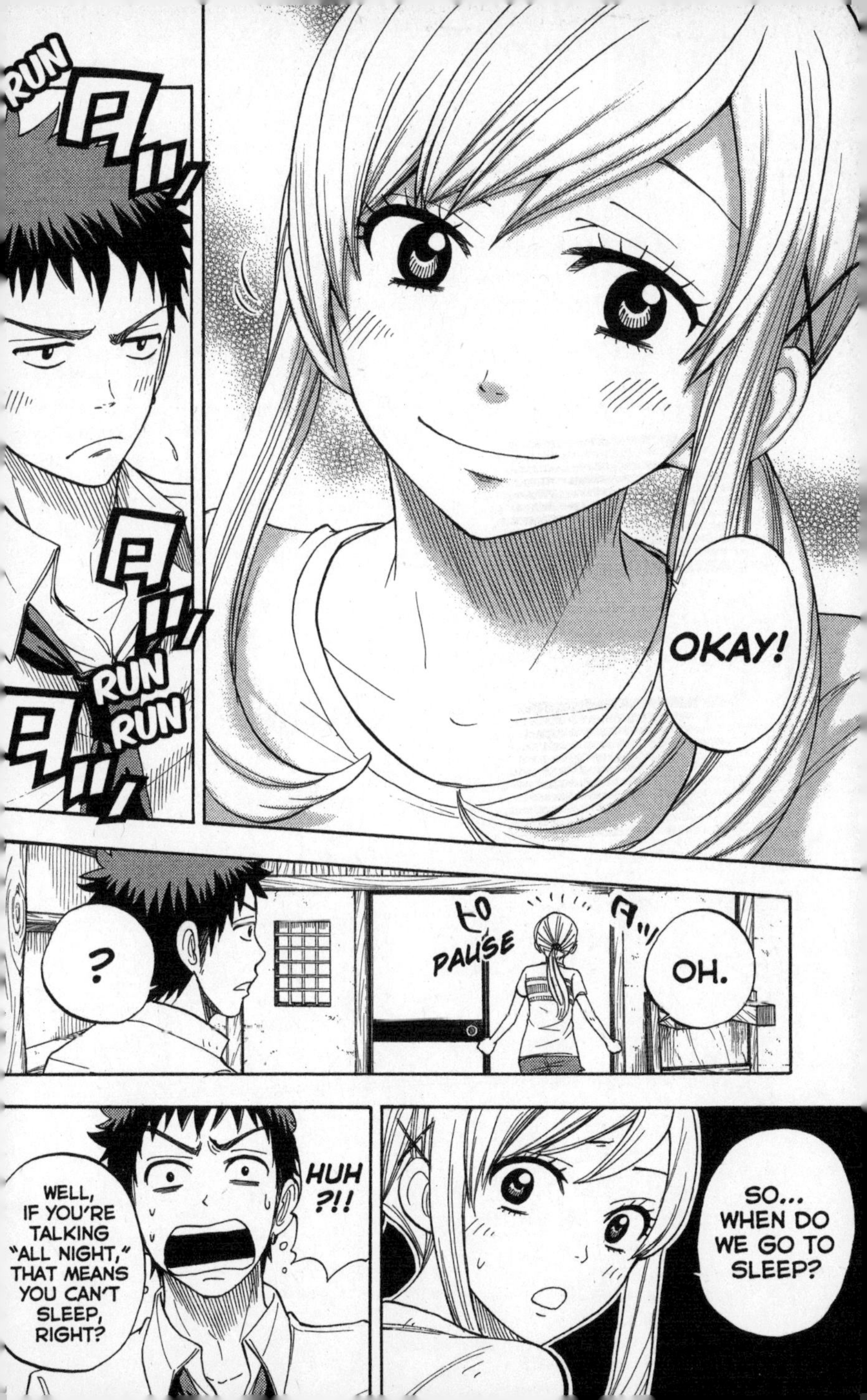
OKAY!
RUN
RUN
RUN
OH.
PAUSE
?
SO... WHEN DO WE GO TO SLEEP?
HUH ?!!
WELL, IF YOU'RE TALKING "ALL NIGHT," THAT MEANS YOU CAN'T SLEEP, RIGHT?

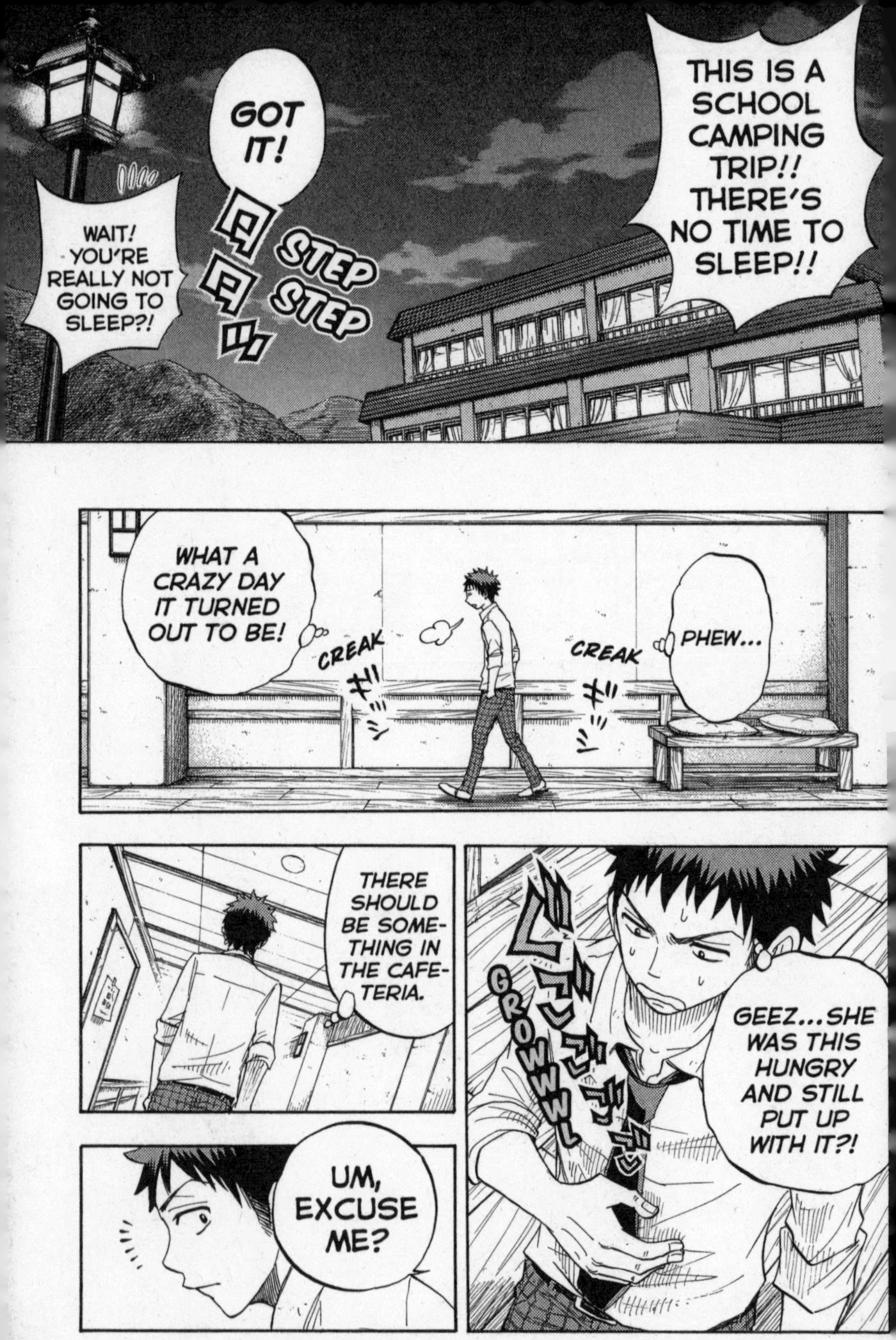
THIS IS A SCHOOL CAMPING TRIP!! THERE'S NO TIME TO SLEEP!!
GOT IT!
STEP STEP
WAIT! YOU'RE REALLY NOT GOING TO SLEEP?!
PHEW...
CREAK
CREAK
WHAT A CRAZY DAY IT TURNED OUT TO BE!
GEEZ...SHE WAS THIS HUNGRY AND STILL PUT UP WITH IT?!
GROWWWL
THERE SHOULD BE SOME-THING IN THE CAFE-TERIA.
UM, EXCUSE ME?

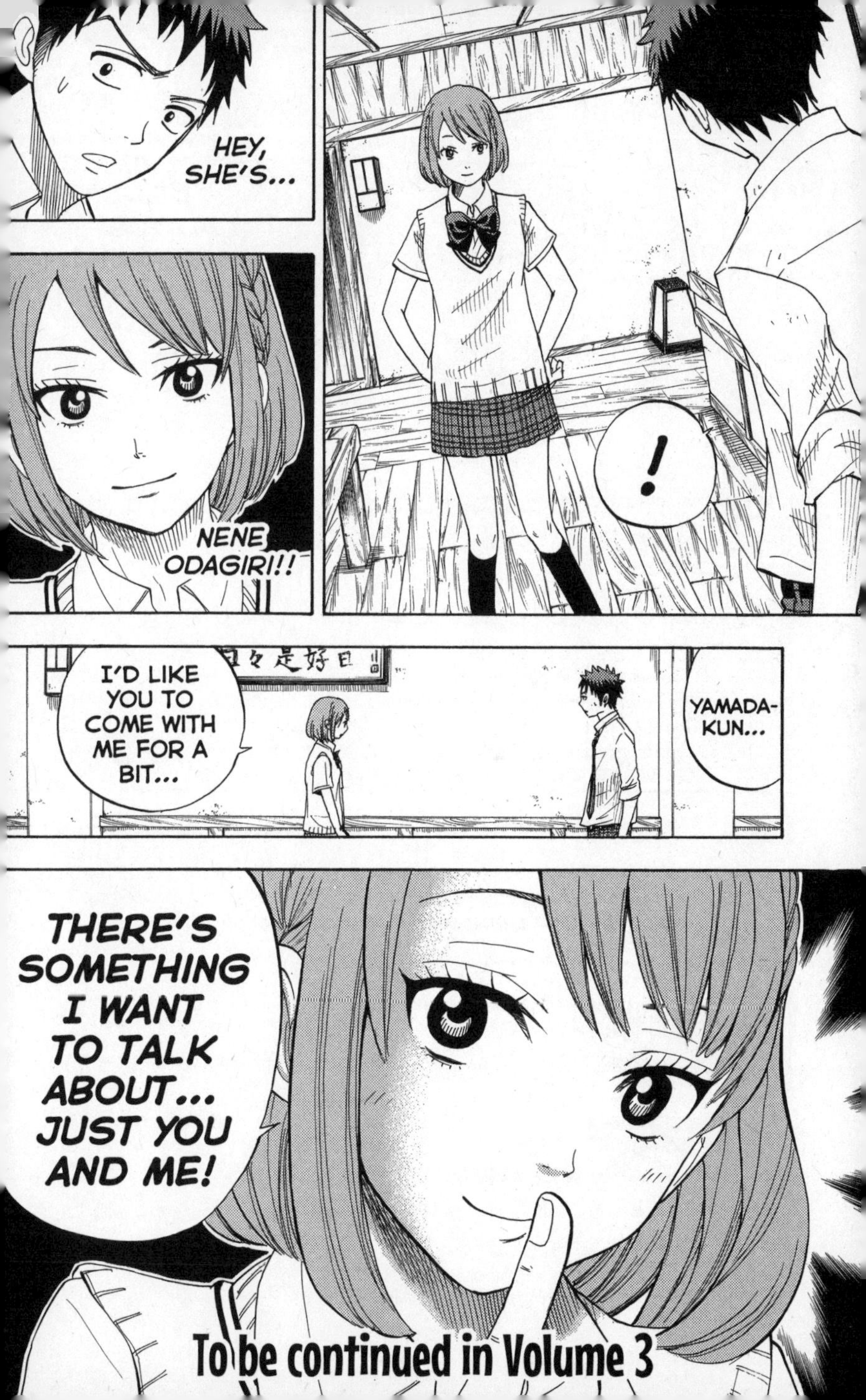
!
HEY, SHE'S...
NENE ODAGIRI!!
YAMADA-KUN...
I'D LIKE YOU TO COME WITH ME FOR A BIT...
THERE'S SOMETHING I WANT TO TALK ABOUT... JUST YOU AND ME!
To be continued in Volume 3

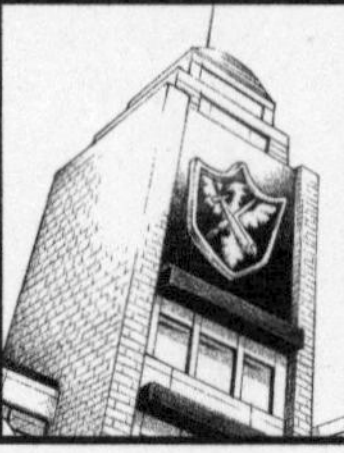

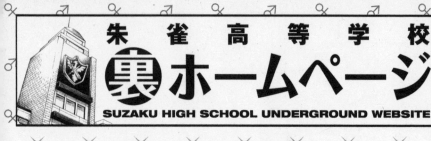

朱雀高等学校 裏ホームページ

SUZAKU HIGH SCHOOL UNDERGROUND WEBSITE

«Notice of Establishment»

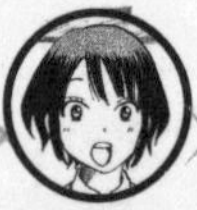

Hi!
I'm Miyabi, the administrator for the Suzaku High School Underground Website!

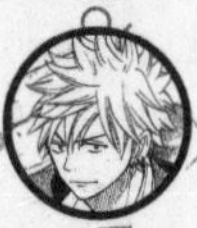

And I'm Miyamura, her assistant. Nice to meet ya.

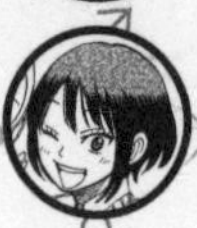

Now then, I know this is all of a sudden, but we've just set up this webpage to request messages from our readers! After receiving your messages, the two of us will answer your questions right here in this column!!

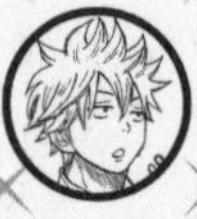

Whether it's questions or problems for us, or something about your own troubles, send us whatever you like. We're taking whatever ya got!! Send your messages to the following address:

Yamada-kun and the Seven Witches: Underground Website
c/o Kodansha Comics
451 Park Ave. South, 7th Floor
New York, NY 10016

***Don't forget to include your handle (pen name)!**

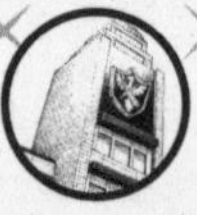

All right, then!
We're waiting for your messages!

Yamada's Mystery Solving Column

TEACH ME! YAMADA-KUN

YEAH!

Part 1

YAMADA, YOU SWITCH BODIES WHEN YOU KISS SOMEONE, RIGHT?
SO WHAT HAPPENS IF YOU KISS US BOTH AT THE SAME TIME?
HUH?
ブチューーッ
SMOOCH
OKAY, LET'S GIVE IT A GO!
WHOA !!
OUR MINDS HAVE BEEN SPLIT APART!
THERE'S NO WAY THAT HAP-PENED!
TEE HEE. ♥
YOU'RE NO FUN.
Nothing happens.

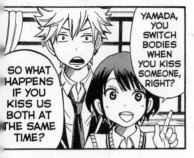

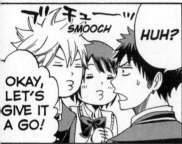

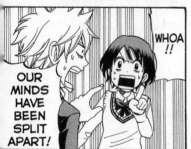

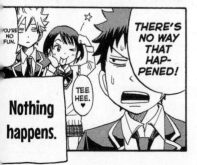

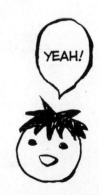

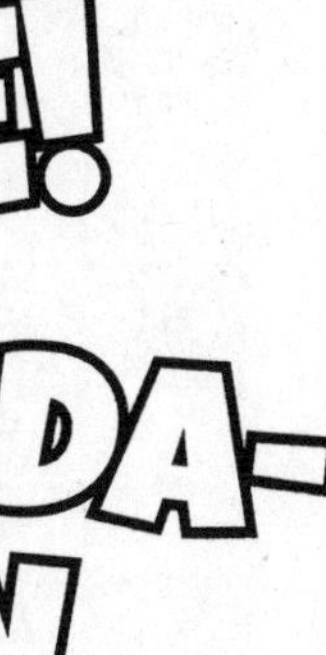

Part 2

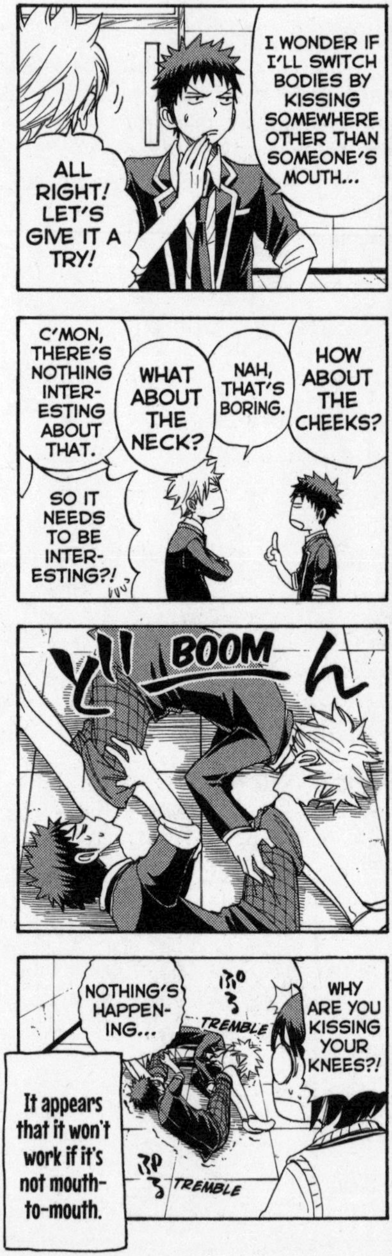
I WONDER IF I'LL SWITCH BODIES BY KISSING SOMEWHERE OTHER THAN SOMEONE'S MOUTH...
ALL RIGHT! LET'S GIVE IT A TRY!
HOW ABOUT THE CHEEKS?
NAH, THAT'S BORING.
WHAT ABOUT THE NECK?
C'MON, THERE'S NOTHING INTER-ESTING ABOUT THAT.
SO IT NEEDS TO BE INTER-ESTING?!
BOOM
WHY ARE YOU KISSING YOUR KNEES?!
TREMBLE
NOTHING'S HAPPEN-ING...
TREMBLE
It appears that it won't work if it's not mouth-to-mouth.

Part 3

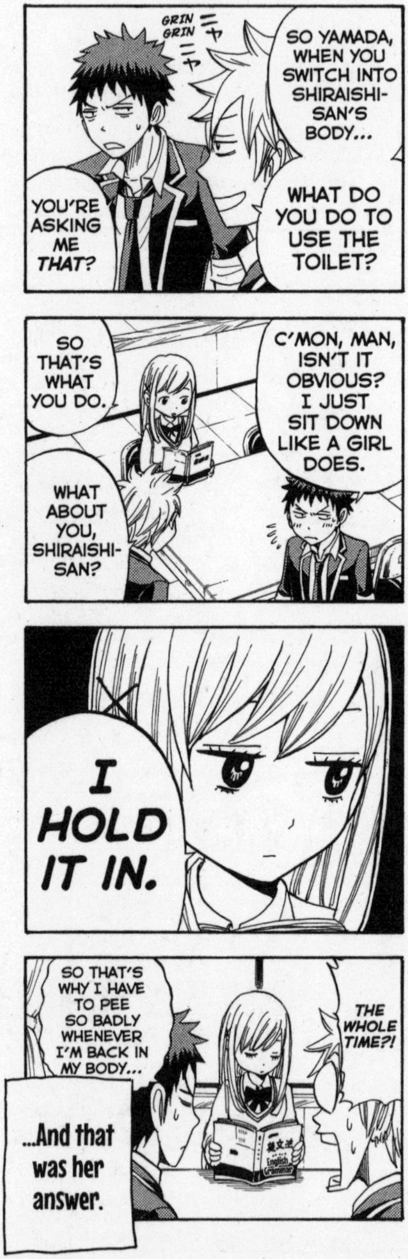
GRIN GRIN
SO YAMADA, WHEN YOU SWITCH INTO SHIRAISHI-SAN'S BODY...
WHAT DO YOU DO TO USE THE TOILET?
YOU'RE ASKING ME *THAT*?
C'MON, MAN, ISN'T IT OBVIOUS? I JUST SIT DOWN LIKE A GIRL DOES.
SO THAT'S WHAT YOU DO.
WHAT ABOUT YOU, SHIRAISHI-SAN?
I HOLD IT IN.
THE WHOLE TIME?!
SO THAT'S WHY I HAVE TO PEE SO BADLY WHENEVER I'M BACK IN MY BODY...
...And that was her answer.

Translation Notes

Ai-ai gasa, page 4

The drawing of an umbrella above Shiraishi and Yamada's names is an ai-ai gasa, and it is similar to the Western practice of drawing a heart shape with the initials of two lovers inside.

The phrase itself roughly means to share an umbrella, but the "ai" in this phrase is also a homophone for "love" in Japanese, which is why writing two names under a drawing of an umbrella signifies that the owners of those names are a couple.

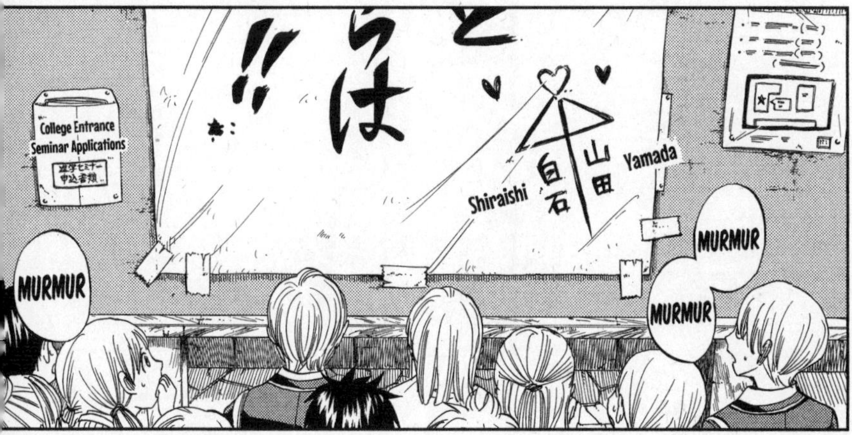

山田
Yamada
白石
Shiraishi
MURMUR
MURMUR
College Entrance Seminar Applications
MURMUR

Bowlegs, page 80

Walking bowlegged, or with "crab legs" as it is called in Japanese, is considered more masculine, whereas walking pigeon-toed is more feminine.

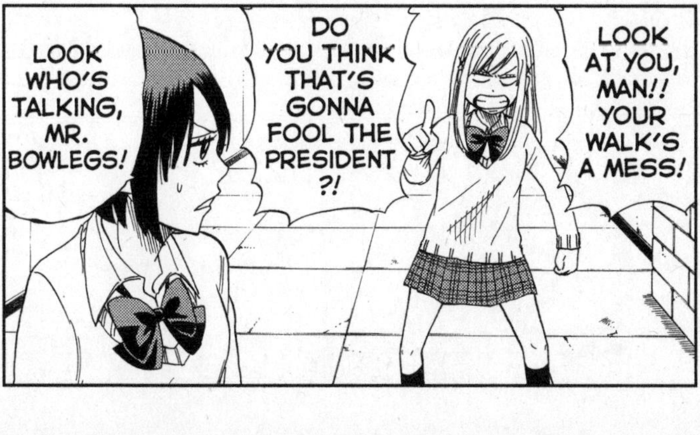

LOOK AT YOU, MAN!! YOUR WALK'S A MESS!
DO YOU THINK THAT'S GONNA FOOL THE PRESIDENT?!
LOOK WHO'S TALKING, MR. BOWLEGS!

A deceitful devil, page 95

In this scene, Miyamura is actually calling student council president a tanuki, or a Japanese raccoon dog. Tanuki, like foxes, often appear as characters in Japanese folklore and are said to have supernatural powers such as the ability to shapeshift. Tanuki are known to use their powers to deceive and mislead humans, so a cunning and deceitful man can sometimes be called a tanuki.

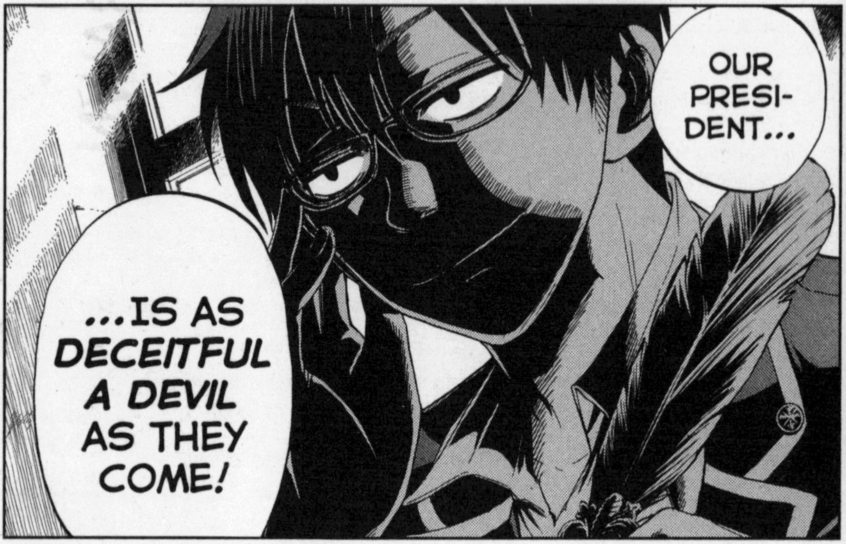
OUR PRESI-DENT...
...IS AS DECEITFUL A DEVIL AS THEY COME!

Shishi odoshi, page 177

A shishi odoshi (literally “deer scarer”) is a contraption that uses sound to scare off wildlife that would otherwise eat or damage one’s crops. A famous type of shishi odoshi that has become synonymous with Japanese gardens is one in which a bamboo tube fills with water until pushed beyond the center of gravity of its pivot, causing the tube to hit a rock or other hard object to produce a distinct “ka-pon” sound (ka-plunk in this translation).

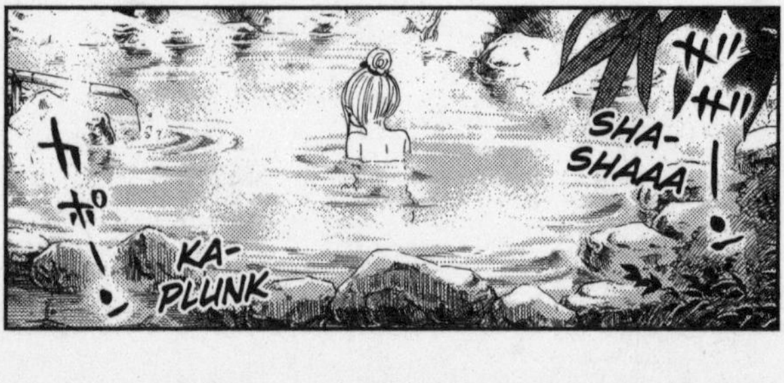
SHA-SHAAA
KA-PLUNK

P9-ECP-601

Yamada-kun and the Seven Witches volume 2 is a work of fiction.
Names, characters, places, and incidents are the products of the author's
imagination or are used fictitiously. Any resemblance to actual events,
locales, or persons, living or dead, is entirely coincidental.

A Kodansha Comics Trade Paperback Original.

Yamada-kun and the Seven Witches volume 2 copyright © 2012 Miki
Yoshikawa
English translation copyright © 2015 Miki Yoshikawa

All rights reserved.

Published in the United States by Kodansha Comics,
an imprint of Kodansha USA Publishing, LLC, New York.

Publication rights for this English edition arranged through Kodansha Ltd.,
Tokyo.

First published in Japan in 2012 by Kodansha Ltd., Tokyo, as *Yamada-
kun to Nananin no Majo* volume 2.

ISBN 978-1-63236-069-4

Printed in the United States of America.

www.kodanshacomics.com

9 8 7 6 5 4 3 2 1

Translator: David Rhie
Lettering: Sara Linsley
Editing: Ajani Oloye
Kodansha Comics Edition Cover Design: Phil Balsman